JACQUE

MICHEL

FAUBOURG   SAINT   HONORÉ

OT

THE
FRENCH
REVOLUTION

ALSO BY IAN DAVIDSON

The Gold War (with Gordon L. Weil)

Britain and the Making of Europe

*European Monetary Union:
The Kingsdown Enquiry*

*Open Frontiers and the European Union:
Report of the Templeman Enquiry*

Jobs and the Rhineland Model

Missing the Bus, Missing the Point: Britain's Place in the World,
in *Moored to the Continent*

Voltaire in Exile: The Last Years, 1753–1778

Voltaire: A Life

THE
FRENCH
REVOLUTION

FROM ENLIGHTENMENT TO TYRANNY

IAN DAVIDSON

PEGASUS BOOKS
NEW YORK LONDON

THE FRENCH REVOLUTION

Pegasus Books Ltd
148 West 37th Street, 13th Floor
New York, NY 10018

First Pegasus Books hardcover edition December 2016

ISBN: 978-1-68177-250-9

10 9 8 7 6 5 4 3 2 1

Printed in the United States of America
Distributed by W. W. Norton & Company, Inc.

To the late Peter Carson, peerless editor and fellow-KS, who urged me, all those many years ago, to undertake this book; and to Jennifer Monahan, my wife, whose multifold talents and tireless support enabled me to write it.

CONTENTS

Maps   ix

Timeline   xvii

1   Introduction   1

2   *États Généraux*   9

3   The Fall of Necker   22

4   The Storming of the Bastille   25

5   The Dismantling of Feudalism   30

6   Declaration of the Rights of Man   34

7   The King Moves to Paris   40

8   The Assembly Starts to Govern France   50

9   The Revolutionaries Reform the Church   59

10 The Flight of the King   66

11 The Rush to War   77

12 The Overthrow of the Monarchy   87

13 The *Commune insurrectionnelle*   103

14 The *Convention*   119

15 The War in 1792: From Valmy to Jemappes   130

16 The Trial of the King   137

17 *Girondins* and *Montagnards*   144

18 The Fall of the *Girondins*   154

19 The Civil Wars of 1793   164

20 The *Gouvernement révolutionnaire*   175

21 The *Terreur*   190

22 The Spasm of Religion to the Fall of Danton   205

23 The Fall of Robespierre   218

24 The Aftermath   232

25 Epilogue   244

In Place of a Bibliography   253

A Note on the Children of Louis XVI   257

A Note on the Franchise for Women   258

The Coups d'État of the French Revolution   259

The French Text of the Declaration of the Rights of Man of 1789   261

A Note on Money and Inflation   263

A Note on the Comité de salut public   266

A Note on Death and the Revolution   269

Notes   278

List of Illustrations   298

Index   300

MAPS

1. France in the 1790s
2. Northern France 1790s
3. Revolutionary Paris
4. Central Revolutionary Paris
5. Versailles

GREAT BRITAIN

UNITED
NETHERLANDS

Antwerp
Brussels
AUSTRIAN
NETHERLANDS

GERMANIC
STATES

PAS DE CALAIS
NORD
Somme
SOMME
AISNE
ARDENNES
Luxembourg
SEINE
MARITIME
Rouen
OISE
Caen
Seine
Varennes
Verdun
MANCHE
CALVADOS
EURE
Paris
MARNE
MEUSE
Metz
MOSELLE
Granville
ORNE
Versailles
SEINE ET
MARNE
Marne
MEURTHE
ET MOSELLE
Strasbourg
Chartres
EURE
ET LOIR
Étampes
Aube
AUBE
Nancy
BAS
RHIN
Brest
ILLE
ET VILAINE
MAYENNE
Châtillion
sur Seine
HAUTE
MARNE
VOSGES
FINISTÈRE
CÔTES D'ARMOR
Le Mans
INDRE
LOIRET
HAUT
RHIN
Rennes
MORBIHAN
Orléans
Loire
ET LOIR
CHER
YONNE
CÔTE D'OR
HAUTE
SAÔNE
LOIRE
ATLANTIQUE
Angers
MAINE
ET LOIRE
LOIR
ET CHER
NIÈVRE
Dijon
DOUBS
Savenay
INDRE
Saône
Nantes
Cholet
DEUX
SÈVRES
Bourges
INDRE
Autun
SAÔNE ET LOIRE
JURA
SWITZERLAND
VENDÉE
VIENNE
ALLIER
AIN
CHARENTE
MARITIME
CREUSE
PUY
DE DÔME
RHÔNE
Chambéry
CHARENTE
HAUTE
VIENNE
LOIRE
Lyon
SAVOY
DORDOGNE
CORRÈZE
ISÈRE
PIEDMONT
Bordeaux
Dordogne
CANTAL
HAUTE
LOIRE
Rhône
GIRONDE
LOT ET
GARONNE
LOT
LOZÈRE
ARDÈCHE
HAUTES
ALPES
LANDES
Garonne
AVEYRON
Nîmes
AVIGNON
ALPES DE
HAUTE
PROVENCE
TARN
Montpellier
BOUCHES DU
RHÔNE
VAR
Toulouse
HAUTE
GARONNE
HÉRAULT
Marseilles
Toulon
PYRÉNÉES
ATLANTIQUES
HAUTE
PYRÉNÉES
AUDE
ARIÈGE
PYRÉNÉES
ORIENTALES

SPAIN

Rhine

0   100   200   300km

N

FRANCE IN THE 1790s

The system of the départements was decided by
the National Assembly on 26th February 1790.

NORTHERN FRANCE 1790s

REVOLUTIONARY PARIS

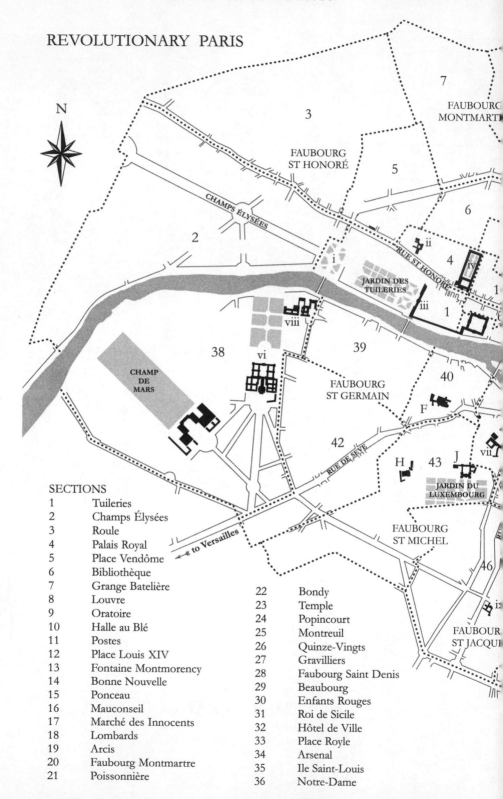

N

7

FAUBOURG
MONTMARTE

3

FAUBOURG
ST HONORÉ

5

CHAMPS ÉLYSÉES

6

2

ii

RUE ST HONORÉ

4   IV

i

JARDIN DES
TUILERIES

1

iii

1

viii

38   vi   39

40

CHAMP
DE
MARS

F

42

H   43   J   vii

RUE DE SEYE

JARDIN DU
LUXEMBOURG

to Versailles

FAUBOURG
ST MICHEL

46

ix

FAUBOUR
ST JACQUI

SECTIONS
1   Tuileries
2   Champs Élysées
3   Roule
4   Palais Royal
5   Place Vendôme
6   Bibliothèque
7   Grange Batelière
8   Louvre
9   Oratoire
10   Halle au Blé
11   Postes
12   Place Louis XIV
13   Fontaine Montmorency
14   Bonne Nouvelle
15   Ponceau
16   Mauconseil
17   Marché des Innocents
18   Lombards
19   Arcis
20   Faubourg Montmartre
21   Poissonnière

22   Bondy
23   Temple
24   Popincourt
25   Montreuil
26   Quinze-Vingts
27   Gravilliers
28   Faubourg Saint Denis
29   Beaubourg
30   Enfants Rouges
31   Roi de Sicile
32   Hôtel de Ville
33   Place Royle
34   Arsenal
35   Ile Saint-Louis
36   Notre-Dame

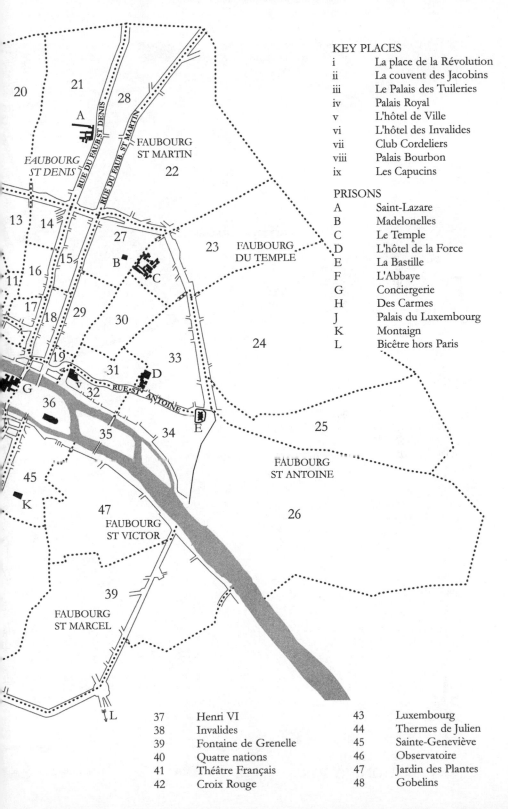

KEY PLACES
i   La place de la Révolution
ii   La couvent des Jacobins
iii   Le Palais des Tuileries
iv   Palais Royal
v   L'hôtel de Ville
vi   L'hôtel des Invalides
vii   Club Cordeliers
viii   Palais Bourbon
ix   Les Capucins

PRISONS
A   Saint-Lazare
B   Madelonelles
C   Le Temple
D   L'hôtel de la Force
E   La Bastille
F   L'Abbaye
G   Conciergerie
H   Des Carmes
J   Palais du Luxembourg
K   Montaign
L   Bicêtre hors Paris

20
21
28
A
FAUBOURG
ST MARTIN
22
FAUBOURG
ST DENIS
RUE DU FAUB.ST DENIS
RUE DU FAUB.ST MARTIN
13   14
27
23   FAUBOURG
        DU TEMPLE
15
B
C
11
16
17
18   29
30
24
19
33
31   D
G   v   32   RUE ST ANTOINE
36
35   34
E
25
FAUBOURG
ST ANTOINE
45
K
47   26
FAUBOURG
ST VICTOR
39
FAUBOURG
ST MARCEL
L

37	Henri VI	43	Luxembourg
38	Invalides	44	Thermes de Julien
39	Fontaine de Grenelle	45	Sainte-Geneviève
40	Quatre nations	46	Observatoire
41	Théâtre Français	47	Jardin des Plantes
42	Croix Rouge	48	Gobelins

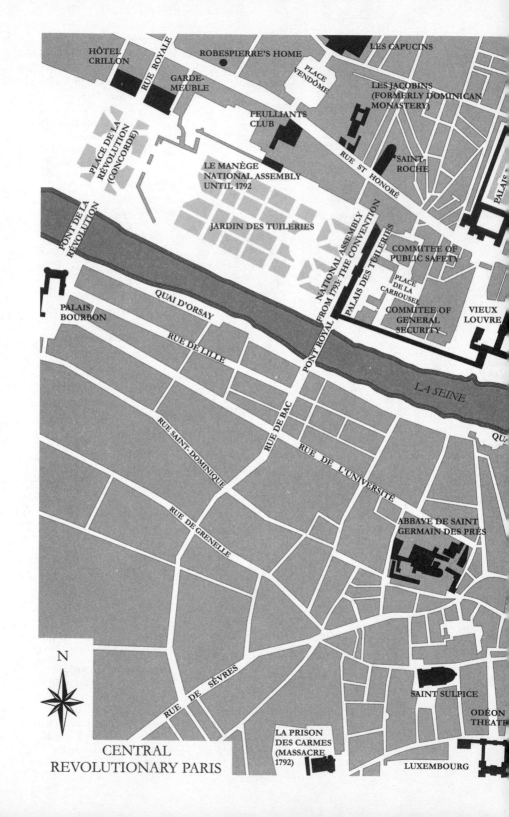

CENTRAL
REVOLUTIONARY PARIS

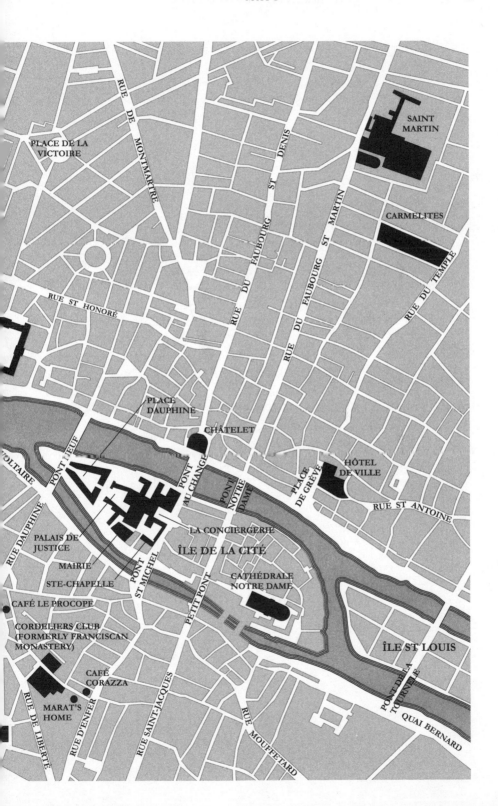

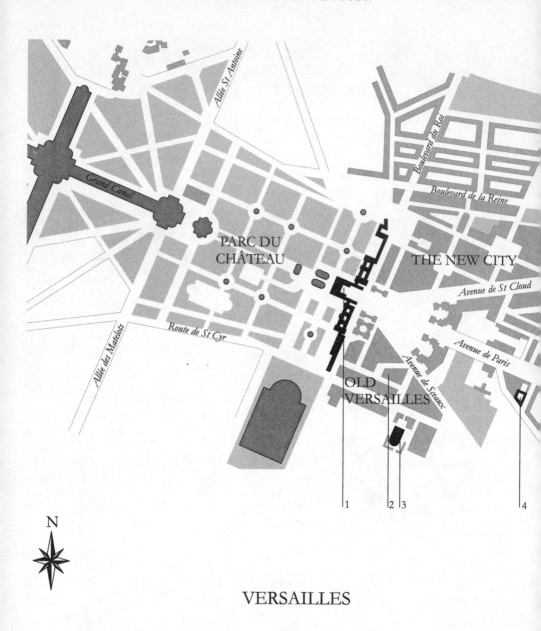

VERSAILLES

1. Château de Versailles

2. Salle du Jeu de Paume

3. Eglise Saint-Louis
   (named 'Temple of Abundance')

4. Salle des Menus Plaisirs
   (meeting place of the National Assembly)

TIMELINE

DATE	FRANCE	UNITED STATES	EUROPE
1762	Jean–Jacques Rousseau (1712–1778), publishes *Le Contrat Social* & *Émile*; 13 editions of *Le Contrat Social* published in 1762–1763; *Petit Conseil* of Geneva orders it burned, & Rousseau banned;		
1763	13 April: Voltaire (1694–1778): publishes *Traité sur la Tolérance* 12 May: Rousseau publicly renounces his Citizenship of Geneva; 27 September: Jean–Robert Tronchin defends the *Petit Conseil*, in *Lettres écrites de la Campagne*; David Hume (1711–1776) stays in Paris; befriends J–J Rousseau		
1764	July: Voltaire publishes *Dictionnaire Philosophique* December: Rousseau replies to Tronchin in *Lettres écrites de la Montagne*		
1765	November: Voltaire publishes *Idées Républicaines,* in defence of the lower orders in Geneva;		January: conflict in Geneva between patricians and burghers; patricians of *Petit Conseil* appeal to outside Guarantors: Bern, Zurich & France;
1766			
1767			December: Geneva conflict: Delolme publishes pamphlet claiming sovereignty of the people;
1768		1st vol *Encyclopaedia Britannica* published	January: Geneva conflict; J-R Tronchin proposes compromise Edict of 1768, called Edict of Pistols;
1769			
1770			Geneva conflict: patricians put down a demonstration by *natifs* by force;
1771			

DATE	FRANCE	UNITED STATES	EUROPE
1772			Sweden: monarchist *coup d'état* by Gustavus III;
1773			Poland partitioned;
1774			
1775		American colonists rebel against British government	Pierre Augustin Caron de Beaumarchais (1732–1799): *Le Barbier de Séville*
1776		July 4: American rebels declare Independence;	David Hume (1711–1776): dies in Edinburgh, age 65; Adam Smith (1723–1790): publishes *The Wealth of Nations*; Thomas Paine (1737–1809): publishes *Common Sense*
1777	Jacques Necker (1732–1804), protestant banker from Geneva, appointed *directeur général des finances* from 1777;	France gives covert support to American rebels; gunpowder, arms, through Beaumarchais's company; total aid to Americans costing so far up to £5m. June: Marie Joseph Gilbert Motier, marquis de La Fayette (1757–1834), travels to America (age 20), joins American rebels, and is made a general by George Washington	
1778		6 February: France signs Treaty of Alliance with United States, and openly joins American War of Independence against Britain	
1779	Voltaire (1694–1778): dies in Paris, age 84; Jean–Jacques Rousseau (1712–1778): dies at Ermenonville, age 66		
1780			29 November: Maria Theresa dies, Joseph II becomes sole ruler of Austrian Empire;
1781	Charles de Calonne (1734–1802) proves that the accounts presented by Necker are wrong; Jacques Necker fired for failing to deal with the budget deficit;	19 October: Siege of Yorktown, defeat of Cornwallis by American troops led by George Washington and French troops led by Comte de Rochambeau;	Beaumarchais: *Le Mariage de Figaro* accepted by the *Comédie Française,* but banned by the censors
1782		September: France exhausted by the costs of the American War; Vergennes, French Foreign Minister, proposes peace negotiations; Americans decide to negotiate directly with the British;	Geneva: counter–revolution; patricians call intervention by France, annul Edict of 1768;

DATE	FRANCE	UNITED STATES	EUROPE
1783	3 Nov: Calonne appointed *Contrôleur-Général des Finances*; Total cost to France of commitment to American War of Independence: over £1,300m; increasing total debt of French state (= monarchy) to around £3,300m	3 September: Treaty of Paris, end of American War of Independence;	Political disturbances in Dutch Republic; lasting until 1787, with intervention of Prussia;
1784	Beaumarchais: *Le Mariage de Figaro* finally allowed, with the support of Louis XVI, by the censors to be performed in public		
1785			
1786	2 August: Calonne presents plan for new land tax, a so-called *subvention territoriale*; 26 September: Commercial Treaty with England;		W A Mozart (1756–1791): *The Marriage of Figaro* performed at Burgtheater in Vienna
1787	22 February: Calonne presents new budget and taxation plan to *Assemblée des Notables*, 144 aristocrats, princes, dukes, bishops, *conseillers* etc; they reject it; 8 April, Lous XVI dismisses Calonne, and exiles him; May; Louis XVI appoints new *Contrôleur–Général des Finances*, Étienne Charles de Loménie de Brienne (1727–1794), archbishop of Toulouse; Brienne dismissses *Assemblée des Notables*;	17 September: US Constitution adopted in Philadelphia;	
1788	16 July; Parlement of Paris rejects tax proposals of Brienne, leading to total deadlock over the King's finances; 25 August: Louis XVI recalls Necker; Necker insists on the calling of *États Généraux,* to solve the finance crisis; 27 December: Louis XVI accepts proposal by Necker to double the number of *députés* for the *tiers état;*	21 June: US Constitution ratified by nine states;	

DATE	FRANCE	UNITED STATES	EUROPE
1789	January: Sieyès publishes *Qu'est ce que le tiers état?*, May 5: Versailles: opening of États généraux; 17 June: Versailles: Revolutionaries call themselves *Assemblée Nationale*: 20 June: loyalty oath in the *Jeu de Paume*; 23 June: Versailles: Séance Royale: 11 July: Louis XVI dismisses Necker; 14 July: Paris: Fall of the Bastille; 15 July: Jean Sylvain Bailly elected mayor of Paris, and La Fayette commander of the *garde nationale de Paris*; 17 July: the King visits Paris; start of emigration: the comte d'Artois (brother of the King) and many others; 29 July: Louis XVI recalls Necker; 4–5 August: Versailles: overthrow of feudalism; 25 August: Versailles: *Déclaration des Droits de l'Homme*; 5 October: march of the market women from Paris to Versailles; 6 October; the King moves to Paris; 2 November: National Assembly places Church property '*à la disposition de la nation*'; 9 November: 1st meeting of the National Assembly in the Salle du Manège at Tuileries; 17 December: National Assembly votes to use Church property to underwrite state debts; 19 December: creation of first *assignats*		
1790	13 February: decree banning closed religious orders; 26 February: creation of the 83 *départements* of France; 15 March: decree suppressing *droits seigneuriaux*; 17 March: first steps in the reform of the Church, sale of Church property; 21 March: suppression of the salt tax (*la gabelle*) 8 September: Louis XVI dismisses Necker;		26 January: 1st performance in Vienna of Mozart's *Cosí fan Tutte*; Edmund Burke (1729–1797): publishes *Reflections on the Revolution in France*; 20 February: death of Joseph II of Austria; succeeded by his brotherLeopold II
1791	2 April: death of Mirabeau; 16 May: Robespierre sponsors decree to exclude existing deputies from election to the new Legislative Assembly; 20 June: Escape of the King to Varennes; 18 July: Demonstration at Champ de Mars; Danton flees to England; 3 September: 1st Revolutionary Constitution; 1 October: *Assemblée Nationale Législative;*	Thomas Paine (1737–1809): publishes *Rights of Man*; 10 December: ratification of 1st 10 amendments to the US Constitution, known as US 'Bill of Rights',	

DATE	FRANCE	UNITED STATES	EUROPE
1792	20 April: *Assemblée Nationale* votes for war against Austria; 9 August: Insurrection by *sans-culottes*, formation of *Commune Insurrectionnelle*; August 10: overthrow of Tuileries; imprisonment of the King; 2 September; fall of Verdun; 2–7 September; prison massacres; 20 September; Battle of Valmy; 21 September; opening of new *Assemblée Nationale,* called *Convention;* 10 December: start of the trial of the King; Johann Wolfgang Goethe (1749–1832): witnesses the Battle of Valmy		20 April: *Assemblée Nationale* votes for war against Austria; 23 August: fall of Longwy; 2 September; fall of Verdun; 20 September; Battle of Valmy;
1793	Thomas Paine (1737–1809): publishes *L'Age de la Raison*; 20 January: King condemned to death; 21 January: King executed; 3 March: *levée des 300,000*; uprising in the Vendée; 10 March: creation of *Tribunal révolutionnaire;* 4 May: 1st price control measure, '*le maximum*', on wheat and flour; 31 May, 2 June: insurrection by *Montagnard sans-culottes*; overthrow of the *Girondins* by coup d'état; 24 June: 2nd Revolutionary Constitution: stillborn; 23 August: mass conscription '*levée en masse*'; 5 Sept: start of the *Terreur*; 5 September: major anti-inflation demonstration, led by Hébert: 29 September: 2nd price control measure, also known as '*le maximum*', covering more foods, as well as wages; 17 October: victory over Vendéens at Cholet; 31 October: execution of the *Girondins*; 4 December: Decree (*loi du 14 frimaire*), setting up centralised Revolutionary Government, under control of CSP: (1) role of *envoyés en mission* curbed; (2) role of *départements* curbed; (3) all mayors replaced by 'national agents'; (4) *Armées Révolutionnaires* abolished; (5) *Comités de Surveillance* strengthened; 5 December: 1st issue of Camille Desmoulins' *Le Vieux Cordelier*, calling for clemency, opening prisons; 13–14 December: Vendéens defeated at Le Mans; 19 December: Toulon retaken; 23 December: Vendéens defeated at Savenay;		6–8 September: French victory at Hondschoote; 16–17 October: French victory at Wattignies;

DATE	FRANCE	UNITED STATES	EUROPE
1794	13 January: arrest of Fabre d'Églantine for corruption; 5 February: Robespierre speech on *'principes de morale politique'*: endorses *vertu* and *terreur*; 6 February: Bonaparte promoted to general; 13 March: arrest of Hébert, Ronsin, Vincent; 18 March: arrest of Chaumette; 21–24 March: trial of *'Hébertistes'*; 2–5 April: trial of *'Dantonistes'*; 19 April: recall of *envoyés en mission*; 7 May: Robespierre's report to *Convention* on *'principes de morale politique'*: *'l'Être Suprême'*; May 10: arrest of Jean Pache, mayor of Paris, replaced by Lescot Fleuriot; 8 June: *Fête de l'Etre Supreme*; 10 June: *loi du 22 prairial*; removing all defence from the accused, in *Tribunal Révolutionnaire*; 11 June– 27 July: *'la Grande Terreur'* 26 July: violent speech of denunciation by Robespierre at *Convention*; 27–28 July, 1794: *'9–10 Thermidor'*; overthrow and execution of Robespierre	2 June: after battle at sea, American grain convoy arrives in Brest	26 June: French victory at Fleurus;

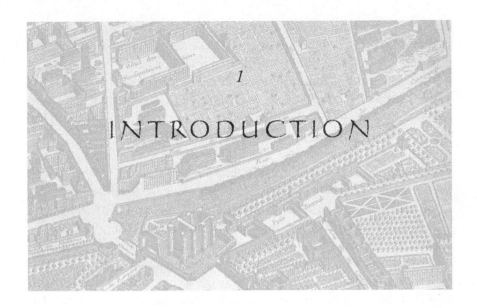

1

INTRODUCTION

THE STORY OF THE FRENCH REVOLUTION is the story of how a group of educated young Frenchmen, many of them lawyers, set about building a new state in France, on new principles based on the rule of law, of how, for a while, they succeeded; and of how, after a while, they failed.

They called it a 'Revolution', but it started almost entirely peacefully, and it went on being largely peaceful for another three years; and when, eventually, it began to descend into failure, chaos and Terror, it was the Revolutionaries who progressively dismantled, piece by piece, their own system of the rule of law.

This story is quite different from that told by the lurid and violent picture-book illustrations which have so often been attached to the French Revolution in some popular mythologies. Anyone who has been taken in by images which imply that the French Revolution consisted mainly of screaming, bloodthirsty mobs and the fearful, repetitive thud of the guillotine blade is bound to be daunted or even confused. Images like that cannot be made sense of, because they are simply misleading.

It is true that the Revolutionaries left behind the guillotine, the Terror and the ingenious institutions of the world's first modern police state. And they also invented the concept of mass warfare, character-ised by mass mobilisation, the large-scale concentration of economic and bureaucratic resources and the ruthless pursuit of victory.

But they did not come to Versailles in the spring of 1789 to destroy anything: their 'Revolution' only started to take shape after the *ancien régime* had collapsed, under the weight of its own bankruptcy, and the 'Revolutionaries' found that they were left in charge.

They went on to change the history of the world forever. They opened the door to a new era of liberation and democracy in Europe; they embarked on the creation of the first modern, would-be rational-ist, secular state, constructed from the ground up and based on the rule of law; and they formulated far-reaching ideas of a fairer society, later encapsulated in the slogan *Liberté, égalité, fraternité*, a slogan more often quoted than practised, by them or anyone else.

The trigger for this Revolution was the King's progressive recogni-tion that the French state was virtually bankrupt and that he needed help to solve his financial difficulties. But the most profound political reason for the Revolution was that the King and his predecessors had, over many decades, repeatedly adopted policies which alienated all those who might have helped him solve his problems, including, cru-cially, both the nobility and the bourgeoisie.

The premises of the *ancien régime* were increasingly unfair and unjust to almost everybody, apart from a tiny minority of the nobility. Over at least the previous century, successive French monarchs, espe-cially Louis XIV and Louis XV, had squeezed the nobility from their inherited political roles in the running of various parts of the country and had concentrated political power at the centre, at the Palace of Ver-sailles. But to compensate the nobility for their loss of political rights, the monarchy had increased their privileges in other ways, partly through a scandalously inequitable regime of tax exemptions, partly by conferring exclusive social status on those rich enough and subservient enough to play along with the narrow rituals of courtly fashion at Versailles and most critically in career advancement.

When the Revolution erupted, the inequity of the tax regime was the subject of the Revolutionaries' most vocal complaints. But at the bedrock, it was the discrimination against the bourgeoisie in the state's most impor-tant professions that was the Revolution's primary driving force.

The traditional avenues of advancement in a France dominated by the monarchy were the army and the Church; but under rules laid down by the monarchy, and significantly tightened earlier in the eighteenth century, under Louis XV, no one could be promoted to any serious level in either field unless they were aristocrats. The nobility was a very small minority of the French population, though even today there is debate about how small. This is partly because the aristocracy continually squabbled among themselves and with the court about who was noble and who was not, from the most ancient *nobles d'extraction* to the less ancient but still knightly *nobles d'épée* to the wholly civilian *nobles de robe* of the law courts; and partly because succeeding monarchs would create new titles, especially Louis XIV, who kept launching new titles and inventing new offices which he sold for cash – and then reinvented, and sold again for more cash. As a result, there is still considerable disagreement both about the number of aristocrats and of aristocratic families; and estimates of the two categories do not coincide: numbers range from 9,000 to 25,000 families, and anywhere from around 110,000 to around 400,000 individuals.[1]

These discrepancies may seem large, but they are trivial compared with the size of the French population, which was probably around 21 million people at the beginning of the eighteenth century and expanded steadily to around 28 million by the century's end. In other words, whatever the number of *noblesse* in France at the end of the 1700s, proportionally it was tiny, somewhere between 0.4 and 1.5 per cent of the total population. Of these aristocrats, whether 110,000 or 400,000, the vast majority were small landowners, known scornfully as *hobereaux*, living remotely on their estates in the depths of the country, in *la France profonde,* and many of them, despite their titles, their dignity, their pride and their privileges, were often quite pinched economically, even poor; in England they would have been called just country gentry, and poor country gentry at that. What this means is that the rich and influential nobility were a tiny minority of a tiny minority; not 'the top 1 per cent', in the phrase often used about extreme inequality in the twenty-first century, but just a very small fraction of that.

The clergy were even less numerous. There were 120,000 of them, of every sort and condition. At the top were 139 bishops, who were very rich, very powerful and very privileged, and all, of course, members of the nobility; at the bottom were 35,000 parish priests, most of whom were almost as poor as their parishioners.

For an ambitious young man who did not come from the nobility, the career options were rather limited: business or the law. The Industrial

Revolution had just started, especially in England, but it was still in its infancy, and industry as a career was still mainly in the future, so business usually meant trade or commerce. But commerce needed capital, which mostly meant having parents with an established business. So the normal alternative, for an ambitious young man without a family business to go into, was the law.

There were many attractions in a legal career. If you were successful, working in and around the royal law courts, you could make a decent living, and you could perhaps, in time, buy one of the valuable official positions in the legal system, which were for sale, and which would make you more money. If you made enough money, you might in theory be able to buy one of the most prestigious legal positions, attached to the higher law courts, known as the *Parlements*, though the *noblesse de robe* were fiercely resistant to the intrusion of commoners. Nevertheless, the law was one route by which a commoner might acquire a title of nobility, and most of the privileges that went with it.

But the law was not just a way for an ambitious commoner to make a living; it was also becoming the basis for a new political class. Typically, the rising lawyer at that time was steeped in the ideas of the Enlightenment. French society, like others in much of Western Europe, was undergoing a colossal transformation. The ultra-intellectual Enlightenment of Montesquieu and Voltaire, Bach and Mozart, Isaac Newton and Adam Smith was just the tip of a vast change that was happening throughout society and producing an expanding, educated, literate and ambitious bourgeoisie. This is how François Furet describes the political implications in France of the Enlightenment:[2]

> In the eighteenth century, French society was desperately in search of intermediaries between the state and the people, because it was too 'developed', as we would say now, to be kept, as in the previous century, in a state of silence and of obedience. After the death of Louis XIV, people naturally turned to traditional institutions, like the *parlements*. But since the *parlements* continued to prove, throughout the century, totally conservative, with the condemnation of the *Encyclopédie*[3] and of the unhappy Calas family,[4] they could not be valid intermediaries in an Enlightened society. That is why French society in the eighteenth century increasingly gave itself other spokesmen: the *philosophes* and the writers. Literature thus effectively acquired a virtually political function.[5]

The political function of literature was even intensified further among the rising young professionals of the legal system, through the enforced development of the characteristic political skills of debate. When the 'Revolutionaries' arrived on the scene, they did not come to overthrow anything: they came to discuss, to argue and to make political speeches.

Alexis de Tocqueville[6] makes a similar analysis to Furet's:

> When you think that the French people, so out of touch with their own affairs and so lacking in experience, so hampered by their political institutions and so impotent to reform them, were nevertheless, at the same time, of all the peoples on the earth, the most literate and the most in love with intelligence, you can easily understand how their writers became a political force and ended up by being the leading force.[7]

In intellectual and moral terms, the Enlightenment was inevitably the antithesis of the closed, conservative and repressive system of the *ancien régime*; but its social and economic implications had broader political consequences, which set the rising class of the educated bourgeoisie in opposition to the absolutist state. The Enlightenment gave the rising bougeoisie a fundamental claim to a political role; the practice of the law gave them the skills to exercise it. The expanding, educated and literate bougeoisie were pushing up and could no longer be stopped. There were now more and more educated and able young men, part of the significant and growing middle class, and they wanted a bigger share in the system and were deeply frustrated by the exclusionary rules of the *ancien régime*. The career privileges given by the monarchy to the nobility virtually forced a large minority of these able young men to look for a career in the law. And that is what they did.

Louis XVI did not recognise the political claims of the bourgeoisie, however: the absolutist state laid down by his predecessors, Louis XIV and Louis XV, was based on the assumption of a tacit alliance between the monarchy, the clergy and the nobility. In 1786, Louis XVI found himself, once again, in deep financial difficulties and turned for help to his traditional class allies: he called a meeting of nobles, but they refused to help. Having shut them out of any recognised political role in the running of the state, Louis XVI found that he had alienated them irrevocably. He then turned to the *Parlement de Paris,* the highest law court in the land, with the formal role of registering royal edicts; but they too refused to help. The *Parlement* had, over time, begun to assume (quite unconstitutionally) that it was entitled to assert its own political rights and had in effect transformed itself into an unofficial opposition to the monarchy. In other words, the cumulative result of the monarchy's exclusionary policies over the previous two centuries was to create a stalemate of the entire French political system.

In theory, a revolution like the French one could have happened anywhere in Europe, because Europe was ripe for it. England, of course, had had its own revolution more than a century earlier and had eventually staggered through to a form of constitutional, monarchical, parliamentary democracy. On the continent, the despotism of Bourbon France, though extreme, was not unique. Most peoples in most of Europe lived under monarchies of one kind or another, most of which were more or less despotic. Some of these regimes had wrestled fitfully with reform, but never very far. A sole exception might have been Geneva, which on paper was ostensibly a democratic Republic, but was really an autocracy under the control of a tiny ruling class. By the last half of the eighteenth century, the repressive regimes of Europe had outlived their operational usefulness or their political acceptability. As a result, from 1760, subject peoples had regularly erupted in protests against their rulers, in Hungary, in Milan, in Sweden, in Belgium and in Geneva, as well as in France itself.[8]

So why did the Revolution succeed in France? The most fundamental fact about its opening phase is that Louis XVI simply surrendered to the advancing tide of the bourgeoisie. Elsewhere in Europe, the authorities more or less effectively suppressed the various protests and eruptions, usually with some degree of violence. In America, the English had tried to suppress the rebels by force and had been militarily defeated in the War of Independence. In France, it was the King who was defeated, but peacefully, without the use of force.

The French Revolution was not just a turning point in French and European history, it was also a highly contentious event, and many historians have felt obliged to take sides. On the one hand there were the Declaration of the Rights of Man and the assertion of the sovereignty of the people; but on the other there were the guillotine and the Terror, and some historians have felt that the French Revolution was fundamentally defined, even invalidated, by the violence of the Terror. Edmund Burke decried the violence and anarchy of the revolution, even though he published his denunciations several years before the Terror started; and even today, some of the most popular accounts in English, like those of Christopher Hibbert and Simon Schama, are steeped in a tone of deep disapproval.

I have tried to take a more neutral position, letting the story tell itself. This is not an academic book, and I make no attempt to register the latest refinements in academic research. My aim is more modest: to tell the central story of the French Revolution in terms that are credible, economical and readable.

I have drawn on many sources – French, English, American, Canadian and others – from many periods. But I have always been conscious that the French Revolution was essentially a French event; throughout the unending swings of political instability during the nineteenth and well into the twentieth century, French politicians never ceased to wrestle with the fact that the problems they faced were part of the aftershocks, so much so that several of them, including three Prime Ministers in the nineteenth century (François Guizot, Adolphe Thiers and Jean Jaurès), wrote multivolume histories of the Revolution. For this reason it is mainly through the prism of French writers that I have tried to understand a story which has become part of France's long-running dialogue with itself; and for this reason I have quoted most heavily from six French writers from three very different periods spanning this long downdraught: Jules Michelet and Alexis de Tocqueville in the mid-nineteenth century, Albert Mathiez and Albert Soboul in the first half of the twentieth century, and François Furet and Jean Tulard in the second half of the twentieth century.

Michelet lived almost within touching distance of the last survivors of the Revolution, and he was an ardent enthusiast of the Revolution, a passionate Republican and a passionate hater of Robespierre; his history is as vivid as Dickens. Tocqueville did not live to complete his history of the French Revolution, but his *L'ancien régime et la Révolution* remains, even 160 years later, by far the most penetrating and evocative analysis of the causes and circumstances which led up to it. During much of the twentieth century, French scholarship was dominated by left-wing interpretations; Mathiez and Soboul were both Marxists and Robespierrists, and both were extremely intelligent and remain extremely readable. Furet was the leading French historian of the Revolution after World War II, and he was influential in helping break the grip of the Marxists on French historiography; his deep analyses and judgements are still essentially unchallenged. Tulard came after him and published his history in time for the bicentenary.

In the past, French historians tended to be divided between passionate admirers of Robespierre and passionate admirers of Danton. Today these controversies have subsided, and in my book there are no heroes; in this respect the French Revolution may be unique. The American Revolution was a milestone in American and Western history, and it threw up a whole series of exceptional individuals, of whom Washington, Hamilton and Madison were only the first in a long line stretching well into the nineteenth century. The French Revolution was quite different, and Furet is surely right when he says that the French Revolution was a great event but that it did not produce any great men.

Many accounts have given the impression that the French Revolution was exemplified by one single, violent event: the overthrow, in Paris, of the prison fortress of the Bastille. This was, of course, a dramatic and shocking episode, the ferocious assault, by a wild and largely undisciplined mob, on the most feared symbolic institution of the repressive French state; but it was an attack without a plan, without a strategy and without a coherent political consequence.

So it is paradoxical that Bastille Day, *14 juillet*, has become the national day of the French Republic[9] and the very symbol of the Revolution. The fall of the Bastille was in fact wholly unrepresentative of the real work of the early Revolution, which started three weeks earlier, 10 miles away, in Versailles, south-west of Paris, in orderly, dignified and well-dressed silence.

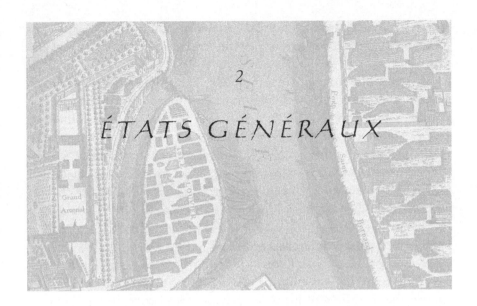

2

ÉTATS GÉNÉRAUX

LOUIS XVI FINALLY REALISED that all the ordinary institutions of the state were systematically blocking him and that he would get no help either from the nobility or the Paris *Parlement*. On August 2, 1788, he decided to go over their heads by calling a meeting of the *États généraux* (Estates General) in the desperate hope that when it convened at Versailles it would rescue him from his financial (and political) predicament. This assembly was so named because it represented all the people of France, whose population was notionally divided into three hierarchically distinct *États*: the clergy at the top, followed by the nobility, and the commoners, the Third Estate (*tiers état*), at the bottom.[1]

The *États généraux* was an antiquated and long-neglected national advisory institution that had been created nearly 500 years earlier, in 1302; its meetings had become infrequent and its function uncertain and unreliable. In more recent times, because of the overweening authority and centralised power of Louis XIV and Louis XV, the *États généraux* had effectively fallen into disuse; it had not met for 175 years, the previous time having been right at the beginning of the reign of Louis XIII (Louis XVI's great-great-great-great-grandfather), to celebrate his coming of age in 1614. That date is significant, for it was Louis XIII who later launched the explicit policy of royal absolutism, which Louis XIV much extended, epitomised by the remote grandeur of the vast and magnificent Palais de Versailles.

By 1788, the situation had completely changed: Louis XVI still lived in splendid isolation at Versailles, but he was not any kind of real successor to the 'Sun King', Louis XIV. Born in 1754, in 1770 he had married Marie-Antoinette, the sister of the Emperor of Austria, when he was the Dauphin and only fifteen years old, and she was only fourteen. Several years passed before she conceived, which prompted much malicious gossip and speculation. But in 1774 he had succeeded to the throne, and on December 19, 1778, Marie-Antoinette gave birth to their first child, Marie-Thérèse, the first of four and the only child to survive their parents for a significant number of years.[2]

Now aged thirty-four, Louis was seriously overweight, pious, weak and indecisive; he was full of goodwill but unable to assert himself against the meddling of his wife's frivolous and conspiratorial entourage. He was no longer making grandiloquent claims of absolutism but modestly asking his 'faithful subjects' to help him 'overcome all the difficulties in which We find ourselves in relation to the state of Our finances ... and to make us aware of the wishes and complaints of our peoples'.[3]

Louis' reference to 'wishes and complaints' was an allusion to the ancient tradition that a meeting of the *États généraux* should be accompanied by the submission, by all the individual delegations, from their constituencies throughout France, of lists of grievances (*cahiers de doléances*). These were to be drawn up by local representatives of each of the three 'orders' (the clergy, the nobility and the commoners, in that order of precedence): in each *bailliage*, or bailiwick, the clergy would meet and together draft their list of grievances; and the nobility would do the same. For the commoners, because they were far, far more numerous than either the clergy or the nobility, the operation was slightly more complex: each parish had to draw up a first draft, and these were then revised and collated at the level of the *bailliage*.

In many cases, the delegations, partly for convenience and partly no doubt for reasons of nervousness and conformism, drafted their submissions with the help of various models, which were freely available and widely circulated; some parishes drew on two or more such models, and in the bailiwick of Nancy, for example, scholars have identified eleven. In rural areas, people were often obliged to rely on these models, since many could neither read nor write. What emerged from all this drafting and collating was 60,000 *cahiers de doléances*, an amazing collection that Tocqueville later described as 'the last testament of the ancient French society, the supreme expression of its desires, the genuine manifestation of what it wanted'.[4]

The *cahiers* contained frequent expressions of shock at the financial deficit and showed general distrust of the King's arbitrary authority in managing the public finances. Strikingly, there was a widespread sense of support, from all three orders, for the idea that the *États généraux* should insist on the establishment of a Constitution before introducing any solution to the financial crisis.

Naturally, the *cahiers* of the commoners contained a wide variety of opinions, depending on local circumstances, but there were a number of converging themes: a profound attachment to the monarchy and belief in the King as the father of the country, a universal desire for an improvement in living conditions, and multiple criticisms of the way the political system was working, or not working. Above all, there were widespread demands for a simplification of the justice system and even more for a reform and lightening of the tax system.

The *tiers état* resented the *corvée*, a form of community duty (often in the form of physical labour) imposed on the lowest order, mainly for the purpose of maintaining the roads; but they resented even more the nobles' monopoly of hunting rights, as well as the obligation imposed on them to use and pay for the nobles' flour mills and bread-making ovens, and the nobles' entitlement to administer local, seigneurial justice. In general, what the *tiers état* wanted was equality before the law; not just non-discriminatory justice but also a non-discriminatory tax system – one which no longer exempted the *noblesse* and the clergy from paying taxes, most of which fell on the *tiers état*.

That said, it seems fairly clear that the system of compiling the commoners' *cahiers de doléances* – with the first drafting at the level of the parishes, followed by the revision and collation at the level of the bailiwicks – led to political filtration, so that the final versions gave more emphasis to the opinions of the more important people higher up: the farmer rather than the farm worker, the master artisan rather than his employee, the skilled craftsman. But there was a general and deep-seated demand for greater equality in taxation.

Significantly, these *cahiers* showed no unanimity of opinion among the commoners about the various quasi-feudal dues or duties that they had to pay to their local seigneurs or lords. Almost all called into question one or the other of these dues or duties, but few demanded the total suppression of the system. Even more significantly, in the light of later events, many of the *cahiers*, from the *noblesse* as well as from the *tiers état*, advocated making use of the value of Church property, either to reduce the state debt or to alleviate poverty. It all added up to a demand, from all sides, for a Constitution which would limit the powers of the King and create a system of national representation with the right to authorise taxation and make laws.

As a result, the meeting of the *États généraux* led directly not to the solution of the King's finances but to the start of the Revolution, because the most important question most commonly raised in the *cahiers* was the unavoidable issue of political legitimacy.

As we have already noted, there was an institution in Paris called a *Parlement*, just as there were a dozen other, less important *Parlements* in different seats throughout France. These were not democratically elected parliaments like the House of Commons or the American Congress; instead, they were law courts at the top of the legal tree. And one of the tasks of the Paris *Parlement* in particular was to register and thus in some sense endorse the King's policy initiatives. This *Parlement* could object if it believed that a royal initiative was in conflict with other legal principles; and sometimes it claimed that this function gave it quasi-democratic legitimacy, as if it represented the nation. But everyone knew that the Paris *Parlement* was a powerhouse of privilege and wealth, a lawyer's paradise, through which members of the rising, educated middle class could acquire the privileged status of *noblesse de robe*, in virtual rivalry with the hereditary nobility at court, the *noblesse d'épée*. There was no recognised basis for the *Parlement*'s claim to political democratic legitimacy.

The *États généraux*, by contrast, were elected and could thus claim to represent the whole of the French nation. By tradition, these three estates were expected to meet, debate and vote separately; also by tradition, each of the three orders had a delegation of roughly equal size. This had the inevitable outcome that the two privileged orders, clergy and nobility, tended to vote in favour of their privileges and to outvote the commoners, even though the commoners represented something like 98 per cent of the population.

The question of the justice of this arrangement dominated political debate in the months leading up to the elections of the delegates.

Astonishingly, in December 1788, Louis XVI had allowed himself to be persuaded by Jacques Necker, the Protestant banker from Geneva who was at the time his chief minister, that the *tiers état* should have twice as many delegates as either of the other two orders. This seemed to imply that the commoners could not simply be outvoted by the two privileged orders if they voted together. But the King had left open the central question: whether the three orders would sit – and therefore vote – separately, according to ancient feudal tradition, thus still giving extra weight to the privileged orders; or whether they would sit and vote together, and thus make it possible for the *tiers état* to outvote the representatives of the other two orders.

The fact that the King had moved halfway towards a more democratic system of representation, but only halfway, was characteristic; and this half-baked compromise turned out to be a serious provocation to the educated members of the *tiers état*, prompting the publication of a positive flood of controversial pamphlets during the second half of 1788.

Many of these works were written by aspiring political activists, some of whom subsequently became famous. One of the most celebrated and scandalous was the delegate Honoré Gabriel Riqueti, comte de Mirabeau. According to Victor Hugo's later characterisation, he was 'of an impressive and electrifying ugliness' (*d'une laideur grandiose et fulgurante*), with an enormous head disfigured by the scars of a childhood smallpox infection. In his youth he was a rebel, a debaucher, a dueller and a wild adventurer, but he became one of the best-known figures of the early Revolution, famous for his popular oratory. He said of himself: 'When I shake my terrible mane, no one dares interrupt me!'[5]

Mirabeau was born in 1749 to a noble family, the son of Victor Riqueti, marquis de Mirabeau, originally from Provence, at Le Bignon, in the Loiret, south of Paris. He joined the cavalry at the age of seventeen, but he soon engaged in disreputable escapades, and his father had him imprisoned on the Île de Ré. After he was released, he was rapidly promoted to captain, but shortly thereafter he left the army and launched himself into a life of adventure, debauchery and scandal. He married a rich heiress but then had a dramatic quarrel with his wife's family, ending in a much-publicised lawsuit. After a particularly shocking later episode, in which he had a quasi-incestuous relationship with his sister, he was forced to flee, and over the next fifteen years his father regularly pursued him with *lettres de cachet*,[6] getting him shut up in a series of prisons. He escaped from one of them, the Fort de Joux, taking with him the charming Sophie de Monnier, the young wife of a very senior judge, at which point he was charged with 'kidnapping and seduction' (*rapt de séduction*), which carried the death penalty, and he had to flee abroad, to Switzerland, to Germany and finally to Holland, where he took citizenship and earned a living by writing hack works for local booksellers. In 1777, when he was twenty-eight, his father had him extradited back to France and imprisoned for three years in the prison fortress at Vincennes. There he met, and disliked, the marquis de Sade, and wrote a number of books, including *Des lettres de cachet et des prisons d'État*, a violent and sophisticated attack on the arbitrary and unjust penal system operating in France at the time.

Mirabeau had already made friends with the young abbé de Périgord, the future Prince Talleyrand, who in Paris introduced him to high society and high finance. After leaving prison, he soon made friends with a number of future Revolutionaries: in 1782 in Neuchâtel he met Étienne Clavière, a banker exiled from Geneva as a result of the recent political upheavals there; in 1784 in Paris he got to know Jacques Brissot and Georges Danton; in Paris, he also worked with Benjamin Franklin, the representative of the new United States. With Brissot, Clavière, Condorcet[7] and others, he founded, in 1788, the *Société des amis des Noirs*, for the abolition of slavery.

When the King convened the *États généraux*, Mirabeau immediately tried to get chosen as a Deputy; but the *noblesse*, to which he belonged, did not want him, and on February 8, 1789, the *assemblée* of the *noblesse* voted to shut him out. Mirabeau then turned to the *tiers état* and published the pamphlet *L'appel à la nation provençale* (*The Appeal to the Provençal Nation*), in which he represented himself as a champion of the Third Estate against the privileges of the nobility – and which led to his triumphant election to the *États généraux* as a representative of the *tiers état* from Aix-en-Provence.

The most influential of all the Revolutionary pamphlets was published in January 1789 by the forty-year-old *abbé* Emmanuel Joseph Sieyès. As an *abbé*, Sieyès was a member of the clergy but not a full priest; yet he held several distinguished Church positions, culminating in 1783 as a canon in the cathedral of Chartres. During his career, he established close relations with Jérôme Pétion, later the mayor of Paris, and with Mirabeau's friend Charles Maurice de Talleyrand, by now the bishop of Autun and one of the rising champions of reform among the clergy. In the summer of 1788, Sieyès was asked to edit a pamphlet written by the duc d'Orléans' secretary, Pierre Choderlos de Laclos (the author of the scandalous and astonishingly successful novel *Les liaisons dangereuses*).[8] He was so stimulated by the experience that he decided to write a pamphlet of his own, which he issued in January 1789 under the challenging rhetorical title *Qu'est-ce que le tiers état?* (*What Is the Third Estate?*).

Sieyès opened his pamphlet with three far-reaching questions, which he also answered.

> What is the Third Estate? Everything.
> What has it been until now in the political order? Nothing.
> What does it ask? To be something.[9]

Sieyès went on to assert that the Third Estate was 'a complete nation' and that the nobility was foreign to this nation, first, in principle, because it did not derive from the people, and second, because, by its very nature, it defended not the general interest, but its own private interests.

Sieyès' pamphlet caused an immediate and enormous political sensation. More than 30,000 copies were sold in the first few weeks, and three more editions quickly followed the first. Mirabeau thanked Sieyès for sending him a copy, and added: 'So there is at least one man in France.' The marquis de La Fayette[10] declared that the Sieyès pamphlet held the first rank 'in that crowd of published writings'.

Almost immediately, Sieyès' denunciation of the privileges of the *noblesse* became the defining thesis of the first phase of the Revolution, starting with the meeting of the *États généraux*. As the Revolution gathered momentum, it did not take long for its leaders to turn against the clergy and the Church as well; eventually they also turned against the King. But to begin with, the central theme of the Revolution was criticism of the nobility and the quasi-feudal privileges that the nobility enjoyed; and it was the pamphlet of Sieyès that brought this first phase into close focus.

During the eighteenth century, France's population had increased by about 35 per cent, reaching close to 28 million, making it by far the most populous country in Western Europe at that time. Its only real rival was Russia in the east, which may have had a population of some 30 million.

Britain, by contrast, mustered only 8 to 10 million, and Prussia even less, 6 million. But the increase in the French population was not matched by economic growth, and wages did not keep pace with prices, with the result that large swathes of the population were regularly afflicted by economic hardship, harvest failures and hunger. The hardship and the hunger became much more severe in the 1780s, with a long succession of cold winters, wet summers and harvest shortfalls.

The vast majority of ordinary French people still lived in the countryside, and it was they who suffered most from hunger and hardship; but France was changing, and the political centre of gravity was moving from the countryside to the towns. The quasi-feudal privileges of the nobility may once have made sense and been more or less acceptable in an essentially rural society, but they were increasingly unacceptable in a country marked by more modern forms of social and economic activity, by the growth of an emerging middle class and, above all, by the growth of towns and the development of urban living. The future Revolutionaries almost all lived in towns; a career in the law was essentially an urban activity.

The elections to the *États généraux* started in February 1789, in the different localities of France. All the nobles had a personal vote. Among the clergy, the bishops and the parish priests (*curés*) had a personal vote; but the closed religious orders had only one vote per monastery. Among the *tiers état*, voting was restricted to men who paid a certain amount of tax, which immediately excluded a large proportion of households; and then voting was conducted in several phases, so as to whittle down the number of commoner delegates.

The elections were slightly chaotic, and we still do not know the exact numbers of delegates chosen. But the broad picture is clear: the clerical delegation numbered 291 *députés*, the nobles 285, and the Third Estate 578.[11] The clerical delegation included 46 bishops, but it was dominated by its 206 *curés*. They were mostly as poor as their parishioners and equally hostile to the principle of privilege, whereas the higher clergy were in many cases themselves rich and privileged, even though some of them, like Talleyrand, were reputed to be liberal. Talleyrand had been born into one of the very great French families, in Paris, in 1754. By virtue of his birth, he might have chosen a military career; but since he was slightly incapacitated by a club foot, he opted instead for the Church, even though he lacked any religious vocation. With the help of his uncle the Archbishop of Reims, he was appointed the bishop of Autun in 1788; he was thirty-four. His contemporaries mainly despised him; but he proved to be one of the great survivors, outliving both Robespierre and the Terror, Napoléon and the Empire, and dying only in 1838 at the age of eighty-four.

When the *États généraux* opened in Versailles in May 1789, the formal arrangements seemed designed to underline the discrimination against the *tiers état*. On May 2, the King received the representatives of the three orders separately; those of the *tiers état* had to wait three hours before being allowed to make their humble bow to the King. On May 4, the Deputies attended a church service at the *Église Saint Louis*, and again the *tiers état* were humiliated: the nobility wore cloth of gold, the upper clergy red or violet capes, but the *tiers état* were expected to wear black, as if at their own funeral; the clergy and the *noblesse* had places marked out for them, but the *tiers état* had to scramble for their seats.

The first formal *séance* of the *États généraux* took place in the Hôtel des Menus Plaisirs in Versailles. This was a large hall, a short distance from the Palace of Versailles, normally used for making sets for court theatricals and for storing sports equipment, such as that required for the *jeu de paume*.[12]

The roll call of the delegates was long and laborious. There was applause, mainly from the *tiers état*, for the arrival of Necker and Louis-Philippe Joseph, duc d'Orléans. Orléans was a first cousin of King Louis XVI and one of the richest men in France, but he was also known for his liberal views and for making the colonnaded garden of his large and luxurious home in Paris, the Palais Royal, available for public debates and for popular entertainment, in the newly established cafés and restaurants under its arches. It had already become a favourite place for political discussions and speeches in the run-up to the *États généraux*, and it soon became even more popular, once the Revolution got going.

The King made a short, wholly conventional little speech, which was applauded with cries of *Vive le roi!*; Charles Louis de Barentin, the Keeper of the Seals, made another short speech, equally conventional but completely inaudible; and then Necker delivered a three-hour disquisition on the state of the public finances, or rather had most of it read out for him, because his voice gave out. As soon as Necker finished, the King closed the session.

Nothing had been discussed; nothing had been settled; nothing had really been started.

There was now deadlock on the most basic procedural preliminaries. The clergy and the *noblesse* embarked on the separate registration of the credentials of the Deputies of their orders; but the *tiers état* refused to move forward on the accreditation of their Deputies, since they would not accept the principle of separate orders meeting separately.

The deadlock over accreditation lasted five weeks. Then, on June 10, the *tiers état* moved to the offensive. It proposed to the two other orders that all three should meet together and declared that it would proceed to the accreditation of all the Deputies from all three orders, meeting together. The *noblesse* rejected this proposal; the clergy hesitated.

This offensive was led by Jean Sylvain Bailly, Mirabeau, Sieyès, Antoine Barnave and Jean-Joseph Mounier. Bailly was a celebrated astronomer, and as the senior member of the *tiers état*, he became, on June 17, 1789, the first *Président* of the *Assemblée nationale* (as the *tiers état* then renamed itself). Barnave and Mounier were two of the most brilliant young lawyers from Grenoble in the Dauphiné in south-eastern France. Barnave, a Protestant and a believer in constitutional monarchy, was among the most eloquent and compelling of the new leaders of the *tiers état* and one of the few to speak without notes. Mirabeau, who was himself a remarkable public speaker, deeply admired Barnave and said of him: 'It is impossible to speak with more reason, more energy or more elegance.' Mounier, another believer in a strong constitutional monarchy, made a name for himself early on with a pamphlet analysing the *États généraux*, and he played a leading part, a little later in the year, in drafting the first three articles of the Declaration of the Rights of Man (*Déclaration des droits de l'homme*).

On June 12 the *tiers état* embarked on a roll call of all the *députés*. The next day, three *curés* from Poitou joined the *tiers état*; on June 14 they were followed by six more, and on June 16 by another ten. The *noblesse* still held out; so did the upper ranks of the clergy; and so did the King.

On June 17, after a debate lasting two days, the Deputies of the *tiers état* decided to pre-empt any further talk and declared that since they represented 98 per cent of the nation, they now constituted an *Assemblée nationale*. Almost immediately this new National Assembly claimed that it had the sovereign authority to take all decisions on taxation and declared that it placed 'the creditors of the state under the protection of the honour and the loyalty of the French nation.' In other words, they were taking the responsibility for the solvency of the state away from the King. The Revolution had begun.

With this dramatic step, the *tiers état* immediately broke its previously declared principle that nothing would be done about the King's finances until there was a Constitution.

The clergy were shaken by the initiative of the *tiers état* and on June 19 voted by a narrow majority, 149 to 137, to join it. But the *noblesse* still held out; and so did the King.

Some of the King's ministers sided with *les Communes* (the Commons), as they occasionally called themselves; but most of his immediate entourage, starting with the Queen, urged him to stand firm against the *tiers état*. Louis decided to convene a special *séance royale* of the *États généraux*, to assert his authority and call the Commons to order. It was announced for June 22.

For practical reasons, the meeting had to be delayed until June 23 and the large hall (*salle*) of the Hôtel des Menus Plaisirs temporarily closed in order to get it ready for this important event. But the delay was not announced, which turned out to be a grave mistake. When the *tiers état* discovered, on June 20, that the large hall was closed against them (as they thought), they spontaneously reconvened in what seemed the most suitable alternative large space immediately available, the Real Tennis Court (*salle du Jeu de paume*). There they swore an oath of solidarity not to allow themselves to be separated from one another until they had drawn up a Constitution for France.

The next day was a Sunday; but on Monday, June 22 the National Assembly convened again, in the large church of Notre Dame de Saint-Louis, founded by Louis XV in 1743 in the centre of the village of Versailles and designed by Jacques Hardouin-Mansart, a grandson of the great architect Jules Mansart. There the *tiers état* welcomed 150 members of the clergy and 2 members of the *noblesse*. But nothing had really been decided, nor could it be until the King declared his position at the *séance royale*, now scheduled for the next day.

Meanwhile, the King had held three meetings of his Council to decide how to proceed. On June 19, Necker set out a plan of action, which had been agreed with several of his more liberal colleagues. He proposed that the tax system be non-discriminatory (i.e., not twisted in favour of special privileges for the clergy and the nobles); that access to all public posts be open to all, including the commoners; and that voting in the *États généraux* be by head, not by orders, if not this time, then at future sessions. He also recommended that the King should not attempt to crush all the demands of the *tiers état*.

On June 21 the King and his Council rejected Necker's plan, and the King resolved to quash all the decisions of the *tiers état* and to insist that the *États généraux* must meet and vote in their separate orders.

Two days later, at the formal *séance royale* in the *salle des Menus Plaisirs*, Louis XVI acknowledged that there could be some minor reforms, and he expressed the hope that the privileged orders would accept equality of taxation; he accepted the principle of taxation by consent and of individual liberty and freedom of the press. But he said nothing about opening up the professions to all, and he resolutely stood by the traditional hierarchies of aristocratic society. In fact, he was still rejecting the principle of equality of rights and would accept only those reforms that the *noblesse* would accept.

The King closed the session with the following words: 'I order you, Gentlemen, to disperse immediately, and to present yourselves tomorrow morning in the halls allocated to your separate orders, there to resume your sessions.'[13]

It seemed as if the nobility had won and had defeated the ambitions of the *tiers état*. Many of the commoner delegates would never before have travelled further than their local town. They were in the presence of their sovereign and surrounded by all the aristocratic splendour of rank, wealth and ostentatious luxury. But they were not intimidated: they kept their seats and silently refused to accept their dismissal by the King.

This is how the historian Jules Michelet described the scene that followed:

> The King walked out, and the nobility and the clergy followed him. The Commons remained sitting, calm and in silence.
>
> The Master of Ceremonies [Henri Évrard, marquis de Dreux-Brézé] returned and said, in a low voice, to the President of the session [Bailly]: 'Sir, did you not hear the orders of the King?' Bailly replied: '… It seems to me that the nation assembled cannot take orders.'[14]

Mirabeau then raised the stakes: 'We are here by the wishes of the nation; only physical force can make us leave.'[15]

This anecdote was so popular with subsequent generations that it has come down to us in many versions; this one was published two days later in the semi-official newspaper *Le Moniteur*:

We have heard the wishes which have been suggested to the King; and you, Sir, who have no right to be his spokesman to the *États-généraux*, you who have no place and no voice here, and no right to speak, you are not made to remind us of his words. Go and tell those who have sent you that we are here by the will of the people, and can only be made to leave by the force of bayonets.[16]

Neither version may be exactly accurate; there were no stenographers present at the time. But this anecdote of a dramatic put-down by commoners of the hitherto unquestioned authority of the King rang round France and has come down to us as one of the legends of the French Revolution; the incident is often referred to by French historians in a shorthand phrase: 'Mirabeau's Retort' (*La réplique de Mirabeau*), and the scene was frequently depicted by painters of the next generation.

The commoners were challenging the legitimacy of royal authority by claiming to represent the French nation. Not all Frenchmen would have been primarily conscious of being French; in practice, most French people of the time would have tended to identify more closely with their home province or smaller locality. But here Bailly and Mirabeau were claiming to speak in the name of the whole of France.

The King's authority had been openly defied, and he did not respond to the challenge. The next day, June 24, the majority of the clergy joined the *tiers état,* and the day after, forty-seven nobles followed them, including the duc d'Orléans.

Two days later, the King simply gave way and invited 'his faithful clergy and his faithful *noblesse*' to join the *tiers état*. On this first and most fundamental point of principle, the *tiers état* had won, not by firing guns, not with bloodthirsty crowds, but with ordinary commoners, sitting in their places, silently, and refusing to be intimidated; just sitting there, saying what they wanted and then going on sitting there.

In short, the French Revolution happened not because a huge crowd of Parisians stormed the Bastille, nor because gangs of marauding peasants periodically set fire to noblemen's *châteaux* in the countryside (which they did), but because the King surrendered to the *tiers état*. When the crisis came, the absolute monarchy of Louis XVI simply fell over like a dead tree. As Furet says, 'the *ancien régime* was dead before it was knocked over.'[17]

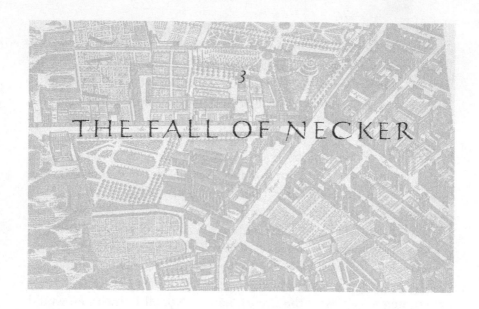

3

THE FALL OF NECKER

AFTER THE CLERGY and the *noblesse* joined the *tiers état* on June 27, 1789, the National Assembly settled down to work, and it formally decided that the first order of business was to be the writing of a Constitution. On July 7 it set up a Constitution Committee, to which thirty Deputies were appointed, and on July 9 it renamed itself the *Assemblée nationale constituante* (meaning, a Constitution-drafting Assembly). On July 11 the marquis de La Fayette proposed that the future Constitution should be preceded by a Declaration of the Rights of Man.

The Revolutionaries were beginning to act on the belief that the King had totally surrendered at the recent *séance royale* and that they were now in charge. As events over the next three years proved, they really were in charge. But right now, at the absolute beginning of the Revolution, the calm and orderliness of their proceedings were about to be shattered, because the King took steps which appeared to signal that he intended to crush them by force. On June 26 he had called up six royal regiments, and on July 1 ten more. All told, there were soon some 30,000 soldiers concentrated in the Paris region, many of them foreign troops in the pay of the monarchy. What is not clear is whether the King was deliberately embarking on a policy of counter-revolution, and if so, whether he had a plan for crushing the Revolution; or whether he had just been jostled into some ill-thought-out gesture by the hardliners at court, led by Queen Marie-Antoinette and his brothers, the comte de Provence and the comte d'Artois.

If there was a pretext for the troop mobilisation, it was that units of the semi-military, Paris-based *Gardes françaises*[1] were proving undisciplined, even semi-mutinous; but in fact it seems that the mobilisation of the troops came first and may have triggered the rebelliousness of the *Gardes françaises*. (At this stage the *Gardes françaises* were all volunteers, generally supporters of the Revolutionary movement but selected by a property qualification, and therefore all bourgeois.) More profoundly, it seems clear that both events were set off by the wave of popular excitement and agitation released by the news of the political events in Versailles. Great crowds of Parisians were milling about, and many were attracted by the excitable oratory of the young Revolutionary speakers in the gardens of the Palais Royal, home of the duc d'Orléans. On June 27, five companies of *Gardes françaises* broke ranks and fraternised with these crowds. Ten of the mutineers were then imprisoned for indiscipline in the Abbaye de Saint-Germain-des-Prés; but a crowd of 4,000 Parisians invaded the prison and released them.

There was already widespread agitation in Paris at the steep rise in the price of bread and the increase in unemployment. Bread was an absolutely vital element in the popular diet and could generally account for half of a working family's budget; in periods of crisis, as in July 1789, it could even rise to as much as 80 per cent. As a result, the supply and price of bread became determining factors in the course of the Revolution. Food shortages and food riots occurred frequently throughout the Revolution and regularly in the summer months, especially during the so-called *soudure* (literally the 'soldering', the gap between when last year's stocks were exhausted and the new harvest was taken in). As it happened, on July 14 the price of bread rose higher than it had at any previous time in the eighteenth century.

As the Revolution proceeded, it was increasingly dominated by the demands of the crowds in Paris, especially their need for bread. Every time there was a food crisis, it almost inevitably provoked conflict between the crowds in Paris, other consumers in the surrounding regions and the producing peasants in the countryside. And every food crisis was liable to trigger another downward spasm in the course of the Revolution.

The National Assembly was immediately alarmed by the King's mobilisation of the troops. On July 8, Mirabeau called for their removal from Paris and their replacement by a bourgeois militia; on July 9 the National Assembly voted to appeal to the King to withdraw the troops.

The King did not respond until the next day, and then he declared that the only purpose of the mobilisation was to keep order in Paris and to protect the debates in the National Assembly. The following day, July 11, the King dismissed Necker and ordered him to leave the country, and he dismissed all the other relatively liberal members of the cabinet. It looked as though the Queen and the King's brothers had won and were declaring a counter-revolution. Yet the new Ministry, under the baron de Breteuil, though wholly reactionary, appears to have had no plan of action, and the King seems to have had not the smallest idea of what the consequences of sacking Necker would be.

When the news of Necker's expulsion reached Paris, it caused widespread alarm. To the moneyed classes, it seemed to spell the bankruptcy of the state and thus the ruin of the *rentiers*, the people who lived off the income from their investments in loans to the state, known as *rentes*. (It is important to be clear that the Revolution affected the rich as well as the poor. The King and his predecessors had long financed the regular shortfall in their budgets by issuing loans to the public, and it was the relatively well-off who bought these loans. In other words, money was a central issue before the Revolution and it remained, for good or ill, a central issue throughout the Revolution.) To the common people, the sense of crisis and uncertainty caused by the sacking of Necker seemed to threaten food shortages and famine. There was agitation everywhere; sidewalk orators in the Palais Royal called for popular resistance to oppression; crowds milling in the Tuileries Gardens were set upon by troops of the King's *Royal Allemand* regiment. Paris was up in arms; or rather, Paris was seeking to arm itself.

4

THE STORMING
OF THE BASTILLE

THE IMMEDIATE CONSEQUENCE of the sacking of Necker on July 11, 1789, was that the centre of gravity of the Revolution shifted abruptly from Versailles to Paris, from the deliberate calm of the *Assemblée nation-ale* to the agitation of the crowds of *sans-culottes* in the streets of the capital. In pre-Revolutionary days, the term *sans-culottes* had sometimes been used as an equivalent of *canaille*, or 'scum', and in March 1791 it appeared in a royalist pamphlet to refer to ordinary people who were poor and down at heel. They were so-called because they did not wear *culottes*, or court breeches, and they did not dress in the smart, courtly fashion, with elegant, braided coats and elaborately powdered hair. But as the Revolution took over, political snobbishness was reversed, and this became the politically correct, Revolutionary term to describe the ordinary, 'patriotic' people of Paris. The *sans-culottes* were not a modern proletariat, and they included all kinds of occupations – shopkeepers, butchers, bakers, artisans, craftsmen – and any kind of employee, literate and sometimes educated as well as illiterate and uneducated. By a new, Revolutionary tradition, the *sans-culottes* wore workingmen's clothes: loose trousers, a tunic and a cap over natural, unpowdered hair; as the Revolution progressed, their dress became a kind of required uniform

of Revolutionary supporters. By contrast, many of the leading Revolutionaries always wore traditional formal dress: Robespierre was always
elegantly turned out, with *culottes* and powdered hair. Naturally, there
were similar ordinary people who lived in towns other than Paris. But
it was the crowd power of the *sans-culottes* in the capital which became
determinant at crucial moments of the Revolution.

The first reaction of the crowds of *sans-culottes* to the news of the
events in the *États généraux* from Versailles and the dismissal of Necker
was to attack and break down the toll houses which charged duty on
goods brought into the city and to set upon the employees of the hated
tax collectors, known as tax 'farmers'. The troops of the *Royal Allemand*
regiment, which had been briefly mobilised by the King to control the
crowds demonstrating in Paris round the Palais Royal, had already
returned to their barracks and so did nothing. Now it was the troops
of the elite *Gardes françaises*, who had previously fraternised with the
demonstrators, who left their own barracks and once again joined the
popular agitation on the side of the demonstrators.

The second reaction of the demonstrators was to find weapons, as a
precaution in case the King's troops came out against them. The Revolution was about to turn violent, in conditions of leaderless anarchy.
Throughout the day of July 13, 1789, thousands of agitated men milled
round the Paris town hall (*Hôtel de ville*) demanding weapons. The
administration of the *Hôtel de ville* proved incapable of dominating the
situation, and a group of leading citizens (who had quite recently come
together as electors to choose delegates from Paris to send to the *États
généraux* in Versailles) now decided to set up an insurrectional civic committee and demanded the right to participate in the administration of the
city. (This would prove an instructive precedent for the creation of the
Insurrectionary *Commune* at the time of the overthrow of the monarchy
three years later.) Jacques de Flesselles, the town's Chief Executive, at first
turned them down; but under the pressure of popular agitation he agreed
to admit twelve electors to the town hall, and this reformed general assembly met at the *Hôtel de ville* for the first time on that day, July 13. Virtually
its first act was to decide the formation of a bourgeois militia, with a force
made up of 800 men from each of the sixty Paris districts, totalling 48,000
men, to quell the agitation and maintain order in the city.

Flesselles announced that this militia would be armed with 12,000
rifles, which would be brought to Paris from Charleville; but the
milling crowds would not wait: they wanted to be armed now. Early on

July 14, they poured towards the large and daunting military hospital of Les Invalides, where they swept aside the objections of its governor and emerged with 3,000 rifles, which they distributed among their fellow-demonstrators.

But these rifles were not enough. The demonstrators wanted more weapons; they wanted ammunition and gunpowder; they wanted cannon; and they believed they would find them at the fortress of the Bastille. Their blood was now up.

The bourgeois Revolutionaries, who had already started to take control of the political system in Versailles through the creation of the *Assemblée nationale*, quickly interpreted the attack on the Bastille on July 14, 1789, as a symbolic attack on a notorious monument of the *ancien régime*. Of course, the Bastille had once been a monument of repression and had been used for the monstrous incarceration of political opponents. In July 1789, however, it held only seven prisoners and was defended by no more than thirty Swiss soldiers and eighty war invalids. Attacking it was not, then, a great demonstration of Revolutionary zeal; it was simply an easy target.

It was still, however, a massive and fearsome fortress, with walls 30 metres high and a wide moat, and its defenders had cannon. The demonstrators tried to negotiate with the Governor of the Bastille, Bernard de Jourdan, marquis de Launay, in the hope that he would hand over some of his cannon to them. But there was a series of misunderstandings, and shots were fired. It is not clear who fired first, but a hundred of the assailants died. To end the massacre, Launay capitulated, and the crowds promised that his life would be spared. He was dragged off to the *Hôtel de ville*, which was not far away; but before he got there, he was struck down and killed. For good measure, Flesselles was shot on the steps of the town hall; and his head, like that of Launay, was hacked off and paraded around on the top of a pike.

To justify these murders, it was claimed that there had been a plot to starve the people of Paris. Two other senior officials, Bertier de Sauvigny and his father-in-law Joseph Foullon, were both lynched on the same pretext later that month.

Those members of the crowd who had brought down the Bastille, or who said they had done so, later claimed the title 'Conqueror of the Bastille'. The *Hôtel de ville* commissioned Pierre François Palloy, a master of public works, to demolish it; he sold off bits as souvenirs.

Following the fall of the Bastille, the Parisian electors inaugurated the new *Commune de Paris* at the *Hôtel de ville*, with Sylvain Bailly as the Mayor and La Fayette as the commander of the militia, which, under its new title of *Garde nationale* – whose soldiers, called *gardes nationaux*, formed units of *gardes nationales* – played a key role in future Revolutionary developments.

At the news from Paris, the conservatives at the court, the Queen and the King's youngest brother, the comte d'Artois, urged Louis to flee to Metz, as a place of safety and close to the frontier, where he would be under the protection of loyal troops. Instead, he decided to stay and resigned himself to giving way to the Revolutionaries. On July 15 he went to the Assembly to tell them that the troops would be withdrawn, and the Deputies applauded him; and on July 16 he recalled Necker and the other Ministers whom he had dismissed five days earlier.

The following day, Louis went to Paris, where he called on Bailly and La Fayette in their new functions at the *Hôtel de ville*. On the way there, the crowd treated him relatively coldly. But when he emerged from the *Hôtel de ville* wearing a rosette in the conspicuous colours of the capital, red and blue, there was some polite applause. It was as if the King were ostentatiously endorsing the principle of a more democratic form of local government in Paris. That seems most improbable; it is more likely that he was simply recognising the existence of the new city authorities and indicating his hope that they would succeed in keeping order. Either way, the fact is that after the fall of the Bastille, the transformation of the role of the Paris *Hôtel de ville* was followed by a wave of similar democratic transformations in towns throughout France.

Meanwhile, in Versailles, the news of the storming of the Bastille prompted the start of a wave of emigration, led, on the night of July 15, by the comte d'Artois, the King's cousins the princes de Condé and de Conti, the maréchal de Broglie, the baron de Breteuil and many more. The King's other brother, the comte de Provence, stayed in Versailles, as did the King and his family.

This exodus was the first of various waves of emigration in the course of the Revolution, usually in response to some upheaval. Nobody knows the total number of people who eventually fled Revolutionary France. One study estimates a figure of 150,000 to 160,000 persons, or about 0.6 per cent of the country's population. A bare majority seem to have been from the *tiers état*, while a quarter were members of the clergy, as a result of the Revolutionary campaign against the Church. The *émigrés* from the *noblesse* were a minority of the total but may have numbered as many as 25,000 people, and they were of course among the most famous names at court and owners of the biggest fortunes. One consequence of the emigration of the rich was a sharp drop in demand for luxury goods and services and a corresponding increase in unemployment among those who had supplied the nobility or had worked for them as servants.

The fall of the Bastille was not, then, the founding event of the French Revolution, as is sometimes suggested in national legend: the King's capitulation to the *tiers état* in Versailles has a better claim to that title, and for the next three years the course of the Revolution would essentially be determined by the bourgeois Revolutionaries through political and parliamentary procedures. But the overthrow of the Bastille did mark the first intervention of the ordinary people of Paris in the Revolutionary struggle, in which the *sans-culottes* became first the allies and later the powerful opponents of the bourgeois Revolutionaries.

5

THE DISMANTLING
OF FEUDALISM

IN THE LAST TEN DAYS of July 1789 a vast wave of panic swept through the French countryside, hitting many regions simultaneously. Historians have called it *la Grande Peur* (the Great Fear), but its causes still remain a mystery.

Rural unrest had started in the spring, prompted in part by widespread shortages of cereals and growing unemployment among landless farm workers. But it was probably also inspired by local political debates during the elections to the *États généraux*, and the articulation and therefore the exacerbation of resentments of the feudal system's many injustices. But since the unrest turned to generalised panic only from about July 20, we can speculate that it may also have been instigated by news of the Revolutionary events in the capital – the fall of the Bastille and the establishment of the new municipal authority in Paris, with its own militia – followed by examples in many towns of France.

The peasantry were also anxious about the forthcoming harvest and obsessed with the idea that the aristocrats might be arming gangs of brigands to destroy their crops. Bands of peasants armed themselves in many provinces and set about attacking *châteaux* and manor houses,

destroying aristocrats' documentary titles of seigneurial feudal privileges, and pillaging grain stores.

On August 3 the National Assembly opened a debate 'on the terrible
reports received from several provinces where the safety of people, the
preservation of property and the payment of taxes have been imperilled.'
One *Député* commented: 'This is the war of the poor against the rich!'
His remark may have summed up the feelings of many of his bourgeois
colleagues, but the Assembly was reluctant to repress the troubles too
violently.

The *Grande Peur* did not last long. It seems to have vanished as suddenly and as completely as it started, melting away on about August 6.
The most probable reason is that two days earlier, in a spontaneous late-
night session, the National Assembly had voted to sweep away all the
paraphernalia of feudal privilege.

The session had started with a formal proposal that the 'sacred
rights' of property be guaranteed. But the young vicomte de Noailles, a
brother-in-law and army colleague of La Fayette, proposed to go much
further. He argued that the Assembly should discuss the complaints of
the peasantry and relieve them of the weight of feudal dues and duties.
In future, he said, taxes should be paid by everybody in proportion to
their income, with no exemptions or special privileges for the aristocracy; all feudal dues should be redeemed for money, at a price related
to the annual income they produced; and all *corvées*, a form of personal
servitude, should simply be abolished gratis.

Although he was a vicomte, and therefore a member of the nobility,
he came from a relatively poor noble family and was only the younger
son; so it might have seemed that he was not offering to make much of a
sacrifice. The duc d'Aiguillon, by contrast, was immensely wealthy, one
of the richest people in the kingdom after the King himself. He did not
go as far as Noailles, insisting that feudal dues were a form of property
and as such were sacred; they could be bought out, but until they were,
they should be imposed exactly as in the past. On the other hand, he did
agree that taxes should be imposed equally on all citizens according to
their means, with no exemptions and no special privileges.

Many other Deputies joined the debate, all vying with one another
in the cause of reform. There were some dissonant voices, but they were
scarcely audible against the din of enthusiasm which swept the hall. By
the time the sitting was closed, at two o'clock the next morning, the
Assembly had voted the dismantling of all the feudal institutions of the

ancien régime: the royal pensions were to be done away with, together with all the municipal and provincial immunities and all tax exemptions and privileges. The Assembly had also approved the idea that the feudal rights of the aristocrats could be bought out by their tenants. With this decision, one of the central principles of the *ancien régime* – a society based on class distinctions and privilege – collapsed in the middle of the night of August 4, 1789.

These decisions of principle had been improvised in the enthusiasm of euphoria. Now they had to be given the force of law; and the Assembly spent the next week, from August 5 to August 11, in often acrimonious debates as it drafted a decree which would turn enthusiasm into legislation. In the end, it decided to abolish all forms of serfdom, all hunting monopolies and all seignorial jurisdictions; all other feudal dues could be bought out, but until they were, they must continue to be paid. The Assembly also decided to eliminate all tax privileges and exemptions.

The common people and the peasantry quickly grasped that the National Assembly had decided a sweeping reform of the feudal apparatus of the *ancien régime*, and they tended to assume automatically that all the old dues, duties and taxes had been done away with. They did not grasp, or at least they did not want to grasp, that the National Assembly intended that the old dues and duties should go on being paid until reformed alternatives could be put in place or until the old dues had been bought out. As a result, the population at large became much more resistant to taxation, with the inevitable consequence that the fiscal crisis of the French state, already close to insolvency, grew almost insoluble.

Even more difficult was the question of what to do about the tithes of the Church – that is, the taxes which the Church raised to pay for the clergy. This was the subject of some of the bitterest debates and a foretaste of what turned out to be a long-running conflict. By the end of the debate on August 4–5, the Revolutionaries had agreed that these tithes would be abolished once an alternative was put in their place; in practice, the tithes lasted another eighteen months, until January 1, 1791, when it was decided that they could be abolished without compensation, since the state would pay the Church's costs.

This conflict with the Church was to create major problems for the Revolution in the months and years to come. Many Revolutionaries were no doubt sceptics on the subject of religion; and it is certain that many of them saw the Church's wealth as an immense resource with which to plug the yawning gap in the public finances. But the more they campaigned against the Church and its property, the more they antagonised the mass of ordinary people in rural areas, who tended to be fervent believers.

The abolition of the feudal distinctions between noble and non-noble property was welcome to many, not just poor farmers and country people. Although France was still heavily dependent on agriculture, its economy was becoming more modern, with new ways of making money. The feudal dues and duties had long been a burden and an aggravation for the poor; but in most cases they were not profitable enough to make the nobles rich. Because of this, some of the nobles were more than willing to sell their feudal dues for ready money, while property-owning commoners were glad of the elimination of the distinction between their land and that of a noble. Whatever their calculations of the economic pros and cons, we can only be impressed by the Revolutionaries' generous exhilaration at the step they had just taken. The great decree finally voted on August 11 said it all: 'The National Assembly is entirely destroying the feudal regime.'

6

DECLARATION OF THE RIGHTS OF MAN

THE PRIMARY TASK that the Revolutionaries had set themselves was to build a better political system for France, based on the rule of law. Three weeks earlier, in Paris, there had been Revolutionary violence; but in Versailles the National Assembly was peacefully debating and legislating for a better future. Early in the Revolution, a large majority of *députés* had been convinced not only that one of their main duties must be to write a Constitution for France but that it should be preceded by a set of political principles, in the form of a Declaration of Rights. The National Assembly formally undertook to embark on this task on the afternoon of August 4, 1789, just before the famous late-night session which dismantled the relics of feudalism (see previous chapter).

The actual drafting of the Declaration did not begin until August 20, just after the National Assembly had finished drawing up the legislation abolishing feudal rights, and it ended less than a week later, on August 26, with a finished text of a preamble and seventeen articles. This Declaration of the Rights of Man is perhaps the most enduring legacy of the French Revolution and symbolises the moment when the Revolutionaries were at their best and trying their hardest to make a better world and a better form of government. Notionally, it was meant to be provisional, to be amended as needed during the negotiation of the future Constitution. In the event, the drafting of the Constitution proved a much more laborious task than the Revolutionaries may have expected, and by the time it was finalised, two years later, in 1791, there was a general agreement that it was no longer possible to revise the Declaration.

One of the chief sources of inspiration for the *députés* was the memorable precedent of the American Declaration of Independence of 1776. In some sense, the parallel is quite close: the American Declaration of Independence was a declaration of war against King George III, while the French Declaration of the Rights of Man was a declaration of war against the *ancien régime*. But the differences are more profound: the Americans were claiming what they believed were the rights of Englishmen; the French were denying the rights of Louis XVI.

The explicit purpose of the French Declaration of the Rights of Man was to act as a detailed and preparatory enunciation of the principles that should underpin a French Constitution. The preamble states that 'the ignorance, the disregard or the contempt of the rights of man are the sole causes of the public ills and of the corruption of governments' and that 'the Representatives of the French People'

> have therefore resolved to set out, in a solemn Declaration, the natural, inalienable and sacred rights of man, in order that the acts of the legislative power, and those of the executive power ... can at any moment be compared with the objectives of any political institution ...
>
> Therefore, the National Assembly recognises and declares, in the presence and under the auspices of the Supreme Being, the following Rights of Man and of the Citizen.[1]

By contrast, the memorable opening of the American Declaration of Independence – 'We hold these truths to be self-evident, that all men are created equal, that they are endowed by their Creator with certain unalienable rights, that among these are life, liberty and the pursuit of happiness' – is really only a rhetorical introduction, in four elegantly turned clauses, to the bulk of the text, which is devoted to a long-winded, pompous and indignant denunciation of the errors and offences of the policies of the English King. The French Declaration not merely says nothing about the offences of Louis XVI; it says nothing even about whether there should be a king at all.

The French Declaration was not the first attempt in modern history
to lay down in law some principles of political rights; in England there
had been a Bill of Rights in 1689 and also, much further back, the great
Magna Carta of 1215. But the French Declaration was probably the first
attempt to draft all the essential principles of an emerging democracy in
a nation state, and in that sense it is an iconic historical document. This
might be said of the American Bill of Rights, but that is fundamentally quite different in purpose: these first ten Amendments of the US
Constitution, adopted on December 15, 1791, were proposed in order to
limit the powers of the federal government. They do not constitute the
enunciation of a set of general principles regarding the Rights of Man
in any way comparable to the French Declaration.

By modern standards, of course, the French Declaration is relatively
limited. Nowadays when we speak of the Rights of Man, in terms of
principles laid down by the United Nations, we tend to understand them
as in some sense absolute and inherent in the very nature of human-
ity. The French Declaration was explicitly much more circumscribed
and really concerned only with the rights of men, but not of women.
Its full French title is *Déclaration des Droits de l'Homme et du Citoyen*
(Declaration of the Rights of Man and of the Citizen). The implication,
repeatedly made explicit in the body of the text, is that the rights of man
are not absolute but almost inherently defined by his characteristics as
a citizen, and are therefore entirely relative, qualified and countered by
the competing claims of the state and the rest of society.

The Declaration's most famous article is, of course, Article 1, which
starts with the proposition that 'men are born and remain free and equal
in rights' (*Les hommes naissent et demeurent libres et égaux en droits*). This
opening statement, of course, echoes the opening rhetoric of the American Declaration; but neither the French Revolutionaries nor the newly
independent Americans thought that equality applied to black slaves or
to women.

The second sentence of the French Declaration's Article 1 qualifies
the principle of equality, saying that 'social distinctions can be based
only on their usefulness to the community' (*Les distinctions sociales ne
peuvent être fondées que sur l'utilité commune*).

Article 2 goes on to state that 'the purpose of every political associa-
tion is the preservation of the natural and imprescriptible rights of man.
These rights are liberty, property, security, and resistance to oppression'
(*Le but de toute association politique est la conservation des droits naturels et*

imprescriptibles de l'Homme. Ces droits sont la liberté, la propriété, la sûreté, et la résistance à l'oppression).

Article 3 declares that the source of all sovereignty is the nation (and therefore not the King), while Article 4 says that liberty consists in being able to do anything which does not harm others.

Article 5 says that the law can forbid only acts that are harmful to society, and that anything which is not forbidden by law is permitted.

At this point the Declaration moves decisively from the enunciation of general philosophical principles to a sequence of Articles setting out the implications of the idea that this new society must be a state based on the law and on individual liberty. In a clear allusion to the theories of Jean-Jacques Rousseau, Article 6 says that 'the law is the expression of the general will', and that 'all citizens have the right', directly or indirectly through their representatives, 'to contribute ... to its formulation.' Moreover, 'all citizens, being equal in [the] eyes [of the law], are equally eligible to all dignities, positions and public employments'.

Article 7 declares that 'no man can be accused, arrested or detained except in circumstances laid down by law'. Moreover, in Article 8, 'the law must prescribe only punishments which are strictly and obviously necessary'. In addition, Article 9 stipulates that 'every man [must be] presumed innocent until he is proved guilty'.

Freedom of thought and expression are provided for in Article 10: 'Nobody can be persecuted for his opinions, even religious opinions, provided their expression does not disturb the public order'. Moreover, Article 11 states that 'the free communication of thoughts and opinions is one of the most precious rights of man'.

Articles 12, 13 and 14 state that 'the guarantee of the rights of man and of the citizen requires a police force', whose costs 'should be spread equally among all the citizens, according to their ability to pay', and that 'all the citizens have the right' to take part, 'directly or through their representatives', in the setting of taxation.

Article 15 declares that 'society has the right to demand accounts of any public official'.

Article 16 says that 'any society in which the guarantee of rights is not ensured, or the separation of powers is not guaranteed, has no Constitution'.

The last article of the Declaration, Article 17, is particularly interesting because of the emphasis that it places on the rights of property. The Declaration does not explicitly include equality as one of the natural

rights of man, and the motto *Liberté, égalité, fraternité*, commonly associated with the French Revolution, does not figure in it; this phrase did
not become common currency until several years later, and then it was
popularised not by the bourgeois Revolutionaries but by their radical
challengers from the *sans-culottes*. By contrast, not only does property
figure as one of the four rights listed in Article 2, but the principle of
property rights gets even more emphasis in this special article of its own,
Article 17: 'Property, being an inviolable and sacred right, none can
be deprived of it unless public necessity, legally constituted, obviously
requires it, and on condition of a fair and prior indemnity' (*La propriété
étant un droit inviolable et sacré, nul ne peut en être privé, si ce n'est lorsque
la nécessité publique, légalement constatée, l'exige évidemment, et sous la
condition d'une juste et préalable indemnité*).

Whereas the four rights listed in Article 2 – liberty, property, security
and resistance to oppression – are described as 'natural and imprescriptible', only property is described, in Article 17, as 'sacred'. At one
level this is quite odd: apart from one reference in the preamble to 'the
Supreme Being' – a formulation which manifestly falls short of a reference to 'God' – there is no indication that the Revolutionaries were
much concerned with the sacred in a religious sense. Their use of the
word 'sacred' was, most probably, the strongest way they had of express-
ing the importance they attached to property in a political context. The
majority of the *députés* were bourgeois; they had the interests of the
bourgeoisie at heart; and what they wanted was a bourgeois revolution.

As we can see from the preamble, the Revolutionaries thought that their
Declaration was a political benchmark of enduring validity. In one sense
they were right; but if one group of politicians can draft a Declaration
of Rights, another group in different circumstances can draft a different Declaration of Rights; and similarly, if one group of politicians can
draft a Constitution, another group can draft a different Constitution.
The American Constitution has been amended several times, but it has
not been replaced. The French Revolution, by contrast, precipitated
the beginning of two centuries of political instability, one of whose
symptoms was the proliferation over subsequent generations of many
Declarations of the Rights of Man, as well as different Constitutions.

There was a second Declaration, linked to the Constitution of 1793, which was extremely democratic in theory but never implemented; and a third Declaration, linked to the Constitution of 1795, which was a straightforward right-wing reaction to the *Terreur* of 1793–94. Napoléon and the restored Bourbons largely dispensed with even lip service to human rights, but with the Revolution of 1830, the tradition of linking Constitutions to Declarations of the Rights of Man was resumed. As far as history is concerned, however, there is only one Declaration of Human Rights of any significance before that of the United Nations in 1948, and that is the French Declaration of 1789.

7

THE KING
MOVES TO PARIS

IN THEIR DECLARATION OF THE RIGHTS OF MAN, the National Assembly had left one problem unresolved and unaddressed: what to do about the King.

They had decided in principle that the source of sovereignty lay with the nation, and not, therefore, with the King. But they had not decided to get rid of the King, nor to turn France into a Republic; another three years would pass before they reached that point. Now, in the late summer of 1789, they were in the anomalous position of claiming full sovereignty for the nation but feeling that they needed to devise new rules so as to include the King, and what was left of his prestige and his popularity, to endorse and facilitate their ambitions.

A small group of moderate Revolutionaries felt that the Revolution was already going too far and too fast. Known as *Monarchiens,* led by Jean-Joseph Mounier, and including the duc de Clermont-Tonnerre, baron Pierre Victor Malouet, and Trophime Gérard, marquis de Lally-Tollendal, they argued that France ought to have a strong King and a two-chamber form of parliament, modelled along the lines of the English system. The implication of such a system, they believed, was that the King would have an absolute power of veto over the actions of the National Assembly. This was a strange position, if they really believed that sovereignty came from the nation; but if the King was to remain, they had to find some role for him.

The more ambitious and more numerous Revolutionaries, led by Adrien Duport, Antoine Barnave and Alexandre de Lameth, who belonged to the radical new *Club Breton* (so named because a significant number of its founding members came from Brittany) and called themselves patriots, wanted to go much further than the *Monarchiens* and argued against giving any right of veto to the King.

For the time being, the question of the future shape of the Constitution remained in abeyance. But the Revolutionaries were in a hurry; they needed the King, or at least they thought they needed the King, to endorse and ratify their recent important decisions: the overthrow of the vestiges of feudalism, and the Declaration of the Rights of Man. Later, but before the overthrow of the monarchy in 1792, the Revolutionaries found that they could override the King; at this juncture, though, they were still in the grip of the assumption that monarchy was a natural and necessary element of government.

In the end, two compromises were struck. First, the Assembly voted massively, on September 10, 1789, by 849 to 89, against the institution of a second chamber. The great achievement of the *tiers état* was to have united the three orders into a single National Assembly, so why undo this by creating two bodies? Moreover, many feared that a second chamber would turn out to be a device for the restoration of aristocratic privilege. Then, on September 11 the National Assembly decreed, by a substantial but much smaller majority, 673 votes to 352, that the King should have just a suspensive or delaying power of veto, which would allow him to hold back actions by the National Assembly for a maximum of two legislatures, or four years.

The Revolutionaries had believed, or at least hoped, that if they voted for a suspensive veto the King would meet them halfway. They were wrong. Louis responded, on September 18, by refusing to ratify either the overthrow of feudalism or the Declaration of the Rights of Man. At the same time, he summoned to Versailles from the north-east of France one of his royal regiments, the Regiment of Flanders; it was due to arrive on September 23. Once again it looked as though he had determined to take on the Revolutionaries, with force if necessary.

The negotiations over the Constitution were made more complicated by the fact that this was not a stable situation; on the contrary, the Revolutionaries found themselves drawn into trying to change almost too many bits of the French political system at once. Moreover, the people of Paris were now in a state of extreme agitation, excited by the turbulence associated with the overthrow of the Bastille and aggravated by the economic crisis and growing unemployment. There was also a growing food shortage, for though the harvest was good, the food had not reached the shops. Supplies were proving difficult to find, there were long queues at the doors of bakeries, and the price of a 4-pound loaf of bread had risen from the normal 12½ to 13½ sous.

In parallel to their negotiations on the new Constitution, the Revolutionaries had embarked on the reform of local government. They had started almost immediately, in July 1789, when (as noted in chapter 4) they had swept away the municipal government of Paris inherited from the *ancien régime* and replaced it with a committee of electors, headed by Sylvain Bailly as the Mayor of Paris, which had also inaugurated the local *Garde nationale*. But this committee was in turn eliminated later in the year, as part of the national reform of local government, and on May 21, 1790, the Revolutionaries passed a law redefining the municipal government of Paris.

This reform gave the people of Paris democratic political institutions through which to raise their previously silent voices. The sixty districts were to elect a new municipal council of 300 members, whose first task would be to draw up a Constitution for the city. But the very act of holding elections, in a period of popular unrest, sharply stimulated political activity in all sixty districts, each of which started to behave like an autonomous local municipality, with its committees and its general assemblies; and this stimulated the emergence of popular leaders, like Georges Danton, the rising Revolutionary lawyer, and Antoine Joseph Santerre, a rich brewer and a powerful local leader. Often, the enthusiasm of these district assemblies fostered an ambitious Revolutionary spirit, which was liable to contest the authority of the *Hôtel de ville* and to denounce any concession to caution or moderation.

Popular ferment in Paris was further whipped up in the spring of 1790 with the holding of municipal elections, when the sixty districts were again reorganised, on May 21, into forty-eight *Sections*, each with an elected assembly. The Paris municipal council, known as the *Commune*, was now to consist of 144 members, three for each of the

Sections. From the beginning, the assemblies of these *Sections* met frequently to debate current political issues, some as often as every ten
days. The *Sections* were increasingly active during the following year
of rising political agitation, and many of them went into permanent
session. ('Permanent session' was a Revolutionary term, meaning that
they were entitled to meet as often as they wanted, not just when they
were given permission to do so.) In principle, the *Sections* were subordinate to the *Commune*; but soon they proved determined to exercise
their own voice in the running of the country. Nonetheless, the Paris
Commune had great powers, going well beyond the simple management
of municipal affairs. It could oversee the supply of food to the capital
and in theory fix the price at which food was sold in the shops; and it
could mobilise the *Garde nationale* and declare martial law.

Popular agitation and political debate were partly kept on the boil by
the appearance of a host of political newspapers which had sprung up in
response to the meeting of the *États généraux*. Among the most eloquent
of the new pamphleteers was Camille Desmoulins, a twenty-nine-year-
old barrister who spent more time in the cafés than in the law courts
and who would harangue the crowds with inflammatory speeches while
standing on a table in the gardens of the Palais Royal, the Paris home of
the duc d'Orléans. Desmoulins was one of those who had stirred up the
Paris crowds against the court in July 1789 after the King had dismissed
Necker, and he was among those who had 'conquered' the Bastille. He
attracted much attention with his brochures *La France libre* and *Discours de la lanterne*; the even greater success of his next news-sheet, *Les
Révolutions de France et de Brabant*, which he launched later that year,
made him the pamphleteer most feared by the court.

Another of the new journalist stars was Jean-Paul Marat, a Swiss
doctor who had once had ambitions as a scientist of medicine and who
was embittered by his failure to win the respect of the scientific community. When, in September 1789, he brought out his violently populist
paper *L'ami du peuple*, Desmoulins offered to contribute to it, but Marat
brutally rebuffed him: 'The eagle always goes alone; the turkey goes in
a troupe.'[1]

So when the Revolutionaries got down to the drafting of their Constitution, in the autumn of 1789, they were increasingly aware that the

people of Paris wanted their say as well. Among the Revolutionaries were conservatives who started from the assumption that any Constitution must derive from the depths of French history and that monarchy must therefore be an essential part of it. For the radicals, there was nothing natural or inherent about the political institutions that France had inherited: they thought the task ahead was to construct an entirely new political system, from scratch. In his groundbreaking pamphlet *Qu'est-ce que le tiers état?*, published in January 1789, Emmanuel Sieyès, the intellectual leader of the radicals in the early phase of the Revolution, had argued that the ultimate political reality, predating all constitutional forms, was the nation. 'The nation exists before everything else, it is the origin of everything. Its will is always legal, it is the law itself.'[2] Most Revolutionaries, like all conservatives, wanted to keep the monarchy; but for many this was a matter of political convenience, not an inherent necessity. The radicalism of Sieyès was directly incorporated in the Declaration of the Rights of Man, which states, in Article 3, that 'the principle of all sovereignty resides essentially in the nation. No body, and no individual, can exercise any authority which does not expressly derive from it.'[3]

On October 1, 1789, the National Assembly pressed the King to accept the Declaration of the Rights of Man and the articles of the Constitution that had been adopted so far. But at first Louis withheld his approval of the Declaration: 'It contains very good maxims suitable for guiding your work, but principles which are susceptible to different applications and even to different interpretations cannot be fully appreciated, and do not need to be until the moment when their real meaning is fixed by the laws for which they should serve as the first basis.'[4] He went on to indicate that he gave his 'accession' but not his 'acceptance' to the first articles of the Constitution, with the explicit reservation that once it had been completed, it should keep in the hands of the monarch the executive power, with all its prerogatives. He seemed to be threatening a veto of both the Declaration and the future Constitution.

This reply was unacceptable to many Deputies, including Maximilien Robespierre, a rising young lawyer from Arras, who stated: 'The King's reply is destructive, not only of any Constitution, but even of any national right to have a Constitution. Anyone who can impose a condition on a Constitution has the right to prevent that Constitution; he places his will above the rights of the nation.'[5] The sharpness of this retort immediately marked Robespierre out from the crowd. Like almost all the other Deputies, he was a newcomer. He was cold, careful and aloof, and not a natural public speaker; yet he rapidly established himself as a leader among the Revolutionaries. His view was endorsed by Jérôme Pétion, another of the leading left-wing Deputies, who subsequently became the Mayor of Paris: 'It is said that there is a social contract between the King and the nation. I deny it. The King can only govern according to the laws which the nation presents to him.'[6] Bertrand Barère, a lawyer from Toulouse, said that the Declaration of the Rights of Man did not need to be approved by the King. The Deputies then instructed Jean-Joseph Mounier, their current President, to go and ask the King simply to accept the Declaration of Rights, and to take steps to improve the food supply in Paris. For several days, the King remained obstinately silent, and instead of responding, summoned the Regiment of Flanders to come to Versailles.

The news, when it reached Paris, in circumstances of popular agitation and inflammatory pamphleteering, that the King had sent for the Regiment of Flanders, and that it had reached Versailles on September 23, 1789, was very badly received. What could Louis want to do with this unit, which, though highly professional, was quite small, only 1,000 men? What was the need for a military unit, with its roots in the *ancien régime*, when the Mayor of Paris and La Fayette, its militia commander, had at their disposal, for keeping order, a newly enrolled bourgeois force of *Gardes nationales*, theoretically 48,000 and even in reality 30,000 men strong? Did the King intend to use force against the National Assembly in Versailles? Or was he, as some rumours had it, preparing to flee abroad?

In this explosive situation, all that was missing was the spark to set it off; this came on October 3, when Paris learned that two days earlier the King's bodyguard in Versailles had given a banquet for the newly arrived Regiment of Flanders, at which many toasts had been drunk to the royal family but none to the French nation. Just to hold a banquet when food in Paris was in short supply was seriously provocative. But the worst of it, it was reported, was that amid the celebrations, the national cockade, a symbol of the Revolution, had been trampled underfoot – deliberately or accidentally, who could tell? By the next day, October 4, every kind of alarmist rumour was abroad in Paris, including the age-old fear that there was some kind of royal or aristocratic plot to starve the common people. It is at this point, or thereabouts, that the Queen, Marie-Antoinette, is supposed to have said 'Let them eat cake'.[7] In fact, there is no evidence that she did say it, then or ever.[8]

On October 5, popular agitation turned into something like an insurrection. Vast crowds of people gathered at the *Hôtel de ville*, demanding bread and above all that the King should supply it. Towards the end of the morning this group formed an enormous cortège, largely composed of women, and set off, on foot, under a growing rainstorm. At their head marched Stanislas Marie Maillard, a sometime bailiff's clerk who was newly famous as one of the 'conquerors of the Bastille' and always a ready volunteer for any Revolutionary street excitement. As they went along, dragging a few cannon and brandishing any weapons they could find, they cheerfully encouraged others to join them. By the time they reached Versailles in the early evening, they were wet and dirty, and some 7,000 strong.

Just how the crowd formed a procession and then was led to Versailles remains, like so much of what happened in the French Revolution, slightly mysterious. Some historians believe that the procession was too well organised to have been purely spontaneous, and some speculate that the duc d'Orléans was behind it; but we just do not know.

The conduct of La Fayette, ostensibly the general in command of the new *Garde nationale*, was almost equally puzzling. After the departure of the procession and while the *tocsin* (the great alarm bell at the former Cordeliers monastery) was sounding, units of *gardes nationaux* began gathering at the *Hôtel de ville*, looking for leadership. But La Fayette was nowhere to be seen and did not arrive until the day was well advanced. It seems clear that he did not know what to do, and it is possible that he was reluctant to lead his men in the wake of the procession, for fear of being accused of leaving Paris unprotected. But his men insisted, and La Fayette eventually set off, in the rain, with 20,000 guardsmen, arriving in Versailles late that night, wet and exhausted.

Meanwhile, late that afternoon at the Palace of Versailles, Louis returned hurriedly from a hunt. Under the combined pressure of the National Assembly, the prospective arrival of the large cortège and the reported approach of La Fayette's force of *gardes nationales*, he submitted; and at 8 p.m. he notified Mounier in writing that he would accept the Assembly's decrees on both the Declaration of the Rights of Man and the delaying veto. He also promised to make available all the bread that could be procured in Versailles and gave orders that wheat should be brought from such neighbouring towns as Senlis and Noyon.

When La Fayette finally reached Versailles, some courtiers greeted his arrival with the sardonic comment 'Here is another Cromwell!' In fact, he proved to be something of a comic-opera hero, with nothing of a Cromwell in him; in the presence of the King he always showed great modesty. But now he formally asked Louis not just to accept the Declaration but also to return with him to Paris. Fatally, the King agreed; and with that, the entire purpose of the massive procession to Versailles seemed to have been achieved. The King went off to bed; and so did Mounier; and so did La Fayette.

But the crowds that had marched from Paris had nowhere to sleep, and they stayed up all night, drinking and dancing. At six o'clock on the morning of October 6, some of the demonstrators invaded the *château* of Versailles, and there was some firing of guns: two of the King's bodyguards were killed, and their heads were stuck on pikes. Finally, La Fayette was woken (the journalist Antoine Rivarol cruelly labelled him 'General Morpheus', after the classical god of sleep), and when he arrived, he calmed things down and persuaded the King's bodyguards and the Revolutionary *gardes nationaux* to make friends with one another. The King, the Queen and the Dauphin then appeared on a balcony before the crowd. 'To Paris!', cried the crowd. 'My friends', Louis replied, 'I shall go to Paris with my wife and my children; it is to the love of my good and faithful subjects that I entrust all that is most precious to me.'

At 1 p.m. a cannon was fired to indicate that the King was leaving Versailles. A vast procession set out, some 60,000 strong, headed by contingents of the *Gardes nationales*, followed by carts of wheat and flour and surrounded by women and market porters. Then came the King's bodyguards, the Regiment of Flanders, the Swiss Guards and the King's carriage, with the royal family in it. La Fayette rode behind, followed by some carriages containing a number of Deputies. A large crowd came on behind, chanting, 'We are bringing back the baker, the baker's wife and the little baker's boy',[9] meaning that they hoped the King would keep them supplied with bread.

At 8 p.m. the vast cortège arrived in Paris, and at the *Hôtel de ville*, the King was welcomed by Sylvain Bailly, the Mayor; and after much ceremony of civic goodwill, Louis and his family finally, at ten o'clock that night, reached the royal Tuileries Palace, which had been allocated to them as their new home.

When they learned that the King was to be taken to Paris, the Revolutionaries in the National Assembly decided that they too must go to the capital, because they thought they must be inseparable from him. And when the King and the National Assembly moved to Paris, so did the entire constellation of political institutions which surrounded them, starting with the political clubs.

Political clubs had started early in the Revolution; the first, called the *Club Breton*, had been set up in Versailles in 1789, during the *États généraux*, by a group of Deputies from Brittany, and they were later joined by others. Now the *Club Breton* established itself in the rue Saint-Honoré, in the monastery of the order of the Jacobins; it adopted the formal name of *Société des Amis de la Constitution*, but it was always thereafter known as the *Club Jacobin*, and it would become by far the most powerful centre of political debate in the later phases of the Revolution.

In February 1790, after the King had moved to Paris, another political club was founded, the *Cercle social*, intended as a centre of correspondence for men of letters from all over Europe and focused on the writings of Rousseau; it held public meetings of 5,000 to 8,000 people at the *Cirque* of the Palais Royal, and it published the comparatively radical journal *La bouche de fer* (meaning 'Mouth of iron', or cannon). The *Club des Cordeliers* was founded in Paris in April 1790 by Danton, Marat and Desmoulins, under the official title *Société des Amis des droits de l'homme et du citoyen*; it acquired its unofficial name from the monastery of the *Cordeliers* (Franciscans) in the rue de l'École-de-Médecine, where it took up residence. It was more populist than the *Jacobins*; its membership was cheaper; it was more radical and rowdier; and it was usually involved, directly or indirectly, whenever there were political demonstrations in Paris.

It was not an accident that most of these clubs took their names from former Catholic monastic orders. The practical reason was that the National Assembly had closed all the monasteries, on the grounds that society no longer required such institutions of idleness, and their property became vacant for possession – including by new groups of Revolutionaries. The irony was that most of the Revolutionaries had necessarily received much of their education from Church institutions, because that was where education was provided; so it was not surprising that the thought processes of some of these new occupants resonated with the harmonics of the thought processes of their monastic teachers and predecessors.

The move from Versailles to Paris was a turning point in the history of the Revolution, and the Revolutionaries did not foresee all of its consequences. The King was now, in effect, a prisoner in Paris and subject to all the physical and moral pressures emanating from the capital; but the same would be true, with some delay, for the Revolutionaries and the National Assembly. At first the Revolutionaries largely kept decisive control of events, through the authority and the legitimacy of the National Assembly, but they would progressively come under political pressure from the people of Paris, partly through formal representatives, such as the *Commune* in the *Hôtel de ville* and the forty-eight individual *Sections*, partly through the mobilisation of popular crowd power. The Revolutionaries in the National Assembly could not foresee how far their policies would alienate a large proportion of the population of Paris, and so they could not fully anticipate how far the turbulent people of Paris would use their new local political instititions to make demands, or how much these demands would come to be in conflict with the principles of the Revolutionaries in the National Assembly.

In most cases, power still lay, in the last resort, with the National Assembly. But the fact that there was now a second centre of power – which could mobilise violent muscle in the streets, first against the King and then against the National Assembly – exacerbated the deep splits between different factions inside the Assembly. As a result, the Revolution turned progressively into a life-and-death struggle among these different factions and between them and the crowd power of the common people of Paris.

8

THE ASSEMBLY STARTS
TO GOVERN FRANCE

THE NATIONAL ASSEMBLY MOVED to temporary premises in Paris later in October 1789, and it started work in a great hurry on a number of radical changes to the government of France. At this stage the Revolutionaries still assumed that France would continue to have a King, but they were determined to cut down his role. In general, the King would now be subordinate to the Constitution; and whereas he had previously been called 'Louis by the Grace of God, King of France and of Navarre',[1] his new title would be 'Louis by the Grace of God and the Constitutional Law of the State, King of the French'.[2] He would be the leader of his people, but he would no longer be their hereditary master. Moreover, he could no longer spend money at will; for the expenses of his household he would have to live within the limits of a civil list, which the National Assembly decreed should be £25m and which would be managed by an independent civil servant.[3]

The King would continue to lead the government, and he would continue to appoint his Ministers; but to prevent any danger of corruption he would not be allowed to appoint as Ministers current or former members of the National Assembly. Moreover, his Ministers would be accountable to the National Assembly, and a retiring Minister would not be allowed to leave Paris unless it approved his accounts. This requirement caused serious difficulties for some later Ministers. When Danton briefly became the Minister of Justice after the overthrow of the King, he repeatedly failed to get Assembly approval of his financial accounts, because his position had given him access to large secret funds and he could not explain where the money had gone; similarly, Jean-Marie Roland de la Platière, the one-time Inspector-General of Industry who was briefly the Minister of the Interior before the execution of the King, never succeeded in getting this approval.

Under the new arrangements approved by the National Assembly, the King would continue to appoint senior civil servants and ambassadors, and admirals and marshals, but he would no longer have the right to decide on war and peace. This question flared up in the spring of 1790 when Spain called on France for support in a colonial quarrel with England. The conservatives in the National Assembly argued that the *députés* were too numerous and too impressionable to take such a heavy decision; but the radicals replied that the King was the servant of the nation and that if he were allowed to decide on war and peace, France would continue to be saddled with dynastic wars, as in the past. In the end, the radicals won: the King would have the right to recommend war or peace, but only the Assembly could decide the issue, and it would have to ratify any peace treaty. Existing peace treaties would continue to be respected, but the Assembly appointed a diplomatic committee to review and if necessary revise them in harmony with the Constitution.

On this central issue, the National Assembly declared solemnly that 'the French nation vows not to undertake any war for purposes of conquest, and would never use its forces against the liberty of any people'. It did not take long, however, for the Revolutionaries to abandon this declaration of principle in the course of the next few years, and to stride vigorously and without apology from wars of self-defence to wars of counter-attack, of liberation, of conquest, of annexation, of pillage and expropriation and eventually of wholesale imperialism.

Though the Revolutionaries had decided to leave the conduct of government in the hands of the King, there was a striking inconsistency in the relationship they were planning to set up between him and the National Assembly. Typically, in a modern democracy it is the government which governs and proposes policies, and the democratic assembly which disposes and either approves or disapproves the government's actions. The French Revolutionaries did not see it that way; once they got the bit between their teeth, they set up a system which was designed to work in exactly the opposite way. There was a King, who was supposed to govern, in the sense that he appointed the Ministers, but in practice the Revolutionaries acted, from very early on, as if the National Assembly were the government, and took many if not most important decisions quite independently of the King and his Ministers; but then, in theory, the King was allowed, for a period, to impose a delaying veto if he did not agree with its actions. As a result, there were times when France seemed to have two separate governments.

Even before the King and all the paraphernalia of government moved from Versailles to Paris, one of the first things the Revolutionaries did was to set about overhauling the French system of local government. Under the *ancien régime*, France was a complete tangle of disparate local and regional entities and provinces. But between the end of September 1789 and the end of February 1790, they determined that all the old relics would be swept away and that France would be divided into eighty-three *départements*, all roughly equal in size, all roughly regular in shape and all so sized that it ought to be possible for all the citizens to reach the departmental capital in a day. Each *département* would be run by a council elected for two years and would be the constituency basis for elections to the National Assembly, as well as for the elections of the leading civil servants and clerics.

Each *département* would have between three and nine districts, themselves made up of cantons, which would be the seats of the locally elected justices of the peace. At the bottom of the pyramid were the *communes*, which were formerly the parishes and were now to be the smallest administrative units, each with an elected council and an elected mayor.

This reform produced a system of local government which is recognisably similar to that in force today and explains why there are currently more *communes* in France (more than 36,000) than in the whole of the rest of Europe. It required an enormous increase in the number of elected officials at each level; and in many cases it proved extremely difficult to find people who were in any respect qualified for the prescribed administrative tasks, especially in the rural *communes*, where the vast majority of the population was illiterate.

The Revolutionaries' next priority was the disastrous state of the public finances, which had previously been virtually equivalent to the finances of the monarchy. They knew that the King had summoned the *États généraux* mainly because he hoped that they would solve his financial problems. But from the beginning they had declined to deal with the King's financial problems with any urgency, because they were afraid that if they did so, he might then summarily dismiss them. This position was adopted by the nobility and the clergy as well as by the *tiers état*: the delegation of the *noblesse* from Troyes was told that they would be disavowed if they voted for any financial rescue for the King before agreement on a national charter. Accordingly, the Assembly passed a decree saying that 'as soon as it shall have, in cooperation with the King, fixed the principles of the national regeneration, it will turn to the examination of the national debt'.

In principle, therefore, the top priority for the Revolutionaries, after their adoption of the Declaration of the Rights of Man, should have been the enactment of a Constitution. In practice, however, the pressure of events, and the temptation to grapple with them, proved too strong. Some elements, like the role and powers of the King, were settled quite early on, but the Constitution as a whole was not finalised until September 1791. Long before then, the National Assembly had got deeply involved with steps intended to deal with the nation's financial problems.

On August 7, 1789, Necker told the National Assembly that the state of the public finances was desperate. For the months of August and September he expected revenues of £37m and expenditure of £68m; he proposed going to the market for a loan of £30m. Two days later the Assembly gave its approval and agreed to an interest rate of 4.5 per cent; but the loan was not attractive to large investors, was seriously undersubscribed, and brought in only £2.6m. When Necker told the Assembly the bad news, on August 27, he proposed launching a state loan of £80m, at an interest rate of 5 per cent. But it too fared badly, bringing in only £52m. Despite what it had said and intended earlier, the National Assembly was already being inveigled by Necker into grappling with the problem of the state's finances.

The most obvious potential source of revenue, as many could see, was the enormous wealth of the Catholic Church. Even before the convening of the *États généraux*, most of the *cahiers de doléances* of the two lay orders had drawn attention to the riches of the Church; and the idea of nationalising Church property began to be discussed quite soon after the abolition of feudal dues on August 4, 1789, and even more frequently after the suppression of Church tithes on August 11. In September, the Calvinist Deputy Pierre Dupont de Nemours estimated that Church revenues amounted to £160m and its expenses to only £113m, leaving a surplus of around £47m which the state could usefully appropriate.

The newly installed bishop of Autun, Charles Maurice de Talleyrand-Périgord, went much further, proposing that the property of the Church be transferred wholesale to the state. He estimated the Church's total income at £150m (£80m from tithes, £70m from other sources) and the total value of its property at £2,100m.[4] He proposed the outright nationalisation and sale of Church property, which he believed would cover the budget deficit, permit the abolition of the hated salt tax (*gabelle*) and progressively pay off the national debt.

Many of the clergy bitterly protested against the idea. The abbé Maury warned: 'Property is sacred, for us as for you. We are being attacked today, but do not deceive yourselves: if we are despoiled today, your turn will come'. But Mirabeau argued that Church property was not genuinely private property and in reality already belonged to the nation; in return for nationalisation, the state would cover the costs of the Church and would still be able to guarantee better living conditions for most of the *curés*. For most of the Deputies the temptation was too strong, and on November 2, 1789, the National Assembly voted 568 to 346 to put the property of the Church 'at the disposal of the Nation' (a form of weasel words which implied but did not quite say 'nationalisation') and went on to promise that *curés* would receive an income of at least £1,200 a year, plus a house and garden.

It seemed too good to be true, and it was. For one thing, it was obviously impossible to put the whole of the Church's property on sale at once, since that would lead to a total collapse of the property market. On the other hand, the state could not simply delay the sale process, since it had a large and pressing need for funds now, to meet the deficit. The solution that the National Assembly adopted was to issue bonds known as *assignats*, whose value was notionally underwritten by the value of the Church property being put up for sale. The reason why the Assembly insisted that these bonds should bear interest and be described as guaranteed by the value of the Church property was that it was desperate for these *assignats* to be accepted as genuine value-based investments, paying their way; for it was haunted by the folk memory of the paper currency which had been launched in France in the early years of the eighteenth century by the ingenious Scottish financier John Law, with disastrous consequences.

The Law scheme had prompted a wave of economic and financial euphoria, leading to a sharp speculative bubble, which had then burst. The scheme collapsed because there were insufficient underlying real assets behind the speculative businesses to sustain the value of the paper currency; the Revolutionaries were trying to ensure that their *assignats* were designed on a basis that would avert a similar fate.

In reality, of course, it was impossible for the value of the *assignats* to be guaranteed by the value of Church property. For one thing, the Church property would be sold at auction, so its value could not be known in advance. One of the Revolutionaries reckoned that the total would be about £4bn, roughly twice Talleyrand's appraisal; but other estimates ranged from £1.8bn to £12bn. Another complication was that the sale process would reduce the value of the property, since purchasers would be offered very easy terms, with a small down payment of between 12 and 30 per cent and twelve years to pay the balance. Finally, it was taking quite a long time to select Church properties for sale and then put them up for auction. Nevertheless, the National Assembly persisted in the fiction, and on December 19, 1789, it authorised the issue of £400m worth of *assignats*, in coupons of £1,000 each, at an interest rate of 5 per cent.

The heart of the problem was that the national tax system was completely ramshackle and universally resented. The National Assembly was quick to dismantle the old taxes but slow to put something more rational in their place.

Over the next sixteen months, until March 1791, it slowly erected a new system, based on three universal forms of income tax: on the income from property (*contribution foncière*), on non-property income (*contribution mobilière*), and on commercial profits (*patente*). These were meant to be administered locally, by locally elected officials: the central government would determine the total sum which each tax was supposed to raise and would allocate collection targets for each area, which local officials were supposed to meet. There were just three problems, all insoluble.

First, the newly elected local officials, as we have seen, were in most cases completely unprepared for their new tasks, and in many cases, at the bottom of the pyramid, they were virtually or even completely illiterate. Second, the process of allocating revenue targets for taxpayers could not fail to be subject to every kind of local corruption or intimidation. Third, the French people were reluctant to pay any taxes, old or new. In August 1789, in their Declaration of the Rights of Man, the *députés* had proclaimed the principle of taxation by consent; what they were not able to do in practice was turn the French into a nation of consenting taxpayers. As a result, the taxes actually collected regularly fell far, far short of their targets.

The Revolutionaries made the tax collection problem even more difficult by largely sacrificing all the old indirect taxes on goods and services, equivalent to modern sales taxes or value added tax. These would have been much easier to collect, but the Revolutionaries rejected the principle of indirect taxes on the grounds that they would be a burden on all, regardless of income, and therefore a particularly heavy burden on the poor.

The first launch of *assignats* seemed to have gone well, so in late September 1790 the National Assembly decided on a second issue. Some of the Revolutionaries were so enthusiastic about this new method of raising money that they wanted to go much further and make a really big issue, of as much as £2,000m, for paying off the national debt, estimated at around £2,300m. Jérôme Pétion, one of the leading radicals, maintained that the only people who were against the *assignats* were the bankers and the speculators; he argued that nothing deters speculation so much as abundance of money. Mirabeau argued that the economy was being stifled by the shortage of monetary assets in circulation: 'We have a pressing need of means to support business: the *assignat*-money, besides paying off the national debt, will also provide a source of greater economic activity. Even if you were to hesitate to adopt the *assignat* as a financial measure, you should embrace it as a certain and active support of the Revolution.' The marquis de Montesquiou, in the name of the Finance Committee, argued that the issue of *assignats* would enable the government to pay off a large amount of the national debt and thus reduce the cost of servicing that debt: 'The *assignat* will save the people the cost of paying interest on £2,300m in national debt. The people will therefore have to pay out £120m less each year, and they will certainly not accuse us of imprudence.'[5]

On the other side were moderates, including those who knew

something about economics, and they argued for a modest issue of *assignats*, of only £300m or £400m; among them were Talleyrand, Dupont de Nemours and Malouet inside the Assembly and Condorcet outside it. Dupont de Nemours specifically predicted that the *assignats* would produce great inflation in the prices of ordinary goods:

> They say that the *assignats* will be as good as money. If so, since there will not be any more bread or wine than before, those who want to get bread or wine with *assignats* or with money will be obliged to give more *assignats* for the same quantity of bread or wine. Those who propose an issue of £2,000m of *assignats* must therefore intend to push up the price of bread, wine and meat. They say that this will not happen, because the *assignats* will be used to buy the property of the clergy, but they are deceiving the people, since the property of the clergy cannot be sold all at once, from one day to the next. The *assignats* will therefore remain in circulation, and meanwhile basic foodstuffs, and above all bread, will cost twice as much as before.

Talleyrand (who may have known about the famous economic principle, commonly known as Gresham's Law, that 'bad money drives out good', first enunciated by Thomas Gresham, a leading financier in Tudor England) told the Assembly that 'the inevitable effect of any paper currency is the immediate disappearance of the coinage' – through hoarding, since the coinage would seem more valuable than the *assignats* – meaning that 'this fictional currency will drive out the real.'

As it turned out, Talleyrand and Dupont de Nemours were right, while Mirabeau and Montesquiou were wrong. But most of the *députés* knew little or nothing about monetary economics and saw no alternative to going ahead with the printing press. In the end, a compromise was struck: the Assembly decided against a massive issue of £2,000m of *assignats* and voted instead, by a narrow majority, for an issue of £800m. Necker was so opposed to this new issue that he resigned on September 3, 1790, amid general indifference; angry crowds harassed him on his way home, and he had to appeal to the Assembly for police protection.

Over the next six years the National Assembly was to repeat the operation of issuing *assignats*, at an accelerating pace and in a rising volume; and whereas at first they had been interest-bearing bonds, soon they became nothing more than paper currency, bearing no interest and simply printed by the state as a substitute for tax revenue.

Quite quickly, the market value of the *assignat* declined against that of the traditional coinage. Already by April 1790 the *assignat* had depreciated by 10 per cent against the metal currency. In September of that year the National Assembly attempted to decree that the *assignat* be legal tender at a fixed rate of exchange with the metal currency; in practice it went on falling. In October 1791 the *assignat*'s value was 18 per cent below par; in November 1792 it was down 28 per cent; in December 1793 it was down 48 per cent. By March 1795, an *assignat* of £1,000 could buy only £80 in metal currency.

France at that time had no recognised central bank and no experience of reliable paper money; and the increasingly reckless proliferation of a new paper currency, in a country which did not trust or want it, had all the negative consequences that some of the more clear-sighted Deputies had feared: rapid inflation, the precipitous depreciation of the *assignat*, the consequent collapse of any popular respect for, or acceptance of, this currency, and the virtual disappearance, through hoarding, of the metallic coinage.

One particularly acute consequence was that the peasants became reluctant to accept the *assignat* in payment; and when the authorities tried to force them to, they preferred to cut back on the sale of cereals, which led to shortages in food supplies and thus to hunger and even near-famine, and in effect to a virtual state of war between the peasantry and the townsfolk.

With hindsight, we can see that the entire *assignat* enterprise, including the way it was recklessly mismanaged, was one of the most serious of all the mistakes that the Revolutionaries made. It may indeed have been the single most important factor that caused the Revolution to go off the rails and descend into the *Terreur* of 1793–94.

THE REVOLUTIONARIES REFORM THE CHURCH

WITH THE DECISIONS TO NATIONALISE and sell off its property and then to launch the new financial instrument of the *assignat,* the Revolutionaries were progressively and fatally embroiled with the Catholic Church. From early on in the Revolution, many of them had had their eyes on the power of the Church. Perhaps even for most of them, this was mainly in order to get hold of its wealth. We can now see that this was a major gamble, since it involved the Revolutionaries in a fundamental power struggle with the Church, as well as with the rest of the population of France, most of whom were more or less fervent believers. But the Revolutionaries do not seem to have thought of it as a gamble at all; for them, it was just part of the logic of the Revolution.

From the moment that they decided, on August 11, 1789, to suppress the tithes of the Catholic Church, the Revolutionaries accepted in principle that the state would have to be responsible for financing the Church's activities. But in return they were determined to be closely involved in the running, and therefore the reform, of the Church; and on the next day they set up an Ecclesiastical Committee in the National Assembly.

On October 28 the National Assembly decreed that there were to be no further recruitment to the monastic orders in France, on the grounds that there was no need for it; the Revolutionaries referred to monks and nuns as 'idlers' or *fainéants* (do-nothings). Three and a half months later, on February 13, 1790, the National Assembly went even further in the same anticlerical direction: it forbade the taking of religious vows and suppressed the closed orders. 'The law', it said, 'will no longer recognise solemn monastic vows by persons of either sex, and declares, in consequence, that orders and congregations where such vows are made are and will remain suppressed in France.' The Church's hospital and educational institutions were exempted, however.

This was the start of another long-running battle between the Revolutionaries and the Church.

The Declaration of the Rights of Man had declared the principle of tolerance, including religious tolerance. Catholic clergy fiercely protested, since they wanted a privileged position for the Church. But the majority of Revolutionaries insisted that it would not be allowed any immunity from the Revolution.

The first to benefit from this principle of tolerance were the Protestants. At that time France had around 1 million Protestants, who had clung on despite the long-standing policies of rigorous discrimination against them. Just before the Revolution, in 1787, Louis XVI had officially recognised their civil rights; and as a result, Protestants had been enthusiastic participants, at every level, in the process of launching the *États généraux*. In 1790 the National Assembly decreed the restitution to the Protestants of property that had been confiscated from them under the Revocation of the Edict of Nantes in 1685.[1] Political tolerance for Jews would take longer: the Sephardic Jews of the south-west of France were admitted to political equality in January 1790; the Ashkenazi Jews of Alsace, who were often targets of acute local anti-Semitism, had to wait another twenty months, until September 1791.

The implication of these policies of Revolutionary tolerance was that the Revolution must be in conflict with the power and the intolerance of the Church. At first, it does not seem that the Revolutionaries were motivated by any significant amount of *anti-religious* feeling; that would come later, as the increasingly violent Revolution searched for new enemies. But even from the beginning there seems to have been a substantial strain of *anticlerical* sentiment, based largely on resentment at the multifarious privileges that the Church enjoyed under the *ancien régime*. One of these was that it was not subject to any legal obligation to pay regular taxation but was allowed simply to make a donation of its own choosing to the state. This so-called *don gratuit* dated back to 1561 and had been instituted as a special measure for rescuing the state's precarious finances in a time of war. But soon it became a customary contribution and reached an average of about £3m every year, or 3 to 5 per cent of Church revenues; the clergy insisted, though, that this was still a voluntary contribution and that the Church must continue to be exempt from any obligatory taxation.

The Revolutionaries would have none of this, and on November 2, 1789, the National Assembly swept this argument away when it decreed that the property of the Church would now be at the disposal of the nation. The corollary of nationalisation was that in future the salaries of the clergy would be paid by the state, but on a more systematic and more equitable basis than in the past. The metropolitan bishop of Paris would receive a princely salary of £50,000, and the other bishops would get £20,000. The *curés* would get a minimum of £1,200 and a maximum of £6,000 per year. Under the old regime, some of the bishops had been fabulously rich, and they would now see their incomes fall considerably; but most of the *curés* would be much better off.

If the state was to pay the salaries of the clergy and the other expenses of the Church, it followed that the Church and the clergy must be reformed in ways that were consistent with the ongoing reorganisation of the rest of France. The debate on this new regime for the Church came to a climax in the spring of 1790, and on July 12 the National Assembly voted in a new *Constitution civile du clergé*. This meant that the clergy, being no longer a separate order, must become part of the civil society of France, subject to the laws of the land. As a first step, the Revolutionaries decided that the political, administrative and geographical structure of the hierarchy of the French Church must mirror the new political, administrative and geographical structure of the government of France. And since they had divided France into eighty-three *départements*, with eighty-three locally elected departmental governments, it followed that the French Church should also have just eighty-three departmental dioceses, with eighty-three bishops. Moreover, in accordance with France's new democratic regime, these eighty-three bishops would not be appointed by the King, nor installed by the Pope, as under the age-old Concordat of 1516, nor even assigned by the national hierarchy of the French Church, but would be elected at the level of the department. By the same token, the *curés* in the parishes (now redesignated *communes*) would no longer be appointed by the bishops but would be elected by the electoral assemblies of the local districts. To qualify for election, a bishop would need fifteen years of experience in the Church ministry, a *curé* five years.

Before agreeing to take on the running costs of the reformed Church, the Revolutionaries demanded another political price. In February 1790 the National Assembly imposed an obligation on the Church that every *curé* must read out, from his pulpit, the texts of all the Assembly's latest decrees. The clergy could no longer just be preachers of the word of God; they must now also be spokesmen for the Revolutionary state.

With hindsight, it seems clear that the Revolutionaries, in taking responsibility for the reorganisation of the Church, were following their Revolutionary logic down a very dangerous blind alley. For they were trying to incorporate the Church into the Revolutionary regime, and it took them some time to grasp that the Church was a foreign body which could not be transplanted inside the Revolution. They tried to finesse this existential problem nine months later by passing another decree, on November 27, 1790, requiring the clergy to swear an oath of allegiance to the new political regime; but it did no good, because the problem was insoluble.

By then the swearing of oaths had become almost a customary feature of the public life of the Revolution, having started with that of the *salle du Jeu de paume* (the so-called Tennis Court Oath) on June 20, 1789, when the Deputies of the *tiers état*, together with a small number of clerical Deputies, had sworn an improvised and solemn collective vow 'never to separate'. Then, towards the end of 1789, the members of the newly formed *gardes nationales* were called on to swear an oath 'on the altar of the fatherland' to 'combat the enemies of the Revolution; to maintain the Rights of Man and of the Citizen; to support the new Constitution of the Kingdom; and to take up, at the first sign of danger, the rallying cry *Live free or die*.' This process went a step further seven months later: on July 14, 1790, at the *Fête de la Fédération* (celebrating the first anniversary of the overthrow of the Bastille), the participants swore 'to be faithful to the Nation, to the Law and to the King (*à la nation, à la loi, et au roi*), and to uphold the Constitution of the Kingdom as decreed by the National Assembly'; Louis XVI was obliged to swear loyalty 'to the nation' and that he would 'uphold and execute the laws'.

This newborn custom of swearing loyalty oaths was incorporated in the drafting of the new Constitution, whose Article 5 seemingly refers to the *Fête de la Fédération* oath, stipulating: 'The civil oath is: I swear to be faithful to the nation, to the law and to the King, and to uphold with all my power the Constitution of the Kingdom, decreed by the *Assemblée nationale constituante* in the years 1789, 1790 and 1791.' This oath, already more specific than its predecessors, was now required of all elected officials: mayors, municipal councillors, judges of the peace and administrators at the district and department levels.

With the reform of the Church, the Revolutionaries went even further, in what was a serious political miscalculation. For they resolved that the clergy must be distinguished from all the civilian officials of the state by being required to take a specific oath of loyalty to the new regime. Both the bishops and the *curés* would now be called on to swear that they would 'take care of the faithful of the diocese, and be faithful to the nation, to the law and to the King, and support with all their power the Constitution decreed by the National Assembly and accepted by the King'. This specifically clerical oath created a tidal wave of problems, first for the Church and then even more, over the years ahead, for the Revolutionaries. It was the final blow to any hope of consensus among believers in France and led to a schism first in the Church and then, indirectly, in the rest of French society. For whereas civilian officials were required only to declare loyalty to the newly configured institutions of the civil state, the clergy were in effect being asked to renounce their long-standing commitment to the hierarchy, the principles and therefore the legitimacy of the Church.

It is not at all clear how far the Revolutionaries appreciated, if at all, the risks of the step they were about to take. The explicit and practical penalty of not taking the oath of allegiance was that a *curé* or bishop would cease to be paid by the state, would no longer be authorised to conduct services or to lead a congregation and would therefore be unemployed. But the implicit and political consequences were much more serious. Any clergy who chose their loyalty to the Church and to their congregation over their loyalty to the Revolution would be judged to have chosen to oppose the Revolution and to be in revolt against the law. In the event, many of the *curés* and many of the congregations would remain faithful to each other, with or without an oath. The danger inherent in the compulsory oath of allegiance was that it had the capacity to alienate not just some part of the clergy but a substantial if unpredictable part of the churchgoing population of France, which was almost everybody.

This radical overturning of the centuries-old independence of the Church was deeply and intensely controversial, not just among the clergy but also among the faithful. Bishops who were members of the National Assembly called on the Pope to take a stand, but Pius VI remained silent. Louis XVI, for his part, let it be known quite quickly, if unofficially, on July 22, 1790, that he would accept the Civil Constitution of the Clergy, but he demanded more time before he would give his official ratification. On the very next day he received private information that the Pope condemned the Civil Constitution. The King must have thought that there was some possibility of a face-saving compromise, for on August 24 he gave it his formal sanction. The Pope offered no compromise, but it was not until the spring of 1791, much too late to make any difference, that he made public his condemnation.

But there was still the question of the clerical oath of allegiance. The King had appealed to Rome for help of some kind, but the Pope had remained immovable and silent. Under pressure from the National Assembly, Louis finally capitulated, and on December 26, he formally accepted the demand for an oath of allegiance. It was now immediately required from all the clergy in France, and the profundity of the schism in the Church became obvious just as immediately.

Among the clerics in the National Assembly, the pressure to swear loyalty to the Revolution was obviously intense, but of 250 clerical *députés*, only 99 consented to swear the oath. The split in the country at large was even deeper: of eighty-three bishops, all but seven refused to swear; one of those seven was, of course, the cynical and worldly-wise Talleyrand. Among the lower clergy, there was massive opposition: of about 54,000 *curés*, nearly half, roughly 26,000, refused to take the oath. These clergy are sometimes called refractory priests, or non-jurors.

Support for the oath was extremely variable in different parts of the country: in Île-de-France, in the vicinity of Paris, 80 per cent of the clergy signed the oath; but in the west and in the east, 80 per cent of the clergy refused to sign. In the department of Bas-Rhin, in Alsace, only 8 per cent of the clergy signed the oath, but in Loiret, near Paris, the proportion was 90 per cent, and in the Var, in Provence, it was 96 per cent.

If the Revolutionaries had assumed that loyalty to the new regime would automatically trump loyalty to the Church, they were profoundly mistaken. And when the Pope's condemnation of the Civil Constitution became known in the spring of 1791, it prompted a wave of retractions among clergy who had sworn the oath; in the end it seems that well over half the clergy were refractory and refused or withdrew the oath.

Those members of the clergy who refused to swear the oath lost their jobs, and many of them emigrated. Their places now had to be filled; and under the rules just introduced by the Revolutionaries, they had to be filled not through appointment by the old Church hierarchy but through local elections, departmental in the case of the vacant bishoprics and communal in the case of the absent *curés*. By definition, almost all the electors were lay members of the electorate; in many cases they may have been non-believers and in some cases, absurdly, Protestants. The turnout was generally very low, and the elections were often extremely agitated, especially in *communes* where the congregation had just lost a valued but refractory priest.

Worse was to follow, for in many *communes* where the old *curé* had refused to swear the oath of allegiance there were often running battles between the supporters of the old and the new. Loyalists threw stones at the new *curés* and refused to take the sacrament from them; conversely, the converts to the new regime took vengeance on the old by physically intimidating those who persisted in loyalty to their former *curés*.

The Revolutionaries had now split France from top to bottom and quite gratuitously launched a long-running clash between themselves and most of the rest of the country. Some historians believe that this conflict, and especially the requirement of a specifically clerical oath of loyalty to the Revolution, was one of the worst of the unnecessary mistakes made by the Revolutionaries. It certainly set in train a sequence of events that was to build up a web of virtually insoluble problems for the Revolution in the years ahead.

10

THE FLIGHT
OF THE KING

TO THE PEOPLE OF PARIS, the transfer on October 6, 1789, of Louis XVI from Versailles to Paris may have seemed a triumphant assertion of the popular will. Yet the position of the King was inherently anomalous. In theory, he would have to cooperate with the Revolution, since he would be permanently under the influence of the people of the capital; he repeatedly succumbed to this pressure and did promise to cooperate. But he was never persuaded of the legitimacy of the Revolution, and his endorsements, when they eventually came, were always reluctant. In fact, as we have seen, the National Assembly was already playing the role of government; in which case, it was not clear what was the function of the King.

Moreover, he was an unwilling prisoner, and the most obvious reaction of any prisoner is to try to escape. The idea that he should flee had long been discussed at court, and his youngest brother, Charles Philippe, the comte d'Artois, had already fled abroad on July 16, 1789, and established himself in a would-be counter-revolutionary court at Turin. Five months later, towards the end of that year, the self-styled marquis de Favras dreamed up a plan to have the King kidnapped and taken to the secure fortress of Metz. But he talked too much, La Fayette had him watched, the plan was discovered, and Favras was hanged on February 19, 1790. The King remained undecided.

Events in early 1791 helped to persuade him that he must try to escape. In February, two elderly aunts of the King set out on a pilgrimage to Rome. On the 19th, they were stopped en route by interfering officials and brought back to Paris. On calmer consideration, the Revolutionaries recognised that there was no law to prevent their journey, so they were allowed to set out again. But it was a disturbing precedent, and the King started to make plans. In particular, he made contact with François Claude Amour, marquis de Bouillé, the commander of French military forces in eastern France (Alsace, Lorraine and Franche-Comté), who had attracted attention in September 1790 when he had suppressed, with extreme brutality, the mutiny of some of the King's traditional troops in the garrison at Nancy. Bouillé now made arrangements for providing six regiments of cavalry to escort Louis along the route of his escape.

The King's mind was made up for him on April 18, 1791, when he attempted to set out for his *château* at Saint-Cloud and was stopped by some officious members of the *Garde nationale* and a crowd of bourgeois demonstrators. They were apparently moved by a rumour that he was going to Saint-Cloud to make his Easter confession to a refractory priest.

To disarm suspicion, Louis made it known that he had addressed a circular to Europe's leading monarchs telling them that he approved of the Revolution and was placing himself at its head. At the same time, however, he sent another, secret message to Europe's monarchs disavowing the terms of the circular. He now decided to try to escape, and on the evening of June 20 he slipped out of the Tuileries with his wife, his two children and his immediate entourage, in a very large rented carriage. Once they were safely past the barrière Saint-Martin, the northern gateway of Paris, they all transferred to a vast and lumbering travelling coach (*berline*), in which they set off for the north-east. Their destination, on the recommendation of Bouillé, was the stronghold of Montmédy, not far from Luxembourg: Louis' aim was to seek a place of safety but not to leave France, since that, he feared, would wreck the reputation of the monarchy with his subjects.

The King's younger brother Louis-Stanislas Xavier, comte de Provence (*Monsieur*), left Paris at the same time, but quite independently, and escaped without hindrance to the Austrian Netherlands, from where he moved to set up his own court at Coblenz.

What Louis would have done if he had reached Montmédy as planned is unclear. He may have hoped that the crowned heads of Europe would muster an army, invade France and rescue him. Certainly, on December 3, 1790, he had written to King Frederick William II of Prussia to ask him to convene a European Congress, backed up by military force, to help Louis restore his authority. But if they did not invade – and there was no evidence that they were planning to do so – Louis would be left hanging in the wind, and his position, alone at Montmédy and far from the political centre of gravity at Paris, would have been even more anomalous than it had been in the Tuileries. Inevitably, he would have come under increasing pressure to rationalise his position by following his brothers into exile.

In fact, Louis never reached Montmédy. To begin with, his progress was regular and unimpeded, but very slow. However, quite soon the cavalry escorts laid on by Bouillé on the King's route started to lose track of his progress and after a while, they began to arouse suspicions in the villages they passed through. At Sainte-Menehould the King was recognised by the local postmaster, reputedly from having seen his image on the coinage, and the alarm was raised. Not much further on, at Varennes, the King was stopped by the local population, virtually arrested and forced to return to Paris. Back in the capital he was greeted by enormous crowds, looking on from the streets and the rooftops in total silence.

The King was relieved of all his functions while the National Assembly worked out what to do with him. From every point of view, his position was now not just anomalous but untenable; but the Revolutionaries were in a frenzy of uncertainty over the alternatives. There was a wave of demands from different parts of the country for the King to be put on trial but, paradoxically, few demands, at least at first, for him to be deposed or for the establishment of a Republic. For the moment, most of the members of the National Assembly could see no good alternative to the monarchy, and they were deeply anxious not to upset the Constitution, which they were in the last stages of elaborating. So they chose to pretend that the King had been kidnapped by a conspiracy of aristocrats led by the marquis de Bouillé.

This was quite difficult to believe, since Louis, on his departure from Paris, had left behind a *Déclaration du roi adressée à tous les Français*, in which he said that he was 'revolted to see the anarchy and the despotism of the clubs which dominated the Assembly' and that he wanted to put himself and his family in safety. But the official line from the

Revolutionaries, however implausible, was made easier to swallow by the fact that Bouillé himself, on learning of the failure of the King's flight, crossed the frontier into Luxembourg and from there wrote a letter to the National Assembly in which he took responsibility for the 'kidnapping'. The Assembly endorsed this fiction and declared that Louis had been the innocent victim of an abduction; on July 16 it restored him to all his functions as a constitutional monarch, on condition that he accept the Constitution when it was presented to him; and from this moment it became illegal to call for a trial of the King or for his replacement as the head of state.

The news of this decision triggered angry protests among the working classes, who were suffering poverty and rising unemployment and felt that the King had betrayed them. One factor behind this rising unemployment was the emigration of their employers and customers, many of whom were aristocrats; after the debacle of the King's flight to Varennes, this emigration accelerated, especially among army officers. By the end of 1791, some 6,000 officers, or about half the entire officer corps, had left the country.

The King's flight to Varennes and forcible return to Paris also intensified alarm in the capitals of the rest of Europe. When he planned his escape, he may have hoped that other monarchs would come and rescue him by force of arms; and after he was taken back to Paris it looked, briefly, as if they might. On August 20, 1791, Leopold II, the Austrian Emperor, let it be known that the European powers would recognise the French Constitution if the French King accepted it. Soon, however, under pressure from French émigrés, notably the comte d'Artois, Leopold persuaded Frederick William II to join him at Pillnitz in Saxony to issue a threatening joint declaration on the situation in France. In this declaration, published on August 27, the two monarchs said, ominously, that the position of the French King was 'an object of common concern to all the sovereigns of Europe':

> They hope that these sovereigns will not refuse to employ, jointly with them, the most effective methods, relative to their power, to put the King of France in a position to strengthen, in the most perfect liberty, the bases of a monarchical government, which is appropriate both to the rights of these sovereigns and to the well-being of the French nation. Then, and in that case, their said Majesties [the Emperor and the King of Prussia] ... are resolved to act promptly, by

common agreement, with the necessary forces to achieve this common objective.'[1]

This looked like a serious threat of military action in some near future; and that was how it was widely perceived in France and how the French King's *émigré* brothers did their best to interpret it. But in fact, Leopold intended this declaration as a purely rhetorical threat that committed him to nothing. For it implied that Austria and Prussia would act only if all the other European powers agreed to do so; and since he already knew that the English were determined to stay neutral, he already knew that the case would not arise. As Leopold is reported to have said in private: '*Alors, et dans ce cas* ["Then, and in that case"] are for me the law and the prophets'.

With the threat – however hollow – of foreign military action, and with thousands of nobles emigrating abroad, the question now was whether the Revolutionaries could continue to rely on popular support at home, crucially that of the *sans-culottes* in Paris. Yet in the summer of 1791 the National Assembly took a radical anti-labour step, which underlined the depth of the gulf in interests between the bourgeois Revolutionaries and the workers in the lower levels of society. In March 1791 the National Assembly had abolished trade guilds and corporations. This could be regarded as an expression of liberal policy, a move against any attempt by employers to restrict competition. But when groups of workers started to combine to demand higher wages, the Revolutionaries turned against them, and on June 14 the National Assembly adopted the *Loi Le Chapelier*, named after the Deputy Isaac Le Chapelier, which banned all organisations of workers and specifically prohibited any form of trade union action.

This anti-union legislation, which remained in force for another seventy-six years, until July 1867, may seem remarkably regressive, considering that it was introduced by a libertarian Revolution; and two weeks later it provoked a demonstration by a crowd of unemployed men. But notions of trade unionism were at that time in their infancy, and the vast majority of the workers in Paris were individually employed, not part of a large-scale proletariat. Their main social preoccupation was not primarily, at this stage, wage rates but the availability of food, in adequate quantities and at reasonable prices; it was when food was scarce and prices high that ordinary people were driven to protest.

In fact, food scarcity was an increasingly serious problem in the autumn of 1791, largely as a direct result of the inflation provoked by the reckless issue of *assignats*. The virtually uninterrupted rise in prices and the erratic shortages of food led to frequent outbreaks of food rioting over the next three years. And on top of the shortages of French-produced food there came shortages of colonial products – sugar, coffee, rum – due to the slave revolt in the French Caribbean colony of Saint-Domingue (modern-day Haiti) in August 1791.[2]

One consequence of the inflation in France was that the exchange rate with foreign currencies collapsed. Foreign trade became even more difficult and the economic crisis at home more serious because imports had to be paid for in gold and silver coinage at a time when French metallic coins were being hoarded and disappearing from circulation.

The King's flight and his acquittal by the National Assembly combined to trigger a strong anti-monarchist movement among some of the more radical Revolutionaries, led by the *Club des Cordeliers*. The *Cordeliers*, founded in April 1790 and dominated at first by Danton and Marat, was more downmarket, more left-wing and above all more populist than the *Jacobins*, and it played a leading role in political activity at the street level in the forty-eight *Sections* and more generally in popular political agitation in Paris. Over the next two years the *Cordeliers* would play a key part in all insurrectional uprisings in Paris. When they learned on June 21, 1791, of the King's flight, they immediately issued an open appeal for 'tyrannicide', the execution of the King; and on the next day they issued a petition calling for a Republic. This campaign was backed up, on July 1, with the appearance of a new journal, *Le Républicain*, which openly called for a change in the political regime. It was jointly edited by the marquis de Condorcet, the celebrated intellectual and friend of Voltaire, and by Thomas Paine, the firebrand pamphleteer from England.

Paine had first caused a stir in America in 1776 with his radical pamphlet *Common Sense,* in which he had championed the cause of American independence. He had raised even more of a commotion in England with his latest pamphlet, the first part of *The Rights of Man*, on

March 16, 1791. This was partially a tirade in support of democracy and against the English system of government, partially a point-by-point vindication of the French Revolution and a rebuttal of its indignant denunciation by Edmund Burke. *The Rights of Man* raised such a storm in England that in April Paine fled briefly to France, where he was received in triumph and joined forces with Condorcet.

In February 1792, eleven months after the first part, Paine published the second part of *The Rights of Man* in England, in which he went much further than before, outlining a spectacular programme of economic and social reform which, without exactly repudiating the rights of private property, went as far as it was then possible to imagine towards a welfare state. This instalment had even greater success than the first; reputedly, it sold 1.5 million copies in Paine's lifetime. But its popularity was too much for the English government, which prosecuted Paine for seditious libel, meaning a libel intended to provoke the overthrow of the government. Once more he had to flee to France, this time never to return to England. But his fame as a libertarian had so far preceded him that before the trial produced its inevitable conviction, he learned that the French National Assembly had offered him honorary citizenship and with it membership in the new National Legislative Assembly, which he accepted.

After the King's enforced return from Varennes to Paris and his (conditional) acquittal in July 1791 by the National Assembly, the question of his position ought to have been closed. Instead it provoked popular anger on the left, and the debate over the King's future raged ever more strongly in the political clubs. The *Cordeliers* argued that a popular referendum should decide his fate. The *Jacobins*, unwilling to embrace republicanism but not wishing to be left silent, released a petition on July 16, 1791, calling for the abdication of the King and his replacement 'by all constitutional means'. These words seemed to rule out a Republic, but they also seemed, by implication, to open the door to the King's replacement by his cousin, the duc d'Orléans. It is difficult to believe that this is what the *Jacobins* had intended. In any case, by the end of the day they had withdrawn their petition, not least because several hundred of their members, including almost all of those in the National Assembly, had resigned and founded a pro-monarchist club, *Les Feuillants*, which took its name from its residence in yet another vacant monastery, the Couvent des Feuillants, in the rue Saint-Honoré.

But the republican campaigners in the *Cordeliers* Club and their allies in the equally radical *Cercle social* pressed ahead with their plan for a petition to be displayed at a public meeting in the large park in central Paris called the Champ de Mars and to be signed by as many as could be persuaded to do so. In its final form, the petition called on the National Assembly to repeal the decrees which had declared the King innocent; it proclaimed 'that the crime of Louis XVI is proved, that this King has abdicated' and that it was necessary to 'convene a new constituent power, so as to proceed in a truly national way to the judgement of the guilty, and above all to the replacement and the organisation of a new executive power'. It made no explicit reference to a Republic, though its republican intention was unmistakable; but it is worth underlining, in contrast with later events, the essential legalism of this petition's spirit.

On July 17 the petition was placed on a newly erected Altar of the Revolution in the Champ de Mars, and a large crowd of peaceful demonstrators gathered; it was a Sunday, and by the end of the day, some 6,000 had signed the petition. But the Mayor of Paris, Sylvain Bailly, decided that it was unconstitutional and, after declaring martial law, sent La Fayette and the *Garde nationale* against the crowd. The soldiers were greeted with a hail of stones, and La Fayette ordered them to open fire. Some fifty of the demonstrators were killed, and hundreds were wounded. The repression which followed was severe. Republicans were harassed and arrested and their publications banned: the house magazine of the *Cercle social*, the *Bouche de fer,* was closed, and so were the *Républicain* of Condorcet and Paine (after only four issues) and the *Journal du Club des Cordeliers*. The *Club des Cordeliers* was itself closed for three weeks, and François Nicolas Vincent and Antoine François Momoro, two of its leading radical agitators, were arrested. Warrants were issued for Camille Desmoulins and others; Marat went into hiding; Danton escaped briefly to England.

Robespierre, a member of the *Jacobin* Club, was (for the time being) careful not to get involved in any of these violent republican events. He may have been a Revolutionary Deputy, but he was highly strung and nervous, and after the demonstration at the Champ de Mars and the massacre of the demonstrators, he began to feel that he might be in some personal danger; so he left his furnished room on the third floor of 64 rue de Saintonge, in the Marais *quartier* of Paris, and accepted the invitation of Maurice Duplay, the prosperous owner of a joinery business, to take lodgings in his family home. Robespierre moved in with the Duplay family, at 398 rue Saint-Honoré, on October 1, 1791, and apart from a brief interval when he went to live with his sister Charlotte, he stayed there for the rest of his life, where the entire family put themselves at his service, cosseted him and protected him from the outside world.

The National Assembly made some last-minute revisions, all of a conservative nature, in the final drafting of the Constitution: the King's role was slightly strengthened; his Ministers would be permitted to attend National Assembly debates; and the property qualification required to be an elector was increased. The revised Constitution was adopted on September 3, 1791, and accepted by the King on September 13. Considering its work done, the National Constituent Assembly (*Assemblée nationale constituante*) decided to shut up shop on September 30 and gave way to an entirely new National Legislative Assembly (*Assemblée nationale législative*). In his closing remarks at the last session of the Constituent Assembly, Jacques Thouret, its President, declared: 'The National Assembly has given the state a Constitution which will guarantee both liberty and the monarchy.'

In fact, nothing had been settled. The King had sworn loyalty to the Constitution, but he did not mean it; and in any case there was no real way to reconcile his role with the claims of the Revolutionaries. Ostensibly, the conservatives in the National Assembly and the Paris municipality had seen off the republican campaigners in the *Club des Cordeliers* and the *Cercle social*; but the massacre at the Champ de Mars left traces that would be long remembered.

From now on, the romantic idea of the Revolution as an idyllic enterprise was overlaid by the grim realities of political conflict; and the idea of a Republic was out in the open and could not be disposed of. The popularity of La Fayette, once universally adulated as the 'Hero of Two Worlds' (that is, of the New World and the Old, because of his youthful engagement in the American War of Independence), was fatally damaged by the massacre at the Champ de Mars. When Bailly resigned as the Mayor of the *Commune* of Paris, La Fayette resigned as the commander of the *Garde nationale* in the hope of being elected as his successor. But when that election came, on November 16, it was Jérôme Pétion, a radical *Jacobin*, who was elected, with 6,728 votes, while La Fayette was ignominiously left behind with only 3,126; he retreated from political life in Paris and resumed his military career, as the commander of the *armée du Centre*.

The first round of elections for the *Assemblée nationale législative* took place in early June 1791, before the flight of the King, and the

second between August 29 and September 5, when the country was in
the maximum state of agitation over the consequences of that flight.
The rules for these elections were much less democratic than those that
had governed the choice of *députés* to the *États généraux*. The electoral
law that had been adopted by the *Assemblée nationale constituante* nearly
two years earlier, on December 4, 1789, and incorporated in the Constitution, divided the citizens into two categories, active and passive. The
active citizens were those who paid taxes equivalent to at least three
days' work, roughly £2 to £3 a year, and they had the right to vote; the
passive citizens paid less than three days' worth of taxes, and they did
not have the vote. Also excluded were all women, all domestic servants
(on the grounds that they were not independent) and all men who were
under twenty-five, charged with a crime or insolvent.

The distinction between active and passive citizens was only the
first step in the exclusion of the lower orders. Although all active citizens were entitled to vote in the first round of elections, these were to
choose the electors proper. To be a real elector, one who would actually
vote directly in a second round of voting for the representatives of the
National Assembly, you had to have paid taxes equivalent to ten days'
work, roughly £7 to £10 a year. And to be eligible to stand as a candidate
for the *Assemblée nationale législative*, you had to have paid taxes equivalent to a *marc d'argent*, approximately £50. According to one calculation,
the active citizens numbered about 4.3 million voters, while the passive
citizens numbered about 3 million non-voters. However, it seems that
the incidence of poverty, even extreme indigence, was much higher in
the towns than in the countryside; in addition, the definition of the price
of a day's work was lower in the countryside than in the towns. The
combined effect of these two factors was that a majority of men in the
countryside could qualify as active citizens, and therefore could vote,
but in the towns barely a third of the men were able to do so.

What this meant was that, while a majority of the adult male population could play some part in the first stage of the electoral system, all
the lower orders were excluded, by design, from any participation in the
political decision-making process proper. From the very beginning the
French Revolution was a bourgeois revolution, and with the electoral
law of December 4, 1789, the bourgeois Revolutionaries had intended
to entrench their dominant role.

Radical patriots were hostile to the rule for eligibility, since they
regarded the test of a *marc d'argent* to be ridiculously exclusive. 'To

expose the full absurdity of this decree', said Desmoulins, 'you only have to point out that Jean-Jacques Rousseau and Pierre Corneille [the celebrated playwright] would not have been able to stand for election'. In their final modification of the draft Constitution the Revolutionaries raised the minimum payment of taxes required of an elector from about £10 to between £15 and £25 but abolished any further restriction on eligibility just described, the so-called *marc d'argent*. This reform did not apply to the current elections to the Legislative Assembly, however, since they had already started.

In any event, the elections which took place between June and September 1791, just like the recent election for the Mayor of Paris, failed to mobilise popular enthusiasm. In the mayoral election, Pétion won an overwhelming victory over La Fayette; but of a total of 80,000 potential voters, 70,000 stayed at home. In the national elections the turnout was as low or lower; it was lower in the towns than in the countryside, and in Paris it was scarcely 10 per cent.

It seems that the French people were increasingly alienated by the Revolution. Whether this was primarily due to recent political events, like the Revolutionaries' growing quarrel with the Catholic Church or the agitation over the King's flight to Varennes and the subsequent schism in the *Jacobin* Club, or whether it was mainly due to inflation, food shortages and economic hardship must be uncertain. Either way, the conclusion was becoming unavoidable: by the end of the *Assemblée nationale constituante* and the transition to the *Assemblée nationale législative*, the people of France and the people of Paris had lost almost all of their enthusiasm for the Revolution.

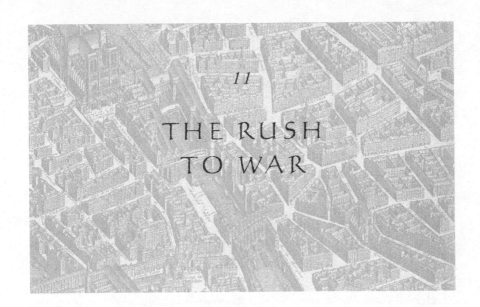

II

THE RUSH
TO WAR

THE NEW NATIONAL LEGISLATIVE ASSEMBLY which opened on October 1, 1791, was, in its composition, almost spectacularly youthful; there were 745 Deputies, and they were all young men. 'Never', said the historian Jules Michelet, 'has there been a more youthful assembly than the *Législative*. A large proportion of its members were less than twenty-six years old.' Gone was the wide variety of ages and classes of the old *Constituante*, gone were all the grey hairs. 'This looked like a uniform battalion of men', says Michelet, 'almost all of the same age, of the same class, of the same speech and of the same dress. A new France was sitting here, all with the dark hair of youth.'

The National Assembly was meeting in Le Manège, the former riding school of the Tuileries Palace, which it had adopted as its parliamentary building when it had moved to Paris with the King in October 1789. This was a very large hall, suitably large for a debating chamber and conveniently close to the King in the Tuileries Palace. It was much longer than it was wide, with the officiating position of the *Président* in the middle of one of the long sides and ranks of seats for the *députés* all round him, to left and to right and in front. At the far ends and at one level higher up there were galleries for the public.

When *députés* were called on, they came forward to speak from the centre. But the acoustics in Le Manège were terrible. Speakers had to shout to be heard, and when the National Assembly admitted the public, speakers were often drowned out by the catcalls and abuse of the spectators.

The seating in the *Assemblée nationale législative*, as in its predecessor, was spontaneous and self-selecting. The more radical Revolutionaries, notably all the members of the *Jacobin* Club, chose to sit together on the left of the President, whereas the supporters of the monarchy, and especially the members of the *Feuillant* Club, tended to sit on his right. So our political terms 'left' and 'right' turn out to be metaphors accidentally inherited from the French Revolution.

The reason for the youthfulness of this National Assembly was that on May 16, 1791, Robespierre had persuaded its predecessor, the *Assemblée nationale constituante*, to decree that no member of that body could be elected to the new one. So the *Assemblée nationale législative* must therefore be composed entirely of new men.

This was Robespierre's first tangible achievement as a member of the National Assembly and the first indication of his emergence as one of the dominant figures of the Revolution. His purpose may have been to promote younger men, in the expctation that they would be more instinctive Revolutionaries. But in practical terms, the decision had unforeseen consequences for the political stability of the Revolution.

The exclusion from the new Assembly of all those who had gained national political experience during the past two and a half years, the first creative years of the Revolution, meant that they were now compelled to divert their political energies elsewhere; and the obvious place for them to go was to the debates in the political clubs, through which some –like Robespierre – continued to lead their factions. As a consequence, the entire Revolutionary movement was now split between two rival sets of political institutions: the newly elected National Assembly at the centre, and the constellation of political clubs around it. The result was a permanently raucous antiphony between debates in the National Assembly and debates in the clubs, especially the *Jacobins*; frequently, the most revolutionary politicians would repeat to the *Jacobins* in the evening the speeches which they had delivered in the afternoon to the National Assembly, in the hope of securing the noisy endorsement of their supporters, as if from a higher court of appeal.

At first the *Jacobins* were a small minority of the *Assemblée nationale législative*. Of its 745 Deputies, only 136 had signed up for the *Club des Jacobins*, and this number probably did not increase significantly during the twelve-month life of the *Législative*. This did not, however, prevent them from becoming an increasingly strident, vocal and eventually dominant minority.

By contrast, 264 members, a little more than a third, declared themselves conservatives or pro-monarchists by signing up with the *Club des Feuillants*. By the end of the year, that number had risen to 334, not far short of half of all the Deputies. This right-wing or *Feuillant* faction was divided: some continued to follow La Fayette, and others the so-called Triumvirate: Alexandre de Lameth, Adrien Duport and Antoine Barnave. These Triumvirs, who were close to the court, were prepared to go a long way down the road of reaction and to accept revisions of the Constitution which might include giving the Assembly a second chamber and the King an absolute veto. La Fayette, on the other hand, was distrusted and detested by the court, not least because he wanted to stick to the Constitution as it stood. Though discredited with progressive 'patriots' as a result of the massacre at the Champ de Mars, he was still a popular and influential figure on the right and was particularly determined to keep to the principles of the Declaration of the Rights of Man, to which he considered he had made an important personal contribution.

Between the *Feuillants* and the *Jacobins* was a large, undeclared centre of some 300 Deputies, unaffiliated with any club, who came to be known as *la Plaine* (the plain) and later, derisively, as *le Marais* (the marsh, or swamp); they tended to support the existing constitutional arrangements, were in favour of the monarchy and were likely to vote with the conservatives.

In other words, after two and a half years of Revolution, fewer than a fifth of the members of the National Assembly were really 'Revolutionary' in a radical modern sense; but that did not prevent this small minority from capturing the Revolution and taking it, two years later, to the most politically extreme destination.

Debates in the National Legislative Assembly were soon dominated by a group of clever young left-wing politicians from south-west France, who were later referred to as *Girondins* because many of their leaders came from the Gironde *département*. One of their most brilliant speakers was Pierre Vergniaud, a thirty-four-year-old lawyer from the Bordeaux bar. His much younger friend, the twenty-six-year-old Jean-François

Ducos, also came from Bordeaux, but from a family of merchants and *plantation* owners, and he had followed his father into trade. Ducos' sister was married to Jean-Baptiste Boyer-Fonfrède, also a member of the Assembly, from another rich *Bordelais* trading and shipping family with property in Saint-Domingue.

Another of Vergniaud's close friends in the *Législative*, also on the left, was Marguerite Élie Guadet,[1] a thirty-three-year-old barrister from Bordeaux; he was a dazzling, passionate speaker and was to prove one of Robespierre's most effective opponents in the National Assembly. A fifth member of the group was Armand Gensonné, also a barrister from Bordeaux but connected to the merchant classes there. He too was thirty-three years old.

Perhaps surprisingly, the leader of these so-called *Girondins* came not from the south-west but from the Paris region. This was Jacques-Pierre Brissot, who was born in Chartres in 1754, the son of a landowner in Beauce. Being three or four years older and much more cosmopolitan, he easily overshadowed his colleagues from the Gironde. He had studied law but had resolved on a career of letters and embarked on a life of freelance journalism, political controversy and financial adventurism. Some people sneered at him as a literary and political adventurer, but his greater international experience and much wider political contacts, even though he was only thirty-seven, made him the automatic leader of this group of Revolutionaries; and they were known at first much more often as *Brissotins* than *Girondins*.

The top priority on the political agenda for the *Brissotins* and their allies was what to do about the King and the foreign enemies of the Revolution; but the most urgent problem facing the Assembly was the worsening crisis in the French economy.

This crisis was epitomised by a series of violent disruptions in the food trade, leading to episodic shortages. In February 1792 the warehouses of a number of food merchants in Dunkerque were pillaged and there was a violent conflict that left fourteen dead and sixty wounded. In March in a number of *départements* in the centre and south of France (Cantal, Lot, Dordogne, Corrèze, Gard), some members of the recently formed *gardes nationales* attacked and pillaged a series of *châteaux* which belonged (they thought) to *émigrés*. Another factor in the food disturbances may have been the rebellion which had broken out in the West Indies, in Saint-Domingue.

Saint-Domingue was one of the richest of France's colonies, and its plantations produced enormous wealth in the form of sugar, rum, coffee and cotton. Its economy was essentially built on the slave trade; the dominant and slave-owning population consisted of 30,000 whites, but all the work was done by 500,000 black slaves. In between were 27,000 mulattoes, who were free but not white. Brissot had founded the *Société des amis des Noirs* in 1788 but failed to get any support from the *Assemblée nationale constituante* for the abolition of slavery. Part of the problem was that some of the Revolutionaries had a personal stake in the plantation business: not just some of the right-wing members of the *Feuillant* Club, like the Lameth brothers, but also, as we have seen, some of the left-wing *Girondins*. On March 8, 1790, the National Assembly passed a decree setting up assemblies of local self-government in the colonies, for which only the whites could vote and in which only the whites could sit. From this point on, the Revolutionaries simply blanked out the question of slavery; the only related question they were prepared to debate was what rights, if any, to give to mulattoes. More than a year later, on May 15, 1791, the National Assembly gave citizenship to mulattoes, but the colonial whites refused to implement the decree. This refusal led to the rising first of the mulattoes, then of the blacks, in August 1791, under the command of Toussaint Louverture.

The rebels set fire to the plantations, which caused an immediate economic backlash. Sugar, coffee and rum, though relatively expensive, had by this time become fairly regular articles of consumption in Paris, and the supplies were now brutally cut short; this, on top of the shortages of other foodstuffs, exacerbated the price inflation caused by the decline in the value of the *assignats*. There was disorder in local food markets, denunciations of food hoarding and demands for government intervention to fix food prices. In the spring of 1792, Jacques Simoneau, the Mayor of Étampes, refused the demands of local crowds that he set fixed food prices, and he was murdered by a mob. But it was the uninterrupted decline in the value of the *assignat* which was the deepest cause of France's economic difficulties, since it was pushing up inflation, disrupting food supplies and causing serious disturbances in France's foreign trade.

The *Brissotins* claimed that the fall in the value of the *assignat* was due not to the fact that it was an unsupported paper currency, counterbalanced by far too little in the way of tax receipts, or that too many had been issued, but to the fact that confidence in the currency was being deliberately undermined by the enemies of the Revolution: the crowned heads of Europe, the brothers of the King, other *émigré* aristocrats and not least the refractory priests, who had refused to swear loyalty to the Revolution. It was only by meeting these external threats head-on, they believed, that they could deal with their worsening domestic social and economic crisis. And to them, meeting these external threats meant confronting the foreign powers, forcing them to recognise and accept the Revolution and getting them to put a stop to the subversive actvities of the *émigrés*. In the last resort, that would probably mean war.

In fact, almost everybody seemed to be set on war, for opposing reasons. The King wanted war because he hoped the Austrians would come to his rescue. La Fayette and his supporters wanted war because many of them were military men and thought they would do well out of it, or at least well enough to be able to bring the Revolution under their control. And some of the *Brissotins* wanted war at least partly for idealistic reasons, in the belief that victory would enable them to extend the benefits of the Revolution to other countries.

Almost the only people who did not want war were a small group of left-wing Revolutionaries led by Robespierre. He had made himself ineligible for the National Assembly, but he made his voice heard often and passionately in the *Jacobin* Club. He was a relentless speaker, delivering more than 500 speeches in the *Constituante* and more than 100 at the *Jacobins* between September 1791 and August 10, 1792. He is said to have been a poor orator, with a high-pitched voice and a harsh provincial accent from his native Artois in the north-east of France.[2] But his speeches must have been curiously compelling, for they seem to have fixed the attention of his hearers, even against their will. Robespierre's rhetoric may not read well today, but what is not in doubt is the verdict of his fellow Revolutionaries: many, even those who disagreed with him politically – and many did disagree with him, on the right and in the centre – were impressed by the force of his character and of his convictions. 'He will go far', said Mirabeau, 'because he believes everything he says'.[3] The historian Jules Michelet, looking back seventy years later, gave an eloquent picture of the fascination that Robespierre exercised on his audience in the National Assembly in the autumn of 1792: 'The inquisitorial figure of Robespierre, sickly, blinking, hiding his dim eyes behind his glasses, was a strange sphinx of a man, whom one watched ceaselessly despite oneself, and whom one disliked watching.'[4]

Robespierre opposed war because he believed that it would come to no good; he warned that France was not ready for one and would not be ready without a massive rearmament effort, and a victorious war might bring to power a victorious general.

'War', he told the *Jacobin* Club on December 18, 1791,

> is always the first wish of a powerful government which wants to become still more powerful ... It is in war that the executive power deploys the most fearful energy and exercises a sort of dictatorship which can only frighten our emerging liberties; it is in war that the people forget those principles which are most directly concerned with civil and political rights and think only of events abroad, that they turn their attention from their political representatives and their magistrates and instead pin all their interest and all their hopes on their generals and their ministers ...
>
> It is during war that a habit of passive obedience, and an all too natural enthusiasm for successful military leaders, transforms the soldiers of the nation into the soldiers of the King or of his generals. [Thus] the leaders of the armies become the arbiters of the fate of their country, and swing the balance of power in favour of the faction that they have decided to support. If they are Caesars or Cromwells, they seize power themselves.[5]

The real enemies of the Revolution, Robespierre insisted, were at home, not abroad. But his warnings, which were to prove uncannily prescient, not just about Napoléon but even sooner about his own *Gouvernement révolutionnaire*, were ignored, and war became unavoidable.

The reason for this was that the question of the King's role remained unsettled at home, and the fundamental claims to legitimacy of the Revolution itself therefore unrecognised abroad. The Revolutionaries should have settled this domestic question at home, but since they could not agree on a legal solution, and since the legitimacy of the Revolution was continuously challenged by *émigrés* and by other crowned heads of Europe (led by the Austrian Emperor), it seemed to the war party that they had no option but to go to war.

Formally, the King had accepted the new Constitution; but everyone knew, or at least suspected, that the court opposed the Revolution. The King's brothers had fled France and were doing their best to muster an *émigré* army and to mobilise the rest of Europe against the Revolution, starting with Austria and Prussia; and the ranks of *émigrés* had substantially increased after the King's flight to Varennes, when half the officers of the army left the country. There was growing debate on all sides over whether France should declare war first, though the Revolutionaries suspected that the King's objective was to incur a French defeat, so as to ensure his triumphant restoration by the other crowned heads of Europe.

Faced with discontents at home, the Revolutionaries stepped up their campaign to make war inevitable, by going after their enemies. On October 31, 1791, the National Assembly passed a decree calling on the King's brother the comte de Provence to return to France or lose his rights of inheritance. On November 9, it passed a decree giving *émigrés* two months to return home; if they refused, their property would be confiscated and they would be guilty of conspiracy, punishable by death. On November 29, sixteen months after the National Assembly had imposed the controversial *Constitution civile du clergé*, the Revolutionaries turned their attack on those recalcitrant priests who had not emigrated, threatening them with the loss of their pensions and two years of prison; this was the start of a long, detailed and unrelenting programme of repression of non-conforming priests.

The King used his delaying veto to block these decrees, but he accepted another one of November 29, which threatened the Electors of Trier and Mainz with war if they did not expel French *émigrés* from their territories. The Electors complied with this ultimatum, but the King now wanted war, which he thought he would be the one to conduct, for either he would be victorious, in which case his authority would be enormously strengthened and he could curb or even reverse the Revolution, or else he would be defeated, in which case he counted on the other crowned heads of Europe to intervene and restore him, and thus put down the Revolution. In fact, he expected defeat, as he had written after Varennes: 'Instead of a civil war, it will be a political war, and things will be much better for it. The physical and moral state of France are such as to make it impossible to carry on such a war.' It is not entirely clear what the King meant by 'a political war', but his conclusion was well founded. The French army was not large and not well prepared or well equipped to fight a war.

But La Fayette also hoped for war: he assumed that he would be the commander-in-chief and that when victory came, as he thought it would, he could drive out the *Jacobins*. As professional soldiers, the Lameth brothers also hoped for war; they thought that a short and limited war would allow the generals to stabilise the Revolution. Part of the left wing of the National Assembly, urged on by Brissot and the leading orators from the Gironde, also wanted war. France and Europe needed a revolutionary struggle, they thought, for that would force the King to declare his real position.

Many of the most enthusiastic advocates of war now became convinced that it would be easy, since French armies would be welcomed in neighbouring European countries, and their populations would rise up to throw off the chains of their feudal oppressors. In any case, it was a duty to help liberate the potential Revolutionaries of the rest of Europe. Robespierre saw this as yet another error. 'The most extravagant idea that can be born in the head of a politician', he told the *Club des Jacobins* on January 2, 1792, 'is to believe that it is enough for a people to enter among a foreign people by force of arms to make them adopt its laws and its Constitution. Nobody loves armed missionaries; and the first advice that nature and prudence give is to reject them as enemies.'[6]

In fact, the Revolutionaries had recently witnessed, and all too vividly, in Avignon, the dangers and the potential conflicts inherent in 'liberation'. Avignon, with 28,000 inhabitants, was one of the five or six most important towns in southern France. But it was an enclave, having been a papal possession since the fourteenth century, together with the neighbouring Comtat Venaissin, whose capital was Carpentras. During the early days of the Revolution, its population had been increasingly polarised between the clergy and the nobles, who remained conservatively committed to the papacy, and the bourgeoisie and the artisans, who wanted to take part in, and benefit from, the Revolutionary advances being tried in France. In 1790 there had been growing conflict between the two sides, and between Avignon (whose more urban population was also more Revolutionary) and Carpentras (where the population was more conservative). At first the Revolutionaries in Paris refused to get involved. But after long discussions, in the autumn of 1791 there was an emotional debate in the *Assemblée nationale* in which Robespierre declared that 'Avignon's cause is that of the whole world; it is that of liberty';[7] and on September 14 the Assembly decreed that Avignon and the Comtat should be attached to France.

Unfortunately, that was not the end of the story. In Avignon the party of the papists and of the nobility did not acquiesce either in the annexation or in the establishment of a moderate municipal administration, and on October 16 they set off a counter-revolutionary riot which led to the death of a Revolutionary 'patriot' named Lescuyer.

This provoked violent counterdemonstrations, led by the local soldier-adventurer Mathieu Jouve Jourdan, subsequently nicknamed Jourdan Coupe-Tête (Head-Cutter). A wave of killings was set in train, leading to the mob massacre of some sixty right-wing suspects in the Palace of the Popes' Tower of the Glacière, from which the victims were thrown. The French Revolutionaries were shocked by the news, and Avignon was for years a divided society.

Meanwhile, in Paris, the momentum towards war was building up. Louis XVI's Foreign Minister, Jean-Marie de Lessart, did his best to keep the peace, but the mood of the Revolutionaries was against him. On March 10, 1792, the Assembly charged him with treason. The King's other Ministers all resigned, and he appointed a new government made up of friends of Brissot, all of whom were in favour of war: Charles François Dumouriez, a lieutenant general, was appointed the Foreign Minister; Étienne Clavière, a banker from Geneva, became the Finance Minister; and Jean-Marie Roland became the Interior Minister. (They all ended badly. Dumouriez betrayed his country by going over to the Austrians; Clavière committed suicide to avoid being condemned to death; Roland committed suicide on hearing that his wife had been guillotined.)

On April 20 the National Assembly voted overwhelmingly for war against Austria. Only seven members voted against. On the day that war was declared, Robespierre totally reversed his position and delivered a speech to the *Jacobin* Club calling for a war of a nation in arms:

> Since war has been declared, I believe that we must also conquer Brabant, the Low Countries, Liège, Flanders, etc. The only thing which should concern us from now on are the means of executing this useful enterprise; that is to say, at this moment we must wage, as I have proposed several times, no longer the war of the court, but the war of the people; the French people must now rise up and arm themselves completely, whether to fight abroad, or to keep a lookout for despotism at home.'[8]

This was prophetic; for it was not until the whole nation was armed for mass warfare, a year or so later, that France started to win those major strategic victories which changed the map of Europe for twenty-five years and transformed the nature of warfare forever.

12

THE OVERTHROW OF
THE MONARCHY

TO BEGIN WITH, the war did not go well. The war strategy adopted by Dumouriez was simple: remain on the defensive in most directions but strike north, through the Austrian Low Countries, corresponding to most of modern-day Belgium. Three years earlier, in the autumn of 1789, the Low Countries had rebelled and briefly driven out the Austrians, who had soon reoccupied the territory. Dumouriez thus assumed that the people there would rise up and welcome the French Revolutionaries as liberators, and he ordered the three French generals, La Fayette, Rochambeau and Lückner, to go on the offensive.

Unfortunately, the French army did not seem to want to fight, and the northwards strike simply petered out. The generals complained that the army was not properly equipped; and Rochambeau, in particular, made it clear that he had no confidence in the volunteers from the *Garde nationale*, whom he thought were undisciplined. All these factors may have played a part, but it seems that the crucial one was the reluctance or indecisiveness of the generals. Rochambeau certainly showed the greatest unwillingness in carrying out the offensive, and the greatest readiness to retreat without cause. Two regiments of his cavalry, after fleeing in panic, rounded on their general, Théobald Dillon, and slaughtered him, accusing him of treason.

Part of the problem was strictly military. France was not well prepared for fighting a war. The army was starved of funds, was short of equipment, arms and ammunition, and had no more than 150,000 men; wholesale emigration had severely depleted the officer class, and desertion was common, especially in the cavalry. Worst of all, the more liberal innovations of Revolutionary ideology in the volunteer units had undermined the morale and discipline of the regular troops alongside whom they fought. For the army was divided between the traditional royalist troops of the line, in their white uniforms (*les blancs*), who were normally drilled to severe, even brutal standards of discipline, and the new, more democratic Revolutionary volunteers from the *Garde nationale*, in their blue uniforms (*les bleus*), who were better paid and used to electing their own officers. The morale problem showed up in the recruiting figures: after the King's flight to Varennes, the government called for volunteers from the *Garde nationale*, but whereas it had hoped for 100,000 new men, it got only 33,000.

Since the start of the Revolution there had been a number of outbreaks of indiscipline among *les blancs*, of which the most serious was a mutiny at the Nancy barracks in 1790, when the troops had rebelled against their officers and fraternised with the local *gardes nationales*. It had been put down with great ferocity by the marquis de Bouillé, the same officer who was subsequently appointed to provide an escort for the King's flight to Varennes. Order had been restored, but the severe repression (one man was broken on the wheel, forty-two were hanged and forty-one were sent to the galleys) aggravated the growing antagonism in the *blanc* regiments between the men and their noble officers. When France went to war in the spring of 1792, these men felt another divide, between themselves and *les bleus*. It was not until 1793 that the Revolutionaries grasped the problem of this division and decided to 'amalgamate' *les blancs* and *les bleus*, in common units with common rules. But this process was slow; it did not really start until 1794 and was not complete until 1796.

The French were saved from disaster in these early weeks of the war by the equal hesitancy of their enemies. Austria had only 35,000 soldiers in the Netherlands, and the Prussians had barely started to mobilise; Leopold II of Austria was in any case personally reluctant to engage in any war, of any kind, against anyone. His sudden death, on March 1, 1792, brought to the throne his son Francis II, who was of a much more belligerent character and was immediately keen to fight the Revolutionaries, in support of the French monarchy.

Russia, however, distracted Austria and Prussia from wholehearted engagement in the war with France. It was aiming at a new partition of Poland behind their backs; and in May 1792 it intervened in Poland when the Polish Confederation of Targowica called on it for help. This resulted in the Second Partition of Poland, in which Russia took 250,000 square kilometres of Polish territory, including western Ukraine, while Prussia got 57,000, including Danzig (now Gdansk). On this occasion Austria got nothing. Prussia now felt free to turn on France, and the Prussian King, Frederick William II, insisted that Karl Wilhelm Ferdinand, the Duke of Brunswick, be appointed the commander-in-chief of the combined Prussian-Austrian forces. This turned out, however, to be a further factor of delay, since Brunswick was not in favour of war with France; in fact, he was not a warlike general in any way, and it was said of him that 'he was one of those who lose the victory by being too concerned to ensure the possibility of retreat'. If the French had only known it, their enemies were not really all that threatening.

But the French did not know it. When their armies failed to carry out their orders to go on the offensive, Robespierre publicly blamed the generals; the generals blamed the troops; Rochambeau resigned; many officers deserted; three regiments of cavalry went over to the enemy; and the French Defence Minister, the marquis de Grave, resigned.

The heart of the problem was political. If France's war management was in a state of catastrophic malfunction, it was mainly because the Revolutionaries in Paris had failed to impose civilian political control on the military leaders at the front. La Fayette, for example, sent a message to the Austrian ambassador in Brussels asking for a suspension of hostilities and offering to march on Paris with his troops to drive out the *Jacobins* and reform the Constitution. The ambassador replied evasively; but on May 18, 1792, the three French generals decided together, on their own responsibility, to suspend hostilities. Critics suspected a treasonous conspiracy between La Fayette and the court, which was an extension of long-standing suspicions of a treasonous conspiracy between the court and the Austrians – that is to say, between Queen Marie-Antoinette and her brother Leopold II, the Austrian Emperor, and now her nephew Francis II.

Another reason for this mismanagement was that the Revolutionaries had gone to war on false pretences. The Prussians and the Austrians had made threatening noises and may have looked threatening, but they had not declared war and they had not invaded. The French

Revolutionaries could quite reasonably have devoted their energies to training and equipping their military forces. Instead, they had rushed into a foreign war in the hope that it would indirectly solve – by diverting attention away from the central political problem of the Revolution, which they had failed to settle – what to do about the King. Within just over three months, they would find that this problem had been solved for them, without their permission and against their will, by the *sans-culottes*.

When the war started badly, the first reaction of Jacques Brissot and his *Girondin* allies was to step up their campaign against those at home whom they suspected of being enemies of the Revolution, starting with the King and the refractory priests. On May 27, 1792, the National Assembly passed a decree for the deportation of refractory priests. Two days later it passed a decree to dissolve the King's Constitutional Guard, which had been created by the National Assembly the previous September. And on June 8 it passed a decree to set up, near Paris, a camp for 20,000 semi-military volunteers from the provinces, known as *fédérés*. Brissot and the *Girondins* claimed that this was needed to protect the capital in the event of a breakthrough by the Austrians; the *Feuillants* and other monarchists claimed that it was part of a *Jacobin* plot to kidnap the King and use him as a hostage in such an event. Louis submitted to the suppression of his Constitutional Guard; but on June 11 he imposed his veto on the other two decrees.

He also dismissed three of his main *Girondin* Ministers, Roland (Interior), Clavière (Finance) and Joseph Servan (War), and replaced them with loyal *Feuillants*. Rumours began to spread that he was planning a conspiracy with the Austrians, through Queen Marie-Antoinette, to break the *Jacobins*, dissolve the Assembly, recall the *émigrés* and end the war.

From his camp at the northern front, La Fayette on June 16 sent the King and the Assembly a long diatribe denouncing the *Jacobins* and the other clubs, the *Girondin* ex-Ministers and Dumouriez. The King kept Dumouriez but moved him to the War Ministry; when Dumouriez next appeared at the National Assembly, to give a long and pessimistic report on the military situation, he was shouted down. He told the King that the political situation was very dangerous and urged him to withdraw his vetoes; Louis refused. Dumouriez resigned and was punished with a posting to command a division at the northern front.

Public opinion was increasingly agitated; an agitation that was most violent at street level and in the political institutions of the Paris *Sections*. The *Sections* were supposed to be controlled, or at least supervised, by the Paris municipality, now known as the *Commune*. The *Commune* was firmly led from the left by Revolutionary leaders: the *Jacobin* Jérôme Pétion had recently secured a large majority in his election as the Mayor of Paris and had taken as his Chief Executive (*procureur-syndic*) Louis Pierre Manuel, who had taken as his deputy the left-wing populist Georges Danton. But while the *Commune* was under firm control, the *Garde nationale* could no longer be relied on, especially after the departure of its hero La Fayette. Moreover, the common people, restless and angry because of their poverty, were now arming themselves, usually with pikes (for lack of rifles). Because of its prevalence, the pike became the symbol of popular protest; as Robespierre said: 'This weapon is in a sense sacred.'[1]

All of this meant that the situation was now ripe for a violent dénouement, a day of crowd action, or what the French call *une journée*, the first of which was set for June 20, 1792. As so often with the big crowd events of the Revolution, the question of who planned or led it remains something of a mystery. Albert Mathiez, the noted Marxist historian of the Revolution, says the *Girondins* started it; but François Furet says it was obscure local figures, who were then led in action by Antoine Santerre, a rich and popular brewer of the Saint-Antoine quarter.

In any event, it seems clear that there had been preparations in the *Jacobin* Club for a big demonstration at least a week before, and probably well before that; and that Robespierre was part of this planning talk. By June 16, everyone was discussing June 20 as the now expected date for the demonstration. The *Directoire* of the *département* of Paris, which had overall responsibility for the region and whose members included Talleyrand, wanted to prevent it; but Pétion, knowing that it could not be averted, simply wanted to contain it, by calling up the whole of the *Garde nationale* and getting them to march alongside the demonstrators.[2]

The popular momentum towards the demonstration was unstoppable, but now most of the *Jacobins* were firmly opposed to it. 'Robespierre', says Michelet, 'far from taking part, was entirely hostile; he did not like these big events. Carefully turned out, bewigged, and powdered, he would not have risked in these roughhouses, nor even in the crude society of a riot, the safety of his person.'[3]

The demonstration duly happened on June 20. It was meant to be in commemoration of the Tennis Court Oath of 1789, but it seems to have been pretty disorganised. Perhaps 10,000 men assembled outside Le Manège, the meeting chamber of the National Assembly; they were organised by *Section* and led by Santerre, Legendre, Fournier, Saint-Huruge and Jean-François Varlet. They demanded to be received by the National Assembly, to present a petition. The National Assembly agreed to receive only a small number of them, a delegation. The demonstrators then demanded the right to hold a parade through Le Manège. Reluctantly, the parliamentarians submitted, and it lasted three hours; many of the demonstrators were drunk.

After wearying of the parade, some of the demonstrators found their way to the doors to the Tuileries, which were neither guarded nor locked. They invaded the palace, and they came upon the King; they jostled him, they insulted him, and they shouted at him: 'Down with the veto!' He remained extremely calm, agreed to put on a red bonnet of liberty and to drink a glass of red wine with them but he refused to withdraw his vetoes.

Meanwhile, Pétion, who had done nothing to lead, impede or control the demonstration, had appeared late in the day, told the crowd that violence was not the way and persuaded the demonstrators to withdraw peacefully. They had achieved nothing. The *département* of Paris suspended him; but he was applauded at the public celebration of the anniversary of Bastille Day three weeks later, where the crowds were intensely hostile to the court, and the National Assembly decided to reinstate him.

Not a single one of the forty-eight Paris *Sections* disavowed the demonstration of June 20.[4] It provoked a brief pro-royalist reaction among the middle classes, however, especially in the provinces. La Fayette, long a monarchist, was one of those who had walked out of the *Jacobin* Club a year earlier in protest at the talk of a republican petition. Now, full of indignation at the way the King had been manhandled, he abandoned his army at the front and rushed back to Paris. On June 28 he presented himself at the National Assembly, where he was applauded. He demanded the dissolution without delay of the *Jacobin* clubs and the exemplary punishment of all those guilty of the violence of June 20. Needless to say, his proposal was not adopted, but a motion reproving his conduct, put forward by Marguerite Élie Guadet, one of the leading *Girondins*, was also rejected, by 339 votes to 234.

La Fayette seems to have thought that his moment for a decisive act had come. Having heard that the King was due to review a parade of the *Garde nationale* the following day, he decided to take command of the troops and march them against the *Club des Jacobins*. He may have thought that he could take control of the situation with a *coup de force*; he may even have thought that he could take power. But word of his plans got out and reached the ears of the Queen, who would have none of it. 'I see well that Monsieur de La Fayette wants to save us; but who will save us from Monsieur de La Fayette?'[5] The royal entourage tipped off Pétion, who cancelled the parade; and the thirty-five-year-old marquis de La Fayette, deflated, went back to his army empty handed.

Meanwhile, the military situation had started to appear much more threatening. The unilateral suspension of hostilities by La Fayette and the other generals had given the Austrians and the Prussians time to regroup. The Prussian army, under the Duke of Brunswick, followed by the army of the *émigrés*, was preparing to invade French territory, and the French forces seemed unable to resist them.

On July 1 the National Assembly declared that all official institutions would now hold their meetings in public, in the hope that this would help to mobilise support for the government's war policy. The next day it circumvented the King's veto on the proposed camp of 20,000 *fédérés* by passing a decree which summoned provincial *gardes nationaux* to Paris for the July 14 celebrations. Public opinion in the streets of the city was increasingly suspicious that the court was conspiring with the enemy; and on July 3, Pierre Vergniaud, one of the leading *Girondins*, delivered a speech accusing the King of working for the enemy and causing France's military setbacks; he virtually called for Louis' overthrow.

On July 6 the King informed the National Assembly that the Prussians had crossed the frontier. On July 10 his *Feuillant* Ministers urged him to lead them to the National Assembly, in order that he should there publicly denounce the mismanagement of the war; he refused, and they resigned. The next day the Assembly proclaimed a national emergency, *la patrie en danger*. This was a new stage in the crisis and a new attempt by the National Assembly to assert its authority. The declaration allowed it to override the King's vetoes, and all public institutions went into permanent session. The whole of the *Garde nationale* was mobilised, and new battalions of volunteers were raised; in a few days, 15,000 Parisians signed up.

It was around this time, according to Mathiez, that Robespierre decided to take over the leadership of the growing popular protest movement:

> In the *Jacobins*, Robespierre and [François] Anthoine ... took over the leadership of the popular movement. The role of Robespierre above all was considerable. He harangued the *fédérés*, the paramilitary volunteers who were arriving in Paris from the provinces, and denounced the treachery of the generals and the impunity of La Fayette. He told them that the National Assembly had been insulted by La Fayette, and that it was now up to the *fédérés* to save the state. He urged the *fédérés* not to swear allegeance to the King. Robespierre, without being intimidated, drafted petitions which were more and more threatening... That of July 17 called for the overthrow of the King. At his instigation, the *fédérés* appointed a secret directorate, which included his friend [François] Anthoine [a radical speaker in both the National Assembly and the *Jacobins*], and this directorate sometimes met in the house of the joiner Duplay, where he lived, as did Anthoine.[6]

This account is tantalisingly ambiguous, and it highlights one of the most interesting questions of the French Revolution: what was the role of Robespierre in the overthrow of the King? Mathiez tells us that Robespierre called for the overthrow of the King, but not how he wanted the King to be overthrown. The tone of the passage implies that Robespierre had joined the insurrectionists; but the use of the word 'petitions' equally clearly implies that he had not. For if there were to be petitions, to whom could they be addressed except to the National Assembly? That was the only political institution which might conceivably have the legal authority to overthrow the King. But here was the kernel of the political dilemma: it had so far balked at the idea.

If Robespierre had changed his mind about defying the National Assembly, it is not clear why he did so, nor what exactly he had decided to do. There may have been two factors at play. The first was that by now the *fédérés* were arriving in Paris in their thousands and being recruited and coached, under Anthoine's supervision, to take part in the planned insurrection. Robespierre may well have felt that this torrent of potential insurgents was simply overwhelming his options for constitutional action.

A second possible factor is that he may have thought that it was difficult, or even impossible, to count on the National Assembly as an instrument for removing the King. As public opinion moved against the court under the influence of the events of the war, Robespierre and other Revolutionaries may have hoped that there would be a corresponding move by the National Assembly to take control of events. By now he may have concluded that this was not going to happen; such a conclusion would have been confirmed on August 8, when the National Assembly voted by a large majority to exculpate La Fayette from any treasonous delinquency.

The *sans-culottes* did not wait for Robespierre to change his mind. On June 20, the day of the demonstration, they had set up a secret insurrectional committee (*Comité insurrectionnelle*) with the support of the *Commune* and especially of Manuel, its Chief Executive, and Danton, his second deputy.

'On July 25,' according to Michelet,

a civic party was given for the *fédérés* on the site of the ruins of the Bastille, and the same night, of the 25th to the 26th, an insurrectionary directory assembled at the Soleil d'Or, a small nearby nightclub. There were five members of the committee of the *fédérés*, plus the two leaders of the *faubourgs*, Santerre and [Charles] Alexandre, three men of action, [Claude] Fournier, known as the American, [François] Westermann and [Claude-François] Lazowski, the *Jacobin* Anthoine, the journalists [Jean-Louis] Carra and [Antoine Joseph] Gorsas, lost children of the Gironde.'[7]

Now Manuel demanded and secured agreement that the *Sections* would be included in the planning of the insurrection. A coordination committee (*bureau central de correspondance*) was set up, which was effectively run from the *Jacobin* Club. What this means is that the leaders of the *Jacobins*, including Robespierre, and the leaders of the *sans-culottes* were all deeply involved in planning the overthrow of the King.[8]

From the main towns of France, messages flowed in calling for the overthrow of the King; and every day, more and more *fédérés* arrived in Paris. On July 17 they had presented a petition to the National Assembly demanding the suspension of the King and the election of a *Convention* by universal male suffrage. On July 29 Robespierre followed their lead, in a major speech to the *Jacobins*, in which he called for the deposition of the King and the election of a *Convention*. On July 30 a company of

600 men from Marseille marched into the city, singing the hymn of the Army of the Rhine, composed in Strasbourg only a few months earlier by the young Captain Claude Rouget de l'Isle; it became famous as *La Marseillaise*, today the French national anthem.

The tide of events was becoming irresistible, and pressure was coming up from below.

In Paris, the forty-eight *Sections*, created in May 1790, had rapidly become active centres of political agitation, to the point that they were beginning to alarm the national authorities. After May 1791 they were not allowed to hold public meetings except with permission, and they were forbidden by the National Assembly from holding meetings for any purpose except debates about the administration of the municipality; that is, they were forbidden from holding debates about general political issues.

But the *Sections* refused to submit, and the war gave them the pretext they were looking for. On July 24, 1792, the *Section des Postes* demanded, and got, from the *Assemblée nationale législative* the right for any *Section* to meet *en permanence*, which meant whenever they liked, without asking permission. The National Assembly had already decided that all meetings of public bodies must be held in public; so the *Sections* now set aside viewing galleries in their meeting halls, which were immediately invaded by political agitators. This had the automatic effect of driving away moderate citizens, who were intimidated by the agitators' threats and insults. Under this pressure, political ferment at these meetings became more and more intense.

In principle, membership in these *assemblées*, as for the *Garde nationale*, was restricted to active citizens, those who paid a certain amount of tax. But on July 25 the *Section du Louvre* demanded that all citizens be treated as active; and on July 27 the *Section du Théâtre-Français* granted this right on its own authority. This guaranteed that when the *bureau central de correspondence* for the *Sections* was organised, the pressure on it from below was already intense.[9]

Although Vergniaud had virtually called for the King's overthrow on July 3, the *Girondins* now thought that the resignation of Louis' *Feuillant* Ministers on July 20 might signal their chance to return to power, and they changed tack. On July 26, Brissot denounced all calls for the overthrow of the King: 'If there are men who aim to establish a Republic on the ruins of the Constitution of 1789, the sword of the law should strike at them as at the counter-revolutionaries of Coblenz'. (It was in Coblenz that Louis XVI's younger brother the comte de Provence had set up his *émigré* court and was trying to rouse the crowned heads of Europe to declare war on the French Revolution.) But the *Girondins'* opportunistic volte-face at this moment of crisis could not turn back the tide of events, which was relentlessly flowing towards the overthrow of the monarchy. Moreover, this sudden change of policy may have been one of the factors that made irrevocable the fatal enmity between them and the more radical *Jacobins*, which eventually led to the *Girondins'* downfall.

The political atmosphere suddenly became much more threatening with the publication of what became known as the Brunswick Manifesto. Although the war was still only half-hearted in purely military terms, on July 25, 1792, the Duke of Brunswick, the commander-in-chief of the Austrian and Prussian forces, issued a long and menacing ultimatum. It read, in part:

> The French, and especially the people of Paris, were called on to submit to the King without delay ... and if the least violence were to be shown towards their Majesties the King and the Queen and to the royal family, [the sovereigns of Prussia and Austria] will inflict on them an exemplary punishment, in subjecting the city of Paris to a military execution and a total overthrow, and the guilty rebels to the tortures which they will have deserved.[10]

The news of the declaration reached the streets of Paris on August 1; but instead of intimidating the insurrectionists, it enraged them and stiffened their determination. Everyone was primed for action; and organising and coordinating committees had been set up in every quarter, in the *Sections*, in the *Commune*, among the *fédérés* and of course in the *Jacobin* Club, not to mention in Robespierre's home in the house of the Duplay family. Yet even at this late stage, when preparations for an insurrection were far advanced and most of the main actors were deeply involved, there were still many influential Revolutionaries who were deeply unhappy about what was being planned and hoped for another way.

The *fédérés* were arriving in Paris in large numbers; and on July 17,

1792, they sent a delegation to the National Assembly, to appeal to it to take action, to punish the traitors, to charge La Fayette with treachery, to suspend the government; in short, to take charge and take power. The National Assembly turned a deaf ear to their appeal. On July 27 the *Section des Cordeliers* under the presidency of Danton, had issued a declaration of loyalty to the Constitution. What that meant was unclear, except that it would seem to rule out an uprising. Then, on July 31, the *Section de Mauconseil* had announced that it no longer recognised the King and said that it would march on the National Assembly on August 5. The obvious implication was that the people of Mauconseil were still, even now, uncommitted to overthrowing the King and still hoping that the National Assembly would do the work for them.

It was too late. The National Assembly was a broken institution, completely overtaken by events. It would recover very quickly, and it would reassert itself; it would even reassert its control of the Revolution. But at this crucial point of crisis, it was broken.

Pétion, the Mayor of Paris, made three last, desperate attempts to avert the insurrection. On August 3, 1792, with the endorsement of forty-seven of the forty-eight *Sections*, he led a delegation to the National Assembly to call for the overthrow of the King. All historians underline the importance of this move; few underline the equally clear implication that the *Sections* wished the King to be removed by the National Assembly – legally, therefore, by deposition, and not by insurrection.

When the *Section des Quinze-Vingts* joined the *Section de Mauconseil* in its plan to march to the National Assembly on August 5, Pétion persuaded them to delay until August 10, to give the National Assembly more time to dethrone the King. Again, few historians underline the significance of this fact.

Finally, on August 7, Pétion went to Robespierre's home to ask him to calm the people.

We do not know how Robespierre responded; in fact, we do not really know where he stood at this crucial moment in French history. He did not speak at the *Jacobins* on August 3; nor on August 4; nor on August 5. It was quite uncanny how little he said in public on those critical days leading up to the uprising. If we do not know where Robespierre stood at this vital moment, the conclusion is unavoidable: he did not want us to know; he was determined to avoid committing himself in public.[11]

But it is clear from subsequent events that he must have been on the verge of deciding to join the insurrectionary movement, probably at the last moment. Claude Mazauric, a Robespierrist historian of the Revolution, tells us that Robespierre was not directly implicated in the August 10 insurrection: 'Like Marat … he helped to prepare peoples' spirits for the insurrection of August 10, of which he was, however, not the organiser.'[12] François Furet goes further and says that Robespierre played no part in any of the intrigues aimed at breaking the constitutional authority of the National Assembly, not that of June 20 nor even that of August 10, and that he was only carried to power by the coup d'état of the following year, 1793.[13]

The circumstantial evidence suggests otherwise. Robespierre's colleague and fellow-lodger at the Duplay's, Anthoine, was a member of the planning committee for the insurrection; and the *bureau central de correspondance* was effectively run from the *Jacobin* Club, of which Robespierre was one of the leading members, if not *the* leading member. He did not, of course, take part in the violence of the August 10 insurrection; but as soon as it had happened, he was there, very much among the leaders of the insurrectionists and the Parisian *sans-culottes*, and within weeks they had elected him as one of the first of their representatives in the new *Convention*. So even though he did not say or do anything in public, he must have told the insurrectionary leaders in private, just before the event, that he was with them. From then on, Robespierre was the principal leader of the street power of the Paris *sans-culottes*.

Exactly who did what on August 10 and during the next ten days, when and with whom remains a mystery, so typical of the history of the French Revolution at its moments of crisis. But everyone in Paris knew that an insurrection was being planned, because almost everyone in Paris was part of the planning process, and that it was the *sans-culottes* from the *Sections* who would lead the overthrow of the monarchy.

Their first step was to overthrow the Paris *Commune* and establish one of their own. (They could have raised a preparatory insurrection against the National Assembly, which would have had the same effect; but it seems they did not quite dare to do that.) On August 9, between eight and nine at night, all the *Sections* held meetings to choose delegates. At eleven, the great warning bell (*tocsin*) of the *Cordeliers* started to ring; and the delegates, three per *Section*, converged on the *Hôtel de ville*, where they took over a large hall and set up their Insurrectionary *Commune*, simply brushing aside the legally constituted *Commune*, and placed Mayor Pétion under nominal house arrest. He offered no resistance.

The *Commune insurrectionnelle* resided in, and asserted its political authority from, the town hall from August 10 to September 2, 1792. These were days of wild improvisation. According to Soboul et al., 'great confusion reigned over the composition of this assembly, which was very unstable and subject to incessant modifications. The *Sections* withdrew, replaced or substituted delegates just as they pleased.'[14] The first delegates, according to Michelet, were mostly obscure, unknown men and did not include any of the great leaders, like Robespierre or Marat. One historian counted the names of 363 *sans-culottes* who were registered as members at some point or other between August 9 and 17, 1792.[15] According to the historian Alphonse Tulard, the *Commune insurrectionnelle* initially numbered more than 526 delegates, far more than three per *Section* – in fact, almost eleven.[16] They were mainly drawn from the agitators who had been making themselves heard in the public galleries of the *Sections*. Within a few days the *Commune* tried to impose some order on what was obviously a rowdy, ill-disciplined, self-selected crew by restricting the number of members to 144, or three per *Section*; but under pressure from the *Sections*, it quickly doubled that number.

Robespierre did become a member of the *Commune insurrectionnelle*, presumably because the insurrectionary leaders co-opted him; but not until the day after the insurrection, August 11.

Meanwhile, on August 9 the Insurrectionary *Commune*'s Council dismissed the legal *Commune*'s Council, which simply withdrew. But the insurrectionary Council reinstated a number of the legal *Commune*'s town hall administrators and a number of its top employees, all of whom were *Jacobins*. Pétion as the Mayor, Manuel as the Chief Executive (*procureur-syndic*) and Danton as Manuel's second deputy.

Antoine Jean Gailliot, marquis de Mandat, commander of the *Gardes nationales* at the Tuileries Palace, was summoned to the *Hôtel de ville* on August 10. As his name tells us, he was an aristocrat; he was also a loyal military servant of the monarchy. He went trustingly, without an escort. On his arrival, he was surrounded, told that he was stripped of his command and shot dead. The defence force of the Tuileries was now without its commander.

Around midnight, a few *députés* went to the National Assembly; most were *Feuillants*, come to save the King. The *Girondins* did not turn up until seven the next morning, August 10; perhaps they were afraid. Furet says that there were now only some 200 *députés* present in the National Assembly, of a total of 745.

Early that day an officer of the new Insurrectionary *Commune*, probably Danton, entered the National Assembly with two other officers to tell it that the sovereign people, meeting in *Sections*, had named Commissioners, who would exercise all powers, and that they had suspended the General Council (*Conseil général*) of the old *Commune*.[17]

Large crowds of demonstrators were by then flooding towards the Tuileries, some from the *faubourg* Saint-Antoine, others from the Left Bank, supported by *fédérés*, notably from Marseille and Brest. By 9 a.m. the first waves had reached the gates of the palace. Quite soon, the *gardes nationales* inside the Tuileries were fraternising with the demonstrators. But the soldiers of the Swiss Guards, the dutiful defenders of the royal palace, put up a fierce resistance, and shots were fired. The invasion now became extremely violent, and the Swiss were soon overwhelmed. By the end of the day, the invaders were victorious, and many of the Swiss had been brutally massacred. But at ten o'clock in the morning, before any violence had broken out, the King had been persuaded to leave the Tuileries with his family and to take refuge in Le Manège, next door, under the protection (as he thought) of the *Assemblée nationale*. He had sent a message to the Swiss Guards telling them not to resist, but it was too late: the battle was already raging, at the end of which 800 men lay dead, both demonstrators and defenders.

After the storming of the Tuileries, the insurrectional *Commune* sent delegates to the National Assembly to say that it wanted the overthrow of the King and the election of a new Assembly. The National Assembly played for time, but finally it submitted and agreed that the King would be suspended 'until a National *Convention* had spoken'.

The next day Vergniaud told the National Assembly that the royal family would be confined in the Luxembourg Palace. Manuel, the *Commune*'s reinstated Chief Executive, simply overturned that decision and declared that only the *Commune* had the right to decide the fate of the King: he and his family would be sent to the Temple, part of the original monastery of the Templars.

Vergniaud accepted the decision and implied that the King would be held in the palace of the Temple. No, Manuel insisted: it must be in the Temple's prison. Again, the National Assembly submitted to the power of the Insurrectionary *Commune*; on August 12, 1792, the King and his family were handed over to the *Commune*, which incarcerated them in the prison of the Temple.

The *sans-culottes* were now in charge. This would not last; but it was a clear sign that the world was changing. And the central fact in this changing world was that the French Revolutionaries had crossed the fatal frontier into illegality.

For more than three years the Revolution had been managed peacefully, and above all legally, by the bourgeois Revolutionaries in the National Assembly. Now the Paris *sans-culottes* had thrust them violently aside. From this point on, the central theme of the Revolution was an uncompromising power struggle between these two groups.[18]

13

THE COMMUNE INSURRECTIONNELLE

WITH THE VIOLENT STORMING of the Tuileries by the *sans-culottes*, the political authority of the National Assembly appeared to have collapsed, and the *Commune insurrectionnelle* immediately started to make demands that were unprecedented, far-reaching and brutal. It sent a delegation to the National Assembly to claim virtually all sovereign powers, overriding those of the elected National Assembly, and to assert for itself a new kind of legality, derived from the insurrectionary will of the people. The delegation was led by Sulpice Huguenin, a lawyer from Nancy who had been working in Paris as an official in one of the customs posts and had been elected President of the new *Commune*.

'The people, who send us to you', he stated,

> have charged us to declare to you that they invest you once more with their confidence, but they have charged us at the same time to declare to you that they can recognize as judges of the extraordinary measures to which necessity and resistance to oppression have driven them only the French people, your sovereign and ours, meeting in its primary assemblies.'[1]

The meaning of this portentous and laborious speech was that the *Commune* did not accept the political legitimacy of the National Assembly and was therefore demanding the election, by the French people, of a new kind of assembly.

It was to be called a *Convention*, in homage to the Constitutional Convention held five years earlier in the newly created United States. But the elections to this assembly would be different from all their predecessors in two crucial respects. First, they would be by universal manhood suffrage, without the previous distinctions between the rich and the poor, the active citizens and the 'passive'. Second, they would not be held by secret ballot; instead, voting would be in public, according to a roll call and out loud (*à haute voix*).[2] The purpose of this innovation was, of course, to expose voters to the maximum political pressure and intimidation from those standing round; and it was soon used again, for the same purpose, in the operation of the new Revolutionary Tribunal.

The National Assembly quickly agreed to elections and to the new electoral conditions. It also agreed to the provisional suspension of the King, but it refused demands for his absolute overthrow. The concept of a legality derived from the popular will of the people was a striking innovation; yet it was immediately clear that the insurrectionary leaders of the *Commune* did not themselves really believe in it. Why else would they demand the election of a new National Assembly, unless they felt that true legitimacy, and therefore legality, must derive from such a properly and nationally elected body?

This first phase of the intimidation of the parliamentary bourgeoisie by the *sans-culottes* did not last very long: from the overthrow of the monarchy on August 10 to the opening of the *Convention* on September 21 was a period of just six weeks, and when the *Convention* started work, it quickly asserted the legitimacy of its authority as the new national assembly. But these six weeks were crammed full of dramatic events: the invasion of France and the seige and capture of two key French fortresses by a Prussian army; the eruption of violent reactions in Paris, including the massacre in a number of prisons of more than one thousand inmates by mobs of bloodthirsty *sans-culottes*; then the lifting of the clouds with a spectacular French victory at the landmark battle of

Valmy, followed by the withdrawal of the Prussians not just from the captured fortresses but from France altogether.

On August 11, 1792, one day after the overthrow of the monarchy, Robespierre became a member of the Insurrectionary *Commune*. This delay must have been of his own choosing, perhaps to see how the situation panned out, for within days he was acting as one of the most forceful and demanding public representatives of the *Commune,* and he quickly became the virtual leader of the *sans-culottes*. He never, of course, imitated the *sans-culottes* in appearance or demeanour: they may have worn traditional workingmen's clothes – tunic, loose trousers, loose hair and a cap – but he was always got up to the nines (*soigné, coiffé, poudré*), as Michelet tells us, with powdered hair and in court dress, including silk stockings and *culottes*.[3]

In the days immediately following the overthrow of the King, Robespierre led three intimidating delegations to the bar of the now-discredited National Assembly, in the name either of the *Commune* or of one of its *Sections*. On August 15 he came to demand the punishment, what he called *la juste vengeance du peuple*, of those who had defended the Tuileries on August 10. What he meant by this became clear almost immediately: the *sans-culottes* wanted a special Tribunal set up to try these men. Already, four days earlier, on August 11, Antoine Santerre, the newly appointed commander of the *Garde nationale*, had told the National Assembly that he could not answer for the consequences if it did not immediately court-martial the Swiss defenders of the Tuileries. The National Assembly stalled for two days; then, just a week after the overthrow of the King, it agreed to set up a *Tribunal extraordinaire* to try, and if convicted, execute, counter-revolutionaries – that is, those who had defended the Tuileries. The remit of this Tribunal did not include the trial of the King; for that, the insurrectionists evidently felt that they needed the legitimacy of a National Assembly.

The judges and jury members of this Extraordinary Tribunal were elected by the various Paris *Sections*, sitting separately, during the night of August 17–18, after which the *Commune* vetted them for political correctness. Robespierre was elected the President of the court, but he declined to serve, on the grounds that many of the accused would be his personal enemies. When the time came to choose a jury, those selected would present themselves to the court individually and say, 'I am so-and-so, and I live at such-and-such address; have you anything against me?' The juries were required to announce their verdicts out loud, one by one.

The new court started sitting immediately and secured its first execution five days later. The victim was Arnaud de La Porte, a former Minister of the King's Household and a regular distributor of the King's secret funds; he was guillotined on August 23, 1792. But the pace of condemnations was not enough to satisfy the demands of the crowd. In the first two weeks of its existence the Tribunal condemned only three victims to death and acquitted another three; and over the next ten weeks, fifty-nine people were brought before it but only twenty-two condemned to death.

The guillotine had been devised in the early days of the Revolution as a method of capital punishment that would be equitable, reliable and, as far as possible, painless. Under the *ancien régime*, nobles were entitled to be beheaded, with a sword or an axe; commoners were liable to many forms of execution, many of them barbaric: hanging, burning, dismembering and breaking on the wheel. Now, under the Revolution, the method of capital punishment would be the same for all, regardless of rank.[4] Dr Joseph Ignace Guillotin, one of the new *députés*, recommended the machine, invented by a certain T. Schmitt, a German maker of harps, and further developed by Antoine Louis, the secretary of the French Academy of Surgery. It was used for the first time on April 25, 1792, at the Place de Grève, to execute a thief named Pelletier.

The Extraordinary Tribunal had been set up by the National Assembly; but now power had shifted to the new *Commune insurrectionnelle*. It was, on balance, as Furet comments, a representative assembly of *sans-culottes*. It contained a number of potentially violent urban roughnecks, but of the (variably) 288 members, about a hundred were shopkeepers or artisans, and it included forty-five professionals, twenty civil servants, twenty-three lawyers and five priests. It was mainly led from the top by bourgeois Revolutionaries, who stood for election to the future *Convention* and became the backbone of the *Montagnard* faction there.

Some of its members, like Robespierre and Danton, already had reputations as leading Revolutionaries. But surprisingly, in view of his populist notoriety, the Insurrectionary *Commune* did not include Jean-Paul Marat, the embittered and sickly former doctor who had become, with his newspaper *L'ami du peuple*, the Revolution's most incendiary and most widely read pamphleteer. It is not clear why he was not elected to the *Commune insurrectionnelle* on August 9–10. It could have been because he had failed to cultivate the right people, and that could have been because he was often physically unwell; but Michelet claims that it was because Robespierre had kept him out, since he disliked and despised him: 'The political man [Robespierre], a man of rigid attitude, careful, well dressed, powdered, was disgusted by the filth of the other.'[5] In fact, each despised the other. Marat was a flamboyant puritan, and he made a point, as a friend of the common people, of being ostentatiously unkempt, unwashed and dishevelled. He was described, memorably, by René Levasseur, one of the *Jacobin* members of the Assembly, thus: 'This demonaic fanatic inspired in us a sort of repugnance and stupor. When they showed him to me for the first time ... I considered him with that anxious curiousity which one feels in contemplating certain hideous insects. His clothes in disorder, his livid face, his haggard eyes had something repellant and frightful which saddened the soul'.[6]

One of the noisiest members of the *Commune* was Jacques Roux, a former priest who became one of the most radical campaigners on the left; and he was matched by Jacques René Hébert, a journalist from the Bonne Nouvelle *Section* who was notorious for his newspaper *Le Père Duchesne,* vibrant with scabrous journalism and replete with uncouth and unprintable words, which he delighted in printing.

More typical of the new intake was Pierre Gaspard Chaumette. He was a sometime cabin boy and medical apprentice who had acquired a certain celebrity as an ultra-revolutionary speaker in the populist *Cordeliers* Club and had established his Revolutionary credentials as an enthusiastic participant in the preparations for the demonstrations of June 20 and August 10, 1792.[7] Later that year he was elected *procureur*, or Chief Executive, of the *Commune*, after Manuel was elected to the *Convention*; and Hébert was made his deputy.

Another leading participant in the insurrection was Jean Nicolas Pache, from the *Section* of the Luxembourg district. He had early acquired a solid reputation as a civil servant, first in the Navy Ministry, then in the royal household and most recently in the Ministry of the Interior. After the insurrection he was promoted to the Ministry of War, first as the Secretary-General and then later, unexpectedly, when the job suddenly became vacant, as the Minister of War. At the Ministry he appointed as his successor as Secretary-General François Xavier Audouin, a former priest who was also a founding member of the Insurrectionary *Commune*. In January 1793, Audouin married Pache's daughter, and the witnesses at the wedding were Santerre and Hébert.

The sudden shift of power from the bourgeois Revolutionaries in the National Assembly to the *sans-culottes* in the *Commune* meant that the *sans-culottes* could use their new power to their advantage. A key point about the insurrectionary regime is that, while the Revolution destroyed many jobs, the war, after a while, although it was going badly, being badly managed and badly led, created many new ones, which the *sans-culottes* were able to hand out to their friends. The Revolution had caused great economic hardship through inflation and food shortages; and the war, to begin with, only added to these difficulties, partly by dragging men away from their jobs, their homes and above all their fields, but also by commandeering economic resources needed in civilian life. But once the French started to get a grip on the military threat facing them, the management of the war began to create considerable civilian employment: directly, in the War Ministry, which was vastly expanded, and indirectly, but crucially, in the arms and supply industries.

Michelet claims that the War Ministry created 10,000 jobs in a rush in 1792 and that in the following year the whole of the *Jacobin* Club was employed in its administration, amounting to another 10,000 jobs, for themselves and for their dependents.[8] Considering that the population of Paris was 600,000, men, women and children, this would have meant that the War Ministry was not just massively expanded, and totally dominated by the *Jacobins* and their *sans-culotte* allies, but also a dominant provider of jobs for the *sans-culottes*. The war, the insurrection and the War Ministry combined as a threefold machine for the mobilisation, radicalisation and advancement of the Revolution of the Parisian *sans-culottes*.

The most pressing problem for the new *Commune* was to reinforce the structures of its own credibility as an arm of government. The insurrectionists had unleashed the crowd power of the people of Paris; now they had to control it. They thought they could do so by trying to appease the anger of the deprived lower classes, by taking the first steps towards a police state. They set up a *Comité de surveillance*, which they attached to the Paris police department and charged with public security, and they called on the Paris *Sections* to establish their own, under the auspices of the *Commune*. The initial purpose of these *comités* was to keep an eye on, or investigate, all suspects and enemies of the Revolution. Ever since November 1791, nine months earlier, refractory priests had been labelled 'suspects of revolt against the law'; in the mass excitement of the events of August 10, 1792, the category of suspects and enemies of the Revolution was expanded almost uncontrollably: to aristocrats, to relatives of *émigrés* and then to anybody who could be accused of being a suspect. The *Commune* gave the *comités de surveillance* authority to make *visites domiciliaires* – that is, to force their way into people's homes without a warrant – and to disarm and imprison suspects. Many *communes* throughout France were inspired to follow the example of the Paris *Commune*, and it is estimated that as many as 20,000 *comités de surveillance* were set up in the days and weeks that followed. This mass delegation of police powers to anybody and everybody inevitably created the ideal institutional conditions for crowd hysteria and panic at moments of political crisis.

One reason for the *Commune*'s establishment of what was, in effect, a secret police committee was to gain credibility as a patriotic force defending the Revolution against its enemies at home and abroad. The war was at a critical moment: the forces of the Duke of Brunswick – who reportedly told his staff that it would be a walkover, *une promenade militaire* – crossed the frontier on August 19, nine days after the overthrow of the monarchy; on August 23 the fortress of Longwy fell to the invaders; and on August 30 the fortress of Verdun was under siege. The *Commune* ordered the imprisonment of refractory priests, the arrest of royalist journalists, the closing of their journals and the transfer of their presses to patriotic printers; and it put out a list of people to be arrested who were thought to be anti-civic, chaplains or *Feuillants*. Over a few short days, some 3,000 suspects were imprisoned in Paris.

Étienne Panis, the President of the *Comité de surveillance*, discreetly co-opted Marat as one of its first unofficial members, even though he was not an elected member of the *Commune*. Robespierre must have acquiesced in his appointment, which implies that Marat's republican credentials outweighed the repugnance which Robespierre felt for him.

The *Commune* endorsed the permanence of the *Sections*, which (as we have seen) meant that the *sans-culottes* could hold meetings and debates whenever they liked without asking permission; at the same time, however, it attempted to exert greater control over them, by subjecting their staffs and even the elected members of their *Assemblées* to a political purge (*un scrutin épuratoire*). The *Commune* also decided to reduce the Paris *garde nationale* to forty-eight battalions, one for each *Section*.

The *Assemblée nationale* tried to resist the claims of the *Commune* by strengthening the role of the *département* of Paris (which was hierarchically superior and included the surrounding region as well as the city itself). But Robespierre led a deputation to the National Assembly to protest, and on August 13 he obtained a decree forbidding the *département* from interfering in matters of security and police, which were now solely within the competence of the *Commune*; the *département*'s authority was confined to tax collection and public finances.

The National Assembly again tried to assert itself, by appointing a new government, which it called the *Comité exécutif provisoire* and to which it appointed a number of former Ministers, mostly linked to the *Girondins*, whom the King had dismissed on June 13: Jean-Marie Roland to the Interior, Étienne Clavière to Finance and Joseph Servan to War. Most provocatively, it plucked Danton out of the administration of the *Commune*, where he had been and was now again the second deputy to Manuel, the Chief Executive, and put him in charge of the Ministry of Justice. In the votes to ratify these new Ministers, who were outside (i.e., not members of) the National Assembly, it was the man whom Mathiez calls the 'equivocal' Danton,[9] from the parallel, populist, *Cordelier* world of the *Sections* and the *Commune*, who was the big winner, for he was confirmed by 222 votes out of 285.

At this crucial moment, everybody in France realised that they had a national crisis of authority on their hands. There was no head of state and no head of government; and the splintered political authority between the National Assembly and the insurrectional *Commune* gave rise to extreme anxiety as to who would be in charge of the war, and specifically who could control the armies, whose generals had already shown a treacherous lack of discipline.

The fact was that Revolutionary France did not have an effective system of national government. Two years earlier the Revolutionaries had instituted a far-reaching reform of French local administration, which was superbly and locally democratic and looked after the affairs of the *communes* and the *départements*; this reform has survived in largely recognisable form ever since. But they had not created a system of national government by which the central political authorities could assert effective control over the whole territory.

Under the *ancien régime*, France was widely decentralised and diversified, with many and varied local jurisdictions. The King had exerted national control partly through the army and partly through the *gouverneurs* of the provinces, who were also military commanders, but

mainly through the *intendants*, who were effectively his personal representatives in the various parts of France and who exercised his authority
over all civil administration, including public works and taxation. It
was essentially through the delegated powers of these *intendants* that
the King was able to rule the whole nation. (When Napoléon Bonaparte
came to power, he imitated the *ancien régime* by instituting a national
system of *préfets*, obviously inspired by the *intendants*, with one in each
département, which still operates today.) Now that the King had been
removed, it was as if he was shown to have been the keystone of the
political system's arch, and the rest of the structure seemed to be betray-
ing all its inherent weaknesses and to be collapsing in on itself.

To deal with this crisis, the main political institutions in Paris, the
National Assembly, the Council of Ministers and the *Commune*, all
created parallel and competing systems of quasi-national government,
which relied on a new tool, the special representative, with far-reaching delegated authority. On the first day of the new regime, August 10,
1792, the National Assembly appointed twelve of its members to go to
the armies, three to each army, to reassert the authority of the national
government, 'with the power to suspend, provisionally, both the generals and all other officers and public officials, civil or military, and even
to arrest them, if circumstances require, as well as to provide for their
provisional replacement.'[10]

The National Assembly also sent eighteen representatives to the
départements of France, while the Council of Ministers sent twelve,
chosen by Danton, to sixteen *départements*. Not to be outdone, the
Commune sent out, in early September, twenty-four special representatives to assert its authority in the *départements* around Paris, as well as in
those *départements* in the west.

This delegation of power to individual representatives was a major
and extraordinary innovation; and after the elections in the autumn, the
Convention extended it to the newly explicit concept of *envoyés en mission*,
or *représentants en mission*. In that phase, these representatives were
given exceptional, virtually unlimited authority, including the power of
summary execution. In principle, those whom the National Assembly
sent out were answerable, on their return, to the National Assembly, and
some of them were called to account; but at the time, their actions were in
practice virtually uncontrollable. Those sent out by the *Commune* were
answerable only to the *Commune*. In short, this was another innovation
taking the Revolution further outside the domain of legality.

The problem confronting the Revolutionaries was not merely that they lacked an effective system of national government; they increasingly found that they lacked national consent. The insurrectionists' uprising was essentially a Paris- and populist-based event, and it set the capital on a collision course with much of the rest of France: this was partly about the overthrow of the King but more about the claim of the Paris *sans-culottes* to sovereign authority over the rest of the country. Much of France had been dismayed by the overthrow of the King; most people were traditionally monarchist and conservative, and many were shocked at the violence of the Paris mob. Similarly, most of France was rather profoundly Catholic and was alienated by the Revolutionaries' running conflict with the clergy and the schism in the Church between the refractory and the loyal priests. Above all, most of France would not accept the visceral hostility of the most radical elements of the Paris *Commune* to all public manifestations of the Catholic Church and then, ineluctably, to Christianity itself.

But the most inflammatory issue was the claim of the Paris *Commune* to national sovereignty. During the first phase of the Revolution, people had no doubt come to terms with the new authority of the National Assembly, since it was nationally elected. But they did not take to the idea that they would be ruled from Paris by the *sans-culottes*. The rise of the Insurrectionary *Commune* was the inevitable prelude not just to a running struggle between the *sans-culottes* and the bourgeois Revolutionaries but also to episodes of civil war between Paris and a number of the provinces of France.

In Paris, meanwhile, the most urgent need was to calm the agitation among the *sans-culottes*. In the immediate aftermath of the storming of the Tuileries, the authorities in the Insurrectionary *Commune* had sought to appease them by demanding a new Tribunal; and within a week the National Assembly had complied. But it was not enough: among the *sans-culottes* a sense of public crisis was still brewing. On the very evening of August 11, the police department of the *Hôtel de ville* had sent Santerre a note warning that 'we have been informed, Sir, that a plan is being formed to invade the prisons of Paris in order to remove all the prisoners and to exact summary justice on them.'[11]

Immediately after the overthrow of the monarchy, about a thousand suspects had been arrested, among them aristocrats, priests and Swiss soldiers who had been defending the Tuileries. The priests were mostly concentrated at the Couvent des Carmes and at the Séminaire Saint-Firmin, which had been turned into prisons; and the number of inmates in the main Paris prisons (Abbaye, Conciergerie, Châtelet) was now around 2,000, two-thirds of whom were common criminals. There was a widespread rumour of a royalist plot to release the prisoners and arm them against the Revolutionary patriots. Journalists of every stripe – Hébert, Antoine Joseph Gorsas and Jean-Louis Carra, among others – were demanding summary justice against the enemies of the Revolution. Louis-Stanislas Fréron, the publisher of the newspaper *L'orateur du peuple*, explicitly called for a massacre: 'The prisons are bursting with criminals; it is urgent to rid society of them right away.'[12]

Some have been tempted to assume that Marat, the political rabble-rouser, was behind these declarations, for already in December 1790 he had made wild but unspecific calls for the massacre of '10,000, or even 100,000'. Now he deliberately added fuel to the flames: 'The last resort', he wrote, 'which is the surest and the wisest course, is to go armed to the Abbaye, to drag out the traitors, especially the Swiss officers and their accomplices, and to put them to the sword.'[13]

The *sans-culottes* were being stirred into a frenzy by this rabid journalistic campaign, egged on by various members of the *Commune*. The *Section* of the Poissonnière district adopted the following resolution: 'This *Section*, considering the pressing dangers to the country and the infernal manoeuvres of the priests, decrees that all the priests and suspect persons held in the prisons of Paris, Orléans and elsewhere shall be put to death.'[14] And its resolution was endorsed by three other *Sections*: those of Luxembourg, Louvre and Fontaine-Montmorency.

Under pressure from the *Commune insurrectionalle*, the National Assembly endorsed the growing campaign against the priests with a sweeping set of repressive decrees. On August 18 it suppressed certain religious congregations and forbade the wearing of religious vestments in public. It ordered the deportation, to the colony of French Guiana, of all priests who had refused to take the oath of allegiance to the Civil Constitution of the Clergy; and it imposed a new loyalty oath on priests, even those who had sworn the previous one: 'I swear to be faithful to the nation, to maintain with all my power the liberty, the equality, the safety of people and property, and to die, if necessary, for the execution of the law.'[15]

The National Assembly went on to forbid religious processions, con-fiscated gold and silver religious vessels used in the Mass, as well as church bells, and removed from the Church the right to register births, marriages and deaths, an official function which was transferred to the civil authorities. This campaign was directed not just, as before, against refractory priests, so-called enemies of the Revolution, but against all aspects of the Christian Church, what the French once called *la prêtraille*, regardless of its relationship to the Revolution.

Opinion in France about the Church was divided. The bourgeoisie and the intellectuals, the inheritors of the Enlightenment, were prob-ably in many cases at least somewhat sceptical about Christian doctrine, and many were no doubt critical of the Catholic Church and its abusive privileges under the *ancien régime*. But most of the vast mass of people in the countryside, especially among the peasants, were no doubt in some sense believers, or at the very least profoundly accustomed to traditional religious rituals and the role of the priests in their local communities.

Just one of the anti-Church measures – the removal of the bells – illustrates the depth of the chasm of incomprehension between the Paris *sans-culottes* and the mass of the population in the rest of the country. Rural France had lived to the rhythm of bells since time immemorial. Church bells announced the morning Mass and signalled the midday break with the Angelus, celebrated marriages and tolled for deaths, rang out for victories and warned of dangers. The first Revolutionaries had conceded the rights of religion, in their Declaration of the Rights of Man; but the *sans-culottes* of the Paris *Commune* – who always rec-ognised the sound of the great bell of the *Cordeliers*, the *tocsin*, as the signal of alarm – now seemed determined that the Revolution would be wholly secular and thought they could simply sweep away the sound of bells from the lives of the peasants. This inevitably put them on a colli-sion course with much of the rest of the French population.

Meanwhile, the military situation was increasingly threatening. The Prussians had captured the fortress of Longwy and were besieging the fortress of Verdun, both believed to be crucial defensive strongholds between Paris and the north-east frontier; but the Ministry of War, the National Assembly and the *Commune* all seemed to be dithering impo-tently. On September 2, 1792, Danton, then the Minister of Justice, came to the National Assembly and delivered a rousing speech of military inspiration which was to become famous in the annals of the Revolution: 'The bell which is about to ring is not a signal of alarm; it is the order to charge against our country's enemies. To defeat them, Gentlemen, we need boldness, more boldness, still more boldness, and France will be saved!'[16] He was loudly applauded. Michelet seems to believe that Danton had been hoping that the National Assembly would give him some form of supreme power. It did not do so.

Danton made no reference to prison massacres, which he must have known were in the air; and then he went home and was not seen again for several hours.

That afternoon, the National Assembly and the *Conseil général* (the assembly) of the *Commune* closed their sessions, but that of the *Comité de surveillance* remained open. In attendance were Panis, its President, Marat and a few other colleagues.

The offices of the *Comité de surveillance* were in the *Mairie*, on the Île de la Cité, in the middle of the Seine.[17] This was not just the official residence of the mayor; it was also part of the same block of buildings as the *Palais de justice* (Courts of Justice) and the prison of the Conciergerie, and it had a set of prison cells, controlled by the *Comité de surveillance*. It also happens that the location of what was then the *Mairie* is now occupied by the current and long-standing headquarters of the Paris police, the *Direction régionale de la police judiciaire de Paris*, whose address is familiar to readers of Georges Simenon and other French detective story writers: 36, quai des Orfèvres.

On September 2, 1792, the cells of the *Mairie* held a number of prisoners. That afternoon, the *Comité de surveillance* ordered or permitted (it is not clear which) twenty-four of them to be transferred to the prison of the Abbaye, not far away on the Left Bank.[18] They were all taken away in six hackney cabs. A number of these prisoners were priests, dressed in ecclesiastical garb. The convoy was surrounded on its slow journey by screaming crowds, and just as they were reaching their destination, the prisoners were attacked and killed with pikes and other makeshift weapons in the cabs or as they were getting out.

Another mixed band of *sans-culottes*, formed of shopkeepers and artisans, *fédérés* and *gardes nationaux*, now made off for the Couvent des Carmes, in the rue de Vaugirard, where it was known that many more refractory priests were imprisoned. They invaded with rifles, pikes, sabres and sticks and massacred 188 priests and three bishops. At the

Abbaye the mob forced its way into the prison, where it found some fifty to sixty of the former defenders of the Tuileries, Swiss Guards or *Gardes du Roi*, and murdered them.

At this point the *Comité de surveillance* attempted to assert its authority: 'Comrades', it declared, 'you are ordered to judge all the prisoners of the Abbaye without distinction. Signed, Panis and Sergent.' (Étienne Panis was the President, and Antoine François Sergent a member, of the *Comité*.) One of the people in the mob at the Abbaye, Stanislas Maillard, thus stepped forward and spontaneously took on the role of unofficial judge. Nicknamed *Tape Dur*, or 'Hit Hard', he was a former soldier and bailiff's clerk who had played a leading role at all the Revolution's major street demonstrations to date. He had been at the forefront of the taking of the Bastille in 1789; he had led the procession of market women from Paris to Versailles later that year; and he had helped to storm the Tuileries on August 10. Now he conducted a series of impromptu 'trials' in the courtyard of the prison, with other *sans-culottes* or bystanders acting as jurors; those declared guilty were cut down on the spot.

The killing went on for several more days and in several more prisons: at the Conciergerie on September 3 and at the Châtelet, Saint-Firmin, and La Salpêtrière on September 4. The massacres did not finally stop until September 7. While they were in progress, Danton, as the Minister of Justice, was asked anxiously about them, to which he is said to have replied, impatiently and indifferently: 'I don't give a damn about the prisoners; let them do the best they can!'[19]

It is not clear whether the *Comité de surveillance* had deliberately sent the prisoners at the *Mairie* to their deaths. But even if it had not, it defiantly endorsed and commended the slaughter, in the name of the *Commune*, in a statement, countersigned by Danton, which it issued the next day, September 3, and circulated to all the *départements*:

> The *Commune* of Paris hastens to inform its brothers in the *départements* that some of the ferocious conspirators held in its prisons have been put to death by the people; acts of justice which seemed to them indispensable to restrain by terror the legions of traitors hidden within their walls, at the moment when they were preparing to march against the enemy; and no doubt, the entire nation, after the long succession of betrayals which have brought it to the edge of the abyss, will hasten to adopt this measure so necessary for public safety.[20]

All told, there were probably between 1,090 and 1,395 victims, or around 40 to 45 per cent of the Paris prison population. And the purpose of these killings? No one knows. The most common theory is that the people had been so aroused and so excited by the violence of the battle for the Tuileries on August 10 that only more killing could appease them. Another is the pretext, adopted by the *Commune* in its circular, that the people were in a state of panic at the imminence of the Prussian invasion and gripped by fantastic fears that as soon as patriotic men left for the front, the enemies of the Revolution at home – refractory priests, *émigrés* and others – would surge out of prison and murder their wives and children. What is certain is that a number of Revolutionaries, not least Marat, had deliberately whipped up a public campaign of bloodlust and frenzied hatred of priests and that the prison massacres left a stain on the Revolution which could not be wiped out.

In any case, the news from the front was alarming enough. By the end of August the Prussians had captured the French fortress of Longwy and were besieging the fortress of Verdun. It may easily have looked, to the people of Paris, that the Prussian invasion was irresistible; and that fear may have seemed even more real when the Prussians captured Verdun, on September 2, though this news did not reach Paris until after the massacres had started. The fall of Longwy and Verdun seemed to open the way for the conquest of Paris, and several Ministers started talking of moving the government to Blois in central France. Danton put a stop to such talk and instead demanded, and got, from the National Assembly an order for the mobilisation of 30,000 men.

The immediate military threat from the Prussians was short-lived. On September 20, less than three weeks after the fall of Verdun, the French defeated Brunswick at the battle of Valmy, and the Prussians retreated. But the disruptive impact of the war was made much worse by a sharp downturn in the economy, linked to inflation and food shortages. Although the authorities in Paris were able to mitigate the inflation in food prices with public buying efforts, these did not solve the problem of food shortages. The recurring instability in the food supply system led to increasingly insistent demands from the most radical firebrands of the *sans-culottes* for rigid food price fixing and a complete break with the economic liberalism which the bourgeois Revolutionaries championed.

After the elections in the autumn, the *Convention* was briefly able to use its democratic legitimacy to rein in the *Commune*. But Robespierre would soon remobilise the *Commune* and the *sans-culottes*, together with their supporters in the War Ministry, as allies in his life-and-death struggles against his political rivals among the bourgeois Revolutionaries, the so-called *Girondins*.

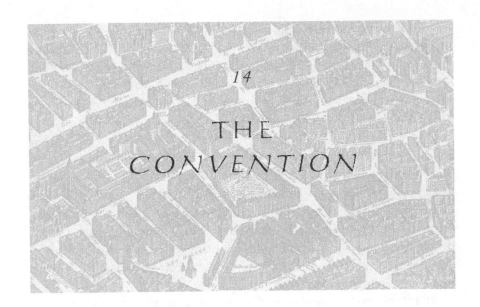

14

THE CONVENTION

THE INSURRECTIONARY *COMMUNE*'S GRIP on power was extreme but short-lived. The monarchy was overthrown on August 10, 1792. Elections for a new National Assembly were agreed and announced the next day. The first round of voting, to elect the Electors proper, took place on August 26 and the days following. The second round of voting, to elect the *députés*, took place during the first three weeks of September. The outgoing *Assemblée nationale législative* held its last session on September 20; the new *Assemblée nationale constituante* held its first session the next day.

In other words, as noted in chapter 13, the time from the spasm of the overthrow of the monarchy to the formal inauguration of a new, properly elected constitutional authority was a bare six weeks.

The new *Assemblée nationale* was an *Assemblée constituante*, that is, a Constitution-writing assembly. When they had stormed the Tuileries, the insurrectionary *sans-culottes* had done what the National Assembly had long balked at doing: irrevocably removed the King from the political equation. Even then, the National Assembly still refused to depose him; the most it would agree to, formally, was his suspension. Either way, the King was no longer part of the political system, so the

Revolutionaries needed a new Constitution. That was the essential purpose of the new National Assembly, as it demonstrated by declaring, at its first sitting, 'The monarchy is abolished in France.'[1]

The elections to the new National Assembly, called a *Convention* in homage to the Constitutional meetings of the newly independent Americans, were by universal male suffrage, without discriminations based on property or income. Women were still completely disenfranchised. A voter had to be over twenty-one years old, self-supporting by employment and not a domestic servant; a candidate for election had to meet these requirements and be over twenty-five. As a result, the basic electorate almost doubled from that of the *Assemblée nationale législative* election in 1791, to some 7 million people. Because voting was still not direct, there was again a large political gap between the ordinary voter and his representative in the *Convention*; but differences of wealth or income no longer defined that gap.

But if the voting rules for the *Convention* were more democratic than those for its predecessors, the new National Assembly turned out to be no more representative than the *Constituante* or the *Législative*, because the electorate showed very little interest in voting. The policies of the Revolutionaries were having results which alienated more and more voters, whether it was the disorder of the economy, the quarrel with the Catholic Church or the strains of the war. Many ordinary people were shocked by the violent way in which the King had been overthrown, and now there was the further trauma of the September prison massacres, which sent waves of horror right across France and beyond. Although the number of votes went up, it was because the franchise had been massively enlarged; the relative turnout remained almost as low as before, at just under 12 per cent, compared with just over 10 per cent in 1791.

But if the Revolution brought much hardship and suffering, and consequently much ambivalence towards voting, certain people did well out of it, especially those who had some money and could afford to buy Church property (newly designated as *biens nationaux*) being put up for sale. Inevitably, those who were already rich – the nobility and the monied members of the bourgeoisie – were best placed to pick up the plum bargains. Land was still, by common consent, the most desirable asset. Everybody wanted some; but the peasants[2] wanted it most.

Many of the peasants were already owners or leaseholders of their land, and they now had the means and the desire to acquire more. After the abolition of Church tithes and the quasi-feudal dues previously paid to the seigneurs, they had a bit more money in their pockets; and the Revolutionaries were selling off Church land cheap and on soft terms. Their wives were not necessarily thinking the same way, however, and questions of the Church and Church property divided many peasant families down the middle. Many of these wives were devoted to the Church and to the traditional, non-conforming (refractory) priests whom they knew, whereas their farmer husbands were impatient to buy Church land.

Michelet has a brilliant passage on this determination: 'Buy or die. The peasant has sworn, whatever happens, he will buy. Public events make no difference; war is declared, he buys; the throne falls, he buys; the enemy arrives, no matter, he buys without question. The news of 60,000 Prussians makes him shrug his shoulders; what can so few do to expropriate a whole people?'[3]

At this point, in the autumn of 1792, the Revolutionaries had already sold off Church property worth £3,000m. As Michelet comments, 'The Revolution had passed into the earth; it had taken root.'[4] In fact, the sale of Church property by the Revolutionaries probably constituted the greatest wave of redistribution of land in French history.

Despite this chance to acquire land on excellent terms, most people did not like the results of the Revolution so far. Public alienation was widespread. On August 10 the organisers of the *Commune insurrectionnelle* had whipped up tens of thousands to invade the Tuileries and overthrow the King; but within weeks the mass of ordinary people had turned away in indifference. The Paris *Sections* were allowed to hold meetings whenever they wanted, but almost nobody came. In one *Section*, with a potential electorate of more than 3,000 citizens, meetings were held where only twenty-five turned up; others might have sixty people present, but only ten taking an active part: the rest would listen and lift their hands to vote, but mechanically and obediently.[5]

There was no political campaigning, in the modern sense at least, in the elections for the *Convention*, and no parties putting together party manifestos. On the other hand, all kinds of tactics were used to ensure the election of like-minded people. In Paris, for example, the *Commune insurrectionnelle* insisted that voting in these elections be not by secret ballot but in public and by public declaration, out loud.[6] Perhaps as a result, the turnout in the capital was particularly low: in June 1791 the election for the Mayor of Paris had been widely shunned, mustering only 10,000 voters; this time, to elect twenty-four members of the *Convention*, only 525 voters turned up. They were carefully shepherded away from the legally assigned polling place, the Paris Archevêché (the former Archbishop's Palace), and herded to a more reliable place for voting: the *Club des Jacobins*.[7]

This method of intimidation proved so successful that when the votes were counted, all but one of the twenty-four Deputies elected by the Paris voters were followers of Robespierre, of Danton or of another leading member of the *Commune*. Robespierre was the first elected, on September 5, followed by Danton on September 6, then Jean-Marie Collot d'Herbois, Louis Pierre Manuel, Jacques Nicolas Billaud-Varenne and Camille Desmoulins; Marat was elected on September 9.

Some *départements* outside Paris followed the example of the *Commune* and imposed the same intimidatory voting procedure. Elsewhere, the absence of party discipline or party campaigning meant that voters were more or less free to reflect local conditions, with the result that the majority of the *Convention* (from outside Paris) was rather moderate and bourgeois and of varying political origins.

This time, Robespierre's 1789 initiative banning the re-election of sitting Deputies was not in force. As a result, of the 749 new Deputies, many of whom were lawyers, advocates or solicitors (*notaires*), about a third were already politicians of national standing, having been members either of the *Assemblée nationale constituante* or of the *Assemblée nationale législative*; many of the rest had held public service jobs in their *départements*. There were a few nobles, including the duc d'Orléans, who had asked the *Commune* to give him a new name after the abolition of all aristocratic titles in 1792, and had been granted the democratic-sounding 'Philippe Égalité'; and about fifty 'constitutional' clergy, who had taken the oath of the *Constitution civile du clergé* of July 1790, including seventeen bishops. One of the priests was Emmanuel Sieyès, the once-celebrated author of *Qu'est-ce que le tiers état?*, who was still trying for a political role in the front rank; and there were a few reforming Protestant pastors, such as Jean-Paul Rabaut Saint-Étienne from Nîmes and Marc-David Lasource from the Tarn, both leading members of the *Girondins*.

Despite the introduction of universal male suffrage, the 749 Deputies included only two men from the working class: Jean-Baptiste

Armonville, a thirty-six-year-old wool carder from Reims, and Noël Pointe, a thirty-seven-year-old blacksmith from Saint-Étienne. This was probably because the elections took a long time, especially in those places which followed the example of the Paris *Commune* and required public voting out loud; it seems likely that most of the potential candidates from the working class were either not interested or intimidated, or felt they could not afford to take the days off work.

The *Convention* also had a few army officers, including Lazare Carnot and Paul François, vicomte de Barras, both of whom played leading parts in the next few years of the Revolution. Carnot was a forty-year-old engineer officer from Burgundy (Côte d'Or) who had been a member of the *Assemblée nationale législative* with a prominent role in the Military Committee. He would play an even bigger role as a special representative of the *Convention* to the armies, then as a member of the new and increasingly powerful *Comité de salut public*, in which capacity he would be largely responsible for turning the French war effort from defeat to victory.

Barras had an even more brilliant career. He had been a young army officer but had resigned at the age of twenty-eight when he reached the rank of captain and had then spent his way through his fortune in Paris before retiring to his home in the South of France. He returned to Paris when his *département* (Var) elected him as a Deputy in the *Convention*. He was soon sent as a special representative to the provinces to speed up the mass mobilisation of troops, in which process he gained a significant reputation as a military commissioner. At the siege of Toulon in 1793 he would establish close links with a young artillery officer from Corsica, the twenty-four-year-old Napoléon Bonaparte, who had been a cadet at the French military school at Brienne in the Aube from the age of ten and had graduated at sixteen as a gunnery lieutenant from the *École militaire* in Paris. In 1789, Bonaparte had signed up for the Revolution, though it was at least as much for opportunistic as for Revolutionary reasons; at that time he was much more interested in the independence of his native Corsica than in the French Revolution. Barras would play a significant role as an enabler of the rise of Bonaparte and in the subsequent fall of Robespierre.

There were also two foreigners in the *Convention*, Anacharsis Cloots from Germany and Thomas Paine from England. In late August, during its dying days, the *Assemblé nationale législative* had been persuaded to give French nationality to a number of deserving foreign supporters of the Revolution and to invite them to sit in the *Convention*. They were Joseph Priestley, the English chemist; Jeremy Bentham, the English philosopher of utilitarianism; William Wilberforce, the English anti-slavery campaigner; Friedrich Schiller, the German poet; the American politicians George Washington and Alexander Hamilton; and half a dozen more, from Germany, Switzerland, Italy, Poland and Holland. Almost all declined the invitation. Priestley was elected but declined his seat; but Cloots and Paine were elected and did sit.

Jean-Baptiste Cloots was an eccentric, ultrarich German baron from Kleve who had rushed to Paris in the early days of the Revolution as a 'groupie'. He called himself 'The Orator of the Human Race', and like other Revolutionaries he gave himself a classical Greek first name: Anacharsis, after the Scythian philosopher who travelled to Athens in the sixth century BC and was much admired as a frank, outspoken 'barbarian'. Cloots endeared himself to the *Girondin* war party by advocating revolutionary war throughout Europe. When the *Girondins* fell, he ended badly under the Terror, guillotined, absurdly, as a foreign agent.

Paine was internationally celebrated as a Revolutionary pamphleteer, and he served in the *Convention* as a Deputy for the *département* of Pas-de-Calais. He fell foul of the *Jacobins*, partly because he joined the doomed *Girondin* faction and partly because he angered the *Montagnards* by publishing, in 1793, *Le siècle de la raison* (*The Age of Reason*),[8] which argued for belief in a deistic God at a time when the *sans-culottes* were pursuing a ferocious policy of atheism. He was imprisoned on Christmas Eve of 1793 in the Luxembourg prison, at the personal instigation of Robespierre,[9] as a sympathiser of the *Girondins*. He stayed there for ten months and escaped the guillotine only by accident: the sign marking him out for execution was placed on the outside of his cell door, which was left open, and at the crucial moment, when he should have been taken away, the sign was invisible.[10] After the reinstatement of the *Girondins* he was eventually released from prison, but he spent the next eight years unhappily longing to return to America; when he finally got there, he died alone, forgotten and in poverty.

It is generally said that the *Convention* had around 160 *Girondin* Deputies, about 200 further-left-wing *Montagnards*, and some 389 moderates. In reality, there were no sharp lines to define the balance of political forces in the *Convention*, any more than there had been in the previous National Assembly. When historians refer to political groups such as these and assign numbers to each, they are more using conventional metaphor than stating hard numerical fact.

There were no parties in the modern sense. But as in the previous National Assembly, all the *députés* chose their own seats, and all the radicals sat to the left of the President. The *Girondins* and other traditionally left-wing members of the *Jacobin* Club, however, were now outflanked on their left by the contingent of even more radical *députés*, notably the followers of Robespierre and other representatives from Paris, who sat not just to the far left but also as high up as possible; as a result, they were known as the *Montagne* (Mountain) or *les Montagnards*.

The numbers of Deputies in each of these factions do not really describe the balance of power. In the *Législative* there may have been only 136 *députés* who were members of the *Jacobin* Club, but the *Girondins* had nevertheless managed to dominate the debates. This was partly because they were led by the flamboyant and celebrated journalist-adventurer Jacques Brissot; partly because Brissot gathered round him some of the most eloquent speakers in the new assembly, such as Pierre Vergniaud, Armand Gensonné and Marguerite Élie Guadet; and partly because Brissot's friends and followers were closely linked with several members of the then government, like Jean-Marie Roland and Étienne Clavière.

In the *Convention* the *Girondins* were outnumbered by the influx of so-called *Montagnards*, who were dominated by a phalanx of Deputies elected from Paris, led by Robespierre and backed by the *Commune*. Outside Paris, the *Montagnards*, as the standard-bearers of the new radical wave, did significantly better in those *départements*, in the north and the east, most immediately threatened by invasion, which were also much more responsive to government appeals for new recruits, unlike the particularly resistant *départements* in the west.

But even if on paper the *Girondins* had been overtaken by the *Montagnards*, by the time the *Convention* met, on September 21, 1792, the French had won their first sensational military victory, at Valmy, the nightmares of Longwy and Verdun were being forgotten, and the *Girondin* war policy seemed triumphant. The *Girondins* secured the election of Jérôme Pétion as the President of the *Convention* and got hold of almost all of the top jobs in its secretariat. The prospect of power and influence so intoxicated Brissot that he claimed to control two-thirds of the assembly's seats. This would not last; Robespierre with the *Montagnards* proved an unstoppable force, and at crucial moments he was able to call on the muscle of the *sans-culottes*.

At one time, as recently as the flight of the King in the summer of 1791, Robespierre and Brissot had been on fairly close terms. But Robespierre never forgave Brissot for defeating him on the war policy, and political enmity replaced their personal friendship. When Brissot had tried to stand for a seat in the *Convention* from Paris, Robespierre made sure that he was kept out, and he had to settle for one from the *département* of Eure-et-Loir. Robespierre had even accused Brissot of treason: 'No one dares name the traitors', he told the *Commune* on September 1, 1792. 'Well, I, for the safety of the people, I shall name them; I denounce Brissot, the destroyer of liberty, and the *Girondin* faction; I denounce them for having sold France to Brunswick and for having received in advance the reward for their cowardice!'[11] The next day a gang of heavies employed by the Paris *Comité de surveillance* and sent by the *Commune* invaded Brissot's house in search of incriminating evidence. They found nothing.

Six weeks later, Robespierre took his revenge one step further by getting Brissot expelled from the *Club des Jacobins*. The Robespierrists were determined to purge this club not just of Brissot and his *Girondin* allies but of all members of the *Convention* who were in any degree tempted to question their authority. They decreed that anyone who belonged to another club would be excluded, and they drove out about 200 members.

The first result was that when the *Girondins* wanted to discuss their political plans, they had to do so mainly in private meetings, at little dinners or, more socially, in the salons and *soirées* of the leading political ladies, like Madame Roland. The second result was that the Robespierrists now had a total grip on the proceedings of the *Jacobin* Club and on the opinions which could be expressed there. From this point on, it held no more political debates; instead, the *Jacobins* would simply rubber-stamp, usually with servile applause, policy positions already adopted by Robespierre and his close allies.

Nevertheless, Robespierre kept up his persistent smear campaign against Brissot, blaming him for, among other things, the September massacres, for which he advanced no evidence. The indirect consequence of this vendetta and the direct consequence of the purge of the *Jacobin* Club was that whereas identifiable groupings in the *Assemblée nationale législative* had been evanescent or even largely amorphous, in the new *Convention* there quickly appeared an open and systematic confrontation between the *Girondins* and the *Montagnards*.

The social origins of these two groups were almost indistinguishable: the members of both were bourgeois and educated, both included significant numbers of lawyers, and both believed in property and economic liberalism. Some historians (especially those on the left) claim that *Girondins* were marginally, or even significantly, more prosperous than *Montagnards*; and there seems no doubt that more of the leading *Girondins* came from commercial and trading backgrounds, notably in or near the important seaports in the west and south-west, from Nantes to Bordeaux (the Gironde).

Albert Mathiez, the noted Marxist historian and fervent Robespierrist, maintains that the *Montagnards* and *Girondins* were deeply divided on issues of political principle, to the point of class difference. He argues that the *Girondins* were instinctively prosperous conservatives who considered property an absolute right and were repelled by the coarseness of common people; and that the *Montagnards*, by contrast, represented the little people, who suffered from the consequences of the war.[12]

This is going too far. What mainly distinguished the *Montagnards* from the *Girondins*, in the autumn of 1792, was a matter less of social origin or of instinctive political sympathy than of naked political strategy. If a class war developed, it was because the *Montagnards* chose to start one. At this crucial moment of the Revolution, they shifted to a winning strategy; the *Girondins* did not. And that strategy was to enlist as allies the street power of the Paris *Commune* and the *sans-culottes*. In the *États généraux* and the *Assemblée nationale constituante*, the vast majority of the *députés* had come, necessarily, from the provinces. But when, in 1792, the Revolutionaries were facing elections to the *Convention*, those on the far left drew conclusions based on the experience of the *Législative* and most recently the insurrection of the Paris *Commune* and the overthrow of the King; and they made new plans.

In the *Législative*, the *Girondins* had regularly defeated those to their left, crucially in the argument over whether to go to war. The radicals could not expect to secure a majority in the new assembly, so they decided to throw in their lot with the *Commune insurrectionnelle* and to seek the help of the muscle power of the Paris *sans-culottes*. This meant securing seats in the *Convention* as Deputies for Paris. Robespierre was a lawyer from Arras, whose voters handsomely elected him to a seat in the *Convention*; but he had already shifted his allegiance to Paris, and he opted for a seat from there, becoming the first of the Paris *députés*.

The *Montagnard* strategy and its electoral success were plain to see, and the question of whether Paris and its Deputies were too powerful, and aiming to become even more powerful, provoked some of the earliest and angriest debates in the *Convention*. 'I do not want', said Lasource, 'to see Paris, led by a bunch of schemers, become in the French Empire what Rome was in the Roman Empire. Paris must be reduced to a 1/83 share of influence in France, just like all the other *départements*.'[13] François Trophime Rebecqui, another *Girondin*, from Marseille, broke in: 'The party which they have denounced to you, whose aim is to establish a dictatorship, is the party of Robespierre; that is what common knowledge has taught us in Marseille.'[14]

The logical follow-up to these fears was that the *Girondins* demanded physical protection against the ambitions of Robespierre and his Paris allies. François Nicolas Léonard Buzot, a *Girondin* from Eure, called for the creation of a departmental guard to protect the *Convention*. 'The *Convention*', he said, 'must be surrounded by so imposing a force that not only should we have nothing to fear but the *départements* from which we come would be reassured that we have nothing to fear.' He proposed a force of four infantrymen and two cavalrymen from each department, or a total of 4,500 men. But his plan was opposed by the *Commune*, and eventually blocked.[15]

It is striking that Robespierre was already being accused of aiming at dictatorship in the earliest days of the *Convention*. Jean-Baptiste Louvet, a *Girondin* and the author of mildly licentious novels, regularly charged him with such ambitions, as on October 25, 1792. 'I accuse you', he said in the *Convention*, 'of marching towards supreme power.'

Instead of denying this accusation, Robespierre chose to brazen it out by responding that many things which were illegal were made necessary by the Revolution. 'All these things were illegal, just as illegal as the Revolution, as the fall of the King and of the Bastille, as illegal as freedom itself. You cannot expect a revolution without a revolution.'[16]

For a while, however, the two sides made real efforts to work together for a semblance of harmony and to build a new regime in the wake of the overthrow of the King: there was no question now but that France must be a Republic. On September 22, in one of its first acts, the *Convention* decreed that all legislative acts would henceforth be dated from 'Year 1' (*l'an I*) of the Revolution; and on September 25, that 'the French Republic is one and indivisible' (*La République française est une et indivisible*).

But this brief moment of harmony did not last; and it was the confrontation between Paris and the provinces which would crucially separate the *Montagnards* from the *Girondins* and ensure the *Montagnards'* victory. The more they emphasised the rights and the power of Paris as the heart of the Revolution, the more the *Girondins*, the involuntary provincials, found themselves defending the independence of the cities and provinces of the rest of France.

The *Montagnards* eventually defeated the *Girondins* by mobilising the Paris *sans-culottes* against them; but the only way they could dominate the increasingly radical demands emanating from the Paris *sans-culottes* was to take France ruthlessly down the path towards centralised, Revolutionary dictatorship and the Terror.

15

THE WAR IN 1792: FROM VALMY TO JEMAPPES

IN THE CRUCIAL WEEKS of the autumn of 1792, the French turned the tide of war from defeat to victory and rolled back the invading armies of Prussia and Austria, which had threatened to overwhelm Paris and reverse the Revolution.

On September 20 at the battle of Valmy, the French Revolutionaries won their first, fantastically important victory, and for the time being the threat of invasion was over. As a military engagement, Valmy was not much. It consisted essentially of a prolonged exchange of cannon fire, and at the end of the day there were not many casualties on either side, probably some 300 Prussian and 200 French. No one quite knows why or how this turned out to be a French victory: Brunswick could have pushed on from there towards Paris. Instead he withdrew, conceding the battlefield to the French.

One explanation is that he was shocked to find that the French army was much better than he had expected. The Prussians had come to assume that in any confrontation between their disciplined, seasoned troops and the disorderly rabble of the Revolution, they could count on an easy victory; but when they saw the disorderly rabble stand firm, with cries of *Vive la Nation!*, they were disoriented and unnerved. Another factor was that Brunswick's army was suffering from widespread sickness and ill supplied with food from home; a third was the long-running distrust between Prussia and Austria, now flaring up over the imminent partition of Poland, which Brunswick's advisers saw as more important than pursuing the war against France.

There were rumours that France's General Dumouriez had somehow brought about the Prussian withdrawal by bribery; but the Revolution was constantly awash with rumours of bribery and betrayal. In this case it seems far-fetched, but it is a fact that Dumouriez was increasingly ambivalent about the Revolution and made no effort to harass the Prussians in their withdrawal; on the contrary, he made their retreat as easy as possible and had frequent and friendly diplomatic exchanges with them.

The German poet Johann Wolfgang von Goethe was present at the battle, on the Prussian side, and he told his companions, or so he claimed, many years later: 'From this place and from this day starts a new era in the history of the world, and you can all say that you were there.' In fact, he wrote this account, in *Kampagne in Frankreich*, between 1819 and 1822, at least twenty-seven years after Valmy. At the time, as he admitted in a letter to a friend, he did not really know what was going on.[1]

Although Goethe took a while to realize it, in France and the rest of Europe the psychological and the political effects of the victory at Valmy were overwhelming. Dumouriez was able to push forward to further victories, and the French were emboldened to launch a whole wave of offensives all round the perimeter of the French frontier, not just to the north, in the direction of Dumouriez' original offensive, but also to the east, the south-east and the south. In the south, General Jacques Bernard d'Anselme seized Nice, for 400 years a province of Savoy, and imposed a *Jacobin* administration. In the south-east, General Montesquiou seized Chambéry, the capital of Savoy, while French troops invaded the bishopric of Basel and proclaimed an 'independent' Republic. In Germany to the east, General Adam Philippe, comte de Custine (whose popularity, according to Tulard, came from the size of his great moustaches[2]), took Speyer on September 25, Worms on October 5 and Mainz on October 21 and then threatened Frankfurt.

After Valmy and the retreat of the Prussians, the Austrians, who had been besieging Lille, withdrew to what is now Belgium. The way was open for Dumouriez to revert to his original plan, a northward offensive, with the aim of liberating the Belgians from their Austrian colonisers. The *Conseil exécutif* (the French Revolutionary government) endorsed his plan and made him the commander-in-chief of an expedition 'to free the oppressed people, and to pursue to their own territory the mortal enemies of the Republic [the Austrians].' Dumouriez took his army, now enlarged to 40,000 men, and led it north. On November 6 he came upon the Austrians just short of Mons and defeated them in a resounding victory at Jemappes. The Austrians withdrew, Mons fell, and French troops entered Brussels a week later; Belgium was conquered in less than a month, and Dumouriez was poised to conquer Holland.

At this point the French Revolution took a decisive turn. Dumouriez had planned and now proposed that Belgium, once liberated, would be free and independent. He imposed strict discipline on his troops; and he issued a rousing declaration to the Belgian population which went far beyond anything authorised by the *Convention*:

> Brave Belgian nation, we are entering your territory to help you plant the tree of liberty, without interfering in any way with the Constitution which you will adopt! Provided that you adopt the sovereignty of the people and that you give up living under any despots, we will be your brothers, your friends, your supporters. We will respect your properties and your laws.[3]

Dumouriez was apparently acting with the support of the French government. On October 30, Pierre Lebrun, the French Foreign Minister, had written to the French ambassador in London that 'France has renounced all conquests, and this declaration should reassure the English government on the entry of Dumouriez into Belgium.' He restated this position after the victory at Jemappes: 'We do not want to interfere by giving to any people this or that form of government. The inhabitants of Belgium will choose that which suits them best.'[4]

But this liberal policy, offered by Dumouriez and endorsed by his immediate superior, was immediately cancelled by the *Convention*. When, on December 4, a Belgian delegation came to Paris to ask for recognition of Belgian independence, the *Convention* turned it down; and three days later the French army brutally repressed a public demonstration in Brussels calling for Belgian independence.

Dumouriez blamed the reversal of his policy on speculators and on a conspiracy of the new regime at the War Ministry: 'My victory over the

Austrians was in vain, this superb expedition will end badly, because all my plans are being frustrated, because they are tyrannising the country, because greedy speculators, supported by the offices of the War Ministry, are hoarding all the supplies, under the pretext of feeding the army, but in fact leave it short of everything.'[5]

Dumouriez' complaint concerned reforms introduced by Jean Nicolas Pache, the new Minister of War. Pache was a conscientious and hard-working civil servant and a long-standing follower of Jean-Marie Roland, the *Girondin* Minister of the Interior. On his surprise appointment as the Minister of War, however, he had abruptly switched loyalty to the *Montagnards* and stuffed his Ministry with masses of *sans-culottes*, most of whom were inexperienced and unqualified and all of whom were committed to the *Montagnard* cause. He also introduced a system of centralised control of all army supplies, which upset many of the generals, who had been used to making their own deals for supplies; some had taken advantage of the situation by helping themselves to a slice off the top. On November 22, Pache ordered the arrest of all the previous suppliers to the army of Belgium. Reforms like these were undoubtedly necessary, but if the new system put a stop to the financial corruptions of the old regime, it also opened the door to those of the new.

Pache did not last long at the Ministry: the *Girondins* and the generals conducted a campaign of vilification, and on February 4, 1793, he was forced to resign. In Paris, however, his mass employment of *sans-culottes* had made him extremely popular among working people, and one week later, on February 11, the *Sections* elected him, by a crushing majority, to be the Mayor.

Dumouriez had wanted to pursue a generous war strategy, one that would liberate Belgium and leave it as an independent, self-governing country. But French foreign policy instead took a brutal turn. Danton and his friend and emissary Jean-François Delacroix pressed for the outright conquest and incorporation of Belgium; and it was their policy which was adopted.

On November 19, less than two weeks after Jemappes, the *Convention* issued a decree offering 'friendship' to all peoples:

> The national *Convention* declares, in the name of the French nation, that it will give friendship and help to all the peoples who want to recover their freedom, and charges the government to give the generals the necessary orders to provide help for these peoples and to

defend the citizens who may have been maltreated, or who could be, in the cause of freedom.[6]

The real reasons for this new, ostensibly altruistic policy were now spelled out by Pierre Lebrun: by annexing Belgium, France would increase its population by 3 million, its army by 40,000 soldiers and its revenue by £400m. The commissioners of the *Convention* added that 'the salvation of the Republic is in Belgium; it is only by the union of this rich country to our territory that we can restore our finances and continue the war.'[7]

This was the voice of realism, and the man whose role was really decisive in convincing the government and the *Convention* to adopt this policy and to speak like this was Pierre Joseph Cambon. Cambon was a worldly politician with a strong *méridional* accent, a former trader and the son of a cloth merchant from Montpellier, and he had become the dominant figure on economic policy in the *Convention*, more influential even than Clavière, the Economics Minister.

'Thirty years old or so', says Michelet,

with a high colour, bitter, pure and savage, such was the man. His knowing but frank air was that of a rough provincial trader, of strong peasant stock … You could tell that the arms suppliers of the Republic must have been ill at ease when he looked hard at them, and have felt before such a man that their heads were at risk.[8]

'Cambon was powerfully placed in the *Convention*', says Michelet in another passage,

representing the enormous question of the *assignat* and of the sale [of Church property], the eminently Revolutionary question. The force of this question carried Cambon along; he wanted war, and he wanted it everywhere, to spread the *assignat* everywhere … His fixed idea at this moment, which was that of Danton, was to revolutionise Belgium completely, to sell all the Church or feudal properties there to pay for the war, and to flatten the country.[9]

As the dominant figure in the *Convention*'s Finance Committee, Cambon knew by heart the lamentable state of the French public finances, the desperate shortage of reliable tax revenue and the large and growing cost of the war; and he drew what he saw as the only logical conclusion: France must annex Belgium, in order to seize Belgium's wealth. It would do this first by nationalising and then by selling Belgian Church property and by securing, with the familiar sleight of hand, Belgian gold and silver coinage in exchange for *assignats*.

'We must', he said, 'declare ourselves a Revolutionary power in the countries we enter; it is pointless to pretend; the despots know what we want. No semi-revolution! Any people which does not want what we propose here will be our enemy and will deserve to be treated as such!'[10]

On December 15, 1792, the *Convention* issued a decree setting out the new principles of Revolutionary war. It claimed that the French were not 'guided by the turbulent ambition of conquest', did not want to dominate or enslave any people and respected the independence of nations. But the new policy was unmistakable: it aimed at conquest, if only, for a while, under another name.

In all foreign countries they entered, the French generals were ordered to suppress, immediately, all tithes and feudal dues and every type of servitude. They would destroy all the existing political authorities and hold elections for provisional administrations, from which all enemies of the Republic would be excluded. All former taxes would be suppressed, but property belonging to the tax authorities, to any princes or to any Church body would be sequestrated, to underpin the *assignat*. From this point on, the need to acquire foreign assets – money and all kinds of wealth, but especially money – was a determining factor in France's war policy. To pay its bills, it needed money, which it could acquire only by seizing it from foreigners: France now had to fight an ever-expanding war of conquest, in order to pay for an ever-expanding war of conquest.

In Belgium, it quickly became apparent that the population did not welcome what had turned out to be an invasion and would not willingly vote for its 'liberation' by the French; in Paris there was a delay of more than a month while the Revolutionaries debated what to do next. Cambon finally prevailed, and though the *Convention* did not dare risk a countrywide referendum in Belgium, its annexation was pushed through, under the threat of French bayonets, by a succession of local votes, town by town, in conditions of violent protest.

Over the next few months France had many ups and downs in the war, and for a period, at least while England stayed out of it, there was some debate among the Revolutionaries over the relative benefits of liberation and conquest. When French victories made it inevitable that England would join the First Coalition, the war became a life-or-death struggle and these debates were largely silenced.

At that point, France had only one choice: victory or defeat; and in that equation, victory involved conquest and theft on a truly heroic scale, probably unprecedented since the Roman Empire, more than a thousand years earlier. France used the war to enrich itself massively, as did some of the generals, all of the arms suppliers, all of the speculators and middlemen and, spectacularly, some of the politicians, especially some of those who were sent out with virtually unlimited powers of life or death, the *envoyés en mission*. When the Revolution started, the Revolutionaries had declared that property was sacred; but when the war got going in earnest, it transformed their values out of all recognition.

Mathiez blames all this on the *Girondins* and their relentless war policy: France could have had peace, on the basis of the status quo, if they had been willing to forgo the trial of the King and allow him to leave France in safety. The problem with this argument is that while the *Girondins* may have been mainly responsible for the war policy, it was also they who would, in many cases, have preferred to save the King's life, whereas the *Montagnards* and the Robespierrists were absolutely determined that he should die. Mathiez ruefully concludes: 'So we can say that the struggles between the parties contributed as much as the development of the external situation to preventing the peace and intensifying the war.'[11]

This struggle between the parties was essentially chosen by Robespierre and the *Montagnards*; and from now on, it would get worse and worse, until the *Montagnards* finally brought down the *Girondins* and had them killed.

16

THE TRIAL OF THE KING

AFTER THE SENSATIONAL MILITARY BREAKTHROUGH at Valmy in September 1792, reinforced by the even more compelling victory at Jemappes in November, the Revolutionaries reluctantly turned back to the thorny question of what to do about the King. He had been overthrown; he was in prison; so should he not be put on trial?

It was obvious that if there were to be a trial, it might lead to his execution. For this reason, some of the Deputies, particularly some of the *Girondins*, put numerous procedural difficulties in the way. Jerôme Pétion, the President of the *Convention*, pointed out that the King had been granted and might legally claim inviolability under the Constitution of 1791; Louis Pierre Manuel, the *Convention*'s Chief Executive, proposed that the first step be to ask the people to vote on the abolition of royalty; others wondered if the King's trial would require a special tribunal.

On November 7 these objections were swept aside by the Legislation Committee of the *Convention*, which dismissed the idea of the King's inviolability and determined that he could be judged only by the representatives of the people – that is, the *Convention* itself. All that remained was to decide the charges against him. The *Convention* started debating this and related questions in detail on November 13, 1792. But its procedural deliberations were interrupted almost immediately, when Louis Saint-Just climbed to the rostrum to deliver his maiden speech.

He was by far the youngest member of the *Convention*, and at twenty-five only just old enough to qualify for membership. He was startlingly good-looking and already arrogantly opinionated. Later he became one of Robespierre's right-hand men and was nicknamed the Archangel of the Terror.

It was a short speech, short and brutal; probably one of the most shocking speeches ever heard in this or any other assembly.

There was only one thing to be done, he told the *Convention*: kill the King.

'The only purpose of the committee', he said,

> has been to persuade you that the King should be judged as a simple citizen; and I say that the King must be judged as an enemy ... I do not see a middle ground: this man must reign or die ...
>
> No one can reign innocently: the truth is too obvious. Every King is a rebel and a usurper ...
>
> Citizens, the tribunal which must judge Louis is not a judicial tribunal: it is a council, it is the people, it is you; and the laws which we must follow are those of the rights of the people ...
>
> Louis is a foreigner among us; he was not a citizen before his crime; he could not vote, he could not bear arms; he is even less a citizen since his crime ...
>
> Everything I have said tends, therefore, to prove to you that Louis XVI must be judged as a foreign enemy. I add that his condemnation to death need not be submitted to the people for their approval ...
>
> Louis has waged war against the people: he is defeated. He is a barbarian; he is a foreign prisoner of war.[1]

Michelet vividly describes the contrast between the youthful good looks of the speaker and the brutality of his words:

> His way of speaking was not vulgar; it denoted in the young man a real fanaticism. His words, slow and measured, fell with a singular weight, and left a shudder, like the heavy blade of the guillotine. In shocking contrast, they came, these coldly pitiless words, from a mouth which seemed feminine. Were it not for his fixed and hard

1. May 5, 1789: The opening of the *États Généraux*, which brought together representatives from all over France, of the Clergy, the Noblesse, and the *Tiers État*, in the presence of King Louis XVI, in the *Grande Salle* of the *Hôtel des Menus Plaisirs* at Versailles.

2. Honoré Gabriel Riqueti, comte de Mirabeau, one of the leading orators of the Revolution, at a meeting of young Revolutionaries in Versailles in 1789. Mirabeau was a nobleman who, in his reckless youth, had been involved in so many scandalous adventures that his father had him imprisoned on several occasions. The nobility refused to accept him as one of their representatives to the *États Généraux*; instead he got himself adopted as a delegate of the commoners, the *Tiers État*.

3. The famous Tennis Court Oath (*le Serment du Jeu de Paume*). In June, 1789, the delegates to the *États Généraux* were due to assemble for a make-or-break meeting with the King, the so-called *séance royale*. On June 20, 1789, the commoners found themselves shut out (as they thought) from the main meeting chamber; and they took refuge in the largest large space nearby, the *Jeu de Paume*, or Tennis Court; and there they swore an oath never to allow themselves to be separated until they had drawn up a constitution.

LE SOUHAIT ACCOMPLI

V'la comme j'avions toujours désiré que ça fût.

4. A cartoon symbolising the final reconciliation of the three Estates.

5. The young revolutionary Camille Desmoulins haranguing the crowds in the colonnaded garden of the Palais Royal, residence of the duc d'Orléans.

6. The storming of the Bastille, *14 juillet, 1789.*

7. On October 5, 1789, a vast crowd of hungry Parisian market women marched to Versailles demanding food; they were followed by a large contingent of the newly-formed *Gardes Nationales*, under their commander the marquis de La Fayette.

8. On arrival in Versailles, the crowd celebrated, and many got drunk; there were violent clashes with the King's bodyguards, and some of them were killed, and their heads impaled on pikes.

Il faut en Goûter.

9. A political allegory, depicting the long-running debate over the role of the King's veto. It shows that the King's veto outweighed the influence of the clergy, the nobility and the commoners combined.

10. *(top left)* Pierre Victurnien Vergniaud, (1753–93), a French lawyer and Revolutionary from Bordeaux. An eloquent orator in the National Assembly, Vergniaud was a supporter of Jacques Pierre Brissot, and one of the leading speakers in the Girondin faction.

11. *(top right)* Jacques Pierre Brissot, (1754–93), was the effective leader of the Girondist movement during the French Revolution.

12. *(bottom left)* Paul François Jean Nicolas, vicomte de Barras, (1755–1829), was a former career army officer who came late to the Revolution. He was elected to the *Convention* in 1792, and he played a significant role in 1793 in the career promotion of Bonaparte; in 1794, he was one of the key figures in the overthrow of Robespierre.

13. *(top left)* Charles Maurice de Talleyrand was a French bishop, politician and diplomat. In 1780, he became Agent-General of the Clergy and represented the Catholic Church to the French Crown. Those he served often distrusted Talleyrand but found him extremely useful. The name 'Talleyrand' has become a byword for crafty, cynical diplomacy.

14. *(top right)* Emmanuel Joseph Sieyès achieved instant fame as one of the leading political theorisers of the Revolution, with his January 1789 pamphlet 'What is the Third Estate?' It became the de facto manifesto of the Revolution, and helped to transform the Estates-General into the National Assembly in June 1789.

15. *(bottom left)* Charles-François du Périer Dumouriez was a French general during the French Revolutionary Wars and was largely responsible for the stunning French victory at Valmy.

16. Louis XVI with his wife, Marie-Antoinette.

17. In the eighteenth century the Palace of Versailles was the symbol, in its majestic isolation, of the absolute power of the *ancien régime*. Originally a country hunting lodge, built by Louis XIII in 1623, it was enlarged and expanded by his successor, Louis XIV, in the 1660s and 70s; the buildings were designed by the architect Louis Le Vau, the vast gardens landscaped by André le Nôtre. The picture shows the *cour royale* in the centre of the palace, and the parade ground, or *place d'armes*, in the foreground.

18. This etching shows the Tuileries Palace, built in the sixteenth and seventeenth centuries, long the traditional residence of French monarchs, until Louis XIV moved his seat to Versailles. On October 6, 1789, the people of Paris forced the King to return to Paris, and re-installed him in the Tuileries. Three years later, on August 10, 1792, a large crowd of angry Parisian *sans-culottes* and volunteers from the provinces invaded the palace, and overthrew the monarchy.

19. This painting conveys the violence of the overthrow of the Tuileries on August 10, 1792.

20. 'The Triumph of Marat', painting by Louis-Léopold Boilly. Jean-Paul Marat, (1743–93), one of the populist fire-brands of the Revolution, was denounced by his political enemies and sent for trial before the feared *Tribunal Révolutionnaire*. He appeared there on April 24, 1793, but all the judges and jurors were his political friends, and he was automatically acquitted and carried back in triumph to his seat as a member of the Convention.

21. The emotional night session of August 4–5, 1789, at which the *Assemblée Nationale* decided in principle to abolish all the privileges of the feudal system.

22. Georges Danton (1759–94), a lawyer in Paris, was one of the most eloquent speakers on the left-wing of the Revolution, and a leading figure in the populist *Club des Cordeliers*.

23. Maximilien Robespierre (1758–94), a lawyer from Arras, in northeastern France, was one of the most compelling speakers in the National Assembly: 'He will go far,' said Mirabeau, 'because he believes everything he says'. In 1792 he transferred his political base to Paris where the *sans-culottes* quickly swept him to a position of absolute power. This is a modern reconstruction of his face.

RÉPONSE À BOULAŸ.

MASSACRE DES PRÊTRES.

Dans l'Église des Carmes.

24. September 2, 1792: following the fall of Verdun to the Prussians, a large mob of *sans-culottes* massacred a group of priests at the *Église des Carmes*.

25. On July 27, 1794, after emotional scenes in the National Assembly, where Robespierre had seemed to threaten everyone and anyone, his enemies brought him down: this picture shows his arrest.

26. January 21, 1793: the execution of Louis XVI.

27. The Battle of Valmy. After the declaration of war, in the spring of 1792, the French suffered several setbacks, including the loss of the key strategic fortresses of Longwy and Verdun. But these defeats were dramatically reversed by the surprise French victory at Valmy on September 20, 1792, which marked the retreat of the Prussian forces from France.

28. Marie-Antoinette (1755–93), daughter of the Austrian Emperor Franz I and of the Empress Maria-Theresa. She was married to Louis, the future King of France, when she was just fourteen, and she became Queen of France when Louis acceded to the throne in 1774. She was unpopular in Paris, where she had a reputation for frivolity and extravagance, and for meddling in politics. Nine months after the execution of Louis XVI, she was tried for treason and guillotined. Here she is pictured at the time of her trial.

29. Four months after the overthrow of the Girondins by Robespierre and the *Montagne,* the arrested Girondins were executed. This image shows the guillotining of Jacques Brissot on October 31, 1793, together with twenty-one other Girondin members of the *Assemblée Nationale.*

30. *The Two Only Make One*: Satirical print depicting Louis XVI and Marie-Antoinette as a monstrous conjoined animal. On the left end of the animal, Louis XVI's head is depicted with goat horns. On the right end of the animal, Marie-Antoinette's head is depicted with snakes and peacock feathers protruding from her hair.

31. This shows a *sans-culotte* crowd, led by a female Revolutionary figure (sometimes known as Marianne) wearing a Revolutionary cap; they are singing the Revolutionary song *La Carmagnole*.

blue eyes, his strong eyebrows, Saint-Just could have passed for a woman.'[2]

The discovery on November 20 in an inner wall of the Tuileries of a concealed iron safe (*armoire de fer*) containing some of the King's papers put a stop to any last-ditch attempts to delay the trial. The papers included the King's correspondance with Mirabeau; with Antoine Talon, a secret policeman and one of the leading royalist conspirators among the Revolutionaries, who had fled to America after the overthrow of the monarchy; with Dumouriez; with La Fayette; with Talleyrand; and with others.

It had long been known, or suspected, that Mirabeau (who had been dead for two years) had been in the pay of the court; and it had long been suspected that he had conspired with the King against the Revolution. These letters demonstrated that the latter suspicion was untrue. Mirabeau never said to the King anything different from what he said in public: he believed in a constitutional monarchy, which ought to be linked to the Revolution. As his friend August Marie, comte de La Marck, said of him: 'He only got paid for saying what he believed.'[3] But these letters would inevitably be produced as part of a case against the King.

In terms of the existential accusation which had been levelled against him by Saint-Just, the papers discovered in the 'iron cupboard' were irrelevant: Louis was guilty not because of what he had done but just by being the King. But in psychological and forensic terms, the discovery was devastating: the question now was not whether Mirabeau and others had been conspiring with the court but whether the King had been conspiring with anybody and everybody against the Revolution; and of course he had. There was no way of avoiding a trial; the only question was the verdict.

On December 3, Robespierre came forward to endorse Saint-Just's absolutist thesis of condemnation, but the agitation was so great among those who feared the imminence of a trial of the King that he had the greatest difficulty in getting a hearing amid the tumult and cries of protestation in the *Convention*.

'It is a crime', he said,

for a nation to give itself a King ... Let there be no ambiguity. The Assembly has not decreed that there would be a formal trial; it has only decided that it would itself pronounce the verdict or the sentence on the former King. I maintain that, according to our principles, we must condemn him to death immediately, by virtue of an insurrection.'[4]

The lawyerly slither in Robespierre's words was all too obvious: What were the principles he was alluding to? If the crime was an insurrection, it was not by but against the King. Or was Robespierre implying that the King was guilty of insurrection against the people? No matter; despite the tumult and the protestations, the die was now cast: the King would be put on trial. On December 6 the *Montagnards* secured a decree by the *Commune* that a new committee of twenty-one members would draw up the charge sheet against the King, that the trial would be held in public and that all members of the *Convention*, called by roll, should vote on the outcome, on the verdict as well as the sentence, in public and out loud.

The trial was 'extremely unjust', according to the account in the Robespierrist *Dictionnaire historique de la Révolution française*: 'The evidence was withheld from the King. Any pieces of evidence which could have constituted an avenue of defence were withheld, in a deliberate attempt to show that he was guilty. The witnesses who could have spoken for the defence had been massacred in the prisons on September 2 or 3, 1792, or executed in Versailles'.[5] Nevertheless, the *Montagnards* expected that public opinion, all too present in the public galleries, would be hostile to the King and would tilt the balance towards a guilty verdict and then a death sentence. It turned out that they were right.

On December 10, 1792, Jean-Baptiste Robert Lindet in the name of the Commission of Twenty-One, presented the charge sheet listing all the duplicities of the King, going back to the beginning of the Revolution. The general charge laid was that 'Louis Capet was guilty of conspiracy against the general security of the state'.[6]

The next day, the King was brought before the *Convention* and questioned on the charges. He denied everything; he refused to recognise any of the documents put before him, even his own signature. It did not make a good impression. When he was again brought before the *Convention*, on December 26, his lawyer read a long defence contesting the legality of the trial, denying the responsibility of the King and proclaiming his many virtues and public benefits. The King declared that 'his conscience had nothing to reproach him for'.

While the trial was in progress, vigorous efforts were made by other

European governments to save the King; and according to some sources, later published, Danton was particularly active in negotiating on behalf of the King and egregiously demanding large amounts of money for himself. It made no difference: the negotiations came to nothing.[7]

The stage was now set for the fatal votes, and everything would depend on the *Girondins*. 'Undoubtedly', says Michelet, 'there were many to defend the life of the King, in the presence of the furious fanatics who, from the galleries, shouted, interrupted the speakers, and shook their fists at them, and who, at his entrance, and at his exit, surrounded him with threats.'[8] But at this crucial juncture of the trial, on January 3, 1793, the *Montagnards* brought damaging charges against three *Girondin* leaders, Vergniaud, Gensonné and Guadet, alleging that they had been compromised in treasonable contacts with the court on the eve of the August 10 uprising; and they produced witnesses to say so.

Voting started on January 15, 1793, on three questions: whether the King was guilty; whether the verdict should be subject to popular ratification; and what the sentence should be. There remained the possibility of further votes on the terms of implementing the sentence.

On the first question, the Assembly voted unanimously, 707 to 0: the King was guilty. (The forty-two other members of the *Convention* were either ill or absent for other reasons.)

On the second question, 287 Deputies voted yes and 424 voted no: there would be no appeal to the population.

Inside and outside the *Convention*, popular agitation was intense. On January 14 the Gravilliers *Section*, usually one of the most radical, had voted to form a special jury to try any *députés* who voted for an appeal to the population. Some began to fear a popular uprising against the *Commune*.

At this moment Danton, who had been *en mission* to the army in Belgium, returned to the *Convention* and found Paris in an uproar. 'The army', says Michelet, 'did not want the death [of the King], and France did not want it; an imperceptible minority wanted it; and yet things had gone so far, the question been placed on a point so hazardous, that saving Louis XVI would put the Republic at risk.'[9]

A significant number of *Girondins* did not, on balance, want the death of the King; and some, like Jean-Denis Lanjuinais and Antoine François Hardy urged that a death sentence should require a two-thirds majority. Danton and the *Montagnards* resisted this idea, on the grounds that the Revolutionaries had decided even more important issues, like the declaration of war and the declaration of the Republic, by a simple majority, and the proposal was dropped.

The vote on the King's sentence started the day after the other votes and lasted thirty-six hours, from 10 o'clock in the morning on January 16 until 10 o'clock at night on January 17; it was, according to Tulard, 'probably one of the most dramatic in the history of the *Convention*'. It took so long because every Deputy had to vote out loud, one after the other, following the roll call; each was expected to give reasons for his vote; and many added riders or additional conditions to their votes.

The first to vote was the *Girondin* Jean Mailhe, a lawyer from Toulouse, whose name was the first to be drawn by lot from the list of Deputies. Quite by chance, it was he who had been entrusted with drawing up the charge sheet against the King. He voted for the death penalty, but he added a rider calling for an additional vote on a reprieve or a delay. 'If there is a majority for a death sentence', he said, 'I think it would be worthy of the *Convention* to consider whether it would not be useful to delay the moment of execution.'

The first count gave 366 votes for the death penalty out of 721 votes cast; 361 were needed for a majority. But the results were challenged, and there had to be a second vote. This time there were 387 votes in favour of death, but it was decided to exclude those with a rider like Mailhe's; this produced a total of 361 votes in favour of the death penalty without qualification, exactly the minimum majority required.

The *Girondins* were clearly divided. Some of their leaders, such as Vergniaud, Guadet, Buzot and Pétion, had voted, like Mailhe, for a delay; others, including Ducos, Boyer-Fonfrède, Carra, Lasource, Jean Debry and Maximin Isnard, had voted for death unconditionally.

There remained the question of a reprieve, and the results of this last vote were declared at around one o'clock in the morning on January 20: of 690 votes, 310 were in favour of a reprieve and 380 against.

Later that day, one of the Deputies who had voted for the death sentence, Louis Michel Le Peletier de Saint-Fargeau, a thirty-two-year-old, ultrarich nobleman, was stabbed to death in a restaurant in the court-yard of the Palais Royal by a nineteen-year-old nobleman, Philippe de Pâris, until recently a member of the King's Constitutional Guard.

That afternoon the King was informed of his sentence; he asked for a delay of three days, which was refused. He said goodbye to his wife and family and spent the evening with a refractory priest, Henry

Edgeworth, a Jesuit from Ireland, who accompanied him the next day to the scaffold.

The execution was carried out on January 21, 1793, at the Place de la Révolution (today the Place de la Concorde).[10] Twenty thousand troops crammed the Place and the surrounding area; the scaffold was erected near the columns of what was (until 2015) the Ministry of the Marine, and a large space was cleared around it, to keep the crowd as far away as possible. The King arrived at ten past ten in the morning, in a carriage surrounded by 1,500 soldiers. He climbed the steps. He tried to speak, to proclaim his innocence, but drums rolled to drown out his voice. Four men seized him and tied him down. At the last moment, he let out a terrible cry.

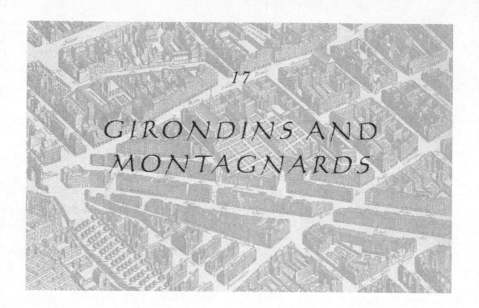

17

GIRONDINS AND MONTAGNARDS

WITH THE DEATH of the King, Robespierre and the *Montagnards* were ready to launch their final assault on their *Girondin* rivals. But first they had to deal with the fact that the execution of the King was leading to an intensification of the war with the rest of Europe, a war for which France was still not really ready.

The war had come and gone the previous year in a rather old-fashioned and episodic manner; with the French victory at Jemappes, it seemed to have reached a temporary pause. Now, in 1793, it moved into a new phase of large-scale conflict, and France expanded its war aims from the 'liberation' of countries which might ask to be liberated, to the 'liberation' of those which had not asked, and then to an explicitly imperial policy of expansion. At the end of January, Danton publicly enunciated a theory, which was becoming fashionable, that France was entitled to its 'natural frontiers'. His speech was characteristically ambiguous, at one point seeming to imply frontiers at the Rhine, the Alps and the Pyrenees; at another, frontiers without limit:

> I say that it is no use trying to make us afraid of giving too great an extension to the Republic. Its limits are set by nature. We shall reach

all four corners of the horizon, towards the Rhine, towards the Ocean, towards the Alps. It is there that the limits of our Republic should end, and no human power can prevent us reaching them.[1]

Pierre Cambon, the *Convention*'s dominant voice on economics, endorsed this theory two weeks later. 'France's ancient and natural limits', he said on February 14, 'are the Rhine, the Alps and the Pyrenees.' During the following month, the *Convention* passed decrees annexing a series of neighbouring states or ministates, starting with the most important, Belgium. For a while, France regularly invoked this doctrine to justify the first phase of its wars of expansion, which helped cement the First Coalition against it.

The execution of the King had alarmed monarchs and their supporters throughout Europe, but it was France's expansionist policy which gave the war its new impetus. The takeover of Belgium threatened maritime access to the Escaut and the Rhine; and it was largely because of this threat to England's trading interests, and therefore to its whole geopolitical strategy, that London at last, reluctantly, abandoned its policy of neutrality, thus massively increasing the strength of the coalition arrayed against France. Towards the end of January, England broke off relations with France; France responded at the end of the month by declaring war in turn. England's rupture with France was echoed across Europe. Spain broke off relations in March, and the *Convention* then declared war against it. Later that month, most of the German princes, followed by almost all of the Italian states, apart from Venice and Genoa, joined Austria and Prussia against France. It was now at war with virtually the whole of Europe.

For this massively expanded war, France needed a much larger army. Those who had signed up in 1791 had been entitled, by their short-term contracts as volunteers, to disband at the end of the season the following year; the army was melting away. At the end of December 1792 it had numbered some 400,000 men; by the beginning of February 1793 it was down to no more than 228,000. The *Convention* accordingly voted on February 24 to raise a force of 300,000 men, the so-called *levée des 300,000*. Unfortunately, the Revolutionaries had not thought through whether this was to be a volunteer force or a modern, wholly conscripted army; and the plan fell between two stools, with disastrous results.

In principle, the levy was compulsory; but its implementation was left, in practice, to each local authority. Each *département* was required to produce a fixed number of men; but if the required number did not come forward voluntarily, each *commune* had to nominate conscripts to fill the gap, by a vote in the local assembly. In political terms, this was the worst possible system, and it was deeply unpopular. The ambiguity of the rules meant that local votes were almost bound to be biased against those who were locally unpopular; and the general sense of injustice was magnified by the perpetuation of the ancient system of *remplacement*, by which a designated recruit could pay someone else to take his place. There were widespread protests at the plan in many *départements*, and the resistance was so great that the whole operation managed to scrape together only 200,000 recruits, and then only after several months of delay and foot dragging.

It was not just that the recruitment plan was not working – it was provoking a national crisis. The recruitment levy met a somewhat more positive response in the north and east, in those *départements* which had felt most endangered by the threat (or the fact) of invasion. But elsewhere several revolts broke out, starting in the Vendée in western France (where it turned into a long-running rebellion against the Revolution) and then in other parts of the west, such as Ille-et-Vilaine and Morbihan, as well as in Haute-Marne and in several *départements* to the south of the Massif Central, from Haute-Loire to Aveyron. This first widespread wave of revolts against the Revolutionary authorities was quickly brought under control; but they were followed, later in the year, by much larger waves of civil war after, and partly in reaction to, the crushing of the *Girondins*.

The recruitment crisis was a challenge to the Revolutionaries' legitimacy, and they gradually reasserted themselves with a rerun of the expedients that they had employed after the overthrow of the King: a strengthening of police repression and the appointment of a large number of special representatives with overarching authority. The *Convention* increased the remit of the local *comités de surveillance* in the *communes*, and then, more decisively, appointed eighty-four of its members to be sent out with unlimited powers to the trouble spots. This Revolutionary institution, *envoyés en mission*, was first proposed by Philippe Fabre d'Églantine, a young lieutenant of Danton's, and its original objective was to check on the defensive arrangements in Belgium. But when the protests against the recruitment levy started, the system was quickly expanded, and on March 9 forty-two pairs of *envoyés en mission* set off as representatives of the *Convention* to investigate all the *départements*.

Envoyés en mission often proved effective in dealing with emergencies, and they were soon regularly employed for all exercises of Revolutionary power outside Paris. Their control extended to military policy on April 9, when the *Convention* sent out more than fifty *envoyés en mission* to all the armies of France. As military commissars they had authority overriding even that of the local generals; some replaced, or even executed, failing generals; and some intervened, sometimes successfully, in the direct management of battles and campaigns. Lazare Carnot, an *envoyé en mission* who was previously an officer in the army engineers, made frequent visits to the front and played a key role in the reorganisation of the armies and the amalgamation of the traditional royalist troops, *les blancs*, with the volunteers from the *Garde nationale*, *les bleus*. Louis Saint-Just, another Deputy who carried out regular missions to the front, was often dynamic and successful in directing the forces and keeping up the military momentum.

The large-scale resort to *envoyés en mission* had profound disadvantages, however. It seriously weakened the *Convention*, by drawing away significant numbers of its leading members for these firefighting activities in the provinces or with the armies; and it destabilised its political balance, thus leading to the destabilisation of the whole political system. The *Girondins*, still the most influential group, increased their relative weight in the *Convention* by getting as many as possible of the eighty-four *envoyés* drawn from their *Montagnard* rivals. This weakened the *Montagnards* in Paris, but it enabled them to strengthen their contacts with some of the more radical *sociétés populaires*, the political debating clubs, in the provinces.

But it was not just the recruitment levy which was causing protests. There was also widespread suffering from high food prices, exacerbated by frequent and erratic shortages. Cereal prices varied wildly from one part of the country to another, while food markets and the transport of foodstuffs were constantly being disrupted by all those, from departmental authorities to local gangs, who tried to divert some of the available supplies by force. There were usually long queues at the bakers' shops; and the food crisis provoked riots and other disturbances in many parts of the country, especially in the large towns where food was most expensive and supplies most erratic: Lyon, Orléans, Étampes, Versailles, Rambouillet. In Paris, the *Commune* spent large amounts of money buying and subsidising bread, but it was not enough fully to alleviate the food crisis or the episodic shortages. There had always been a high incidence of real poverty in Paris, and now it had become much worse, first by the Revolution, then by the war. One contemporary estimate, even at the beginning of the Revolution, was that around one-tenth of the French population was indigent and needed public support in periods of crisis. In Paris, the rate of indigence reached one-fifth, with higher proportions in the poorer quarters: in the *faubourg* Saint-Antoine, every third inhabitant needed support.[2] By 1793, the situation had become much more severe.

The most general and long-lasting consequence of the food crisis was that it broke the previous political consensus supporting the operation of the free market. Ordinary people could see that the free market was not working, or at least that it was not working well enough to produce enough food in regular quantities at prices they could afford. So there sprang up a rising demand from the lower orders for the control and fixing of food prices. Brissot and other free marketeers blamed the disruptions in the food markets on 'agitators' or speculators. But among the *sans-culottes* in Paris, a number of radicals, led by the abbé Jacques Roux of the Gravilliers *Section* and Jean-François Varlet, a raucous street orator, started a noisy campaign for fixed price controls, or, as it became known, *le maximum*.

At first, during the spring of 1793, this demand was resisted by the *Girondins*, while the *Montagnards* tried to equivocate. In a diversion clearly designed to appease the masses, the *Convention* proposed a new *Tribunal révolutionnaire*, to try all traitors, conspirators and counter-revolutionaries. This proposal was hotly debated, and some of the *députés* fiercely resisted it. François Buzot, a lawyer from Évreux, a young and austere figure, 'ardent and melancholy', according to Michelet, and passionately committed to Revolutionary principles of justice, protested fiercely:

> They want a despotism even more frightful than that of anarchy. I offer thanks for every moment of life remaining, to those who are willing it let me have it … Let them just give me time to save my memory, to escape from dishonour, in voting against the tyranny of the *Convention*! When you received unlimited powers, it was not for usurping public liberty. If you confuse all the powers, if this is everything, where will this despotism finish, of which I am myself now so tired ?[3]

Buzot had started on the extreme left of the *Convention*, but he gradually joined the *Girondins*. At the trial of the King, he had voted that the verdict be subject to ratification by a popular vote, and he now voted against the establishment of a *Tribunal révolutionnaire*. But it was nevertheless voted through on March 9 and set up the following day.

The task of this fearsome *Tribunal* was to try people accused of attacking liberty and equality, the unity and indivisibility of the Republic or the internal and external safety of the state. In short, its brief was a holdall designed to catch anyone and everyone. On March 21 the *Convention* backed up the *Tribunal*'s threatening role by reinforcing the role and responsibilities of the local *comités de surveillance*, sometimes also called *comités révolutionnaires*. These *comités*, drawn from *communes*, had been set up a year earlier as the local instruments of Paris policing policy, and there were some 20,000 spread across the country. Now the *Convention* instructed every *commune*, all 44,000 of them, to establish a *comité de surveillance*. Initially, their task was just to keep an eye on all foreigners and suspicious persons; but this national police network was tailor-made for any and every purpose.

At first the *Tribunal révolutionnaire* had five judges, one public prosecutor and a jury of twelve citizens. Later that year it became the main instrument of the *Terreur* and was massively expanded. Even before it was established, Jacques Alexis Thuriot, a populist lawyer from the *Commune*, had secured a rider to the decree ordering that its judges and jurors must vote in public and out loud, *à haute voix*. 'The Terror', as Michelet put it, 'was in this phrase, more than in the rest of the project.'[4]

The *Tribunal révolutionnaire* was a new step into the territory of lawlessness: its rules were designed to short-circuit normal judicial procedures, and within a short time it would be stripped of all forms of legal protection for the accused or for witnesses.

France's ambitious policy of military expansion to 'natural frontiers' had been adopted in the middle of February, but within a month the war was going badly and the French were in headlong retreat. On March 18 the Austrians defeated Dumouriez at Neerwinden, in Belgium, to the north-east of Liège; by the end of the month he had to evacuate the whole of Belgium. Within another week, almost all of France's other conquests to the north and east had been lost, and it had withdrawn, virtually to its original frontiers.

France's war policy was in crisis. The armies were divided and short of essential supplies of food and clothing. Dumouriez blamed Pache, the Minister of War, and the administrative upheavals which he had created in the expansion and reorganisation of the War Ministry. There may have been something in this; no doubt the expansion of the Ministry *was* causing confusion. But it also seems likely that the expanding war was intensifying the stress of the reorganised Ministry's attempts to intervene against the old regime of corruption, with its special deals between individual generals and private army suppliers. The fundamental problem was that France was in the throes of learning to create, and to expand on an unprecedented scale, a modern war machine.

Matters were made much worse by the fact that the political authorities in Paris were increasingly riven by factional infighting between the *Girondins* and the *Montagnards*. The *Girondins* backed the generals and campaigned against the *Montagnard* reformers in the War Ministry, and in February they succeeded in getting Pache fired as the War Minister and replaced by Pierre de Riel, comte de Beurnonville, a colonel at Dumouriez' headquarters.

In this crisis, Danton seems to have played a large but murky role; no one has a confident and coherent account of what he was up to. He certainly spent a great deal of time from December 1792 to February 1793 with Dumouriez and with the French armies at the northern frontier and in Belgium, and when he returned to Paris in January 1793 he was only just in time to vote for the death of the King. His official purpose, as an *envoyé en mission*, was to help Dumouriez in organising the newly conquered territory of Belgium. But it is sometimes alleged that he took steps to enrich himself illicitly, through the old, corrupt system of army supplies or even by soliciting direct payments from the enemy; there is evidence that he was in communication with some of the *émigrés*, though to what purpose is not clear.

Shortly before his defeat at Neerwinden, Dumouriez had adopted a defiant posture towards the authorities in Paris, and on March 12 he had sent an insolent letter to the *Convention* in which he denounced the interference of War Ministry officials. Danton and Delacroix were sent north to remonstrate with the general: 'We shall cure him', they said, 'or we shall strangle him!' (*Nous le guérirons ou nous le garrotterons!*) They reached Leuven on March 20; but Dumouriez refused to withdraw his letter, and Danton returned to Paris to report to the government.

But Danton did not reach Paris until the evening of March 26, five days after he left Dumouriez, although the journey normally took a maximum of two days. To this day, no one knows what he did or where he went during the missing days. His critics suspect that he was up to no good.

While he was gone, Dumouriez turned traitor and opened secret negotiations with the Duke of Coburg, the Austrian commander. In Paris, the *Comité de défense générale*, created on January 1 to fill the hole at the top of the government resulting from the overthrow of the King, decided to send four *envoyés en mission*, together with Beurnonville, the new War Minister, to strip Dumouriez of his command and place him under arrest. But when they got there, it was they who were arrested, and Dumouriez handed them over to the enemy on April 1. They remained in captivity for two years.

Dumouriez tried to turn his army round, to march on Paris and overturn the Revolution. But he had not managed to have all the *envoyés* arrested, and those that remained at liberty forbade the army to follow him, while a local commander sent his young aide-de-camp, the twenty-five-year-old Louis Lazare Hoche, to Paris to warn the *Convention*. (Hoche started as a plain soldier and had risen to Captain; six months later he was promoted to General of Division and became one of the hard-fighting heroes of the Revolution's wars; the grand avenue Hoche in Paris is named after him.)

Thwarted, Dumouriez crossed over to the Austrians on April 5, 1793, taking with him the nineteen-year-old Louis-Philippe, duc de Chartres, the eldest son of the duc d'Orléans. From this point on, Dumouriez' fate was pretty miserable: unlike that other traitor, La Fayette, he was not imprisoned by the Austrians but wandered for many years from country to country, in exile and unwanted; he offered his services to the Russian Tsar but was turned down; and in 1823, at the age of eighty-four, he died poor and forgotten in England, where he had been living on a miserable government pension.

The young duc de Chartres came off much better. He avoided the fate of his father, who was now arrested and seven months later guillotined on manifestly trumped-up charges; and though he spent twenty-two years in exile, he returned to France with the restoration of the French monarchy in 1815. He himself ascended the throne in 1830, instituting the July Monarchy, as Louis-Philippe, the Citizen King.

In response to the public alarm caused by the treachery of Dumouriez, the *Convention* in March and April introduced a far-reaching series of measures to penalise *émigrés*, aristocrats and other enemies of the Revolution: the disarmament of 'suspects', by which they meant nobles and their servants but also anyone accused by the public authorities; a law against *émigrés* which included the confiscation of their property; and the death penalty for anyone who published subversive writings.

The most sinister measure was a decree on April 1, 1793, which revoked the Deputies' immunity from prosecution. From now on, the *Convention* could prosecute any of its members 'against whom ... there are strong presumptions of complicity with the enemies of freedom, of equality and of the republican government.'[5] The elastic words of this decree, with its deliberately imprecise, slithering definition of the offences targeted, were obviously a weapon aimed not at the enemies of the state but at the political enemies of the *Montagnards*: the *Girondins*.

Four days later, on April 5, the *Convention* substantially expanded the powers of the *Tribunal révolutionnaire*. Previously – that is, in the four short weeks since its creation on March 10 – it could only prosecute crimes of conspiracy if the *Convention* drafted the charge. But now the public prosecutor could arrest and try anyone denounced by any public authority, though not a Deputy, a Minister or a General.

Dumouriez' treason set off an explosion of recriminations between the political parties, with everybody accusing everybody else. Robespierre denounced the links between Dumouriez and the Gironde; the *Girondins* retorted that Philippe Égalité, the father of the duc de Chartres, who had escaped with Dumouriez, was a member of the *Montagnards*. Marc-David Lasource, a Protestant pastor from Tarn and one of the leading *Girondins*, accused Danton of complicity with Dumouriez; and Jean Bonaventure Blaise Hilarion Birotteau, another *Girondin*, a lawyer from Perpignan, claimed that Fabre d'Églantine, one of Danton's closest friends, had proposed the restoration of the monarchy.

The *Girondins* called for a Committee of Enquiry to investigate the circumstances of Dumouriez' treason. But Danton brazenly answered accusations with accusations, explicitly accusing Brissot, Gensonné and Guadet, leading members of the *Girondin* clan, of being close friends of Dumouriez; and the *Montagnards* urged on his counter-attack with rounds of applause. His compelling oratory did the trick, and the Committee of Enquiry was never formed.

The shocking news of Dumouriez' treachery seemed to prove that the Revolutionaries had not found an effective system of national government for managing the war. The *Comité de défense générale* was composed of *députés* from all seven policy subcommittees of the *Convention*: War, Marine, Colonies, Finance, Trade, Diplomacy and Constitution; but it proved incompetent and ineffective, and it had manifestly failed to prevent Dumouriez' defection.

Immediately after receiving this news, the *Convention* decided, on April 6, 1793, to set up a centralised policy committee of nine *députés*. Some members of the *Convention* wanted to call it an executive commission and have it directly take over some functions of government. But most were deeply convinced of the principle, absorbed from Enlightenment thinkers like Montesquieu, that it was imperative in any democratic system to split the executive and legislative authorities (the so-called separation of powers), and they were reluctant to give the new committee an executive title. So they decided to call it instead the *Comité de salut public* (CSP), or Committee of Public Safety, with the apparently more modest functions of stimulating and supervising the action of the Ministers and of overseeing national defence, internal and external.

Its original purpose was to manage the war effort; that was why it was created. It was intended to work alongside a pre-existing police committee, the *Comité de sûreté générale* (CSG); and they were designed to become, jointly, the two supreme institutions of government, the CSP for defence and the CSG for police and internal security. There were permanent rivalries between them, but within a matter of months the CSP asserted its pre-eminence and became the dominant Robespierrist instrument of government. In principle, it was answerable to the *Convention*, which could change its membership at will – and did, in fact, several times during the next six months. But the *Convention* would itself become dependent on, and subservient to, the new committee, which became the all-powerful instrument of government, totally dominating the *Convention* and deciding and then organising all aspects of policy, especially the Terror.

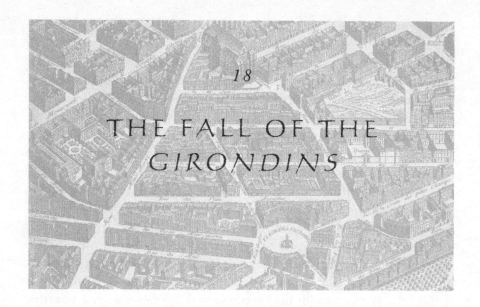

18

THE FALL OF THE GIRONDINS

IT WAS SOME MONTHS before the *Comité de salut public* (CSP) finally emerged as the dominant institution of government. In the meantime, the overthrow and execution of the King had created a vacuum where once there had been a supreme institution of government. France had neither a head of state nor a head of government. The removal of the King had also released the increasingly intense antagonism between the rival factions in the *Convention*. He had been in some sense the keystone of the political institutions of France, maintaining a kind of negative stability. While he was there, he was the main preoccupation of the Revolutionaries; when he was removed, there was nothing to distract them from their lethal competition for power.

The *Girondins* had been a dominant force, but they were beginning to lose their grip. Roland, who had been one of their most powerful allies as the Minister of the Interior, had resigned after the execution of the King. His successor, Dominique Garat, was a nobody whose guiding political principle was to stay out of trouble. The *Girondins* had succeeded in getting rid of Pache, the pro-*sans-culotte* Minister of War, and shifted him across to be the Mayor of Paris; but the next Minister of War (after Beurnonville, whom Dumouriez had handed over to the Austrians) was Jean-Baptiste Noël Bouchotte, another close ally of the *sans-culottes*.

Bouchotte was a long-serving and rather pedestrian soldier who had just about risen to the rank of colonel and was now catapulted, for populist political reasons, into the office of Minister of War. He was hated on many sides. In the field, he had angered the Dantonists by widely promoting the distribution of *Le Père Duchesne*, the vulgar and inflammatory pamphlet published by the left-wing agitator Hébert. The generals despised him as an upstart from the ranks; and they resented the attempts of the reformers in his Ministry to interfere in their cosy and profitable private supply contracts. But like Pache, he stuffed the offices of the Ministry with *sans-culottes*, as well as with left-wing agitators known as *les Enragés* (The Infuriated). Under attack, he twice tried to resign, but nobody else wanted the poisoned chalice of the War Ministry.

The *Girondins* could still count on the support of Clavière, the Finance Minister, and Pierre Lebrun-Tondu, the Foreign Minister; but the Council of Ministers, or *Comité exécutif*, as it was now called, was beginning to come under the control of the CSP. This committee was still feeling its way, since its membership represented a cautious, middle-of-the-road compromise among the factions in the *Convention*. Of the nine *deputés* originally elected to it, seven came from the centre (*la Plaine*) and two from the Dantonist wing of the *Montagne*, Danton himself and his close lieutenant Jean-François Delacroix; but none from the *Girondins*, and none from the hard-line, Robespierrist wing of the *Montagne*.

Not surprisingly, the CSP started out weak, divided and incapable of taking effective charge of policy: it failed to drive back the Austrian invaders, it failed to deal with the civil war, and it failed to resolve the problems of the *assignat,* inflation and the food shortages. Most seriously, Danton had started to break ranks with the French war policy and was urging the case for sounding out the possibility of peace terms; in the process, he raised the suspicion of some people that he was taking money from the Austrians.

For a while, therefore, the centre held the balance of power in this CSP. The main figures were Bertrand Barère, an able and eloquent lawyer from the south-west, and Pierre Cambon, the dominant speaker in the *Convention* on finance and economics. These two were supple middle-of-the-roaders: they were from *la Plaine*, but they would always vote with the *Montagne* whenever they thought it was necessary to save the Revolution. On the other hand, they deeply mistrusted the *Commune* and therefore Danton and his affiliates, who were closely associated with the populists and the *sans-culotte* street orators of the *Cordeliers* Club; so whenever the *Convention* had to vote on questions affecting the people or politics of Paris, Barère and Cambon tended to vote with the *Girondins*. This meant that the *Montagne* could not, at the start of the struggle, hope to defeat the *Girondins* under normal procedural rules.

A few weeks later at the end of May, the political balance shifted in favour of the *Montagnards* when the CSP was expanded to take in five new members. But by that time, the *Montagnards* had already decided to escalate the conflict by taking it right outside the rules of the *Convention*, with a direct appeal to the Paris *sans-culottes*.

In the trial of the King, it had been the *Girondins* (or some of them) who had tried to save his life, by arguing that any verdict ought to be subject to ratification by the people. On April 5, 1793, the *Montagne* raised the stakes by sending out a circular from the *Jacobin* Club in Paris to all the sister *Jacobin* clubs across France, appealing for petitions demanding the recall – that is, the expulsion from the *Convention* – of any *deputés* who had tried to save the life of 'the tyrant'. When they heard of this circular, the *Girondins* angrily blamed Marat, who, as the President of the *Jacobin* Club, had signed it, and they called for his impeachment before the *Tribunal révolutionnaire*. After violent arguments, the *Convention* carried the accusation against Marat, by 226 votes to 93; one reason for the large majority was that many *Montagnards* had been sent out as *envoyés en mission* to the *départements*, to push through the recruitment (known as the levée) of 300,000 men. But it was a short-lived victory, for the *Tribunal révolutionnaire* was of course packed with supporters of the *Montagne*, and when Marat surrendered to it on April 24 he was immediately and easily acquitted, and carried in triumph back to his seat in the *Convention*.

Well before Marat's acquittal, a large and threatening crowd of Parisian *sans-culottes*, representing thirty-five of the forty-eight *Sections* and led by Pache, the newly elected Mayor, came to the *Convention* on April 15 in response to the *Jacobin* circular, with a menacing petition calling for the indictment of twenty-two of the leading *Girondins*, starting with Brissot, Vergniaud, Guadet, Gensonné, Buzot, Pétion, Lasource and Lanjuinais, and accusing them of being 'guilty of the crime of felony against the sovereign people'.[1]

The *Girondins* responded with an appeal to the other half of popular opinion in Paris. Towards the end of April, Pétion published a pamphlet entitled *Lettre aux Parisiens*, in which he accused the *Montagnards* of

deliberately fomenting class war and called for the help of supporters
of law and order:

> Your properties are being threatened, and you are closing your eyes
> to this danger. People are stirring up war between those who have
> and those who have not, and you are doing nothing to prevent it. A
> few intriguers, a handful of factions are imposing on you, are leading
> you into violent and unconsidered actions, and you do not have the
> courage to resist; you do not dare to go to your *Sections* to oppose
> them. You see all the rich and peaceful people leave Paris, and you
> just sit there ...[2]

At first this appeal seemed to work: some of the better-off Parisians,
already irritated and alarmed at the way the *sans-culottes* had been using
the far-reaching powers of the recently created *comités révolutionnaires*
to penalise them by imposing special war taxes, started to retaliate by
going to their local *Sections* and voting down the war taxes. During
working hours, the members of the working classes could not get to
their *Sections*; so the better-off were able, during the week, to muster
purely temporary daytime majorities in a number of the *Sections*: Buttes
des Moulins, Mail, Champs-Élysées. But the *sans-culottes* fought back,
and outside working hours there were frequent and rowdy clashes
between opposing factions in different *Sections*. The *Jacobins* and the
Commune, vigorously backed the *sans-culottes* and ordered a number of
arrests.

The *sans-culottes* were increasingly being readied by the *Montagnards* for mobilisation. For some weeks, Robespierre had been regularly
denouncing the *Girondin* leadership, accusing them of complicity first
with the suspected disloyalty and then, after April 5, 1793, with the
demonstrated treachery of Dumouriez; and on April 10 he had come to
the *Convention* to call for the indictment of the duc d'Orléans, as well as
Brissot, Vergniaud, Gensonné and Guadet.[3]

Later that month Robespierre started preparing the ground for
insurrection by shifting to a more domestic, party-political discourse,
in which he openly embraced the case for class war against the *Girondins*. In a speech to the *Jacobins* at the end of April and then again to
the *Convention*, he openly questioned the 'sacred' principle of property
rights and said that they must ultimately be subordinated to the general
interest.

Class-war politics was a new development. During the first three years of the Revolution, under the *Assemblée nationale constituante* and the *Assemblée nationale législative*, the *sans-culottes* had been relatively willing to put themselves at the service of the bourgeois Revolutionaries against the *ancien régime*; their reward was the overthrow of the aristocracy and the removal of the burden of feudalism. But those days were well past. Feudalism and the King had been overthrown, but the *sans-culottes* were worse off than before, with high unemployment, high and rising prices and above all repeated food shortages. To some extent, the *sans-culottes* of Paris were protected from the inflation of food prices, because the *Commune* subsidised the price of bread, keeping it at just 3 sous for a 1-pound loaf. But for most articles the rate of inflation was frightening and painful. On June 21, 1793, in the working-class quarter of the *faubourg* Saint-Antoine, a man was heard shouting out: 'Once upon a time, soap cost only 12 sous; now it costs 40. *Vive la République!* Once, sugar cost 20 sous, today it's 4 livres. *Vive la République!*'[4] He was arrested.

If the *sans-culottes* were to be enlisted in the struggle between factions of the bourgeoisie, they would have to be paid for their support; and the first down payment would be control of food prices.

Despite the disorders in the food markets and the suffering of ordinary people, the *Girondins* were still arguing in favour of free market forces. But pressures were growing for government intervention: more and more delegations came to the bar of the *Convention* to press for price controls, and in a number of provincial towns, such as Lyon, Marseille and Rouen, the municipal authorities were buying up supplies of wheat, which they distributed either free or at subsidised prices. In Paris, the *Commune* was spending £12,000 a day on bread subsidies, but this made the supply situation worse, since the private millers and bakers could not meet the price competition from subsidised bread, and some simply shut up shop. The queues at the bakers' grew longer, and the protests among the *sans-culotte* agitators, led by the priest Jacques Roux and the street orator Jean-François Varlet, only grew louder.

Robespierre's opening salvo against property rights was immediately seconded by his allies on the left at a meeting of all the mayors and municipal officers of Paris and the suburban *communes* called by Louis Marie Lhuillier, the *procureur-général-syndic* (chief executive) of the Paris *département*, who drafted a manifesto to denounce the economic policy of the *Girondins*:

Let no one raise objections based on property rights! The right of property cannot be the right to starve one's fellow citizens. The fruits of the earth, like the air, belong to everybody. We come to demand: 1. The fixing of the maximum price of wheat throughout the Republic; 2. The abolition of the grain trade; 3. The suppression of any intermediary between the farmer and the consumer; 4. A general census of all the wheat after each harvest.[5]

Under this growing pressure, the *Convention* on May 4, 1793, passed a law of price control for wheat and flour, known as *le maximum*. Each *département* was required to fix the prices for these goods in relation to average market prices during the early months of the year and to police the system by keeping a record of available stocks: every farmer and trader was required to declare the quantity of cereals he held, and his local authority was entitled to inspect his premises to check if he was telling the truth. Anyone convicted of having spoiled, lost or hidden cereals could face the death penalty.

Having given in to the key demand of the *sans-culottes*, Robespierre pressed ahead with his strategy of class war. In early May, in a speech to the *Jacobins*, he urged the *sans-culottes* to rise up against the rich: 'You have aristocrats in the *Sections*; drive them out! You have your freedom to preserve; proclaim the rights of your freedom, and make use of all your energy. You have an immense people of *sans-culottes*, so pure, so vigorous; they cannot get away from their work, so let them be paid for by the rich!'[6]

The conflict between the *Girondins* and the *Montagnards* was now increasingly heated. Camille Desmoulins, the popular journalist and friend of Danton, published a pamphlet accusing the *Girondins* of having been in league with the English and the Prussians and of planning to divide France into twenty or thirty federal Republics. Of course, he had no evidence for the accusations, because they were not true; but he impudently retorted that 'in a case of conspiracy, it is absurd to ask for positive evidence'.[7]

At the *Convention*, after rowdy interrruptions from the galleries, Guadet, one of the leading *Girondins*, called for the closing of all the political institutions in Paris and the convening of a backup *Convention*, composed of the substitutes for the elected *députés*, to be held at Bourges, in the centre of France and therefore well away from the capital. But he got no support, and the *Convention* decided instead to set up a Committee of Twelve to calm things down. This only made matters worse, however, since the first thing it did was arrest Hébert for an offensive article in *Le Père Duchesne*. He was not just a vulgar journalist, though; he was also the deputy *procureur* of the *Commune*, whose representatives came to demand, and of course secure, his immediate release.

There was now a tug of war over the Committee of Twelve. On May 27 the *Montagnards* and their supporters rounded up enough votes to have it suppressed; the next day, by a large majority, the *Girondins* got it restored. The procedural struggle between the factions in the *Convention* was in total deadlock, so Robespierre called for another insurrection.

'When the people are oppressed', he had told the *Jacobin* Club on May 26, 'when it has nothing left except itself, then only a coward would not tell it to rise up. When all the laws are broken, when despotism is at its peak, when good faith and modesty are trampled underfoot, that is the time when the people should rise up. That time has arrived.'[8]

Three days later a large number of *sans-culotte* delegates from thirty-three of the forty-eight *Sections* convened at *l'Évêché*, the former bishop's palace in Paris, and there they appointed a nine-man insurrectionary committee. Two days later they sent this committee to the *Hôtel de ville* to assert the sovereign powers which they claimed a majority of the *Sections* had conferred on them. They tried, in effect, to depose the members of the legal *Commune*; they were there, they said, to punish the traitors. It was virtually a rerun of the insurrection of August 10, 1792.

In the face of this challenge, the legal authorities proved impotent. The CSP, notionally the supreme governing authority in France, simply did nothing. In the afternoon of May 31, 1793, the *Commune* and the *Sections* drafted a joint motion in fourteen points, whose threatening terms were read out to the *Convention*:

1. A charge sheet against twenty-two named *Girondin* Deputies
2. A charge sheet against the Committee of Twelve
3. A demand for the creation of a Revolutionary army of *sans-culottes* in every town of France, including 20,000 men in Paris
4. The establishment of workshops for the manufacture of arms for the *sans-culottes*
5. Bread to cost no more than 3 sous per pound
6. The arrest of Lebrun-Tondu and Clavière

7. The closing of the postal administration and the purging of all
   other administrations
8. The disarmament, arrest and condemnation of all suspects
9. Voting rights to be restricted to *sans-culottes*
10. Expansion of the *Tribunal révolutionnaire*
11. The establishment of workshops for the old and infirm
12. The exaction of a forced loan of £1bn from the rich
13. The immediate payment of indemnities to defenders of the
    country
14. A purge of the CSP and of the *Conseil exécutif*

Fearing what was to come, many *Girondins* stayed away from the
Convention, and many did not sleep in their own beds. But when it came
to it, on this first day of insurrection the *Convention* stood up to the
intimidation of the *sans-culottes* pretty well. It conceded that the Committee of Twelve would be disbanded and that the CSP would conduct
an enquiry into the conflict; but it would go no further.

In that sense, the insurrection of May 31, 1793, failed to come off.
The insurrectionists were not entirely sure of their position, since they
did not have unanimous support from all forty-eight *Sections*; and in
contrast with the insurrection of August 10, 1792, they had failed to
ensure that the menace of their declaration was backed up by a big
enough threat of physical violence. They immediately gathered for a
new attack, and this time they made better arrangements. On the night
of June 1 the *Comité insurrectionnel* ordered the arrest of Roland and
Clavière. Roland escaped, but his wife was captured; Clavière remained
at liberty. At the same time, the *Comité insurrectionnel* ordered François
Hanriot, the young Revolutionary who had only just, two days earlier,
been appointed commander of the *Garde nationale de Paris*, to surround
the *Convention* 'with a respectable armed force'.

He did as he was told. The *Convention* was due to meet the next
day, a Sunday, June 2. Hanriot mustered a force of 80,000 armed
men from the *Sections*, including a troop of gunners, with which he
entirely surrounded the *Convention*. A delegation of the *Commune
insurrectionnelle* came to the *Convention* and demanded in menacing
terms the immediate arrest of the twenty-two *Girondin députés*, plus
the members of the Committee of Twelve. Danton proposed a compromise: the twenty-two would not be arrested but instead invited to
resign. There was uproar. Many *Girondin députés* indignantly refused

to resign; many complained loudly that Hanriot's troops were threatening the *Convention*.

Finally, after a long and heated debate, the members of the *Convention* attempted to challenge the forces arrayed outside by simply walking out of the building. They were led by Marie Jean Hérault de Séchelles, the young, rich and popular *deputé* who had just been appointed to the governing CSP and was currently the President of the *Convention*; he was followed in turn by all the members.

But outside they were confronted by Hanriot, who was immovable: 'Gunners, to your guns!', he ordered. The Deputies stopped; they retreated; and they returned, defeated, to their places inside.

On a proposal of Georges Auguste Couthon, the semi-paralysed friend of Robespierre, the *Convention* agreed to surrender the twenty-two named *Girondins*, plus the members of the Committee of Twelve, but on the condition that they would not be put in prison, only subject to house arrest. Then Marat had three of the twenty-two excused, on the grounds that they had been led astray.

These were significant concessions. Those who accepted house arrest remained provisionally at liberty and were in principle allowed to lead fairly normal lives, going about their business, visiting their friends. But most foresaw that house arrest could only be the prelude to trial and probable execution, and many escaped as soon as they could. Many other (non-*Girondin*) *députés* protested at the overthrow of the *Girondins*, and seventy-three were indicted for their protests and put in prison; but they were not brought to trial – largely, Robespierre claimed the day before his own downfall, because he had intervened to prevent it.

The arrest of so many *Girondins* and then of so many of their sympathisers meant that Robespierre and the *Montagnards* now had complete control of the *Convention*, even if they did not constitute a formal majority.

The overthrow of the *Girondins* was the latest and the most fatal step of the French Revolution into illegality. It was not as dramatic as the overthrow of the monarchy, but the essential fact about that insurrection, on August 10, 1792, was that while the insurrectionists of the *Commune* had intimidated the National Assembly, they had not violated its integrity, nor the immunity of its members: their central demand was the election of a new National Assembly, a *Convention*. In May and June 1793, by contrast, the central demand of the insurrectionists was precisely the violation of the immunity of the members of the *Convention*. On April 1, the *Convention* had been pressured into removing from the Deputies their immunity from prosecution by the *Convention* if there were 'strong presumptions of complicity with the enemies of freedom, of equality and of the republican government.'[9] But now the insurrectionists went further, violating the immunity not just of individual *députés* but of the *Convention* itself. For that reason, this uprising has been described as not so much an insurrection as a *coup d'état*.

In their fourteen points, the insurrectionists of the *Commune* had sketched out some elements of a new social agenda which would have marked a clear break with the liberal principles of the bourgeois Revolutionaries. But for the moment it was not fleshed out or acted upon. The bourgeoisie still firmly held the main political discourse of the Revolution, and they resisted and tried to crush left-wing agitators. Nevertheless, the overthrow of the *Girondins* on June 2, 1793, had broken all remaining political restraints. All hope of a legal Revolution was now over; and Robespierre, a lawyer, must have known it.

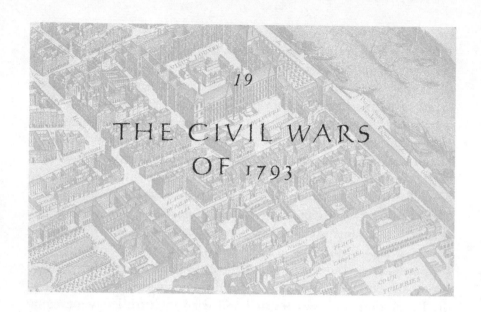

19

THE CIVIL WARS
OF 1793

IN THE SUMMER OF 1793, after the overthrow of the *Girondins*, France faced war on three fronts: a rebellion in the region of the Vendée, in the west of France; the so-called civil war in several other parts of France, partly precipitated by the overthrow of the *Girondins*; and the foreign war against the European coalition.

There were similarities between the Vendée and the civil war: both were certainly wars of rebellion against Paris. But they were quite distinct in their origins, in their conduct and in their outcomes.

The Vendée was a local war of protest against the Revolutionary authorities in Paris, and it was precipitated not by the fall of the *Girondins* but by the demand of the *Convention*, on February 24, 1793, for a conscription quota of 300,000 men. On March 3, hundreds of young men rose up near the town of Cholet in protest, ostensibly at the method of selection but in reality at the fact that they were being asked to fight in a war that was far away and none of their business. From that moment the whole of the surrounding region was in flames.

According to some accounts, there were up to five wars of the Vendée, lasting serially almost eight years, until the end of the decade. But the main war happened in 1793, mostly in and around four *départements* near the mouth of the Loire – the Vendée itself, Loire-Inférieure, Maine-et-Loire and Deux-Sèvres – with a ferocious amount of killing on both sides.

In some respects, the word 'war' is a misnomer: this was an almost spontaneous uprising, mainly of country peasants, and the rebels had no formally organised armies as such and little in the way of military weapons, systematic supplies or even regular leaders. At first they relied on all kinds of improvised rural weaponry, such as pikes, scythes and shotguns, and they acquired proper military weapons, like rifles, mainly from Republican soldiers whom they captured or killed. They made little attempt to fight formally organised battles and instead tended to come together almost as episodically recruited bands for hit-and-run attacks.

Sometimes the Vendéen rebellion is characterised as pro-Catholic or pro-royalist, but that is not what it was about. No doubt most of the local peasantry were regular churchgoers and supporters of their familiar priests; and no doubt some supported the monarchy. Some of the local nobility did come forward as officers to lead the insurgents, like the romantic twenty-one-year-old Henri du Vergier, comte de La Roche-jaquelein, who did so with heroic and dashing distinction and made himself famous locally both for his bravery and for his legendary and inspiring battle cry: 'If I go forward, follow me; if I retreat, kill me; if I die, avenge me!'[1] He was killed in battle the following year, aged only twenty-two. But the local nobility did not start the war of the Vendée; and there had been no sign of a Vendée revolt following the execution of the King earlier in the year. Various royalists and Catholics came together after the start of the uprising, giving themselves grandiloquent titles such as *Armée catholique et royale d'Anjou*; but these were impro-vised afterthoughts rather than coherent or consistent armies.

On June 9 the rebels won their first significant victory, at Saumur; on June 18 they took Angers; and on June 29 they beseiged Nantes. But they made no serious attempt to take the fight further. Some of their leaders, like the gamekeeper Nicolas Stofflet, supported by La Roche-jaquelein, wanted to march on Paris, but the majority resisted; they preferred instead to withdraw to the west. The rebels were in the main local protesters, not counter-revolutionaries, and they were reluctant to go far from home.

In Paris, the uprising in the Vendée took the Revolutionaries by sur-prise, and their confusion was complete. They were not yet organised for a foreign war, and even less for the suppression of a domestic rebellion. There was in theory a domestic army in the west, the so-called *Armée des côtes maritimes*, divided into three: *de la Rochelle*, *de Brest* and *de Cherbourg*; but these forces were largely disorganised and their soldiers the locally raised flotsam and jetsam of France. So it took time for the *Convention* to organise a systematic response, and one of the first elements was the dispatch of numbers of its own members as *envoyés en mission*, with far-reaching powers, to take charge of local authorities and exercise command over local military and civil bodies. At first the element of improvisation and the large number of *envoyés en mission*, all with undefined and competing claims, rather added to the confusion. But gradually the Revolutionaries in Paris reasserted control, and on October 1 the *Convention* gave orders to the *armée de l'Ouest* to finish the war of the Vendée. It was at Cholet, where the rebels had first risen up, that the Republican army on October 15–17 inflicted a crushing defeat.

This phase of the rebellion dragged on a bit, but it drew to a close towards the end of the year, when the rebels were defeated in a battle that finished in a massacre, on December 23, in the marshes of Savenay in Loire-Inférieure (now Loire-Atlantique), not far from Saint-Nazaire. After his victory, the Republican General François Westermann wrote proudly to the *Convention*: 'The Vendée is no more. I have just buried it in the marshes of Savenay. I crushed the children under the hooves of the horses, and massacred the women. I have not one prisoner to reproach myself with. I have exterminated all.'[2] But he was wrong: he had not exterminated them all, and episodically they went on rebelling.

What is normally called the civil war, by contrast, was much more widespread, with outbreaks of armed resistance in several provinces and provincial towns throughout France. Some historians have called it a 'federalist revolt', but this is really just a term of propaganda: the *Montagnards* tried to smear the various rebellious movements by claiming that the civil war was part of an anti-Revolutionary conspiracy devised by the treacherous *Girondins*, and aimed at setting up a federalist government in France. Of course it was nothing of the sort. When the *Girondin* Lasource had said, a year earlier, that 'Paris must be reduced to a 1/83 share of influence in France, just like all the other *départements*',[3] he had meant not that France should be a federation but that it should be ruled nationally, by the National Assembly, and not by the Paris *Commune*.

Some of these rebellions were in part uprisings in support of the *Girondins* and in protest at their expulsion from the *Convention*, while others were in part protests at the assertion of supreme political power by the *Montagnards* and the Paris *sans-culottes*, which provided two reasons for the *Montagnard* propaganda. But other rebellions were triggered by quite distinct local power struggles between pro- and anti-Revolutionary factions.

In any case, the relationship between Paris and the provinces was ambiguous for a while. It was a fact that the *Montagnards* and the Paris *sans-culottes* had carried out a coup d'état against the National Assembly; yet after they had done so, the *sans-culotte* insurrectionists seemed to have ambivalent intentions. They had been mobilised to bring down the *Girondins*, but they did not then challenge the legitimacy of the *Convention* by demanding the election of a new *Assemblée nationale*.

Moreover, the fate of the arrested *Girondins* was so far unclear. The CSP was meant to be the centre of political authority, but its membership was still mainly composed of moderates, and during the latest insurrection in Paris it had remained completely inert. On June 5 it made a half-hearted effort to intervene on behalf of the *Girondins*, calling on Jean Nicolas Pache, the former Defence Minister, who was now the Mayor of Paris, to produce the evidence against the accused, 'in the absence of which it will be forced to announce to the *Convention* that it does not exist'. But Pache paid no attention and did nothing, so the question of the trial of the *Girondins* and the case against them remained in suspense, but not removed.

Twelve of the proscribed *Girondins* had fled Paris immediately, and another eight left in the days following. But those who remained were defiant: the flamboyant Vergniaud, the prosperous lawyer from Bordeaux, loudly demanded to be put on trial. Colleagues of the *Girondins* who had been driven out raised complaints on their behalf. On June 6, fifty-two *députés* made a collective public protest, and they were joined by another nineteen on June 18 and another five shortly thereafter. Several of them left Paris to follow their *Girondin* colleagues and help them rouse their supporters in the provinces. Outside Paris, the reactions to the coup d'état were mixed. The *départements* in its immediate vicinity remained loyal to the new masters of the *Convention*, the *Montagnards* and the *Commune*, and so did those in the centre of France

(Indre, Cher, Creuse, Corrèze, Cantal, Allier). But elsewhere there were protests in a number of major population centres, especially those with a long history of regional importance and a strong sense of local identity, such as Caen and much of Normandy in the north-west, Bordeaux and Bayonne in the south-west, Marseille and Toulon on the Mediterranean, and above all Lyon in central France.

Six weeks after the overthrow of the *Girondins*, on July 13, 1793, Marat was murdered in his bath[4] by Charlotte Corday, a pious twenty-four-year-old who had come specially for the purpose from her home in Normandy, with a knife concealed in her skirt. She was not in any real sense a *Girondin*, but she believed that Marat was responsible for the June 2 coup d'état and that his death would bring peace. She was guillotined four days later.

In many parts of the country, however, what is called the civil war, though brought into focus by the coup d'état of the *Montagnards* in Paris, was in fact an almost coincidental reflection of a sequence of local power struggles in different centres. The vast changes set off by the Revolution had released much political agitation, discontent and unresolved conflict in many parts of France; and in most places the questions of the violation of parliamentary immunity in Paris and of the predicament of the *Girondins* were largely secondary to local political fights. In some larger towns, these outbreaks were the manifestation of urban conflicts pitting local republicans and *Jacobins* against local bourgeois conservatives; in other cases, they were partly clashes between town and country, since the authorities running the surrounding *départements*, reflecting the opinions and interests of the peasants, tended to be more conservative, whereas the authorities running the towns tended to be more Revolutionary and republican.

The first of the provinces to rise after the overthrow of the *Girondins* was Normandy, starting with Eure and Calvados, and it was quickly joined by five *départements* of Brittany: Finistère, Ille-et-Vilaine, Côtes-du-Nord (now Côtes-d'Armor), Morbihan and Mayenne. Caen, the capital of Calvados, became the headquarters of the western resistance; and Félix Wimpfen, the commander of the Republican forces at Cherbourg, went over to the insurrection, taking with him two regiments of cavalry.

In the south-west, the authorities in Bordeaux expelled two representatives of the *Convention*, then another two who had been sent to negotiate in response, ordered the raising of a force of 1,200 men and called for an assembly of all the rebellious *départements*. In Toulouse, also in the south-west, the authorities released royalists from prison and imprisoned *Jacobins* in their place; in Nîmes, in the south, the *Jacobins* were disarmed and imprisoned and their club closed.

In Lyon, local issues almost completely outweighed the national dimension of civil war. It was a very large city for its time, second only to Paris in France, with a population of significantly more than 100,000. In social terms too Lyon was unique, as the only city in the country dominated by a single advanced manufacturing industry, silk production, and therefore the only one with anything remotely resembling a proletariat. Silk had made Lyon very rich; but the Revolution had caused a massive emigration of aristocrats and a collapse in demand for silk products, leading to wholesale unemployment among silk workers. Already in 1790, it has been estimated, 25,000 workers in Lyon were on public assistance; this implies an unemployment rate of 50 per cent.[5] Poverty and popular suffering were extreme and deep-seated, and by 1793 deprivation was even more acute.

The stresses caused by this profound local economic crisis precipitated a long-running and increasingly violent political conflict which swung back and forth between shifting alliances of populists, bourgeoisie, *Girondins*, *Jacobins* and even royalists. Sometimes it seemed to chime (or alternate) with the struggle in Paris, but in reality it had its own, local dynamic.

At one point in early June the moderates in Lyon gained the upper hand, and after first declaring loyalty to the *République une et indivisible* (one and indivisible) they abruptly swung the other way and made contacts with neighbouring insurrectionary *départements* and some of the rebel cities, such as Marseille, Nîmes and Bordeaux. On July 15 they guillotined Joseph Chalier, the rabble-rousing leader of the populists, who thus became, with Louis Michel Le Peletier (the member of the *Convention* who had been assassinated on January 20, 1793, by a royalist *député* after voting for the death of the King) and Marat (assassinated on July 13 by Charlotte Corday), one of the three martyrs of the Revolution.

Marseille, the third or fourth largest town in France, after Lyon and Bordeaux, with a population of around 100,000, was in the early days of the Revolution one of its most important centres, and in January 1793, radical *Jacobins* had taken it over and begun intimidating the rest of the population with a policy of Terror, forced taxes, intrusive police visits and the imprisonment of suspects. By the spring of that year, the ordinary people had had enough: at the end of April the local *Sections* rose up against the *Jacobins* and ordered the expulsion of two representatives sent down by the *Convention*, and in May the *Sections* had the leaders of the city's *Club des Jacobins* arrested. When the people of Marseille heard the news of the overthrow on June 2 of the *Girondin* Deputies in the *Convention*, the rupture between them and Paris was complete, and the local authorities put out feelers to other rebellious centres, like Toulon, to cooperate in resisting the tyranny of the Paris *sans-culottes*.

For a short while the rebellious Marseillais seemed to be demanding some kind of federalism independent of the authority of Paris while claiming fidelity to the principles of the Revolution, because they were exercising direct democracy through the local *Sections*. But the municipal institutions were soon taken over by the leaders of the merchant and business class, many of whom were anti-revolutionary or even royalist, and despite a *Jacobin* uprising in the working-class districts, they openly declared a non-revolutionary policy of federalist independence from Paris.

The nearby port of Toulon was the headquarters of the French Mediterranean fleet, and the area had for some time been the scene of intense political struggles between the town and the surrounding district: *Jacobins* and military loyal to the Revolution had tended to dominate the town, whereas royalists had dominated the authorities of the local district and *département*. During the summer of 1792 there had been repeated incidents of popular anger and violence against public officials, but after the overthrow of the monarchy on August 10 of that year, the *Jacobins* took control and restored order. A year later, however, on July 12, 1793, the population rebelled against the oppressive *Jacobin* dictatorship, and the royalists again took power. They closed the *Jacobin* club and hanged twenty-four of its members. The *Convention* attempted to intervene by sending two *envoyés en mission*, but the royalists had them arrested. On August 27, under the threat of the imminent arrival of two Revolutionary armies, the royalists surrendered the town, the naval port and the French Mediterranean fleet of fifty-eight warships to Admiral Samuel Hood, the Commander-in-Chief of the English fleet in the Mediterranean, and English soldiers entered the town. They also sent a message of allegiance to the King's brother, the comte de Provence, but he did not answer. The Allies placed the town under the authority of a new Governor-General, Major Charles O'Hara.

The so-called civil war had surged to a peak in the middle of June 1793, when some sixty French *départements* out of eighty-three were nominally in rebellion against the regime in Paris. But this was not in any meaningful sense a concerted rebellion, and it was, in general, shallow, fragile and localised; even where the ostensible supporters of the *Girondins* were strong, they never had a coherent strategy of fightback and were relatively easy to defeat. So, unlike the Vendée, the civil war was short-lived. But the worst of it was that when the Paris Revolutionaries defeated the rebels, as they eventually did, they were seldom magnanimous or generous. Instead, they often inflicted a level of punishment that was in many cases extreme, sometimes barbaric and by definition counterproductive.

In Normandy, the rebellion was quickly defeated, and Jean-Baptiste Robert Lindet, sent to pacify the region, kept repression to a minimum. In Bordeaux, the *sans-culotte Sections* overthrew the rebellious pro-*Girondin* authorities, and the rebellion was soon over.

In the south, it took an army led by Jean-Baptiste François Carteaux to defeat the rebels. He was a one-time boy-soldier who had given up life in the army to become a painter in enamel. In 1789 he had rejoined the army as an aide-de-camp to La Fayette, and after a series of rapid promotions he had reached the rank of Lieutenant-General in charge of the Army of the Alps. One of the junior gunnery officers in this army was the twenty-four-year-old Napoléon Bonaparte.

Carteaux took Marseille on August 25. He was just in time to prevent it from falling into the hands of the English but not in time to save Toulon, which was handed over to Admiral Hood two days later. Carteaux' army started a siege of Toulon in September, which lasted more than three months; they finally retook it on December 19, partly thanks to a plan of artillery bombardment of the naval port proposed by Bonaparte. By then the army besieging Toulon was swarming with powerful *envoyés en mission*, including Paul Barras, his inseparable side-kick Louis-Stanislas Fréron, Christophe Saliceti[6] and Robespierre's younger brother, Augustin.

Barras (Paul François, vicomte de Barras) was a once wealthy noble from Provence who had joined the army at sixteen as a gentleman cadet; he left it at twenty-eight when he reached the rank of Captain, and moved to Paris, where he proceeded to enjoy life and spend his way through his fortune. At thirty-seven, he got himself elected to the *Convention*, and he voted for the death of the King; but he spent most of his time out of Paris, as an *envoyé en mission* with the armies. At Toulon, Barras established close links with Bonaparte and used his authority as an *envoyé en mission* to have him promoted from Lieutenant to Captain; after the city's recapture, the *envoyés en mission* jointly recommended that Bonaparte be promoted to Brigadier.

With the fall of Toulon, Barras became one of the masters of the town, and he made use of his sweeping powers to enrich himself through corruption, embezzlement and extortion. His venality was so notorious that Robespierre, from the CSP, had him recalled to Paris. It is said that when Barras returned there, Robespierre cut him dead, so in retaliation he mustered against Robespierre all the allies he could find. Others say this story is at best oversimplified. What is certainly true is that Barras played a key role in Robespierre's downfall and execution on *10 thermidor*.

Barras' reputation for corruption was spectacular but by no means unique. During this phase of the Revolution, lasting until after the fall of Robespierre, the opportunities for and the temptations of corruption grew at an exponential rate. The expansion of the war, with its increased demand for army supplies, created colossal opportunities for business deals, legal and illegal; the rising wave of inflation generated enormous scope for financial speculation; significant amounts of the new money generated by the war and by this inflationary spiral were funnelled into the speculative buying and selling of Church property; and the political fallout from the disturbances following the civil war resulted in unprecedented transfers of unmonitored power into the hands of *envoyés en mission*, some of whom used it without restraint for personal or criminal purposes.

At Lyon, the siege by the Republican army started on August 9, 1793, and lasted two months; the town surrendered on October 9. The Revolutionaries in Paris were determined to inflict a unique and terrible punishment on these rebels, partly as vengeance for the execution of the local *Jacobin* leader Chalier. Its terms were published in detail in a decree that the *Convention* sent two *envoyés en mission*, Jean-Marie Collot d'Herbois and Joseph Fouché, to carry out. Collot d'Herbois, a former travelling actor and theatre manager, had played a leading role in the Insurrectionary *Commune* and was a newly appointed member of the CSP. Fouché was the son of a shipowner in Nantes, where he had received an intense Catholic education and almost qualified as a priest; instead he became an itinerant schoolteacher of maths and physics in various towns of France, including Arras, where he grew close to Robespierre, to whose sister Charlotte he was almost engaged.

'Lyon will lose its name', said the decree,

> it will be called 'Liberated-Town' [*Ville-Affranchie*]. It will be destroyed; everywhere the rich lived will be destroyed; there will remain only the houses of the poor, the homes of misguided or proscribed patriots, buildings specially employed for industry and monuments consecrated to humanity and to public education. On the ruins of Lyon there will be raised a column which will bear witness for posterity to the crimes and the punishment of the royalists of this town with this inscription: 'Lyon made war on liberty; Lyon is no more.'[7]

In practice, the physical destruction of Lyon was less extensive than the threat: all the fortifications were razed, but of the 600 houses of the rich, only about 50 were destroyed.

The punishment of the population, on the other hand, which was carried out over two months, from October 9 to December 9, was massive, wholesale and horrific. A first tribunal carried out 106 executions by firing squad; a second, 79 by guillotine. But a third tribunal moved on to mass executions, by what were called *mitraillades*, the point-blank firing of cannon filled with shot into crowds of people, in the so-called Plaine des Brotteaux, where 268 people died. In all, the number of those executed at Lyon, according to the most detailed history of the affair, was probably nearly 1,900.[8]

The punishment of the defeated rebels of the Vendée was even more savage, notably in Nantes. Nantes was a large port with a population of some 80,000, and though it had not rebelled, many thousands of defeated Vendéen rebels had flooded it in the hope of finding a port where the English would come and help them. The local authorities did not welcome these refugees, many thousands of whom they put in prison. By the late autumn of 1793 the prisons of Nantes held some 6,000 prisoners and suspects, all of whom were simply being starved and many of whom were sick or diseased. The *Convention* sent Jean-Baptiste Carrier to Nantes as an *envoyé en mission* to pacify and to punish the former rebels there.

Carrier was a strange man, an Auvergnat, ill tempered, solitary and

silent, at times dark humoured and withdrawn, at others of an excit-
ability which was at the limits of sanity, and always liable to drown his
solitude in drink. When he arrived, he assumed that he would be surrounded by traitors, and so hired a forty-man Red Guard and set up a
secret police force. His next step, on December 17, 1793, was to condemn
to death, on his own authority and without any judicial procedure, a
group of twenty-four so-called *brigands* (four of whom were teenagers),
followed two days later by a group of twenty-seven. At first the victims
were taken out in groups and then shot; some 2,600 died in this way.
Then, when that proved too slow and troublesome, Carrier instituted
what became known as *les noyades*, 'the drownings', in which men and
women were tied together naked, in so-called *mariages républicains*, and
placed in barges which were towed to the middle of the river Loire and
then scuttled. These killings took place mainly at night, and Carrier
also 'organised nightly orgies, using women *suspects* from Nantes high
society'.[9] It is estimated that between November 1793 and February
1794, 2,000 to 5,000 people were killed in these wholesale drownings.
At the same time, a military committee rounded up 4,000 rebel fugitives
from the defeats at Le Mans and Savenay and had them shot. All told,
Carrier may have been responsible for some 10,000 killings at Nantes.

He was recalled to Paris in February 1794. But that was not the end
of the slaughter and the vengeance. Despite their defeat at Savenay on
December 23, 1793, some of the rebels of the Vendée refused to give up.
General Louis Marie Turreau, the Commander-in-Chief of the *armée de
l'Ouest*, resolved to put an end to the rebellion by destroying everybody
and everything in his path, killing, burning, pillaging and raping men,
women and children. It has been reckoned that his so-called *colonnes
infernales* slaughtered as much as half the population of the *département*
of the Vendée. This was virtually a policy of genocide; but Turreau's
barbaric methods, so far from putting an end to the uprising, in fact kept
it smouldering for many more years.

20

THE GOUVERNEMENT RÉVOLUTIONNAIRE

IN PARIS, THE POLITICAL SITUATION was becoming increasingly unstable. Although Robespierre and the *Montagnards* had gained complete control of the *Convention* with the overthrow of the *Girondins*, this left Robespierre exposed to another, even greater challenge, from the explosive discontents of the *sans-culottes* below.

Robespierre had been able to overthrow the *Girondins* by enlisting the street power of the *sans-culottes*. The problem was that, in political terms, they and he were never really on the same side. The bourgeois Revolutionaries in the *Convention*, and this was true of most *Montagnards*, believed in liberal values, including the independence of elected representatives. The *sans-culottes*, by contrast, believed in direct democracy, voting out loud and in public, meaning the daily control of elected representatives, and the right to recall them. Robespierre no longer subscribed to either of these views. For the purposes of mobilising a mass war effort, and even more of staying in control, in the face of rising protests he needed a centralised, authoritarian and essentially non-democratic government.

At the height of the crisis, he scribbled in a notebook:

We must have a single will. It must be republican or royalist. If it is to be republican, we must have republican Ministers, republican newspapers, republican *députés*, a republican government. The internal dangers come from the bourgeois, and to defeat the bourgeois we must rouse the people. Everything had been prepared to place the people under the yoke of the bourgeois, and to make the defenders of the Republic perish on the scaffold.[1]

Robespierre seemed to be implying that he thought his enemies and critics were all royalists; of course he knew that this was not true. Some of the *Girondins* might have preferred to save the King's life, but they were Revolutionaries, in many cases founding Revolutionaries, just like the *Montagnards*. It is true that there was a deep split in the country, as the civil war had shown, between supporters of the Revolution and royalist sympathisers, and that this split, exacerbated by the struggle between the *Montagnards* and the *Girondins*, had led some supporters of the *Girondins* to look for allies among royalist sympathisers (and elsewhere). But this happened after the overthrow of the *Girondins*, not before.

Robespierre's phrase 'a single will' no doubt derived from the Rousseauist notion of a 'general will', as described in Rousseau's *Du contrat social* (1762), and meaning an almost creationist act of association. But what he really meant here was that France needed a single, central government and should totally suppress any possibility of opposition to it. He may have believed this was necessary partly to fight the war against the rest of Europe, but mainly to fight and win the civil war and reassert the authority of Paris over the rest of France.

What is not clear is whether Robespierre thought it was possible to reconcile his ideal of 'a single will' with the will of the French people, whose opinions and interests were manifestly widely divergent, let alone with the rule of law. There is no doubt that almost all of the founding Revolutionaries had wanted to make a Revolution which was based on the rule of law. The dilemma facing them now, especially since the overthrow of the monarchy, the execution of the King and then the civil war, was whether they could contain their Revolution within the constraints of the laws which they had created. The question was all the more acute because the challenge from the *sans-culottes* was becoming so severe that the Revolutionary leaders were able to contain it only with the Terror and the imposition of centralised, autocratic government.

Moreover, Robespierre was presiding over a deep economic split within the Revolutionary movement. The *Montagnards* were all bourgeois by upbringing and instinct, and many, despite the Revolution, were still relatively comfortably off; but the *sans-culottes* were suffering increasingly severe economic hardship. Periodically, food shortages provoked food riots, when shops were pillaged and food transports hijacked; and inflation and the uninterrupted slide of the *assignat* created an extreme widening of inequality between the haves and the have-nots. These economic difficulties generated unavoidable political conflict.

Already in February 1793, before the overthrow of the Girondins and the civil war, the *sans-culottes* had started raising their economic demands in explicit terms. On Februry 12 the forty-eight *Sections* had sent a delegation to the *Convention* with a petition demanding *le maximum*, the popular shorthand for a fixed price control for wheat. The *Convention* categorically and indignantly rejected it, and the *sans-culottes* responded with a wave of rioting and pillaging of food shops. Robespierre's reaction, on February 25, was lordly and contemptuous. 'When the people rise up, should they not have an aim worthy of themselves? Should they be concerned with miserable shopping lists? The people should rise up, not to collect sugar, but to strike down the brigands.'[2]

The annals of the Revolution have long remembered this ill-advised reference to 'miserable shopping lists', and within a few months Robespierre changed his tune. To maintain the support of the *sans-culottes*, he and his allies reluctantly made a few concessions. On April 11 they agreed to freeze the value of the *assignat* by arbitrary fiat; but of course this did not work, since they did not change their policy of issuing *assignats*. On May 4 they agreed to introduce limited price controls for cereals, and that did not work either. And on May 20 they agreed to a forced loan of £1bn to be exacted from the rich, which was popular with the lower classes but did not change the problem of food supplies.

These concessions were obviously tactical, but they may also have reflected the start of a shift in Robespierre's values, as emerged in debates in the *Convention*. It had seen many fierce disputes in the weeks leading up to the overthrow of the *Girondins*, one of which had been over the terms of a new Constitution. One of the central issues had been a question of rights: should the new Constitution, like each of its predecessors, assign the highest value to individual rights, especially the right of property (which had, at the very beginning of the Revolution, been described as 'sacred'), or should it attach greater value to social rights, such as the right to work, or even the right to life? The *Girondins* clung to the primacy of individual rights, whereas Robespierre and the *Montagnards*, under the pressure of their *sans-culotte* supporters, acknowledged the legitimacy of a swing of emphasis in favour of social rights.

In a speech to the *Jacobins* Club on April 24, Robespierre proposed a number of new articles for a Declaration of Rights.

On property he proposed:

Article 1. Property is the right which every citizen has to enjoy and dispose of that portion of goods which is guaranteed by law.
Article 2. The right of property is limited, like all others, by the obligation to respect the rights of other people.'[3]

On social rights he proposed:

Article 1. The purpose of every political association is the maintenance of the natural and imprescriptible rights of man, and the development of all his faculties.
Article 2. The principal rights of man are that of providing for the preservation of his existence, and his freedom.'[4]

The overthrow of the *Girondins* interrupted this debate. But the quarrel with the *sans-culottes* over food supplies did not go away; on the contrary, it became more acute in the months ahead.

Just before and as a preparation for the overthrow of the *Girondins*, the CSP had been stiffened, on May 30, by the addition of five new members, who included the rich and clever Marie Jean Hérault de Séchelles but also, more significantly, two of Robespierre's closest allies in the *Convention*, the crippled lawyer Georges Couthon and the young, strikingly handsome and arrogant Louis Saint-Just. This enlarged and strengthened CSP quickly drafted a new Constitution, putting it together in a week and getting it endorsed by the *Convention* on June 24, 1793, almost exactly three weeks after the overthrow of the *Girondins*.

This Constitution looked much more democratic than its predecessors. Whereas all previous Revolutionary Constitutions had seriously restricted voting rights according to property or income, the new one mandated 'universal' suffrage, though women would still be excluded.[5] It also looked as though it would go much further in meeting the demands of the more radical *sans-culottes*. These appearances turned out to be deceptive.

Like all its predecessors, the new Constitution was preceded by a *Déclaration des droits de l'homme et du citoyen*. Its first innovation, as a sop to the *sans-culottes*, was to state in its first article that 'the purpose of society is general happiness' (*le but de la société est le bonheur commun*); and it went on to proclaim all kinds of new and unprecedented liberal principles, including the right to work, the right to state support and the right to education. Even more significantly, in political terms, the new Declaration recognised the right to rebel against an unjust political authority. Article 33 said: 'Resistance to oppression is the consequence of the other rights of man';[6] and the last article, number 35, went even further: 'When the government violates the rights of the people, insurrection is for the people, and for every part of the people, the most sacred of rights and the most indispensable of duties.'[7]

But these promises of a right to resist oppression soon proved entirely empty. And despite what Robespierre had proposed in April, the new Constitution offered no limitation on the existing scope of property rights; on the contrary, it explicitly re-emphasised the value of economic liberalism.

The Constitution was submitted to a national referendum in the autumn of 1793. Because it was conducted during the civil war, some of the voting dragged on until the spring of 1794. But the Constitution passed, massively: almost nobody voted no. Yet of some 7 million qualified electors, fewer than 1.8 million voted yes. Once again, the Revolutionaries had held an election; once again, the electorate had shown complete indifference. The Constitution was ratified, but it was not popular, and that was because the Revolution was not popular. There was too much hardship: too much inflation, too many food shortages and too much unemployment. The people were no longer excited by political theories; they wanted food.

Popular protests at the government's economic policy began almost immediately. On June 25, 1793, three weeks after the overthrow of the *Girondins* and just one day after the endorsement of the Constitution, Jacques Roux led a delegation to the *Convention* in the name of the Gravilliers *Section*, together with the Bonne Nouvelle *Section*, as well as the populist *Club des Cordeliers*, to read an address which

became celebrated as the *Manifeste des Enragés*, in which he accused the
députés of passing laws 'made by the rich for the rich'. A former priest
from Angoulême who had been one of the first to swear the *Constitution civile du clergé*'s oath of conformity binding the clergy to obedience
of the Revolutionary regime, he had become one of the leaders of the
popular Gravilliers *Section*, which, after August 10, 1792, elected him as
a member of the *Commune*.

The bourgeois Revolutionaries were outraged and almost had him
arrested on the spot. But Robespierre began to realise that the mood of
popular discontent was so severe as to represent a serious threat to the
government, and that his most pressing need, now that he had brought
down the *Girondins*, was to fight off the protest movements of those
same *sans-culottes* who had enabled him to win that very recent battle.

The civil war had already made some of the Paris Revolutionaries
realise, belatedly, that the Revolution had become seriously unpopular
with far too many people in far too many parts of the country, and that
they had to do something to answer those discontents. On July 8, 1793,
Saint-Just, who had recently been elected to the CSP, suggested that
some of the rebels were less guilty than others. In his view, there were
only nine outright traitors (Charles Jean-Marie Barbaroux, Bergoing,
Jean Birotteau, Buzot, Gorsas, Lanjuinais, Jean-Baptiste Louvet, Pétion
and Jean-Baptiste Salle and five accomplices (Gardien, Gensonné,
Guadet, Mollevaut and Vergniaud); the others were merely misguided.
But Robespierre realised that it was too late to go in for word games and
persuaded the Revolutionaries that they had to make serious changes in
their policies if they were to win the support of the masses.

On June 3 the *Convention* had eased the rules governing the sale
of the property of *émigrés* to make it easier for poor people to buy. On
June 10 it had taken similar steps to ease the splitting up of communal
property. On July 17 it finally abolished, totally and without indemnity,
all remaining feudal rights, including those based on ancient historical
documents. What is so significant about this last step is that almost all
the bourgeois Revolutionaries, including the *Montagnards*, believed profoundly in legally protected property rights; it was only in the face of the
mounting political crisis that they were prepared to disavow a property
right which might be based on a written legal contract.

The *Convention* also took steps to improve the economic condition
of the middle classes. On June 8 it had raised the salaries of public officials and exempted from any contribution to the forced loan of £1bn

all married couples with an income of less than £10,000 a year and all bachelors with an annual income of less than £6,000.

Despite these concessions, popular discontent was still acute, and agitation was kept up by the *Enragés*, who were demanding direct action by the government in the economy: price controls on food, the requisition of cereals by public authorities, higher taxes on the rich, the death penalty for speculators and food hoarders. They were led by Roux, who regularly denounced the inequalities of French society: 'Liberty is only an empty phrase when one class of men can starve another with impunity; equality is only an empty phrase when the rich exercise the right of life and death over their fellow men.'[8]

Robespierre retaliated with a campaign of intimidation against Roux and through the influence of the *Jacobins* got him suspended from his editorial job at the *Commune*, with orders to change his behaviour. In fact, he would easily crush Roux and the *Enragés*; but he faced a much more serious challenge in the political campaigning of Jacques René Hébert and his supporters. For whereas Roux and his friends were scattered individuals, virtually isolated agitators without any strength of organisation, Hébert and his allies were highly organised, widely backed and strongly entrenched. Yet the two movements were similar in their origins and their political aims, and the one followed hard on the heels of the other.

Hébert was a successful popular journalist with a wide personal following and a strong political base, thanks to his senior position on the staff of the *Commune* and connections to a large network of people with radical views in the political bureaucracy, especially in the Ministry of War. He was born in 1757, the son of a jeweller, and in his youth he was more royalist than Revolutionary. But in July 1791, after the King's flight to Varennes, he had signed the petition at the Champ de Mars calling for the deposition of the King. On August 10, 1792, his *Section*, Bonne Nouvelle, had sent him as a delegate to take part in the uprising of the *Commune insurrectionnelle* and the overthrow of the King; and from there he was elected to the *Commune*, where he became the deputy to Pierre Gaspard Chaumette, who in December 1792 replaced Louis Pierre Manuel as the *procureur* (chief executive). Hébert was in a strong political position, with the *Commune* behind him, and he played a leading role the following year in the *sans-culotte* campaign against the *Girondins*.

His popularity as a journalist dated back to 1790, when he had become notorious as the publisher and the distinctive voice of the vulgar popular newspaper *Le Père Duchesne*. Le Père Duchesne (Old Man Duchesne) was ostensibly its narrator, a fictitious character of fairground farces, notionally a travelling seller of stoves, a sort of Punch and Judy figure. *Le Père Duchesne* was an eight-page publication in a small format which appeared three times a week. What made it popular among the *sans-culottes* was the tone that Hébert adopted as its voice: ultracolloquial, ultrapopular and shockingly coarse. He appealed to ordinary readers by filling up his prose with unprintable swear words, of the kind that many ordinary people use all the time but never see in print. Snooty people sneered at his vulgarity (one later critic called him 'the Homer of the dung heap'), but Hébert was not in the least abashed: 'All those who love frankness and integrity will not be alarmed by the *buggers* and the *fucks* with which I sprinkle, here and there, my joys and my angers.'[9] The snooty people were wrong and Hébert was right: within a couple of years, *Le Père Duchesne* was by far the most widely circulated newspaper in Revolutionary France.

Another reason for its success was that Hébert was well connected, and his many friends in the political bureaucracy were useful in promoting his paper's circulation. One of his most important allies was Jean-Baptiste Bouchotte, the Minister of War. Bouchotte was a plebeian army officer of quite modest talents and lowly rank, but he was a loyal supporter of the Revolution, and in April 1793 – after the treacherous Dumouriez had handed over Beurnonville, the then Minister of War, to the Austrians – he had unexpectedly been catapulted into Beurnonville's job.

As the War Minister, Bouchotte used his spending power to promote the circulation of *Le Père Duchesne,* and his Ministry bought many thousands of copies to distribute to the soldiers in the armies. In the summer of 1793 the French war machine was a large and growing administrative operation, and by September the Ministry was regularly taking 12,000 copies of *Le Père Duchesne*, or about a quarter of the circulation of 50,000 copies. What this meant was that Hébert's voice was the voice of a substantial and well-organised propaganda machine, with a large audience among the soldiery as well as the *sans-culottes*. So when he and his friends protested at food prices and food shortages and at the shortcomings of government policy, the government had to take notice.

Bouchotte also stuffed his Ministry with many other friends and supporters of Hébert. François Vincent had been an administrative clerk with a reputation as one of the leading radical speakers at the populist

Club des Cordeliers; Bouchotte plucked him up and put him in the top job, *secrétaire général*, at the Ministry of War. Also at the Ministry was Charles Philippe Ronsin, one of Bouchotte's assistants. He too was an old soldier, who had given up soldiering to write patriotic plays and had then returned to military service at the start of the Revolution, as a Captain in the *Garde nationale*. In 1793, on the strength of his relations with Bouchotte, he was promoted at high speed up the ranks, from Captain to Brigadier in the space of a week, and fought in the Vendée, where he defeated La Rochejaquelein; in September 1793 he was promoted to General-in-Chief of the *Armée révolutionnaire* in Paris.

Another influential *Hébertiste*, not at the Ministry of War but an administrator with the *Commune* of Paris, was Antoine Momoro. Born in 1756, he was a qualified letterist, printer and librarian, and in 1789 he published a printer's manual; he then acquired the valuable position of printer to the *Commune* of Paris. He joined the *Cordeliers* Club, where he rose to become Secretary; as a good radical, he took part in the demonstration at the Champ de Mars in July 1791, and was briefly imprisoned. In September 1792, after the overthrow of the King, he published the radical pamphlet *Déclaration des droits*, in which he demanded restrictions on the property rights of landowners. In the campaign in the Vendée, he worked for Ronsin.

Momoro is usually credited with the popularisation of the slogan *Liberté, égalité, fraternité*. Some Robespierrists claim that it had been devised three years earlier by Robespierre, but most people believe that it did not become widespread until June 21, 1793, when Momoro persuaded Jean Nicolas Pache, then the Mayor of Paris, a fellow *Hébertiste* and a fellow critic of the ruling *Montagnard* clique, to have it inscribed on all the public monuments of the capital.

Hébert was more than just a journalistic protestor at food shortages: he was also a political agitator with a wide-ranging agenda. When the *Convention* seemed to be dragging its feet on the annexation of Savoy and on the trial of General Custine, the joint Commander-in-Chief of the Armies of the Rhine, the North, the Moselle and the Ardennes, who was accused of defeatism if not actually of collusion with the Austrians, Hébert began to suspect that some of the *députés* must be pacifists or royalists, and he did not hesitate to use *Le Père Duchesne* openly to accuse the *Montagne* of harbouring traitors (*les traîtres qui siègent à la Montagne*). As a result of this intimidating pressure, Custine's trial was cut short, and he was guillotined on August 28, 1793.

Hébert also campaigned against the increasingly authoritarian powers of the government, especially the so-called committees of government. He was not wrong in his choice of target; for Robespierre was moving towards the establishment of a centralised, all-powerful Revolutionary government, mainly through the CSP. When that committee was reappointed on July 10, 1793, with a revised membership, Robespierre's allies Couthon and Saint-Just were kept on but Danton was dropped. Later that month, on July 27, Robespierre himself became a member; and a fortnight later the military authority of the Committee was substantially stiffened when it brought in two ambitious young army officers, Lazare Carnot (whose fame would later be popularised with the nickname *l'Organisateur de la Victoire*) and his friend Claude Antoine Prieur-Duvernois, known as Prieur de la Côte d'Or, both captains in the engineer corps.

Hébert's verdict was uncompromising: 'So long as the *comités* usurp all the powers, we shall never have a government, or we shall have a terrible one ... We shall never have liberty, and our Constitution will be only a chimera so long as the Ministers are no more than urchins at the beck and call of the lowest sweepers of the *Convention*.'[10]

This was dangerous talk, but Hébert was undeterred and started to plan a major protest demonstration against the regime. In August 28, at the *Jacobins*, he proposed leading a delegation to the *Convention* with a petition backed by the forty-eight Paris *Sections* and their *sociétés populaires* to demand a purge of the general staffs, the dismissal of all nobles from public employment and other measures of public safety (*salut public*).

The *sociétés populaires* were political clubs frequented by *sans-culottes* in each of the Paris *Sections*. They sprang into much greater activity in the autumn of 1793 when the government tried to suppress political agitation by the *sans-culottes* by restricting the frequency of the meetings of the *Sections'* official *Assemblées générales*; so the *sans-culottes* transferred much of their political energies into their unofficial *sociétés populaires*.

Hébert was backed by his friend and ally the *Montagnard député* Jacques Billaud-Varenne, a writer of violently radical left-wing tracts and an unemployed lawyer who had just returned from a visit to the *armée du Nord* at the front. Billaud-Varenne came to the *Convention* with a sweeping denunciation of the paralysis of the government and proposed the establishment of a commission to supervise the execution of the laws and to send the guilty to the guillotine.

Robespierre immediately objected to this plan. 'There is a danger', he said, 'that such a commission would busy itself more with personal rivalries than with loyal supervision and thus become in fact a *Comité* of denunciation. This is not the first time that I see that there exists a deceitful system for paralysing the *Comité de salut public* while seeming to help it in its work.'[11]

Danton offered a compromise: rather than create an independent commission to supervise the action of the CSP, the *Convention* should instead appoint three additional members to it. The *Convention* passed his proposal on to the CSP, which simply sat on it; for if it accepted the idea of three new members, Billaud-Varenne would have to be one of them, and he was an open critic of the government.

Events were also pushing hard against the regime. For on September 2, 1793, the first reports reached Paris of the surrender to the English of Toulon and the entire French Mediterranean fleet, which was confirmed officially on September 4. Hébert's planned demonstration was unstoppable.

Some historians think that he had ulterior motives. 'Was he planning to seize power?' ask Tulard et al. 'His behaviour fully proves it.'[12] Mathiez takes a similar view: 'The moment had come, [the *Hébertistes*] thought, to take power for themselves.'[13] They offer no specific evidence to back their speculation; but Hébert's protest movement could easily have been seen as a threat to the government.

In any case, popular pressure for a radical change in government policies was rising irresistibly from below. The first partial price control measure, the so-called *maximum*, introduced on May 4, was backfiring badly. Because it was limited to the local price of wheat, it was provoking speculative movements of the commodity as each *département* tried to secure supplies from elsewhere, amounting to an economic tug of war and causing spasmodic shortages of wheat and bread in many places.

In Paris on the morning of September 4, 1793, a crowd of some 2,000 angry *sans-culottes* poured into the Place de Grève in front of the *Hôtel de ville*, crying out, 'Bread, bread!' (*Du pain, du pain!*). Some accounts suggest that Roux led the demonstration, and no doubt he was there. But it seems clear that the main instigator was Hébert. Chaumette, the chief executive of the *Commune*, tried to calm things down by telling the protestors that the *Convention* had undertaken to introduce general price controls on all foods within a week,[14] but they shouted him down: 'It is not promises we need, but bread, and right away.'[15]

Seemingly abandoning the idea of appeasement, Chaumette then climbed on to a table to harangue the crowd: 'Well, I too have been poor, and as a result I know what it is to be poor! This is an open war of the rich against the poor; they want to crush us; well, we must prevent them, we must crush them ourselves; we have the strength to do so!'[16]

As Chaumette's second in command at the *Commune*, Hébert persuaded the demonstrators to disperse, but to meet again the next day, this time at the *Convention*. Thus on September 5, 1793, a large mob turned up at the *Convention*, with Hébert at their head; they stormed right into the hall and intimidated the *députés* into passing a sweeping series of repressive laws: the arrest of suspects; the creation of an *Armée révolutionnaire* of 6,000 foot soldiers and 1,200 gunners; the expansion of the *Tribunal révolutionnaire* and its division into four parts; and a forced loan of £100m to be exacted from the rich.

But if Hébert had been thinking of a coup d'état, he was decisively outplayed by Robespierre; for later that day another deputation came to the *Convention*, this time from the *Club des Jacobins*, led by Robespierre and accompanied by delegations from all forty-eight *Sections*. They demanded that the *Girondins* be put on trial; and they too called for the creation of an *Armée révolutionnaire* (whose task would be to commandeer all necessary food supplies, by force if necessary) and for the dismissal of all nobles from public employment. But the crucial new demand of the *Jacobin* deputation was that the Terror be 'put on the agenda' (*mise à l'ordre du jour*).[17]

No one could possibly have known exactly what this would mean. Versions of this tempestuous day differ somewhat, and there are different accounts of when the term *Terreur* was first used in a Revolutionary sense and by whom. Mathiez tells us that it was Jean-Baptiste Royer, a *député* of the *Convention* and a constitutional bishop (that is, one who had taken the oath of the *Constitution civile du clergé*), who had first used the precise words *Qu'on place la Terreur à l'ordre du jour*, and that was five days beforehand.[18] According to Michelet, Bertrand Barère said that it was 'the *Armée révolutionnaire* which, in the words of the *Commune*, "would put the Terror on the agenda"'.[19] This kind of confusion about details is characteristic of accounts of the Revolution at its most turbulent moments. Yet it is now a widely accepted tradition that it was on this turbulent day, September 5, 1793, when the *Terreur* began and was well and truly 'put on the agenda'.

There is also some uncertainty about exactly what Robespierre and his *Jacobin* delegation said, but the deep message was unmistakable: they had decided to upstage the *sans-culotte* demonstrators by subsuming their demands in a new and far-reaching political agenda. Robespierre was massively raising the political stakes in his determination to stay in charge at whatever cost. On September 6, 1793, one day after the declaration of the Terror, he and the CSP accepted two new members: Jean-Marie Collot d'Herbois, a frustrated actor; and Billaud-Varenne, both *Hébertistes*. If Hébert had had any subversive plans, this would have dealt them a blow, as two of his leading supporters had now been effectively co-opted by the government.

On September 11, 1793, as Chaumette had promised the demonstrators on September 5, the *Convention* passed a regime unifying the price control of cereals throughout France, and on September 29 it passed a comprehensive *maximum général* covering prices and wages. For all foods other than cereals, the prices would be those of 1790 plus one-third; for wages the rates would be those of 1790 plus 50 per cent.

Almost immediately after the introduction of these price control laws, the *Montagnards* changed their mind about the new Constitution, and in early October they made clear that they had no intention of implementing it. A new Constitution implied that there would be new elections, and they did not dare to jeopardise their hold on power. They would instead continue governing – without a Constitution. In a melodramatic gesture, which they hoped would be taken as a symbolic earnest of their democratic sincerity, they solemnly placed the text of the stillborn Constitution in an ark of cedar wood, as if in preservation for some indefinite future. It was never taken out again, and never implemented. But it remained for many years afterwards the benchmark for nostalgic Revolutionaries of a radical, democratic Constitution. Whenever things went wrong, their demand was always 'Bring back the Constitution of 1793'.

It is not clear what, if anything, had happened to make the *Montagnards* change direction so dramatically. They might have been thrown off balance when the meagre results of the constitutional referendum started to come in. It is also possible that Robespierre and others had only just appreciated the severity of the various crises ahead, when France was fighting wars on so many fronts at home and abroad, and had concluded that the country could not afford a liberal Constitution. It seems just as likely that the *Montagnards* had never intended to implement their new Constitution in the first place, and that the entire exercise, from the drafting to the referendum, was simply a public relations manoeuvre.

In any case, on October 10, 1793, the *Montagnards* got the *Convention* to announce that 'the provisional government of France [would] be Revolutionary until the peace' (*le gouvernement provisoire de la France serait révolutionnaire jusqu'à la paix*).[20] As Saint-Just explained: 'In the circumstances in which the Republic finds itself, the Constitution cannot be set up; it would be destroyed by means of itself, it would become the guarantee of attacks on liberty, because it would lack the force necessary to suppress them.'[21]

The *Montagnards* made many efforts over the next few months to justify and explain this anomalous situation. In December 1793, Robespierre contrasted the constitutional order and the Revolutionary order: 'The latter submits to less uniform and less rigorous rules, because the circumstances in which it finds itself are stormy and unstable and above all because it is forced constantly to deploy new and rapid resources to meet new and pressing dangers ... We must organise the despotism of liberty to crush the despotism of kings.'[22]

The expression 'despotism of liberty' needs little comment.

From this point, the CSP became the government of France. At first there were thirteen members; but one of them, Jacques Thuriot, a firm supporter of Danton, resigned on September 20 because of irreconcilable differences with Robespierre. The resulting membership of twelve remained permanent for the next ten months, until the fall of Robespierre and his allies on July 28, 1794. Of the twelve, nine were lawyers; two were in their twenties, six were in their thirties, another two were just forty, and only two were significantly into their forties.

In principle, the CSP was subject to the legislative jurisdiction of the *Convention*. In practice, it dominated the *Convention*, and in almost every respect it established methods of operation that were a total departure from the traditions of the *Convention* and of all the previous National Assemblies.

The plenary meetings of all of the previous National Assemblies, like those of the Paris *Sections*, were very large, public occasions, always noisy, usually rowdy, with many people coming and going and with much rude clamour from the galleries. The debates were managed, sometimes with difficulty, by the elected President of the day, who tried to keep them under the control of parliamentary rules of procedure, which had been developed relatively recently by the Revolutionaries themselves.

These debates were dominated by great set speeches, often literary and intellectual and almost always, by modern standards, interminably long and elaborately rhetorical. The noise was great, because the accoustics of all the chambers where they met were terrible, and the speakers usually had to shout to be heard. Even then they were always liable to be interrupted, not only by noisy heckling by other members but even more by barracking from the galleries.

There was no official record of the proceedings of the National Assemblies, but there was an extended, unofficial account in the daily journal *Le Moniteur*, issued by the celebrated publisher and editor Charles Joseph Panckoucke, which many people treated almost as if it were an official record. In addition, the National Assembly might order some of the best-received speeches to be printed and distributed.

The debates in the leading clubs were followed almost as assiduously as those of the National Assembly, especially, of course, those at the *Jacobin* Club; and these clubs too might order the most popular speeches to be printed and distributed. There was also a proliferation of private pamphlets and news-sheets, reporting or commenting on the proceedings in the National Assembly or the political clubs. So anyone interested in the political events of the day was faced with a vast array of printed information, fact and interpretation.

The proceedings of the CSP were utterly different, but in a most modern, and sinister, sense: for the meetings were closed, private and totally secret. The Committee met twice a day, at 9 a.m. and 7 p.m.; there was no published record of the proceedings and no voting record. The only reports were those spread by rumour and alarm. It was this secrecy which gradually made it powerful and then feared; it would evolve into the archetypical institution of a police state.

Of the twelve members of the CSP[23] (excluding Thuriot), only six survived the turbulence of the Robespierre Terror. One was guillotined in the spring of 1794, on Robespierre's orders (Hérault de Séchelles); three were guillotined when Robespierre fell (Robespierre, Couthon and Saint-Just); and two were deported in the settlement of accounts after the fall of Robespierre (Billaud-Varenne and Collot d'Herbois). This rate of fatality corresponds, very approximately, to my own rough estimate of the average danger to life of taking part in the Revolution.[24]

21

THE *TERREUR*

THE *TERREUR*, which was announced on September 5, 1793, lasted until the fall of Robespierre ten months later, on July 28, 1794. It came without any clearly defined aims or policy, and it was carried out without any detectable rules; its main rationale seems to have been to prop up the authority of Robespierre and his *gouvernement révolutionnaire*, and its method the indiscriminate threat of death to anyone who was, or who could be accused of being, a threat to the Republic.

The most immediate challenges to the new government were to combat a wave of protests from the rest of France at what was perceived as the dictatorship of the Paris *sans-culottes* and to face down the growing protests of those same *sans-culottes* at the increasing harshness of their conditions of life.

The Terror went into operation officially with the *Loi des suspects* (Law of Suspects), on September 29, 1793, followed by the mobilisation of the *Armée révolutionnaire*. This army was something the mob had demanded at the insurrectionary demonstration of September 5, to enforce the new system of price controls, *le maximum* (described in earlier chapters). This price control regime did not work any better than the old one and in many ways was much worse. It was far more detailed and required more and more policing to make it function, often increasingly intrusive and repressive, because more and more people tried to get round it. The wage controls upset almost everybody: in the countryside, many farmers found they were required to pay their workers more than they could afford; in the towns, many of the *sans-culottes* found they were expected to take a sharp pay cut because the war, military conscription and the consequent labour shortages had already increased effective wage levels well above the legal maximum.

The primary purpose of the *Armée révolutionnaire* was to ensure adequate food supplies by physically commandeering what was required, by force if necessary. It consisted of 6,000 men and 1,200 gunners, each paid 40 sous a day, and was under the command of the *sans-culotte* General Charles Ronsin, who had joined the *Garde nationale* as a Captain and then climbed the ranks to become deputy to the Minister of War, Jean-Baptiste Bouchotte. The second purpose of the *Armée révolutionnaire* was to act as the paramilitary arm of the *Terreur* and to enforce the Law of Suspects. The insurrectionists' demand had been meant for Paris only; but in imitation of that precedent, many *armées revolutionnaires* sprang up spontaneously all over France on the initiative of local *Jacobins*, of local *sociétés populaires* or of locally based *envoyés en mission* from the *Convention*, and they too became an important part of the apparatus for carrying out the policy of the Terrorist regime. At one point there were fifty-six Revolutionary armies in the provinces, totalling around 30,000 men.[1]

The Law of Suspects was loosely drawn, and no one knows exactly how many people were arrested during the period of the Terror; it was certainly tens of thousands and may well have been hundreds of thousands. The American historian Donald Greer has estimated the total at around 500,000, Mathiez and Soboul at 300,000. To put these figures into perspective, the French population at the time was around 28 million, so the top estimate of arrests would have been about 1.8 per cent of the total, which must represent something like 5 per cent of the adult males.[2]

In general, suspects were arrested locally, either by the *armée révolutionnaire* or by the *comité révolutionnaire* of the local *Section*, notionally under the supervision of the *Comité de sûreté générale*, the national police committee in Paris. The *comités révolutionnaires* were offshoots of the Parisian *Sections* or their equivalents elsewhere in France. On March 21, 1793, in reaction to the wave of panic caused by bad news on two fronts, a series of victories by the rebel forces in the Vendée in the west and the defeat of the French army by the Austrians at Neerwinden in the northeast, the *Convention* had ordered the setting up of *comités de surveillance*, which were in effect local police committees; and after the launch of the Terror the *Loi des suspects* gave them the power to arrest all 'enemies of liberty'.

So though France did not have an effective system of national government, it did, from the spring of 1793, have a national network of some 20,000 police committees, which, though completely untrained, undisciplined, unorganised and uncontrolled, had the power to set the Terror in motion. This locally based system for arresting suspects obviously responded to local demands and reflected local sentiment. Many of those arrested were nobles, and many were foreigners; but many others were described in the records of their arrests simply as 'suspects', which implies that they might have been just strangers or outsiders. The law was designed to appease and to feed on local paranoia, which it did, and must have been used for the settling of local scores. Since many suspects were not accused of specific crimes, many did not stand trial and were instead just held in prison until after the fall of Robespierre, on average probably for about eight months.

The Law of Suspects constituted a virtually explicit abandonment of the Revolutionaries' founding principle of a state based on law, and Robespierre made it clear that he did not think there was any need to prove the charges against a suspect: 'Public notoriety accuses a citizen of crimes of which no written proofs exist, but whose proof is in the heart of all indignant citizens.'[3] Tocqueville took a rather different view of the Terror. 'The Revolution had been prepared', he wrote, 'by the most civilised classes of the nation and carried out by the most uncivilised and the roughest of people.'[4]

The first and most spectacular challenge to the Revolutionary government, and one of the main reasons for its existence, came from the civil war that had broken out in many parts of France after the overthrow of the *Girondins*. In fact, it turned out to be a double challenge: could the central authorities in Paris defeat the rebels, and could they discipline the forces which they had sent out to inflict this defeat?

They seemed to succeed at the first challenge: by the end of 1793 the rebellions in the French provinces had been put down, with the recapture of Lyon on October 9, the crushing victory over the Vendéens at Cholet on October 17 and the fall of Toulon on December 19. The

second challenge was more difficult. After General François Westermann boasted publicly of how many rebels he had killed in the Vendée
in December 1793, he was recalled to Paris and bundled up with Danton
and a miscellaneous cluster of friends and associates to be sent before the
Tribunal révolutionnaire, which condemned him to death by guillotine.
General Louis Marie Turreau took over the command of the campaign
later in the year, and when he bragged of his *colonnes infernales* and
of his virtually genocidal extermination of enormous numbers of Vendéens, he too was recalled to Paris and put on trial; but he was acquitted.

Jean-Baptiste Carrier, notorious for his wholesale slaughter of rebels
at Nantes, including the infamous *noyades*, was eventually denounced
and on February 8, 1794, recalled to Paris; but it was not until December
of that year, long after the fall of Robespierre, that he was sent before
the *Tribunal révolutionnaire*. It condemned him to death, but he was the
only one of the many *envoyés en mission* from the *Convention* to suffer
that extreme penalty.

The Revolutionaries in Paris mostly gave local commanders or
envoyés en mission a free rein in the civil war, but not in the case of Lyon.
During its seige, the *Convention* sent nine *envoyés en mission* to supervise
operations. The most highly placed was Georges Couthon, a member
of the CSP and one of Robespierre's closest allies. Soon after Lyon fell
he was recalled to Paris, on the grounds that he was too moderate, and
Jean-Marie Collot d'Herbois and Joseph Fouché took his place. These
two were much more ferocious, and they permitted, if they did not
order, the execution of almost 1,900 people, including the notorious
mass slaughter, with cannon firing grapeshot, in the Plaine des Brotteaux. Fouché was recalled to Paris, where Robespierre denounced him
and got him expelled from the *Club des Jacobins*, but that was all. Collot
d'Herbois was also recalled; but as a member of the CSP he was virtually untouchable. It was not until after the fall of Robespierre that he
was put on trial and deported to French Guiana.

It seems clear that one of the central weaknesses of the management
of the Revolution was the lack of a dividing line between those whose
job it was to formulate political policy and those whose job it was to
carry it out. This ambiguity of responsibility was encapsulated in the
role of the *envoyés en mission*.

At the same time, the extreme ruthlessness of the Terror may have played an important part in shifting the French military effort from a series of defeats towards the beginnings of victory. The first mass mobilisation decree, the so-called *levée des 300,000*, launched at the start of 1793, had failed to raise the required number of men. This was partly because it was deeply unpopular among the peasants in many areas, most of whom did not want to join the army, especially if they lived far from the front, partly because it was not universal and partly because the government had left to local bodies the controversial choice of whom to send. But on August 23, 1793, the *sans-culottes* succeeded in pushing through the *Convention* another *levée en masse*, and from that moment military service became universal and compulsory for unmarried men and widowers aged between eighteen and twenty-five. The Revolutionaries expected this to bring in 483,000 men, and in the end, despite long delays, shortage of equipment and a certain amount of 'leakage' through desertions and medical certificates for exemption, it succeeded in raising 300,000.

With these new forces, the Revolutionaries started rolling back the Austrian invaders with a handful of important victories: Hondschoote on September 6–8, Wattignies on October 15–16, Wissembourg on December 26–29. This crucial shift from defeat to victory transformed popular enthusiasm for recruitment, and by the spring of 1794, through the growing success of mass mobilisation, the progressive requisitioning of supplies and the nationalisation of arms manufacture, the CSP had created a military force of about 1 million men divided into twelve armies. The most important feature of these armies was their uniformity. In the early years of the Revolution there had been a clear division between the traditional regiments of the line, with their formal loyalty to the King, and the *Gardes nationales*, created by the Revolutionaries. The traditional regiments had been led by noble officers and were distinguished by their white uniforms (which gave them the nickname *les blancs*); the *Gardes nationales* elected their own officers and wore blue uniforms (and were called *les bleus*). In the spring of 1793, the Revolutionaries had decided that they must have a single army, and gradually, against resistance, they amalgamated *les blancs* and *les bleus*. This was a slow process, but it resulted in standards of discipline applicable to all ranks, a systematic clean-out of the officer corps and an impressive wave of promotions of promising young generals.

Unlike *envoyés en mission*, military leaders were often ruthlessly punished for failure. In 1789, Jean Nicolas Houchard was still only a captain after thirty-five years of service and now fifty years old; with the Revolution, his plebeian origins served him well and favoured his rapid promotion in 1793, first to command the *armée de la Moselle*, then the *armée du Rhin*, and then the *armée du Nord*, with which he brought off the major victory of Hondschoote. At that point, however, things went seriously wrong for him: against the orders of the CSP, he decided on a withdrawal, which he could not control, and it turned into a rout; he was stripped of his command, arrested, sent before the *Tribunal révolutionnaire*, condemned to death, and guillotined on November 15, 1793. Lazare Hoche was luckier: after his precocious promotion from ordinary soldier to Captain to General of Division, he was beaten by the Austrians at the battle of Kaiserslauten but recovered to get his revenge at Woerth in December; and although a jealous young rival, General Jean-Charles Pichegru, enlisted the support of Saint-Just to get him arrested, on April 1, 1794, he escaped execution and was released from prison after the fall of Robespierre.

The *Terreur* had risen in intensity, with denunciations based on the *Loi des suspects*, show trials in the *Tribunal révolutionnaire* and public, spectacular guillotinings in the Place de la Concorde. If it was meant to stop anti-government agitation, it failed; for while Robespierre's domination of the *Convention* was uncontested, his allies the *sans-culottes* continued to protest at their hardships and at the shortcomings of government policy. He responded by cracking down on the most public protesters, the *Enragés*, and he had their leader, Jacques Roux, arrested. Roux spent the next few months in and out of prison, but he kept on with his newspaper and his political campaigning until he learned that he was to be sent to the *Tribunal révolutionnaire*. Seeing that all was lost, he stabbed himself and died of his wounds on February 10, 1794.

After Roux's arrest, Robespierre found it relatively easy to intimidate the other *Enragés*. Jean-Théophile Leclerc, an employee in the Paris postal service from the *Section des Droits-de-l'Homme*, had been publishing an inflammatory newspaper in memory of Marat, but after he received a sharp warning from the *Jacobins*, he closed it down and left Paris. Jean-François Varlet, another Paris postman and a popular but noisy street orator, was imprisoned for a couple of months and effectively silenced. Two leading protesters who stood out in this all-male world were women. One was the thirty-year-old Claire Lacombe, a one-time actress from the South of France who had come to Paris to join the Revolution. She rose to prominence through the women's Revolutionary group *Club des citoyennes républicaines révolutionnaires*, which she cofounded and in which she served as Secretary and then as President. When the authorities put a stop to her Revolutionary activities, she went back on the road as an actress. The other was Pauline Léon, a twenty-five-year-old chocolate seller who had joined the Revolution at the beginning and was the other founder of the *Club des citoyennes républicaines révolutionnaires*. She married Leclerc in 1793 and, under governmental intimidation, gave up her Revolutionary agitation for married life. The shutting down of the *Enragés* demonstrated the determination of Robespierre and the other bourgeois Revolutionaries to stay on top. They had reluctantly enacted some price and wage controls, but they would go no further. Their response to protests was more Terror.

Another woman who achieved notoriety by protesting at the shortcomings of the Revolution was Olympe de Gouges (1748–93), but she was an intellectual, a novelist and a playwright, and she expressed her protests through her writings rather than as an agitator in street demonstrations. She campaigned ceaselessly for the abolition of slavery and for the rights of women, political as well as sexual. It was at the home of her friend Sophie de Grouchy, the wife of Condorcet, that she made her most famous remark: 'A woman has the right to mount the scaffold. She must have an equal right to mount the speaker's platform.' After the fall of the *Girondins*, Gouges was arrested as a sympathiser and a covert royalist; she was sentenced to death for sedition and royalism on November 2, 1793, and executed the next day.

The main instrument of the Terror was the *Tribunal révolutionnaire*. It had been set up in Paris in March 1793 with the task of trying those who were accused of having committed any of a number of vague offences: against liberty or equality, against the unity or indivisibility of the Republic or against the internal or external safety and security of the state. The Law of Suspects expanded its remit by severely restricting freedom of the press, calling for the arrest of 'all those who by their writings have shown themselves partisans of tyranny or federalism and enemies of liberty';[5] a decree on December 5, 1793 (*décret du 14 frimaire*), banning any expression of a challenge to the powers of the CSP continued the trend. A number of provinces had established regional *tribunaux révolutionnaires*, on an ad hoc basis, but on May 21, 1794, the government decided that the Terror would be centralised, with all the *tribunaux* in the provinces closed and all trials held in Paris.

In its first months, the *Tribunal révolutionnaire* had proved rather legalistic and reasonable and had produced more acquittals than condemnations. After the fall of the *Girondins* and the outbreak of the civil war, the *Montagnards* decided that it must achieve more politically acceptable figures. Its President, Jacques Montané, a traditionally trained lawyer from Toulouse, was charged with *moderantisme* and hustled out of office. The Tribunal was substantially strengthened and expanded, with Montané replaced as the President by Martial Joseph Herman, a thirty-four-year-old criminal judge from Artois and Pas-de-Calais and an old acquaintance and loyal follower of Robespierre. He was a man of calm demeanour, quiet speech and sinister appearance; he squinted terribly, to the point where he seemed one-eyed. He was a dutiful servant of the Terror, but when he failed to satisfy Robespierre's expectations, he too was removed and in April 1794 replaced by another Robespierre crony, René François Dumas.

The Tribunal's new chief prosecutor was Antoine Quentin Fouquier-Tinville, a forty-seven-year-old lawyer from a modest family of minor nobility in Picardy who had been a prosecutor at the court of the Châtelet in Paris. In 1783, in his late thirties, he had fallen on hard times, lost his job and got deeply into debt. For the next nine years his life and his career had remained in the doldrums; but in 1792 he was rescued by Camille Desmoulins, the Revolutionary journalist, who happened to be a distant cousin of his. Desmoulins was also a friend and protégé of Danton, and when Danton was briefly the Minister of Justice, he had given Desmoulins the powerful position of Joint Secretary General of the Ministry. Thus Desmoulins was able to help his cousin become a jury foreman in the *Tribunal du 17 août*, created specially to try the defenders of the Tuileries Palace.

This first political Tribunal was closed down three months later, on November 29, 1792. But when the *Tribunal révolutionnaire* was set up, Fouquier-Tinville was appointed its chief prosecutor, and he quickly turned himself into a model petty bureaucrat of death, a sort of butler in the service of Robespierre and the Terror. He was always at the office at eight o'clock in the morning, where he would meet the public executioner to arrange the number of tumbrils required for the day's executions. In the evening, after the day's session, he would leave the court to report to the CSP on the Tribunal's performance. There he was constantly reproached by Robespierre and his allies for the slowness and moderation of the Tribunal; and Robespierre progressively got the rules of the court stripped down so as to whittle away all possibilities of defence. Fouquier-Tinville faithfully followed the new rules as they were introduced.

When, after the fall of Robespierre, the Terror was finally closed down, Dumas, Fouquier-Tinville and Herman were all guillotined for their part in it: Dumas fell with Robespierre and was executed on the same day, July 28, 1794; Fouquier-Tinville and Herman were executed, with fourteen other members of the *Tribunal révolutionnaire*, ten months later, on May 7, 1795.

The first manifestation of the Terror was the mass arrests under the Law of Suspects, possibly as many as 500,000. Many of these people were never charged, because there was no evidence against them, but they stayed in prison anyway for varying lengths of time between September 1793 and August 1794. The number of people who died as a result of the Terror was much smaller: according to Donald Greer, it may have totalled 35,000 to 40,000. The reason why this figure is so imprecise is that it includes all those who were slaughtered indiscriminately in wholesale killings in the civil war, like the mass executions at Nantes, Lyon and Toulon. If one counts only those executed after trial before some kind of formal tribunal, and killed one by one, the recorded number of Terror victims falls to 16,594, of whom half were executed during the first wave of the Terror, between November 1793 and January 1794.

My impression is that significantly more than 40 per cent of those who played any notable role in the Revolution may have died a violent death. During my work on this book, I gradually built up a list of people whose names occurred in various episodes of the Revolution, and by the end it totalled 290 names. Of this total, eighty-four, or 29 per cent, were executed, mainly by guillotine; and forty-one, or 14 per cent, died violently in other ways, some of them by suicide to avoid the guillotine. In other words, 43 per cent of those who played a big enough role in the Revolution for history to have recorded their names had a violent death. This list is of course wholly unscientific; it is just a stochastic sample, of those who cropped up in the course of my reading. Almost all of these deaths occurred in 1793–94.

In the *Tribunal révolutionnaire* of Paris alone, the number of people indicted was 5,343, of whom 2,747 (or just over 51 per cent) were condemned to death and executed. Of those executed, 20 per cent were members of the former (*ci-devant*) nobility, 9 per cent members of the clergy and 71 per cent members of the Third Estate, of whom 41 per cent were artisans and 28 per cent farmers. The vast mass of the victims of the Terror were not particularly significant, except that they had been individually marked down, no doubt by some local adversary or other, as enemies of the Revolution: four-fifths of those condemned were charged with such intangible offences as *complôts* (plots), *attitudes*, *sentiments* or *écrits* (writings), and even the possession of a picture of a crucifix could lead to the guillotine on an accusation of *fanatisme religieux*.[6] If such a large majority of cases was of such manifest absurdity, at least some of the proceedings of the *Tribunal révolutionnaire* must have occurred in a general miasma of paranoia or public hysteria.

The Terror was intended to strengthen the authority of the Revolutionary Government, and in many ways it did; yet the Revolution now entered a period of frenzy and fear, of public and private accusations, of secret denunciations and betrayals, of noisy protests and furtive political conspiracies and of increasingly ferocious repression.

Almost from the beginning, the policies of the Revolutionaries, starting with the wholesale disposal of Church property (*biens nationaux*) and the massive issue of *assignats*, had created conditions that could only encourage speculation and therefore corruption. Even in those early and relatively innocent days, the corruption was so widespread that Robespierre was conspicuous by not being part of it, hence his nickname: *l'Incorruptible*. Now the deliberate dismantling of the principles of law underlying the state created the conditions for lawlessness by all, while France's plunge into hyperinflation and economic confusion, caused essentially by those policy mismanagements, resulted in even more rampant speculation, corruption and embezzlement, especially by the few who were clever enough, unscrupulous enough and brave enough to take maximum advantage of the chaos and the risks. It was not an accident that the authorities brought accusations of corruption and financial wrongdoing in two of the key show trials at the peak of the Terror. The real purposes of these trials were political, but that was wholly concealed and the legal cases largely or partly trumped up; yet it was also a fact that corruption and financial wrongdoing had penetrated to the heart of the Revolution.

Besides helping to corrupt the Revolution's heart, the Terror became the centre of a life-and-death struggle for its soul. In this struggle, the *Jacobin* Club was the theatre where moral and political issues were debated and settled, under the increasingly dominant shadow of Robespierre, who demanded conformity and punished dissenters, in the last resort with expulsion from the club. It had long been one of the principal centres of debate in the Revolution; it now became one of the main moral instruments of the Terror.

Michelet memorably described the *Jacobins* as a latter-day equivalent, in the Revolutionary context, of the Inquisition. Desmoulins had already drawn the analogy in 1791, in his newspaper *Les Révolutions de France et de Brabant*, where he had said: 'The *Jacobin* Club is the nation's true research committee … Not only is it the Grand Inquisitor, which frightens the aristocrats; it is also the great reformer, which puts right abuses and comes to the help of all the citizens'.[7] By 1793, under the Terror, its role had transformed from reform to repression.

After the crisis of 1791, following the flight of the King, the *Jacobins* had expanded enormously, and by September 1793 their national membership may have amounted, through provincial sister clubs, to about 500,000, so at the time of the Terror they constituted a complete national network, almost a shadow government. Their main meeting place in Paris was what had once been a Dominican monastery (*Couvent des Jacobins*) in the rue Saint-Honoré, and Michelet believed that the members of the *Jacobin* Club had insensibly absorbed some of the key characteristics of the previous occupiers, whose order had been the driving force behind the Catholic Inquisition in the thirteenth to sixteenth centuries:

> As was the building, so were its inhabitants. The new, like the old, had, as a fixed idea, a narrow orthodoxy … Their rigidity of attitude, their outward fixity, were all the more necessary to them because in reality their creed was very fluid. Whatever change the situation produced, whatever deviations it imposed on their doctrines, they insisted on unity.[8]

Michelet's history vividly underlines the character and the power of the *Jacobin* Club as the thought police of the Revolution. If the *Jacobins* believed some new doctrine, that was the required orthodoxy, and to protest against it was to risk expulsion from the club, which could easily be the first step towards being denounced to the *Tribunal révolutionnaire*.

'It was not a small matter to be excluded from the *Jacobins*', says Michelet. 'This formidable society, while keeping the form of a club, was in reality a grand jury of accusers. Its membership list was the book of life or death.'[9]

One of the first high-profile victims of the Terror was the former Queen, Marie-Antoinette, the widow of Louis XVI. She was born in 1755, married to Louis in 1770 and became Queen at nineteen, when he succeeded to the throne in 1774. Their first son, Louis Joseph François Xavier, was born in October 1781 but died in June 1789. Their second son, the Dauphin Louis Charles, was born on March 27, 1785, and remained in prison after the execution of his parents. It seems likely that he died there, at the age of ten, probably on June 8, 1795.

After the execution of the King, Marie-Antoinette was transferred from the prison-palace of the Temple to the grim prison of the Conciergerie on the Île de la Cité in the middle of the Seine, now becoming known as the antechamber of death. She was brought before the *Tribunal révolutionnaire* on October 14, 1793, and tried for high treason. Her trial caused no difficulty, for she was widely unpopular and often suspected, as a member of the Austrian ruling family, of being in league with France's enemies. She was condemned two days later, October 16, and guillotined the same day.

Much more problematic was the long-deferred trial of the *Girondins*. Some of those who had been proscribed at the time of their overthrow, on June 2, 1793, and placed under house arrest had stayed in Paris, even when they might easily have got away; but others had escaped and were still on the run, like Charles Barbaroux, Guadet and Pétion, the former Mayor of Paris. The overthrow of the *Girondins* had elicited angry constitutional protests from many of their (non-*Girondin*) fellow *députés*, seventy-three of whom had been indicted for their protests and placed under arrest; but they were not put on trial, largely because Robespierre intervened to prevent this from happening – or so he claimed. Of the overthrown *Girondin députés*, twenty-one were finally brought before the *Tribunal révolutionnaire* on October 30, 1793.[10]

The charges were ludicrous: they included 'perfidious ambition', 'hatred of Paris', 'federalism' and vicarious responsibility for the attempts of their escaped colleagues to precipitate the civil war.

The crowd power of the *Commune* had brought down the *Girondins*, and the principal witnesses for the prosecution were Chaumette, the *Commune*'s chief executive and chief prosecutor, and Hébert, his deputy. Both were committed supporters of the *sans-culottes* but fierce critics of Robespierre; and both would later be guillotined, on different trumped-up charges, within three weeks of each other in the spring of 1794.

The twenty-one *Girondins* who were standing trial included Brissot, the flamboyant thirty-nine-year-old journalist-adventurer who was the founder of the group; Vergniaud, the forty-year-old lawyer from Bordeaux who had risen to be the parliamentary star of the *Girondins* in the National Assembly; Boyer-Fonfrède, the thirty-eight-year-old wealthy merchant from Bordeaux; his close friend and brother-in-law, Ducos, from a rich trading family in Bordeaux and Nantes; and Gensonné, the thirty-five-year-old advocate from Bordeaux whom both Herman and Fouquier-Tinville feared for his intelligence and his forensic skills.

'There was', says Michelet, 'no hypocrisy in the trial. Everybody saw right away that it was just about killing. They disregarded all formalities still customary at this period in the *Tribunal révolutionnaire*. No documents were produced. There were no lawyers for the defence. Several of the accused were not allowed to speak'.[11]

The trial started on October 24, 1793, and went on for several days without making any progress. On October 30 the CSP introduced a decree to the *Convention* which would allow the President of the Tribunal, after three days of a trial, to ask the jury if their consciences were sufficiently enlightened to declare a verdict. It took time to push the decree through the formalities of the *Convention*, so Herman stalled the trial for several hours. The decree did not reach the Tribunal until eight o'clock in the evening, at which point the jury, without any new discussion, suddenly found itself enlightened and condemned all the *Girondins* to death. They were executed the following day, October 31, 1793.[12]

Those condemned, in addition to Brissot, Vergniaud, Boyer-Fonfrède, Ducos and Gensonné, included Jean-Louis Carra, a fifty-one-year-old self-educated writer and passionate Revolutionary; Charles-Éléonor Dufriche de Valazé, a forty-two-year-old lawyer from Alençon; Marc-David Lasource, a thirty-year-old Calvinist pastor from Tarn; and Charles Alexis Brulart Sillery, marquis de Genlis, a wealthy fifty-six-year-old retired officer of the nobility from Paris. On the announcement of the verdict, Valazé stabbed himself and died in the courtroom.

Most of those who had been sentenced to house arrest but had escaped were eventually captured. Jean Antoine Lafargue de Grangeneuve, a forty-two-year-old advocate, got home to Bordeaux, but he was captured in December 1793 and executed there. Guadet, a thirty-five-year-old lawyer from Saint-Émilion, took part in the abortive rising in Calvados, then escaped to Bordeaux, where he was captured in June 1794 and executed. Barbaroux, a twenty-six-year-old lawyer from Marseille, had escaped to the west and then to Saint-Émilion with Pétion and François Buzot, a thirty-three-year-old lawyer from Évreux; they remained hidden in the countryside for about ten months, but in June 1794 they were tracked down, and all three committed suicide, but separately. Finally, there was Marie Jean Antoine Nicolas Caritat, the fifty-year-old marquis de Condorcet, who, though not formally one of the *Girondins*, had protested at their fall. He had escaped from Paris but was condemned to death in absentia. He was discovered in the countryside outside the capital and arrested; he died in a country police cell, poisoned, probably by suicide.

But a few got away. Maximin Isnard, a thirty-eight-year-old perfume dealer from Grasse in the Var, escaped and remained hidden until after the fall of Robespierre; he returned to resume his place as a *député* in the *Convention* in February 1795. Jean-Denis Lanjuinais, a forty-year-old advocate and law professor from Rennes, escaped to his home town, where he remained hidden for eighteen months, and then rejoined the *Convention* in March 1795. Finally, Jean-Baptiste Louvet, a thirty-three-year-old novelist and librarian from Paris, escaped to the west, then to Bordeaux and finally to safety in Switzerland; he too rejoined the *Convention* in March 1795.

But the show trial and execution of the *Girondins* was just the beginning of the Terror. Jean-Marie Roland de la Platière, the former Minister of the Interior, and his wife, Jeanne Marie Philipon, had been friends and patrons of the *Girondins*, and they were both targeted by the proscription of the *Girondins*. He escaped, but she was arrested and tried on November 8, 1793, on a charge of conspiring against the unity of the Republic. She was condemned and executed the same day; on the scaffold, she cried out: 'Liberty, what crimes are committed in your name!'[13] Her husband managed to stay hidden in Rouen for five months. When he heard of her death, he thought at first of returning to Paris to demand the exoneration of a public trial; but he changed his mind and committed suicide on November 15, 1793.

Philippe Égalité, formerly Louis-Philippe Joseph, duc d'Orléans, the richest man in France, was an elected member of the *Convention*, where he had voted for the death of Louis XVI, his first cousin. Not even Robespierre believed that he need have gone this far: 'Égalité was perhaps the only member who could have recused himself.'[14] But when his son, the duc de Chartres, deserted to the enemy with Dumouriez, Orléans was arrested, on April 6, 1793, and kept in prison in Marseille for several months. On September 3 he was sent to the *Tribunal révolutionnaire*, where he was tried on the same charges as the *Girondins* and condemned to death. He was executed on November 7. 'Really', he said as he prepared to mount the scaffold, impeccably dressed as usual and beautifully powdered, 'this seems a bit of a joke.'[15]

'In the end', says Michelet, 'he got what he wanted above all: he saved his money and lost only his head.'[16]

22

THE
SPASM OF RELIGION TO
THE FALL OF DANTON

THE PEAK OF THE TERROR, in the winter of 1793–94, was highlighted by what is sometimes called Robespierre's 'War Against the Factions', in which he progressively brought down his critics, rivals and other opponents, as well as those whom he believed to be undermining the principles of the Revolution with crime and corruption. At the same time, however, and just as important, the Terror dragged him and his allies into an intense debate about the future of the Revolution, between those who wanted to accelerate it and those who wanted to slow it down.

From very early on, people had been asking the basic question: when will the Revolution end? As its first years passed without producing any improvement in the lot of ordinary people, more and more wanted it to stop. But there was no way of answering the basic question, because the Revolutionaries had not gone to Versailles with an agreed plan, and they did not have a conceptual picture of any final destination.

For the most committed and most radical Revolutionaries, the Revolution itself was the destination. For them, as Tocqueville pointed out, it was virtually the equivalent of a new religion, even if many of the central terms were transposed.

The French Revolution was not geographically limited … It created, above all the particular nationalities, a common intellectual home-land, of which men of all the nations could become citizens … So it is to religious revolutions that we must compare the French Revolution if we want to understand it with the aid of analogy …

The French Revolution functioned, in relation to this world, in precisely the same manner that religious revolutions act in relation to the next; it treated the citizen in an abstract fashion, independent of any particular society, just as religions consider man in general, inde-pendently of place and time …

As it seemed to aim at the regeneration of humankind more than at the reform of France, it ignited a passion which, until then, the most violent political revolutions had never been able to produce. It inspired proselytizing and gave birth to propaganda … It became itself a sort of new religion, an imperfect religion, it is true, without God, without forms of worship and without an afterlife, but which nevertheless, like Islam, has inundated the whole world with its sol-diers, its apostles and its martyrs.[1]

So when Desmoulins, and much later Michelet, compared the *Jacobin Club* with the Catholic Inquisition,[2] they were perceiving the same kind of intolerant religious characteristics which Tocqueville saw and which, for some radical patriots, were at the heart of their Revolution. For some, it was essential to put these quasi-religious characteristics into words, practice and ceremony; for others, it was even more important to fight all other forms of religion, starting, of course, with the Catholic Church.

The declaration of the Republic on September 21, 1792, was not the only symbolic enactment of the new dispensation which the Revo-lutionaries thought they had brought to this world: the next day they announced that this was 'Year One' of the Republic. Inspired by the general idea of wiping out the past and making a fresh start, they instructed their Public Education Committee to devise a new calendar. This committee, composed of scientists and men of letters, adopted a year of twelve months of thirty days each, with five extra days (six in leap years); the seven-day week would be replaced with a ten-day *décadi*; and newly invented names with rural overtones relating to the seasons supplanted all the old names of days and months, with their Christian connotations.

The Revolutionary who was most responsible for devising the names in this calendar was the poet and playwright Philippe Fabre d'Églantine. Those he gave to the autumn months were grave: *vendémiaire*, *brumaire*, *frimaire*; those for winter were heavy: *nivôse*, *pluviôse*, *ventôse*; those for spring, gay: *germinal*, *floréal*, *prairial*; those for summer, sonorous: *messidor*, *thermidor*, *fructidor*. The *Convention* adopted this calendar on October 5, 1793; the world, the Deputies thought, had started from a new beginning, but they decided it had been a year earlier, on September 22, 1792.

So when the *Convention* announced that 'the provisional government of France [would] be Revolutionary until the peace',[3] the date by the old calendar was October 10, 1793, but by the new one it was *19 vendémiaire an II* (Year 2) of the Revolution.

Many traditional French historians of the Revolution tell the story from now on according to dates in the Revolutionary calendar. I shall mainly stick to the familiar modern calendar: it is easier for the reader to understand; and the Revolutionaries did not, in fact, succeed in inaugurating a new era in the secular world. The French may have stuck to their Revolutionary calendar until 1806, long after the end of the Revolution, but the rest of the world did not follow them. On the other hand, some of the most celebrated Revolutionary events and influential laws are still quite often referred to according to the Revolutionary dates on which they were introduced. Where appropriate, I shall use dates from both calendars.

The launching of the new calendar marked the beginning of a campaign among the most radical *sans-culottes* of *déchristianisation*, first against all refractory priests, then against all priests, whether refractory or conformist, then against the Church as a whole, then against Christianity and finally against all religions. Eventually, the radicals demanded rationalism, atheism and a public Cult of Reason. It was a mysterious campaign, since no one knows quite where it came from or what drove it. It started, almost spontaneously, in a number of rural communities in the vicinity of Paris and then spread rapidly elsewhere in France, with burlesque anti-religious ceremonies, the closing of churches, the forced marriage of thousands of priests, the forced retirement of thousands more and the transformation of churches into Temples of Reason.

This anti-Christian campaign was quite confused, and even today confusing. Michel Vovelle is the most authoritative historian of this episode of the Revolution, and he points out that it was not imposed by the Revolutionary government in Paris, but sprang up impulsively in different places.[4]

Most dramatically, on November 7, 1793, Jean-Baptiste Joseph Gobel, the Bishop of Paris, was physically intimidated by Pierre Gaspard Chaumette, the *procureur-syndic* of the *Commune*, into a humiliating abdication of his position, symbolised by his public surrender of his pectoral cross and ring in person to the office of the *Convention*. But this did not save him: four months later he was bundled into the show trial of the left-wing *Hébertistes* and guillotined.

Three days after Gobel's abdication, the anti-Christian campaign climaxed in the *Fête de la Liberté et de la Raison*, celebrated in the Cathedral of Notre-Dame in Paris with a large pageant of dancers and singers, with young girls parading in white and with a caricature of Christian ritual in which the Christ was replaced by a figure of Lucius Junius Brutus, the hero of Republican Rome. The campaign was whipped on by a number of ultraradical members of the *Convention*, including Joseph Fouché, Marie Joseph Lequinio and Jacques Léonard Goyre de Laplanche, who used their positions to force their anti-Christian views on local populations. In Nièvre, Fouché conducted a ferocious anti-Christian crusade, including many acts of vandalism on local churches and, most notoriously, the fixing of a slogan at the entrance to all cemeteries reading 'Death is an eternal sleep.'[5]

Robespierre tried to resist this wave of de-Christianisation and in an eccentric counter-initiative attempted to impose an alternative Revolutionary creed of his own devising, of a belief in some kind of God, described as a 'Supreme Being'. (In the process, of course, he powerfully confirmed Tocqueville's insight into the meta-religious nature of the French Revolution.)

In the spring of 1794, Robespierre tried to give quasi-religious credibility to this creed by celebrating it in a newly invented public pageant, in which he cast himself in the principal ceremonial role, leading a procession of members of the *Convention* up an artificial hill erected on the Champ de Mars, where they sang hymns and swore oaths of detestation of all kings. Perhaps he understood that most people in France, in contrast with the more radical *sans-culottes*, were not ready to do without Christianity or something like it. But most bourgeois members of the *Convention* despised and secretly derided Robespierre's attempt to impose his cult, with himself as high priest; and when he fell, his cult fell with him.

The struggle between Robespierre and the ultraradicals for the meta-religious or anti-religious heart of the Revolution petered out, because neither side was able to clothe it in any sufficiently appealing ceremonial or emotional form. But the struggle between Robespierre and his opponents over earthly issues was just as ferocious as ever. The frequent food shortages had not been significantly alleviated by the new price control regime and were now aggravated by the poor 1793 harvest. Hébert had joined in the anti-Christian campaign, but he also continued with his noisy denunciations of the government. In the autumn of 1793, therefore, Robespierre decided to put an end to him. In October the *département* of Paris shut down Hébert's paper, *Le Père Duchesne*, and in a speech to the *Jacobins*, Robespierre attacked the '*Hébertiste* faction'. Hébert took the hint and kept quiet, and for a while was left in peace. But on December 17 two of his chief followers, General Charles Ronsin, a Republican commander in the War of the Vendée, and François Vincent, the Secretary General of the Ministry of War, were arrested, together with Stanislas '*Tape Dur*' Maillard.[6] They were released six weeks later, on February 2, 1794. But that was just a warning: on the night of March 13–14, 1794, Hébert was himself arrested, together with Ronsin and Vincent, plus Antoine Momoro, the printer for the *Commune*; and the next day Saint-Just gave a speech accusing the *Hébertistes* of plotting against the *Convention* and of conspiring with foreign powers.

These were fabricated charges, but the trial started less than a week later, on March 21, wrapping up the *Hébertistes* with a whole clutch of disparate foreigners or quasi-foreigners, starting with Jean Conrad de Kock, a Dutch banker; Anacharsis Cloots, a wealthy German baron who was not just a devotee of the French Revolution but also a naturalised French citizen and an elected member of the *Convention*; Pierre Proly, probably the natural son of Count Wenzel Kaunitz, the Austrian diplomat; and Jacob Pereyra, a Jewish Portuguese tobacco trader. No significant evidence was produced against these nineteen so-called *agents de l'étranger* (foreign agents); nevertheless, on March 24, 1794, after three days of trial, eighteen were condemned to death and guillotined. The one man who was acquitted, a certain Dr Jean-Baptiste Laboureau, was a police informer.

The second phase in the 'War Against the Factions' was the trial of Danton and his supporters, called *Dantonistes*, which opened nine days later. In this case, the political aim – to bring down a popular and plausible challenger to Robespierre – was partly disguised by an attack on the genuine corruption of a number of Danton's friends, but again with the implication that the accused were all somehow in league with foreigners and other enemies.

The *Dantonistes* are sometimes called the *Indulgents*, on the grounds that Danton and some of his friends had become, in the autumn of 1793, dismayed or disillusioned by the Terror and urged a return to a more normal life. In November of that year, Danton argued for a policy of greater moderation: a curb on the endless bloodletting, the repeal of the Law of Suspects and even the creation of a Committee of Clemency. He and his friends also urged a moderation of the Terror's economic policies, such as price controls and food requisitions (which they had never liked), and the exploration of a compromise peace with France's European enemies.

Danton's proposals were backed by Desmoulins, a close friend and protégé who, at the start of the Revolution, had been one of France's most influential Revolutionary journalists. On December 5, 1793, he started publishing, with Danton's support, a new political pamphlet, *Le Vieux Cordelier*, whose first issue called for clemency for prisoners under the Law of Suspects. It got a rapturous response from the public and for a while resuscitated Desmoulins' reputation. *Le Vieux Cordelier* was so popular that it sold, in its lifetime, more than 100,000 copies; but its lifetime was short, since only six numbers were printed: Robespierre made sure that the seventh did not appear.

In the celebrated third number of *Le Vieux Cordelier*, which came out on December 17, 1793, just before the arrest of Ronsin, Vincent and Maillard, Desmoulins violently attacked the policy of the *Tribunal révolutionnaire* and the entire rationale of the Terror and called for the restoration of freedom of the press. 'The Committe of Public Safety thought', he wrote, 'that to set up the Republic, they needed for a while the jurisprudence of despots'.[7]

Robespierre knew Desmoulins well, since they had been at school together, at the Collège Louis-le-Grand in Paris, and he quite liked him; yet Robespierre always slightly condescended to him, perhaps in part because Desmoulins was two years younger – he was widely and familiarly known as Camille, and Robespierre once described him as 'a spoiled child' (*un enfant gâté*). On this occasion, Robespierre's instinctive response was conciliatory: on December 20 he made a counterproposal, to set up a Committee of Justice to examine some of the cases under the Law of Suspects. Coming from Robespierre at the height of the Terror, this was an astonishing offer, if it was serious. But Desmoulins rejected the proposal and he argued in the fourth number of *Le Vieux Cordelier*, which came out on December 24, 1793, that there was a much better way of foiling any conspiracies: 'Unlock the prisons for the 200,000 citizens whom you call suspects, because, in the Declaration of Rights, there are no houses of suspicion ... You want to exterminate all your enemies by the guillotine! But was there ever a greater madness? ... Believe me, liberty would be strengthened and Europe conquered if you had a Committee of Clemency!'[8]

On the next day, December 25, thoroughly provoked by Desmoulins' insistent challenges, Robespierre produced his *Report on the Principles of Revolutionary Government* (*Rapport sur les principes du gouvernement révolutionnaire*), whose central purpose was to justify the case, in a Revolutionary situation, for an authoritarian, Revolutionary government, as against a law-based, constitutional one.

'The purpose of constitutional government', he wrote,

> is to preserve the Republic; that of Revolutionary Government is to set it up ... Under a constitutional regime, it is almost enough to protect individuals from abuse by public authorities; under a Revolutionary regime, the public authorities themselves are obliged to defend themselves against all the factions which attack them ... These ideas are enough to explain the origin and the nature of the laws which we call Revolutionary. Those who call them arbitrary or tyrannical are stupid or perverted sophists who seek to confuse their opponents.[9]

Though increasingly irritated by Desmoulins' challenge to his authority, Robespierre was still willing, up to a point, to be conciliatory. On January 7, 1794, he told the *Jacobins* that there was no need to expel Desmoulins from the club; instead, he said, 'we will burn his pamphlet'. If this was intended as a friendly offer, Desmoulins immediately and contemptuously rejected it: 'Burning is not an answer.'[10]

Desmoulins' crisp response is legendary in the annals of the French Revolution, and some people seem to think that he was echoing Rousseau. In fact, Rousseau was not given to one-liners, and this retort was drawn from Voltaire, Rousseau's enemy. Rousseau's revolutionary tract

Du contrat social had been published in 1762, and it caused such a scandal that it was publicly burned in Geneva, his home town, by the official executioner. Voltaire, whom Rousseau had long irritated, was by then in open and irreconcilable conflict with him; but on this occasion he was outraged on Rousseau's behalf, and on behalf of all writers, as he wrote about the incident at the time: 'They have burned this book in our country [Geneva]. The operation of burning it was just as odious as that of writing it. There are some things that a wise government must ignore. To burn a book of argument is to say: "We do not have enough wit to reply to it."'[11]

A final showdown between Robespierre and the *Dantonistes* was now virtually inevitable, and it was triggered by widespread accusations against Danton and several of his friends and associates of corruption and money laundering. This was particularly ironic because Fabre, the primary deviser of the Revolutionary calendar and one of Danton's closest associates, had, during the previous summer, together with a number of his colleagues in the *Convention*, been at the centre of a noisy campaign of denunciation of all financial speculators, focusing specifically on the *Compagnie des Indes*, the large colonial trading and plantation company.

Their main accusation had been that financial companies, especially the *Compagnie des Indes*, were fraudulently avoiding paying taxes. The campaigners included François Chabot, a dissolute and fleshy *député* who had once been a Franciscan friar but now dressed ostentatiously downmarket, as if he were a secular *sans-culotte*, a man of the people; Jean-François Delacroix, a former advocate and judge who had briefly been, with Danton, a member of the first CSP; and Joseph Delaunay, a former *advocat* from Angers, who was subsequently denounced (by Chabot and others) for conspiracies of corruption and blackmail. This campaign had been so successful that the *Convention* had decreed the suppression of all these companies and the closing of the stock market and entrusted Fabre and others with key roles in liquidating the *Compagnie des Indes*, including confiscation of much of its property owned by foreigners.

But this legislative coup did not put a stop to the uproar in the *Convention* or outside it, and the accusations and counter-accusations of depravity and corruption continued flying around in a rising storm. The extreme stresses and distortions in the economy had created the ideal conditions for speculation and profiteering; and the Revolutionaries had not built an administration with the required ethos and professionalism to keep such abuses in check.

Moreover, it was public knowledge that significant numbers of *Convention* members, including some of its leading *envoyés en mission*, had taken advantage of their positions to enrich themselves illegally. Danton was one of those most regularly suspected of corruption. Before the overthrow of the monarchy, he was almost certainly on the payroll of the court, though it is not clear what if anything he did in return for the money; but it should be remembered that until August 1792 there were many people, including many good Revolutionaries, who wanted to save the monarchy, and as emerged in the evidence at the trial of the King, some of them (like Mirabeau) were prepared to work with and to take money from the court. After the overthrow of the monarchy, Danton was briefly the Minister of Justice, where he had access to large secret Ministry funds, and he was never able to give an account of what he had done with them. He was also widely suspected of having enriched himself during his many missions to French army forces at the front in Belgium between December 1792 and February 1793, where he may have made large amounts of money from army contracts or even from treasonous dealings with the Austrians.

Robespierre publicly accused Delacroix of having illegally enriched himself in Belgium; Chabot undoubtedly enriched himself in Tarn and Aveyron, and he allegedly married the sister of two Austrian nationals in return for a mysterious dowry of £200,000. When Toulon was recaptured, Barras, another leading *député* from the Convention, became the town's master and used his position to get rich quick.

The storm of accusations and counter-accusations grew so intense that Chabot, one of those most frequently targeted, took fright and, in an effort to exculpate himself, went to see Robespierre in person and then to the *Comité de sûreté générale* (CSG), of which he had at one time been a member, where he laid his own accusation against Fabre, confessed that he had received £100,000 as his share of the pay-off and alleged that the fraud in the *Compagnie des Indes* was deeply entangled with a much larger conspiracy of foreign bankers, led by a certain Baron Batz. At first the CSG paid little attention to these allegations, believing that Fabre was innocent.

On January 13, 1794, however, the anti-speculation campaigning of the Dantonists blew back sensationally, when Fabre was himself arrested on a charge that he had used his position as a *député* fraudulently to rewrite the terms of the liquidation of the *Compagnie des Indes*.

The *Convention* had decreed that government officials should wind

up the *Compagnie*. But at some point the text of this law had been modi-
fied so as to allow the company to conduct its own liquidation, and thus
evade the enormous tax payments which it owed. It emerged that Fabre's
fingerprints were all over this modification and that he and his friends
had taken a £500,000 pay-off from the company in return. Chabot and
Delaunay were also implicated; and it was alleged that Fabre and his
associates had launched their campaign against the *Compagnie des Indes*
in order to destabilise it on the stock market and thus facilitate their
speculation in the company's shares before its liquidation. This fraud
became a centrepiece of the trial of the Dantonists, which Chabot's allegations helped to expand into a trial of a largely imaginary international
bankers' conspiracy against the Revolution.

Robespierre's immediate reaction to the sensational arrest of Fabre
was to make a public protest against the betrayal of the ideals of the
Revolution, with an implied claim not just that the Revolution needed
to be guided by virtue but that he himself embodied that virtue. On
February 5, 1794, he came to the *Convention* to deliver a speech of
remonstration, titled *On the Principles of Political Morality Which Should
Guide the National Convention in the Interior Administration of the Republic*. But this was not just a speech proclaiming the necessity of good
behaviour and virtue; it was also a speech to justify the Terror.

'The time has come' he said,

> to set out clearly the aim of the Revolution, and the final state where
> we want to arrive ... What is the goal toward which we aim? The
> peaceful enjoyment of liberty and equality ... But since the essence of
> the Republic or of democracy is equality, it follows that love of one's
> country necessarily embraces love of equality ... Not only is virtue the
> soul of democracy, but it can exist only in such a government ... If the
> spring of popular government at a time of peace is virtue, the spring
> of popular government at a time of Revolution is *virtue and Terror*
> together: virtue, without which Terror is fatal; Terror, without which
> virtue is impotent. Terror is nothing else than justice, prompt, severe,
> inflexible; it is thus an emanation of Virtue ...[12]

This was Robespierre's last gasp of an attempt to justify the meta-
religious soul of the Revolution. But his rhetoric failed to damp down the
protests of left-wing agitators, because it had no effect on the sufferings
of ordinary *sans-culottes*. The new and expanded *maximum* was largely

ineffective in holding down food prices, and it did nothing to solve the problem of food shortages; there was some easing of the controls on wage rates, but for most *sans-culottes*, life was getting steadily harder. There were queues and near-riots at the shops and in the markets; there were strikes and threatening public demonstrations; and some of the *Hébertistes* and their friends were calling for a new insurrection. The arrest of Ronsin and Vincent on December 17, 1793, only inflamed the anti-government protesters in the populist *Club des Cordeliers*, because the economic crisis was getting worse.

The members of the CSP and the CSG began to realise that they must do something urgent to ease the plight of the poor; and on February 26 and March 3, 1794, Saint-Just pushed through a clutch of laws, the so-called *décrets de ventôse*, which were designed to carry out a massive redistribution of property from the 'enemies of the people' to the very poor.

'Necessity', he said,

> is perhaps leading us to results about which we have not thought. Wealth is in the hands of a fairly large number of enemies of the Revolution; need puts working people into a state of dependence on their enemies ... The property of patriots is sacred, but the property of conspirators is there for all the needy. The poor are the powers of the earth. They have the right to talk with authority to governments which fail to look after them.[13]

Under these *décrets*, all the *communes* were ordered to draw up lists of the deserving poor (*patriotes*), and the *comité de surveillance* of each *Section* or *commune* to provide lists of *émigrés* and of all those who had been imprisoned for political reasons since May 1789. After review by the CSG, the property of these 'enemies of the Revolution' would be summarily expropriated and sold and the proceeds distributed to the poor. The *décrets de ventôse*, if fully enacted, would have brought about a colossal redistribution of property to the poor, since they would have dispossessed about 300,000 suspects and *émigrés*.

Some historians, like Mathiez, think that this represented a decisive, egalitarian shift to the left by the CSP to satisfy the demands of the *sans-culottes*. Robespierre had said a year earlier, in a speech to the *Convention* on April 24, 1793, that 'extreme inequality of wealth is the source of many evils and many crimes.'[14] And on May 24, 1794, the CSP ordered the distribution of 15 to 25 sous a day to the poor and infirm of Paris. In the rest of the country, local authorities were slow to follow suit. Other historians doubt whether these decrees represented a fundamental change of *Jacobin* policy and suggest that they were simply a tactical gesture to appease protesters. Their operational details were not spelled out, and the government did nothing more to intervene directly in the economy to ease the plight of the *sans-culottes*. We shall never know the truth of the matter, because the decrees had barely started being enacted by the time Robespierre fell, and they were repealed shortly thereafter.

The trial of Danton and his friends became inevitable after the arrest of Fabre, and it followed hard on the heels of that of the *Hébertistes*. On March 18, 1794, the *Convention* ordered the trial of all those compromised in the *Compagnie des Indes* affair: Fabre, Claude Basire, Chabot and Delaunay. Eleven days later, on the night of March 29–30, Danton was arrested, together with others charged with being *Indulgents*: Desmoulins, Delacroix, Pierre Nicolas Philippeaux. Friends had warned Danton of the dangers, and some had advised him to escape, but he rejected the idea. 'One doesn't carry the country on the soles of one's shoes', he said.[15] Before his arrest, he went to see Robespierre on two or three occasions, to appeal to him on grounds of old loyalties; but Robespierre remained unmoved. Jean-Baptiste Robert Lindet, a lawyer from Normandy, was the only one of the twelve members of the CSP who refused to sign the arrest warrant. 'I am here to save the citizens', he said, 'and not to kill patriots.'[16]

    On April 1, 1794, the *Convention* listened in silence as Saint-Just read out the lengthy charge sheet against Danton and his fellow-accused; it consisted almost entirely of circumstantial innuendos alleging past intrigues with Mirabeau (who had died three years earlier, of overwork and debauchery, at the age of forty-two), covert dealings with the court (now all dispersed or in exile), secret relationships with Dumouriez (now languishing in an Austrian prison), treacherous transactions with the *Girondins* (most of whom were now dead), attempts to save the royal family (who were now dead, in prison or in exile), insidious campaigns for clemency and peace, silent resistance to all Revolutionary measures, links with corruption and friendships with suspect foreigners. No one could have been in any doubt: this was to be another show trial.

For good measure, and to ensure that the judicial process would be entirely muddied, the *Convention* swept in a job lot of foreigners, speculators, profiteers and mere friends of Danton: Marc René Marie d'Amarzit, the abbé d'Espagnac, a notorious speculator and profiteer in the army supply business, deeply implicated in the speculation round the *Compagnie des Indes*; Andres Maria de Guzman, a Spanish adventurer and political agitator; Sigmund and Emmanuel Junius, Moravian Jews who had changed their last name to Frey, suspected of being Austrian spies and implicated in the affairs of Chabot; General François Westermann, a friend of Danton's, denounced for his massacres in the Vendée; and finally Marie Jean Hérault de Séchelles, a rich and popular aristocrat whom Robespierre had long hated and envied for his easy charm.

The trial started on April 2, 1794, in the Grand Hall of the former *Parlement de Paris*, and it did not take long. The first day was devoted to the affair of the *Compagnie des Indes*, and the evidence against Fabre and his friends was damning. The second day was spent in the interrogation of Danton, who not merely defended himself but vigorously attacked his accusers, whom he denounced as imposters. He was a powerful speaker, and his loud voice echoed into the street outside. More and more people crowded into the public galleries to watch; and several members of the CSG appeared in the courtroom to stiffen the resolve of Herman, the President of the *Tribunal*, and Fouquier-Tinville, the Chief Prosecutor. The third day was devoted to the questioning of the other accused, and they imitated Danton, loudly demanding the calling of witnesses for their defence. Fouquier-Tinville panicked and wrote to the CSP for advice. Following the example set in the trial of the *Girondins*, it decided to silence Danton by inventing yet another device to cut through the obstacles of the law: Saint-Just went to the *Convention* and pushed through a decree that 'anyone accused of conspiracy who will resist or insult the national judicial system will be excluded from the proceedings immediately'.[17] It was approved unanimously; Danton could be silenced. The next day, April 5, 1794, Fouquier-Tinville read out the terms of this decree, and the jury was persuaded to pass the required guilty verdict. Later that day, Danton and fifteen others, of whom nine were *députés* of the *Convention*, went to the guillotine.

On the scaffold, Danton said to the executioner: 'Show my head to the people: it will be worth seeing.'[18]

23

THE FALL OF
ROBESPIERRE

IN THE THREE MONTHS following the fall of Danton, Robespierre tried desperately to ride the Revolution by intensifying the Terror and by advancing more and more arguments to explain the steady dismantling of the laws underpinning the state. Eventually, the atmosphere of fear became so frenzied that his enemies brought him down.

The intensification of the Terror went hand in hand with a further centralisation of the government. After Robespierre's victories in the spectacular show trials in March and April 1794, first of the *Hébertistes*, then of the *Dantonistes*, the CSP moved swiftly to tighten control of all political institutions, and in particular to rein in any activities which were most directly influenced by the *sans-culottes*. The *armées révolutionnaires*, which had been created the previous autumn in direct response to the demands of the *sans-culottes*, were now closed down, as were the special commissioners for investigating food hoarding (*commissaires aux accaparements*); both were deemed too close in political sympathy to the *Hébertistes*. The government also removed virtually any outlet for the expression of popular anger: all denunciations to the *Tribunal révolutionnaire* would now come directly from one of the two governing *comités*, at first, officially, from the *Comité de sûreté générale*

(CSG) and soon, encroachingly, after it set up its own police depart-ment, from the CSP.

One significant date in the insanity of the Terror was April 22, 1794, when the *Tribunal révolutionnaire* sent to the guillotine two notable and thoroughly respectable Revolutionaries, together with an extremely dis-tinguished public servant of the *ancien régime*.

Jacques Guillaume Thouret was a leading constitutional lawyer who had played a key role, in the early days of the Revolution, in the reorganisation of France into its eighty-three *départements* and in the development of the new French judicial structure, notably the jury system. His crime under the Terror was simply to become a suspect. Isaac René Guy Le Chapelier was another Revolutionary lawyer, who left his name to posterity with the *Loi Le Chapelier*, which forbade the formation of trade unions, earning him the hatred of the *sans-culottes*. His crime before the *Tribunal révolutionnaire* was *modérantisme*, or moderation, which was newspeak for being an anti-revolutionary. The *Montagnards* sent him to the guillotine but did not repeal his law, which remained on the statute book until 1864.

The third of these victims was Guillaume Chrétien de Lamoignon de Malesherbes, from one of France's most distinguished families of legal and royal servants. He was a liberal, and he had protected Voltaire and the *Encyclopédistes* of the Enlightenment from the censors of the *ancien régime*; his crime against the Revolution was to have agreed to act as one of the lawyers defending the King at his trial.

Most trials before the *Tribunal révolutionnaire* were now dressed up as conspiracy cases. The first was the 'Conspiracy of the Prisons', in which a disparate clutch of twenty-six people was alleged to have plotted to attack prisons and release their prisoners. This conspiracy was purely imaginary, and the trial did not take long. It started on April 10, 1794, and ended three days later with seven acquittals and nineteen death sentences, including for Pierre Gaspard Chaumette, the leader of the Paris *Commune*; Jean-Baptiste Gobel, the deposed Bishop of Paris; Arthur, comte de Dillon, a disgraced general who had repeatedly been suspended for suspected royalist conspiracies; and Lucile Desmoulins, the widow of Camille.

Robespierre immediately replaced Chaumette as the leader of the *Commune* with Claude François de Payan, one of his loyal bureaucrats on the staff of the CSP. Payan was not, of course, elected, and his title in his new job was not *procureur* but *agent national*. In fact, ever since

December 4, 1793, all the elected *procureurs* throughout France had been progressively purged or, if approved, reappointed as *agents natio-naux*, representatives of the central government, as part of the Terrorist regime.

On May 10, 1794, Jean Nicolas Pache, the Mayor of Paris, previously the Minister of War, and a leading *Hébertiste*, was abruptly arrested and replaced by another loyal Robespierrist, Jean-Baptiste Édouard Lescot-Fleuriot, the deputy public prosecutor of the *Tribunal révolutionnaire*. The *Commune* was effectively under the direct control of the national government.

Robespierre ordered the closing down of all the *sociétés populaires*, the previously independent debating clubs around the country. The author-ities had previously tried to curb the grass-roots political activities of the *sans-culottes* by limiting the frequency with which the *Sections* were allowed to hold official *Assemblées générales*. The *sans-culottes* had cir-cumvented this restriction by setting up unofficial debating clubs, called *sociétés populaires*, which the authorities banned in retaliation. Thus in April and May 1794, thirty-nine of the *sociétés populaires* in Paris simply disappeared[1] or were displaced by offshoots of the *Jacobin* network, which now exercised a monopoly of political debate and opinion.

This move may have tipped the odds fatally against Robespierre. For while the immediate effect was to reinforce the concentration of political power at the centre, it also underlined, in the most public way possi-ble, the fundamental split between the *sans-culottes* and the bourgeois *Montagnards*. Political contact between Robespierre and the mass of the *sans-culottes*, whose popular movement had brought him to power, was now largely lost, and Saint-Just virtually admitted as much: 'The Revo-lution is frozen'.[2] When it came to the moment of crisis, a few weeks later, and the choice had to be made between Robespierre and his enemies, an essential minority of the *sans-culottes* were no longer behind him.

Robespierre next took overt control of the government. After the overthrow of the King, on August 10, 1792, the Council of Ministers had been replaced by the six-member *Conseil exécutif provisoire*, which carried on the role of government under the authority of the National Assembly. On April 1, 1794, it was itself replaced by twelve *Commissions exécutives*, which, although nominally appointed by the *Convention*, in fact came directly under the control of the CSP.

On April 19, the CSP further curbed the independence of the *Con-vention* by summoning home twenty-one of its members who had been sent out as all-powerful *envoyés en mission*. They were recalled for abuse of power or corruption and included Paul Barras, Jean-Baptiste Carrier, Joseph Fouché, Louis-Stanislas Fréron and Jean Lambert Tallien. From now on, the CSP sent out its own representatives: Saint-Just was frequently away from Paris on duty with the armies.

This proved a fatal error on Robespierre's part, since the recall of the offending *envoyés en mission* meant that they were in imminent danger of prosecution before the *Tribunal révolutionnaire*. Barras had played a leading role at the siege of Toulon, and after the town fell he had made himself scandalously rich. Louis-Stanislas Fréron was a member of the Convention who had made a ferocious reputation as a *missionnaire de la Terreur*; he had teamed up with Barras in the pacification of Toulon, where he boasted that he had had 200 shot each day; and he had gone on to similar exploits in Marseille. Carrier was notorious for his savage repression of the rebels of Nantes and Fouché for his ruthless campaign of de-Christianisation in Nièvre and for the later massacres he authorised with Jean-Marie Collot d'Herbois during the suppression of Lyon. Tallien was infamous for his brutal repression of rebels in Bordeaux. Barras, Fréron and Tallien were all widely suspected of corruption and embezzlement.

In June the government propelled the Terror into its final spasm. The pretext was an attempted assassination, on May 20, of Collot d'Herbois, followed by the arrest three days later of a woman with a knife, who was claimed to be planning an attack on Robespierre. In reaction, the government passed the infamous Law of 22 *prairial* (June 10, 1794), which deprived those who were accused in the *Tribunal révolutionnaire* of any form of defence: there was to be no interrogation of the accused; no evidence was to be produced against them; they were to have no lawyers; they could call no witnesses; and the tribunal could only choose between two verdicts, acquittal or death, and that based not on evidence but on the moral conviction of the jurors.

This law's Article 6 substantially enlarged the description of 'enemies of the people':

> Those who will have supported the projects of the enemies of France, by persecuting and speaking ill of patriotism, those who will have sought to inspire discouragement, to deprave the morals or to reduce the purity and the energy of the principles of the Revolution, all those who, by whatever means, and whatever their concealment, will have

attacked the liberty, the unity or the safety of the Republic, or worked to prevent its reinforcement.[3]

It was not, said the law, a question of punishing these people, but simply of destroying them.

This was the beginning of the *Grande Terreur*. The intention was massively to speed up the trial process: each session of the Tribunal might be presented with large batches (*fournées*)[4] of dozens of prisoners, often on completely unrelated charges. Like the reorganisation of the armies, this bundling together of unrelated prisoners was known as *l'amalgame*.

An early priority for the Tribunal was to deal with the thousands of people who had already been arrested as suspects, many on indeterminate charges. The Paris prisons were crammed with about 8,000 prisoners, some of them common-law criminals and some of them simply 'suspects', many of whom were now suspected of, and put on trial for, conspiring to release other 'suspects' from prison. In June 1794 three batches of prisoners drawn from a range of gaols (Bicêtre, Luxembourg, Carmes and Saint-Lazare, all former monasteries) were sent to the Tribunal and accused of a prison conspiracy; and another seven batches were sent in July.

For a while in Paris, the rates of conviction and of execution kept pace: from March 1793 to June 1794, a period of fifteen months, 1,251 people had been guillotined, but from the passage of the Law of 22 *prairial* in June 1794 to the fall of Robespierre six weeks later, the number of people executed reached 1,376. 'Heads were falling like slates off the roof',[5] in the memorable phrase of Fouquier-Tinville, the chief prosecutor of the *Tribunal révolutionnaire*.

But some figures suggest that the Terror was starting to slow down. If we look at the whole of France, not just Paris, the dramatic acceleration in the rate of executions under the Law of 22 *prairial* seems to disappear. From March to September 1793 there were 518 death sentences; from October 1793 to May 1794 there were 10,812, or an average of 1,351 per month; and in June and July 1794 there were 2,554, or an average of 1,277 per month, followed by only 86 in August 1794.[6] In principle, all convictions should have been taking place in Paris. Yet it may look, nevertheless, as if France were beginning to weary of the Terror, and as if, despite Robespierre's efforts, it were in fact slightly slowing down. Danton and Desmoulins had argued for a policy of clemency and had been guillotined for their pains; it seemed that others thought the same way, but silently, and in fear. The Revolution was no longer buoyed up by the hysteria of bloodlust: public executions, which had previously attracted vast, screaming, bloodthirsty mobs, were now greeted with aversion; people turned their backs and shops closed their doors on the daily processions of the tumbrils to the place of execution, the objects of sullen and frightened apathy.

Although Robespierre's plans for the Terror were backfiring, by the spring of 1794 mass mobilisation was beginning to pay off. France was building up a large force of several armies in the field. The navy was being substantially rebuilt, both in ships and in manpower. The government began to believe in the real prospect of significant victories in the European war. But under the pressure of economic shortages at home, it set its sights on a strategy that was not idealistic or theoretical but brutally realistic. In the run-up to war in 1791–92 there had been high-minded talk of wars of liberation or of revolution, or even of friendly emancipation; a second phase had begun in January 1793, after the war had started, with a policy of greater realpolitik launched by Danton: a war of expansion, but only to reach 'natural' frontiers (though Danton had gone on to demand the 'unification' of Belgium with France). In the spring of 1794 the food shortages at home and the economic hardships of the French people had become so severe that the government abruptly decided that it must change strategy: the new order of the day would be conquest and plunder.

This was announced to army leaders at the end of March by Lazare Carnot, the government's chief military strategist in the CSP. 'I cannot hide from you', he wrote, 'that we are lost if you do not very soon cross over into enemy territory to get food and resources of all kinds, because France cannot long bear the strained state in which it finds itself at present ... We must live off the enemy or perish.'[7] He wrote again to the generals in May: 'We must live off the enemy; we are not going over there to bring them our treasures.'[8]

The turning point in the war came on June 26, 1794, with the sensational victory at Fleurus by the *armée de Sambre-et-Meuse* under General Jean-Baptiste Jourdan. Fleurus is a small village in Belgium near Charleroi, of which this was essentially a battle for control. When the Austrians conceded defeat at the end of the day, after heavy losses of 4,000 to 5,000 men on each side, the way was open for the French to reconquer Belgium, and the tide of the war had turned.

One of the most significant features of this battle was how many of the Generals or Junior Generals on the French side were young men, often very young men, who had come up from the bottom and won extremely rapid promotion in this war or, more often, in the civil war.

Jourdan was a thirty-two-year-old career soldier who had fought in the American War of Independence. In July 1789, after the Revolution, he had become a captain in the *Garde nationale* when he was twenty-seven; four years later he fought at Hondschoote under Houchard and was then promoted to commander of the *armée du Nord* and defeated the Duke of Coburg at Wattignies. With him at the battle of Fleurus were Jean-Charles Pichegru, a former career soldier who had reached the rank of Sergeant-Major in 1789 when he was twenty-eight, had been promoted to commander of the *armée du Rhin* in 1793 and was now a full General at the head of the *armée du Nord*, aged only thirty-three; Jean-Baptiste Kléber, a former architect who became a grenadier in the *Garde nationale* at the time of the Revolution in 1789, when he was thirty-six, and was promoted to Lieutenant-General on the field of battle after defeating rebels in the Vendée in 1793 when he was forty; and François Séverin Marceau, another former career soldier who became a member of the *Garde nationale* in 1789 after the Revolution and who was promoted to Lieutenant-General on the field of battle in the Vendée in 1793, at only twenty-five years old.

All of these men, and more, won great military glory for themselves and for France; and prominent places in central Paris still remember the names of two of them: Kléber, in the avenue Kléber and the Métro station Kléber, in the sixteenth *arrondissement*; and Marceau, in the avenue Marceau, one of the most elegant streets on the Right Bank, in the eighth and sixteenth *arrondissements*. Marceau died young, mortally wounded at the battle of Aaltenkirchen in 1796, aged twenty-seven; Kléber followed Napoléon to Egypt in 1798 and died in 1800 in the confusion of the French evacuation, assassinated by a young Syrian.

Jourdan won more victories in Belgium, and Carnot wrote to him at the beginning of July 1794: 'You must strip the country, and make it impossible for them [the Belgians] to give our enemies [the Austrians] any means of coming back.'[9] As French forces advanced, they carried out this strategy to the letter. Thousands of sacks of grain, thousands of cattle, millions of pints of wine, hundreds of thousands of rations of fodder were ferried back to France, as well as £50m in coin from the people of Brussels, £10m from Tournai, £3m from Deux-Ponts and £4m from Neustadt.[10] Meanwhile, a large naval convoy bringing food from America had arrived off the French coast and after a fierce battle with the English had been safely escorted into the port of Brest.

France's war aims in the north-east, as Carnot defined them to the generals of the *armées du Nord*, were ostensibly modest and limited; 'We want to keep', he wrote to them in July 1794, 'only what can secure our own frontier – that is to say, on the left all of West Flanders and Dutch Flanders, on the right the country between the Sambre and the Meuse, and in the middle only what is on this side of the Escaut and the Aisne.'[11] But any such frontier implied that Antwerp would remain under French control, and even Mathiez concedes that this would obviously be unacceptable to England.[12]

That month, July 1794, is one of the great mysteries of the French Revolution. With the victory at Fleurus and those that followed, France might have believed that it was provisionally saved in military terms and that, with the plunder that followed, it could be saved economically, again at least provisionally. Yet the government did nothing to respond with new policies. Nine months earlier, in the autumn of 1793, it had told the world that the Terror and the centralised, unconstitutional government would be 'Revolutionary until the peace';[13] yet, though victories were finally arriving and peace theoretically within reach, it did nothing to ease the Terror.

On the contrary, Robespierre simply stayed away from public affairs. For at least three weeks, from July 3 (*15 messidor*), 1794, he did not appear in the *Convention*, and he did not turn up at the office of the CSP until July 23, when it was in joint session with the police committee, the *Comité de sûreté générale* (CSG), ostensibly to affect a reconciliation between them. Between those dates, it seems he may have gone occasionally to the *Jacobin* Club, but he did not give any speeches there. He does not appear to have been physically ill, at least not in the ordinary sense, since he received some government papers at home and signed five of them.[14] Yet for three weeks of maximum crisis, Robespierre remained physically absent from the affairs of government.

No one knows why he went absent, nor what he did; I have seen nothing which claims to give a factual and contemporaneous account of these things. That is how secret he was determined to be, and how effective his secrecy. My guess is that while the Terror was feeding on itself, everywhere generating wild, unlimited fears and suspicions, similar forces were working on Robespierre's mind; but that is just a guess.

What is not in question is that the pressures which the Terror generated in Robespierre's absence sent fissures right across the political scene. Inside the CSP, the regular absences over several months of many of his allies had already weakened his position. After September 25, 1793, according to Michelet, about half the members of the CSP were usually away *en mission*, and most of the remainder were not supporters of Robespierre. These included Carnot, a moderate who was virtually in control of military policy; Claude Prieur de la Côte d'Or, also a moderate and a close ally of Carnot; Bertrand Barère, a moderate from *la Plaine*; and, of course, the *Hébertistes* Jacques Billaud-Varenne and Collot d'Herbois.[15]

Carnot was in conflict with Saint-Just over control of war policy and in partnership with Billaud-Varenne against Robespierre, whom they accused of aiming to be a dictator. Mathiez maintains that this suspicion was unfounded; but he admits that Robespierre's character and behaviour generated much of the resentment against him. He was immensely secret as a matter of principle, and Mathiez says that he 'seldom gave himself away, and maintained with most people a cold and distant reserve which could seem calculation or ambition. He felt misunderstood, and he suffered for it'.[16]

There was also growing friction between the two governing *comités*. The CSG, which was primarily responsible for police matters, was irritated that Robespierre had created a rival police bureau inside the CSP. One of the members who spoke out about this was Marc-Guillaume Alexis Vadier, officially one of the chief managers of the Terror. Mathiez describes him as 'a cynical and libertine old man, who had at heart only one faith, that of atheism.'[17] Vadier had helped to ensure the death of Danton by engineering the curtailing of his trial; he detested Danton, whom he characterised as a 'stuffed turbot'.[18]

But the biggest threat to Robespierre came from those twenty-one members of the *Convention* who had been sent out as *envoyés en mission* but recalled for disciplinary reasons, including such prominent figures as Barras, Carrier, Fouché, Fréron and Tallien. On their return they had each called on Robespierre or written him a letter of supplication, to ask for his help and protection. 'He rejected them with contempt', says

Mathiez. 'Not merely that, he made no secret of the fact that he would seek their punishment.' In fact, according to Mathiez, Robespierre was set on sending four or five of them to the *Tribunal révolutionnaire*, which implied the threat of a death sentence.[19] In principle, a long-standing constitutional law which gave members of the *Convention* immunity from prosecution protected these offending *envoyés*, though it had not saved the *Girondins* or Danton and his allies; and as they had witnessed in those trials, the government had no scruples against rushing through anti-constitutional laws. It now repeatedly attempted to get that immunity lifted, through the back door of the infamous Law of 22 *prairial* (June 10, 1794), but was blocked by protests from other members of the *Convention*. This on-and-off threat of retribution played a key role in the final crisis over Robespierre, and he paid a heavy price for turning down the supplication of the *envoyés*.

The dénouement came on July 26 (*8 thermidor*), 1794, when Robespierre re-emerged from his self-imposed seclusion to deliver a long speech to the *Convention* denouncing his enemies and the enemies of the Revolution. He started by denouncing William Pitt the Younger and England's allies; but then he turned on Pierre Cambon, the dominant speaker in the *Convention* on economic affairs. 'The counter-revolution is based in the administration of our finances', he declaimed and argued that Cambon was just a follower of Chabot and Fabre, two members of the *Convention* who had recently been executed for corruption.

The *Convention* was now agog and trembling with fear: whom would Robespierre accuse next? Instead he launched into a rambling tirade against the members of his own government:

> Let us say that there is a conspiracy against public liberty; that it owes its strength to a criminal coalition which is conspiring right in the heart of the *Convention*; that this coalition has its accomplices in the *Comité de sûreté générale* and in the offices of this committee, which they dominate; that the enemies of the Republic have set this *Comité* against the *Comité de salut public*, and thus created two governments; that members of the *Comité de salut public* have joined this conspiracy ...

'What is the remedy of this evil?', he asked rhetorically. 'Punish the traitors, renew the offices of the *Comité de sûreté générale*, purge this committee itself and place it under the *Comité de Salut Public*; purge the

Comité de salut public itself, and set up a united government under the supreme authority of the national *Convention*.'[20]

The *Convention* was stunned. Robespierre had accused almost everybody of some kind of counter-revolutionary conspiracy; he had attacked all the main institutions of the national government; but he had named no names, except that of Cambon. Robespierre's loyal ally Georges Couthon proposed the traditional vote of thanks and that Robespierre's speech be printed and distributed; and the *Convention* dumbly voted its approval. But then Cambon stood up and demanded the right of reply: 'Before being dishonoured', he said, 'I shall speak to France!' He accused Robespierre of paralysing the *Convention*. His vehemence changed the course of the debate, for it gave courage to Billaud-Varenne, who proposed that Robespierre's speech, instead of being automatically printed and distributed to all the *communes* in the country, in the normal way, should first be re-examined by the two governing *comités*. Robespierre's position started to look shaky. Étienne Panis, once one of the most Revolutionary leaders of the *Commune*, challenged Robespierre to name those members of the *Convention* whom he was accusing of conspiracy; Robespierre simply refused. The *Convention* was in an uproar and cancelled its decision to have his speech printed. It began to look as if Robespierre's position were in the balance.

That evening he went to the meeting of the *Jacobins*, where he again read his speech; and there he was wildly applauded by his loyal supporters. Collot d'Herbois and Billaud-Varenne, who were present at the meeting, were booed, hissed and forced to leave. Later that evening, at the office of the CSP, they had a violent scene with Saint-Just, who had been deputed to speak on behalf of the Robespierrists at the *Convention* the next day. The altercation was brought to an end, but only just, when Saint-Just promised that he would read out the final text of his speech the next morning at the CSP before delivering it at the opening of the *Convention*.

But the next morning Saint-Just did not appear at the CSP but went straight to the *Convention*. It was now the morning of July 27 (9 *thermidor*), 1794. Amid mounting uproar, he went up to the rostrum and tried to read his speech, but Robespierre's enemies were determined that he should not be heard. Overnight there had been secret negotiations between the four or five leading *envoyés en mission*, who were most threatened by the danger of prosecution in the *Tribunal révolutionnaire*, and the moderates in the *Convention*, known as *la Plaine*, who were determined that there should be an end to the Terror. Robespierre's government and the Terror were in jeopardy. Tallien and Billaud-Varenne constantly interrupted Saint-Just at the rostrum, with the complicity of Collot d'Herbois from his seat as the President of the *Convention*. Robespierre stood up and tried to speak, but his voice was drowned out by loud shouts and angry protests. The meeting was firmly controlled by Tallien, Barère and Vadier, while the role of President had been handed over to Thuriot, a former member of the CSP who had resigned after quarrelling with Robespierre.

Billaud-Varenne stood up and accused Robespierre of having sole responsibility for the *Loi du 22 prairial* and, in short, of being a tyrant; and Tallien came forward, brandishing a dagger and demanding the arrest of Robespierre's closest followers. The *Convention* immediately voted the arrest of François Hanriot, the Robespierrist General who commanded the *Garde nationale*, and of René François Dumas, the Robespierrist President of the *Tribunal révolutionnaire*. Robespierre again tried to speak, but his voice was again drowned out, by the shouting and the incessant ringing of the President's bell. Finally a voice from the depths of the *Convention*, from an obscure *député*, Louis Louchet, a Dantonist, was heard shouting above the hubbub: 'It's time to conclude! Vote now on the arrest of Robespierre!'[21]

The vote was held straight away and Robespierre's arrest adopted unanimously. His younger brother, Augustin, asked to be included with him; so did Saint-Just, and so did Couthon, followed by Philippe François Lebas, an obscure and devoted follower of Robespierre from Pas-de-Calais. All five were immediately arrested.

What is astonishing is that this penultimate act of the Revolutionary drama was still being played out, despite the rising frenzy of the Terror, according to formal rules of parliamentary procedure which had been invented, by the Revolutionaries themselves, only four years earlier.

The drama should now have been virtually over; yet in the next few hours, events descended once more into chaos and confusion. Robespierre had been arrested, but the leaders of the *Commune* made desperate efforts to have him rescued. Fleuriot-Lescot, the loyal Robespierrist who was now the Mayor of Paris, ordered the city gates to be closed and the great alarm bell (*tocsin*) to be rung; he forbade the city's prisons from accepting Robespierre or the other *députés* under arrest; and he called on the *Sections* to send gunners and other men to the *Hôtel de ville*.

At first his summons seemed successful. Gunners from some *Sections*

– but by no means all – gathered in the Place de Grève in front of the *Hôtel de ville*, and Robespierre's loyalists met in the *Club des Jacobins*, where they tried to coordinate policy with the leaders of the *Commune*. They sent men to release Hanriot from arrest, and they brought him back in triumph to the *Hôtel de ville*.

But this insurrection petered out. The men in the Place de Grève waited for a lead; but though Robespierre and his colleagues were all released from prison during the course of the evening, they seemed oddly in no hurry to take charge of the situation. At first Robespierre refused to go to the *Hôtel de ville*; and Couthon insisted on staying in his prison until midnight. Late at night, rain began to fall; and the men sent by the *Sections* drifted away. The insurrection had failed.

For its part, the *Convention* was slow to counter-attack. When it realised that the insurrection was failing, it instructed Barras, because of his reputation as an experienced former army officer, to raise a counter-force from the moderate and relatively bourgeois *Sections*; and it passed a decree declaring that the insurrectionists and all those who had escaped from arrest were now outlaws. This meant that Robespierre and his colleagues could be executed on sight. Mustering the counter-force took time, and it was not until two o'clock in the morning that Barras put together a sufficient contingent, which then converged on the *Hôtel de ville* in two columns and rushed in unexpectedly but with prearranged shouts of the secret password, which Hanriot had betrayed: *Vive Robespierre!*

In the main hall they found Robespierre and his allies writing an appeal to the armies. Robespierre's younger brother, Augustin, threw himself out of a window and broke his leg on the stone pavement below. Lebas killed himself with a shot from a pistol. A pistol shot smashed Robespierre's jaw, fired either by him in a suicide attempt or by one of the invading guards. In all versions he lay for many hours on a table in the *Hôtel de ville*, in great pain, with his jaw bandaged and bleeding, until his execution.

After their identification, Robespierre and his brother Augustin, Saint-Just, Couthon and Hanriot, together with another seventeen Robespierrists, were all convicted as outlaws. At 5.30 p.m. that day, July 28 (*10 thermidor*), 1794, they were executed. On the scaffold, before Robespierre was guillotined, the bandage was brutally ripped from his jaw, and he screamed in pain.

The following day, July 29 (*11 thermidor*), 1794, another seventy-three people from the insurrectional *Commune* were summarily executed as rebels against the *Convention*, and twelve more the next day. If you include Lebas, the faithful Robespierrist who committed suicide before he could be executed, and Jean-Baptiste Coffinhal, one of the notorious judges of the *Tribunal révolutionnaire*, who escaped but was captured and executed later, the death toll directly connected with the coup d'état against Robespierre was 107.

The Robespierrist phase of the French Revolution was over. 'Numerous would be those', says Mathiez, 'who would repent in the evening of their lives for their participation in 9 *thermidor*. In Robespierre they had killed, for a century, the democratic Republic.'[22] The problem with this judgement is that Robespierre did not, unfortunately, ever pursue policies which were likely to lead to a democratic republic, and in 1793 he had deliberately put aside the new democratic-populist Constitution which might conceivably have led in that direction.

Nevertheless, the fall of Robespierre remains, even for a non-Marxist historian like Furet, a deeply moving event. 'That is why 9 *thermidor*', he says,

> is such a profound dividing line in the history of the Revolution, and in fact in all of our history, that at this point, quite often, the pen of the *Jacobin* historian finds itself taken, without quite understanding it, by a strange lassitude. It is the end of the Revolution because it is the victory of representative legitimacy over Revolutionary legitimacy ... and as Marx says, the revenge of real society over *the illusions of politics*. If the death of Robespierre has that meaning, it cannot be because he was honest, and the *Thermidoriens* [those who overthrew him] corrupt. It is because he was, more than anyone else, the Revolution in power.'[23]

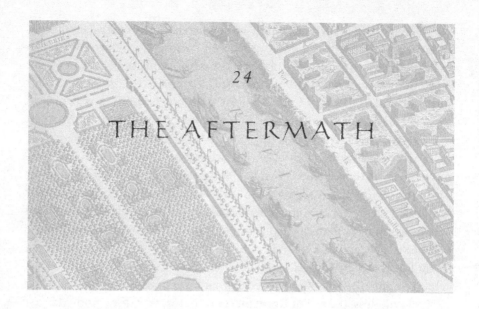

24

THE AFTERMATH

WITH THE FALL OF ROBESPIERRE, the French Revolution came to a juddering halt; but it did not come to rest for nothing had been settled.

In August 1792, Robespierre had thrown his weight behind the *sans-culottes* for the overthrow of their enemy, the King. In May and June 1793 he had used the *sans-culottes* for the overthrow of his enemies, the *Girondins*. Yet it turned out that the gap between his political aims and those of the *sans-culottes* was so profound that only the Terror and the abandonment of all the principles of legality underlying the foundations of the Revolution could contain it. The Terror alienated and frightened so many of Robespierre's most powerful bourgeois colleagues in the *Convention* that they rebelled and brought him down. Was the French Revolution over?

This question dominated political debate in France, interminably, over the next century and more; and the upheaval of the Revolution drove constant waves of political instability over the next five years, only to be halted, provisionally, by the coup d'état which brought Napoléon Bonaparte to power in 1799.

Some of the Revolutionaries had long been disillusioned, and Danton and the *Indulgents* had argued for winding down the Revolution. But while there were many who wanted to know where the Revolution was going, the only answer they had had was the *Convention*'s sybilline declaration on October 10, 1793, arranged by the *Montagnards*, that the government of France would be *révolutionnaire jusqu'à la paix*.[1] But peace did not come for another twenty-two years, and when it did, it was not with the triumph of the Revolution but only with the defeat of France and the overthrow not just of the Revolution but also of the Empire that had followed and subsumed it.

Many of the surviving Revolutionaries in the *Convention*, especially all those who had voted for the death of the King (and were therefore liable to be marked down as regicides in the books of any new, less Revolutionary regime), stood by the Revolution and insisted that it was still under way.

But the immediate aftermath of Robespierre's fall was uncertainty and confusion. On July 28, 1794, the day of his execution, Bertrand Barère, a middle-of-the-road *député* in the *Convention* and one of the founder members of the CSP, came forward to announce that the government would continue to function as usual. But the conspirators who had brought down Robespierre, known as *Thermidoriens* (from the date of his overthrow, *10 thermidor an II*), could not wait to dismantle the whole of the Robespierrist system. This was relatively easy because, with the execution of so many of his followers, the balance of power in the *Convention* had shifted sharply to the right. The *Montagne* was much reduced and had lost all influence; its remaining members were known as *Crêtois*, meaning 'those on the crest of the mountain'. Many of them gradually defected to *la Plaine*, in the middle, which was now the *Convention*'s centre of gravity. The seventy-three Deputies who had been ejected and arrested for protesting at the overthrow of the *Girondins* a year earlier were released from prison; and in December 1794 they and the few *Girondins* who had escaped to safety, like Pierre Claude François Daunou, Jean-Denis Lanjuinais and Jean-Baptiste Louvet, returned to their places in the *Convention*, where some of them joined forces with the *Thermidoriens*.

The *Convention* overturned the institutions of the *gouvernement révolutionnaire* with a systematic reform of the governing committees and the instruments of the Terror. It imposed a progressive, rolling purge of the CSP. Billaud-Varenne, Collot-d'Herbois and Bertrand Barère were the first to go; they had been denounced in the *Convention* as if they were accomplices of Robespierre, and in the spring of 1795 they were put on trial, and condemned to deportation to Guiana; Barère managed to evade the sentence, but the other two were deported. The Convention also immediately decreed, after the fall of Robespierre, that no *envoyé en mission* could be a member of the CSP; which meant that Jean-Bon Saint-André (in Toulon) and Pierre Louis Prieur de la Marne (in Brest) were automatically excluded. Lindet, the younger Prieur (de la Côte d'Or) and Lazare Carnot retired by ordinary rotation on October 6, but Carnot was reappointed by special arrangement, because he was too useful in helping organise the war effort; which meant that by the end of that month, he was the only one of the original members who was still there.[2] Moreover, the CSP was downgraded from its position of dominance: now it was just one of sixteen committees, each with responsibility for a closely circumscribed area of policy. The CSG continued to have responsibility for police matters, and the CSP was confined to war and diplomacy.

Even more telling, the *Convention* suppressed the machinery of the Terror and restored previous elements of legality. Antoine Fouquier-Tinville, the chief prosecutor of the *Tribunal révolutionnaire*, was arrested four days after the fall of Robespierre; and the Tribunal virtually ceased to function. It was formally closed in May 1795 and Fouquier-Tinville guillotined with fifteen other members. The role of the *comités révolutionnaires*, the police committees which had been set up in each *Section* and each *commune* to feed the Terror, was sharply reduced and their number cut back to twelve for the whole of Paris, instead of forty-eight for the forty-eight *Sections*. The *Convention* also repealed the Law of 22 *prairial* (June 10, 1794), which had been introduced to deprive the accused of any form of defence in court. Many hundreds of prisoners, previously arrested as suspects under the Terror laws but not yet put on trial, were released, nearly 500 in Paris alone in the first few days after the fall of Robespierre. The Terror was at an end.

When Robespierre had mobilised the *sans-culottes* against the *Girondins*, he had opened the door to class war. With his fall and the lifting of the Terror, the bourgeoisie set about getting their own back. This phase of this new class war burst out immediately in the wake of the change of government, with waves of punitive demonstrations against known groups of *Jacobins* in Paris and in the leading provincial towns by gangs of violent young men from the well-off bourgeoisie, known as *muscadins* (fops) or *jeunesse dorée* (gilded youth). These demonstrations were mobilised by some of the Revolutionaries who had played key roles in bringing Robespierre down, Tallien, Antoine Merlin de Thionville and

Louis-Stanislas Fréron; the demonstrators were popularly known as *la jeunesse dorée de Fréron*.

Soon the *Convention* officially clamped down on the whole *Jacobin* system; in October 1794 it forbade the networking of affiliated *Jacobin* clubs and the organisation of joint petitions, and on November 12 it closed down the *Jacobin* Club itself. Those Paris *Sections* that *Jacobins* had dominated were invaded by noisy and threatening gangs of *muscadins*, then by moderate bourgeois.

In the provinces there was a violent backlash against the Revolution, especially in the south and the south-east, where a number of reactionary and royalist gangs formed, calling themselves, for instance, *Compagnie de Jésus* in Lyon or *Compagnie du Soleil* in the south. This *Terreur blanche*, in the shape of massacres of *Jacobins* who had been thrown out of power and put in prison, started in Lyon, where more than 100 were murdered on May 4, 1795, and was followed in Aix-en-Provence, where another 40 were killed. The worst episode was the massacre at Fort-Saint-Jean in Marseille on June 5, 1795, where a representative of the *Convention* urged on a gang of young men who slaughtered about 100 *Jacobin* prisoners with sabres and grapeshot. There were other outbreaks of counter-revolutionary violence, in Nîmes and Avignon, but gradually the *Convention* turned against the *Terreur blanche* and by the end of the summer put a stop to it.

The *muscadins* were also known as *les Incroyables* (the Unbelievables). They wore their hair long, down to their shoulders, and went about in eccentric clothes: wide-brimmed round hats, enormous cravates, velvet britches, silk stockings and pointed shoes. In short, their dress was intended to advertise that they were not *sans-culottes*. They were called *Incroyables* partly because of their exaggerated dress but partly because they adopted an affected, ostensibly upper-class form of speech. It including a pretended inability to pronounce their Rs, so they were always referred to, derisively, as *Incwoyables*.

It was no longer smart to be a *sans-culotte*; in fact, even looking like one could be dangerous. The outfit worn by the politically correct *sans-culottes* – the loose trousers, the workingman's smock and the red bonnet on top of flat and unpowdered hair – was so unfashionable that its appearance could be a sufficient pretext for arrest. And whereas it had recently been compulsory to address people simply as *citoyen* or *citoyenne* (citizen) and to use the ultrafamiliar or vulgar *tu* form of address, it now became conventional to address people with more formal politeness, as *monsieur* or *madame*, and as *vous*.

Among the rich and privileged minority, austerity was lifted, and the release of tension at the end of the Terror in turn released a frenzy of self-indulgence. The uncertainties of the Revolution, exacerbated by speculation in Church property, inflation and economic chaos, had made it possible for some to become unimaginably rich by initiative or corruption – the financiers, the bankers, the traders, the arms manufacturers and the speculators, not to mention the *envoyés en mission* who had made vast sums through embezzlement and extortion; and many of the newly rich threw themselves into extravagant and spectacular self-gratification.

Social life was dominated by the private salons of the wives of the rich; the carriages came out, servants were once again in demand, and the balls and the parties began. The beautiful and scandalous twenty-one-year-old Thérésa Cabarrus, a divorcée and the very new trophy wife of the *Thermidorien* Tallien, was one of a number of ultrarich and gorgeous young women, all friends, libertines and rivals, who created sensations by appearing in public in daring costumes, almost semi-naked. Conspicuous among them were the eighteen-year-old Fortunée Hamelin, the wife of a *fermier général*; the sixteen-year-old Jeanne Récamier, the wife of the banker Jacques Récamier; and the newly widowed, thirty-one-year-old Joséphine de Beauharnais. Fortunée and Joséphine were friends and Creoles, Fortunée from Saint-Domingue, Joséphine from Martinique. Joséphine's late husband, General Alexandre de Beauharnais, had been guillotined just five days before the overthrow of Robespierre, for having failed adequately to defend Mainz from seige by the Austrians. She was remarried less than two years later, on March 9, 1796, to Napoléon.

Eventually, the new regime turned against some of the most notorious Revolutionary Terrorists. In September 1794, Carrier was tried and condemned for the mass murders (*les noyades*) of hundreds of rebels at Nantes. He was guillotined on December 16. Towards the end of that month, the *Convention* set up a committee to examine the records of other controversial Revolutionaries: Barère, Billaud-Varenne, Collot d'Herbois and Vadier, the member of the CSG who was formally most responsible for the conduct of the Terror. In the spring of 1795, Barère, Billaud-Varenne and Collot d'Herbois were condemned to deportation to French Guiana and Vadier to Madagascar; but Barère and Vadier escaped before they could be deported and survived long into the next century.

The new regime also had to deal with urgent problems of policy. France was struggling to work out how to fight and win the war with most of the rest of Europe. Above all, its economy was still in a mess, with rampant inflation, increasingly acute food shortages and rising waves of angry protests from the populace. The system of price controls known as *le maximum*, which was badly designed, widely unpopular and largely circumvented, was simply abandoned at the end of 1794. The weather that winter was particularly harsh, with the most extreme frosts of the century, and many people died of cold or hunger. The *assignat*, which had fallen to 31 per cent of its face value at the time of the fall of Robespierre, fell further, to 20 per cent in December, and by the spring of 1795 was worth no more than 8 per cent. Peasants were increasingly reluctant to sell food for *assignats*. The consequent shortages, and the galloping inflation, were especially severe that spring, and food rioting broke out in many parts of France. In Amiens and in Rouen the demonstrating crowds shouted the slogan 'Some bread and a King!' (*Du pain et un roi!*); in Paris the cry was more Revolutionary: 'Some bread and the Constitution of 1793!' (*Du pain et la Constitution de 1793!*). In such circumstances, the conspicuous self-indulgence of an ultrarich minority could only be a provocation to the mass of the population, many of whom were suffering severe deprivation and some of whom were starving.

In Paris the daily bread ration fell steadily, yet the queues at the doors of the bakers' shops got longer and longer, often in vain. In the first three months of 1795 the Paris cost of living index went up 55 per cent. As the weeks went by, the signs grew of an impending conflict between the *sans-culottes* of the working-class Paris *faubourgs* and the bourgeois Revolutionaries of the *Convention*. In March two of the *Sections* in the workers' district of Saint-Antoine sent a tumultuous delegation to the *Convention* to appeal for help; the *Convention* responded with a decree threatening the death penalty for anyone who insulted its members. On April 1 (*12 germinal*) a large but leaderless crowd of *sans-culottes* invaded the *Convention*, but it was easily brought under control by the forces of law and order, backed up by a gang of *muscadins* mobilised by Tallien. On the same day, the *Convention* appointed General Jean-Charles Pichegru, one of the heroes of the battle of Fleurus and now the commander of the *armée du Nord*, as the new (if temporary) commander of the *Garde nationale*.

This set an ominous precedent. The *Garde nationale* had been created and mobilised by the Paris municipality as a militia of local bourgeois citzens; and in the innocent and heady days of 1789 its figurehead had been the flamboyant, self-important and boyish marquis de La Fayette, prancing about on his white horse. The appointment of Pichegru was the first time that the *Garde nationale* had been entrusted to a war-hardened professional soldier and was a symptomatic response to a manifestly unstable political situation, in which the military was eventually called on to play a decisive role.

With the bread ration still falling, from 1.5 pounds per head in February 1795 to 1 pound in March and 0.5 pounds in April, agitation in popular quarters steadily intensified. In May the bread ration was down to a starvation level of 0.25 pounds a day, and on May 20 (*1 prairial*) a large crowd of hungry protesters from the working-class quarters of Saint-Antoine and Saint-Marcel invaded the *Convention*, swamping the proceedings with their tumultuous numbers. There was a scuffle, and one of the Deputies was killed: Jean Bertrand Féraud, a sometime friend of the *Girondins* who had participated in the overthrow of Robespierre on that fatal night. Regardless of his history, the demonstrators cut off his head on the spot, stuck it on a pike and waved it in the face of the *Convention*'s President, François Antoine Boissy d'Anglas, a moderate conservative and monarchist. Despite the implied threat and the noise and confusion in the hall, from which virtually all the Deputies had fled, apart from a few *Montagnards* (who had stayed behind in support of the *sans-culotte* protestors), Boissy d'Anglas kept his self-control, and stood up and bowed respectfully to the head on the pike.

For a while the result of this demonstration seemed in doubt. The handful of *Montagnards* remaining in the hall voted through a few measures favourable to the *sans-culottes*, who gradually dispersed. But after midnight the conservative Deputies returned to their places, repealed these measures and had the *Montagnards* arrested. Over the next few days the conservatives made some conciliatory gestures towards the demonstrators, but in the background they were gathering their forces for a counter-attack. After the *sans-culottes* had invaded the *Convention* on April 1, it had ordered on April 10 'the disarming of the men known in their *Section* as having taken part in the horrors committed under the tyranny',[3] meaning all those who had contributed to the Terror launched by Robespierre. Since the carrying of arms had become, in the course of the Revolution, a symbol of Revolutionary citizenship, this implied the beginning of an overt class war against the *sans-culottes*, a sort of *Loi des suspects* in reverse. On May 23 the *Thermidoriens* mustered a force of 20,000 men, including 3,000 cavalry, and sent them into the rebellious *faubourg* Saint-Antoine. The leaderless *sans-culottes* surrendered without a fight: the protests of *prairial* were over.

Retribution followed their surrender. The new Military Commission, a right-wing successor to the left-wing *Tribunal révolutionnaire*, tried 149 rebels and sentenced 36 to death, 18 to prison and 12 to deportation. Those condemned to death included six of the *Montagnard députés* who had sided with the protestors; three of them committed suicide, but the other three went to the guillotine. There followed a vast wave of 1,200 arrests of suspects in the *Sections*, *Jacobins* and former Terrorists, even if they had had nothing to do with the demonstrations at the *Convention*. The *Garde nationale* was purged of anybody who was politically unreliable, and on May 23 the CSG announced that the prisons were full.[4]

The failure of the protests of the spring of 1795 (*germinal* and *prairial an III*) marked the decisive defeat of the *sans-culottes* and of all their hopes, as Albert Soboul laments: 'Exhausted, disorganised, deprived of its leaders and of its cadres by repression, the popular movement saw ranged against it, from Republicans to partisans of the *ancien régime*, the bloc of the bourgeoisie supported by the army. Its spring, the popular movement, having been broken, the Revolution was over.'[5]

The problem with this judgement, understandable though it may be, is that in one crucial respect it simply does not square with the facts. The spring of the Revolution was not the popular movement, as Soboul says: it was the bourgeoisie.

Members of the bourgeoisie had started the Revolution, devised its rules and kept it going. It was always most likely that they would be on top of whatever was left, and that Robespierre and the *sans-culottes* he had mobilised would lose out.

In some narrow sense the French Revolution was over. But politics is not necessarily a zero-sum game, and there is no last move. The only serious political question after the fall of Robespierre was whether the bourgeoisie would know how to make any sense, in terms of their own ideals, of their victory. The evidence of the next few years, if not the next two hundred, was that they did not.

In the year after the overthrow of Robespierre, between March and August 1795, the *Thermidoriens* devised a Constitution with election rules bent to favour the better-off: to be a simple voter, a man had to be more than twenty-one years old and to have paid some direct tax; but an elector at the next tier up – that is to say, someone who actually voted for a member of parliament – had to have paid tax equivalent to 100 to 200 days' work, depending on his district. This cut the number of electors to 30,000 for the whole of France, or just over 0.1 per cent of the population of 28 million.

In contrast to its predecessors, all of which based the national government in a single-chamber National Assembly, this Constitution created two houses of parliament: a lower house of 500 younger men at least thirty years old, called *Le Conseil des Cinq-Cents* (the Council of the Five Hundred); and an upper house of 250 men over forty, called *Le Conseil des Anciens* (the Council of the Seniors). The role of the lower house was to draft laws and put them forward to the upper house, whose role was to adopt or reject – without amending – them. This structure was topped off by a new institution called the *Directoire*, consisting of five *Directeurs*, whom the two houses nominated and elected. There were rolling elections for both houses, one-third of the members each year, and for the five *Directeurs*, one each year.

The apparent thinking behind these arrangements was that two chambers and frequent elections would optimise the chances of stability and reduce the risks of any kind of dictatorship. In reality, the annual elections made instability much more likely, above all because there was no mechanism for resolving conflicts between the government and the two houses of parliament. Worse, the *Thermidoriens* added a special twist to the election rules to ensure themselves a place in the new system. They knew that they were deeply unpopular on the left and as regicides with the resurgent royalist right. So they decreed that two-thirds of the houses of parliament, that is, 500 of the 750 members, must be outgoing Deputies of the *Convention*. By definition, the *Convention* included all the surviving regicides. If the number of Deputies who were elected to the new houses did not reach the required complement of 500, those who had been elected would be entitled to name enough additional Deputies to make up the full quotient. It would have been hard to devise a system more likely to lead to uproar.

The Constitution was submitted to a plebiscite on September 6, 1795, and in one sense it was massively endorsed: 916,334 voted yes and only 41,892 voted no. But the turnout was once again lamentable, fewer than 1 million voters of a possible electorate of 5 million, which was tantamount to a repudiation. The 'Two-Thirds Decree' was even more unpopular: only 205,498 voted yes, while 108,754 voted no, and it was rejected by a majority of the voters in a quarter of the French *départements* and in all but one of the forty-eight Paris *Sections*, eighteen of which challenged the validity of the results.

Nevertheless, the Constitution was formally adopted on September 23 (*1er vendémiaire*), 1795, but popular discontent with the new arrangements soon erupted on all sides. There was royalist agitation in Paris on September 24, and another major demonstration on October 4. Conscious of the dangers facing it, the *Convention* pre-empted the implementation of the Constitution by appointing a sort of embryo five-man *Directoire*, including Barras, one of its members most experienced in military matters. When there was an even bigger insurrection on October 5 (*13 vendémiaire*), the *Convention* ordered General Jacques Menou to deal with it. Menou, a forty-five-year-old regular officer, was the General commanding the military division in Paris, and he had already, that May, put down a popular uprising in the *faubourg* Saint-Antoine. But this time he hesitated, and for a few hours a large part of the capital fell into the hands of the insurgents. The *Convention* removed Menou from his command and handed over the organisation of the repression to Barras, who gathered round him a number of Generals he trusted, including Bonaparte, at the time with the titular rank of Brigadier but temporarily without a job.

General Louis Michel Danican led the insurrection. He was a regular officer and a Republican, but he had fallen out with the *Convention* after denouncing a number of his fellow officers for the atrocities they had committed in the Vendée, and he offered his services to the royalist insurgents. He led his force, some 20,000 strong, along the Seine towards the Tuileries, where the *Convention* was housed, but artillery mobilised by Bonaparte mowed them down. The insurrectionists suffered about 200 dead or wounded, the defenders of the *Convention* slightly fewer. By six o'clock in the evening the forces of the *Convention* were victorious, and that was the end of the last Parisian insurrection of the Revolution.

Bonaparte was well rewarded by Barras. Three days after helping to suppress the insurrection of *vendémiaire*, he was promoted to Deputy Commander of the *armée de l'Intérieur*; eight days later he was promoted from Brigadier to Lieutenant-General; and ten days after that, on October 26, 1795, he was the Commander-in-Chief of the *armée de l'Intérieur*. The next spring, on March 9, 1796, he married Joséphine de Beauharnais, and two days later he left Paris for Italy at the head of the *armée de l'Italie*, with which he was to make a fortune, for the army, for France and for himself, and a reputation as the country's principal military hero.

The suppression of the *vendémiaire* insurrection coincided with the beginning of better days for the Revolutionary government. The rebellion in the Vendée was running out of steam, and the armies of the Republic were winning significant victories there. One rebel leader, Nicolas Stofflet, was captured on February 23, 1796, and executed by firing squad two days later; another, François Charette, was captured on March 19 and executed ten days later. The war with the rest of Europe was going well too. French forces conquered Holland, which surrendered Dutch Flanders and agreed to pay an indemnity of 100 million florins. Prussia simply withdrew from the war to concentrate on getting its share in the Third Partition of Poland, and in the first Peace of Basel (April 5, 1795) it formally accepted French occupation of the left bank of the Rhine.

The trouble was that six years of Revolution had split France from top to bottom with deep political divisions, from the stubborn *Jacobins* and their sometime *sans-culotte* allies on the left to the vengeful and unreconstructed royalists on the right. Since the Constitution devised by the *Thermidoriens* offered no mechanism for negotiating or reconciling these divisions, the almost inevitable consequence was a series of unconstitutional explosions.

Some French historians refer to these explosions as the four coups d'état of the *Directoire*. In fact, the whole second phase of the French Revolution, from the overthrow of the King in 1792 to the overthrow of Robespierre in 1794, can be considered a sequence of large coups d'état, punctuated by an accelerating series of minor ones.

The first of the new coups d'état, known as the *coup d'état de fructidor*, erupted in the autumn of 1797. The elections in April of that year had produced a right-wing parliament, which was automatically in conflict with the policies of the Revolutionary rump of the *Directoire*, led by Barras, Louis Marie de La Revellière-Lépeaux and Jean-François Reubell. Barras called on Bonaparte for support, and he agreed to help, but on one condition: that the *Directoire* back the Treaty of Campoformio,[6] a temporary peace with Austria which Bonaparte had negotiated on his own initiative, on terms entirely disregarding the instructions from the authorities in Paris. When Barras acceded, Bonaparte sent Charles Augereau, one of his Generals in the *armée de l'Italie*, to Paris where Augereau was appointed the commander of the capital's seventeenth military division. He then flooded Paris with troops, and on September 4, 1797, the results of the April elections were simply cancelled in 49 *départements* and 177 right-wing *députés* disqualified.

One of these *députés* was Pichegru, who had played a significant role in the repression of the *Jacobin* insurrection of April 1, 1795. After the *coup d'état de fructidor*, he was one of sixty-five politicians deported to French Guiana.[7]

The immediate result of this coup d'état was another one the following spring. The expulsion of the *députés* after the elections of the previous year had created a large number of vacancies for the elections in the spring of 1798 to fill, and it seemed likely that the vote would produce a large swing to the left. In the *coup d'état de floréal* on May 11, 1798, the *Directoire* simply disqualified 106 undesirable *députés* so as to ensure a comfortable majority of moderates in the *Conseils*.

Symptoms of political instability inherent in the system reappeared the following spring, but this time it was the neo-*Jacobins*, victorious in the parliamentary elections of April 1799, who took pre-emptive steps against the *Directoire*. They cancelled the election of one of the *Directeurs* who was hostile to them; pressured Barras to change sides; and forced another two *Directeurs*, La Révellière-Lépeaux and Merlin de Douai, to resign, then replaced them with two others who were more cooperative.

Two of this group of *Directeurs*, Emmanuel Sieyès, the intellectual leader of the radicals early in the Revolution, who had finally got a political role in the front rank, and, of course, Barras, decided to have done with the instability of the whole system, and this time they wanted a real coup d'état and a change of regime. Sieyès called on Bonaparte, who had just returned to France on October 9, 1799, covered with glory despite the fiasco of his absurd and abortive expedition to Egypt; and on November 9, 1799 (*18 brumaire an VIII*), Bonaparte's troops overthrew the constitutional authorities and replaced them with a regime called the Consulate, with Bonaparte as the First of the three Consuls. The Revolutionaries and the regicides may have thought or hoped that Bonaparte would support their ideas for a system of representative government; they found, almost immediately, that he intended to be their master. The Napoléonic era had begun, and the Revolution really was over.

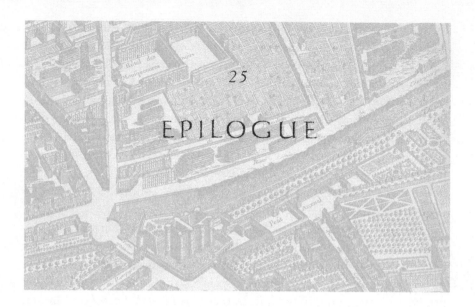

25

EPILOGUE

IN ANY ATTEMPT TO ASSESS the legacy of the French Revolution, the central dilemma is how to strike a meaningful balance between the pragmatic and the philosophical, between the hard-headed and the existential.

From a philosophical and existential point of view, the French Revolution has long been justly celebrated as one of the greatest sources of inspiration for republican and liberal ideals, the foundation story of the French Republic and French republicanism and in some ways the foundation story of democracy in continental Europe.

But from a practical, operational perspective, one must conclude that the French Revolution was, for at least the next hundred years, a deep and damaging failure. The Revolutionaries succeeded in pushing over the *ancien régime*, but they did not succeed in setting up a durable alternative system of government, even in theory. Their most important political innovations, no doubt, were to have declared overtly the principle of the sovereignty of the people, as opposed to the sovereignty of the King or of any other intermediary institution; and to have set out their political principles in a Declaration of the Rights of Man. They created many democratic institutions in many fields and at many levels, and they held many elections at different times. But they never grappled meaningfully with the idea of a working democracy that a majority of the people would accept.

There was, of course, a deep disconnect between their declaration of the sovereignty of the people and their failure to put this principle into practice. As François Furet says, 'There is a gulf between the record of the French Revolution and the intentions of the Revolutionaries'.[1]

In overthrowing the monarchy, they claimed an inspirational, insurrectional legitimacy, but it was spurious, imaginary and invented for the occasion. When the Revolution came to the years of heavy weather and crisis, they abandoned all ideas of democracy or constitutionality and steadily dismantled the legal institutions which they themselves had set up; at the point of crisis it seemed that legimacy was, for the Revolutionaries, the antithesis of democracy. In the end, the explosions they precipitated with the violent overthrow of the old institutions and the deep and divisive animosities which they unleashed with the Terror set off a tsunami of internecine political and social conflict which took at least a hundred years to calm down, and arguably much, much longer.

Of course, the hard-headed, operational perspective is certainly not the only, nor even necessarily the ideal, perspective for viewing the French Revolution. On the contrary, many people over the centuries have found it a puzzling event, and many of its aspects are still puzzling today. Throughout the nineteenth century the Revolution fascinated many of France's leading intellectuals and all of its leading politicians, because it confronted them with problems and had created tensions which they found they could not resolve. Indeed, many of France's leading politicians were so obsessed with the Revolution that they wrote long books about it, including François Guizot, Adolphe Thiers, Alphonse de Lamartine, Louis Blanc, Edgar Quinet and Jean Jaurès. None of them, as Furet points out, ever took the Revolution for granted:

> The greatest historians of the first half of the nineteenth century were still hypnotised by the event which had dominated their lives; but none of them, neither Guizot nor Michelet and certainly not Tocqueville, thought they were entitled to consider it familiar, 'normal', easy to understand. On the contrary, it is astonishment in the face of *the strangeness* of the phenomenon which constitutes the existential orientation of their historical work.[2]

They knew, as we know, that the Revolutionaries had bequeathed a vibrant legacy of political values going far beyond anything that they achieved, which are with us today. I have tried to tell the story of the Revolution in neutral terms, without engaging in the heated controversies which bedevilled so much of its historiography for well over a century. Yet there seems no point in denying that the Revolution had consequences that were for a long time disastrous for the polity and the society of France.

The first and most obvious was an apparently interminable legacy of political instability, with ceaseless and violent swings from one regime to another. The Revolutionaries were shunted aside in 1799 by Napoléon's coup d'état; but when he was finally defeated in 1815, he was succeeded not by a restoration of the Revolution but by a restoration of the Bourbon monarchy, with the two brothers, in succession, of the dead Louis XVI. In 1830 the second of these, Charles X, was himself overthrown and succeeded by a Bourbon cousin, Louis-Philippe, the surviving son of the guillotined duc d'Orléans. But in 1848 this King too was overthrown, and succeeded, after some turmoil, by a new Republic. Napoléon III (Bonaparte's nephew) overthrew this Second Republic in 1871 and installed a Second Empire. And so it went on.

After the fall of the July Monarchy in 1848, Tocqueville wrote mordantly about the repetitiveness of this cycle:

> I began to review in my mind the story of our last sixty years, and I smiled bitterly in observing the illusions we gave ourselves at the end of each period of this long Revolution ... The constitutional monarchy had followed on the *ancien régime*; the Republic on the monarchy; on the Republic, the Empire; on the Empire, the Restoration. Then came the July Monarchy. After each of these successive mutations we said that the French Revolution, having completed what we presumptuously called its task, was over. We said it, and we believed it. Alas! I had hoped it myself under the Restoration, and again ever since the government of the Restoration fell; and here is the French Revolution which is starting again, for it is always the same.'[3]

Different kinds of regimes not only alternated but were themselves unstable. The restored Bourbon monarchies had nine governments over their fifteen years. The July Monarchy of Louis-Philippe lasted eighteen years, from 1830 to 1848, and he had fifteen governments.

The Second Republic lasted three years and had six governments. The Second Empire was more stable, but then it was an Empire. The Third Republic was the most unstable: it lasted for sixty-nine years, from 1871 to 1940, and had eighty-six governments.

This instability did not merely take the form of frequent changes of government; such changes were so violent and so politically charged that they often seriously disrupted the lives of harmless politicians and intellectuals. Academic lecture courses in politics or history, even at the Sorbonne, were liable to be suspended or (later) restored depending on whether they offended or appeased the latest change of guard in the political establishment.

The Revolutionaries had regularly rejected any suggestion that they take account, in their debates on a new French state, of the example of events and institutions in England in the century which had passed since the English Civil War. This was partly because England was the old enemy and partly because the successor regime to the Restoration there was a distinctly non-revolutionary monarchy with a strong aristocratic element in the shape of the House of Lords. Yet with each wave of turbulence in France, many of the leading members of French society who found life too uncomfortable or too dangerous often sought refuge in England, where conditions were safer and stabler. When he felt in danger in 1791, after the affair of the Champ de Mars, even Danton fled for safety to England, though only very briefly.

When the change of regime in 1830 forced King Charles X out of France, he took refuge in England, first at Lulworth Castle, then at Holyrood in Edinburgh. When his successor, Louis-Philippe, was in turn driven out, this time by the Revolution of 1848, he too fled to England, to Claremont, where he died two years later. The 1848 Revolution also drove out Guizot, the conservative politician and historian, who also went to England, to a modest house in Pelham Crescent, now one of the most sought-after addresses in south-west London. But the list of exiles was not confined to kings and conservatives: it included Blanc and Quinet, two distinctly left-wing intellectuals. When the 1848 Revolution compelled Blanc to leave, he too escaped to England, where he wrote a history of the French Revolution in twelve volumes, returning to Paris only in 1870, with the fall of Napoléon III and the Second Empire. Quinet was in exile for almost as long, from 1851 to 1870, but in his case in Switzerland. Louis Napoléon sought refuge in England three times, the third time after his fall as Emperor Napoléon III. In

September 1870, after his defeat at Sedan, he was at first imprisoned by the Germans; but when they released him in March 1871 he left for England, to Camden Place in Chislehurst, where he died two years later.

The irony of this interminable sequence of instability is that almost all of these regimes started with the equivalent of a new Constitution, which most of them, with the exception of Napoléon and the first Restoration, prefaced with a new (but of course different) Declaration of the Rights of Man. So when Tocqueville made a mordant reference in 1856 to 'the nine or ten Constitutions which have been set up in perpetuity in France in the past sixty years',[4] it was not because he could not count, nor because there had been so many Constitutions *à perpétuité* that they were no longer worth counting, though that was probably part of his meaning. No, the prosaic fact is that between the first Revolutionary Constitution, of 1791, and the Constitution of the Second Empire of 1852, there were seven Constitutions, two Charters (one for the first Restoration, of 1814, and one for the July Monarchy of 1830) and one *Acte additionnel* (for the brief restoration of Bonaparte in the 100 Days of 1815). In other words, there really were, as Tocqueville had said, nine or ten Constitutions, depending on your definition of the term.[5]

There were two constants in this story of instability, besides instability itself. The first was the decisive influence of war and the consequent fact that, just as Robespierre seems to have predicted, the military kept intervening in the political process. Napoléon Bonaparte, of course, brought the Revolution formally to an end with the coup d'état of 1799. Napoléon III was overthrown in 1870 after his defeat in the Franco-Prussian War, and his Empire was followed, after a brief resurgence of the Parisian Revolutionaries in the bloody *Commune* of 1870, by another Republic, the Third. With the 1940 defeat of France in World War II, the Vichy regime of Philippe Pétain, a military hero of World War I, replaced this Third Republic, quite unconstitutionally.[6] Finally, the Fourth Republic, which governed France after World War II, was replaced in 1958, just as unconstitutionally, by the Fifth Republic of Charles de Gaulle, another military hero, of both World War I and World War II.

Neither Napoléon I nor Pétain nor de Gaulle could conceivably have come to power as the head of state of a new regime in France if they had not been national war heroes.

The second constant in the instability of nineteenth-century France was the deep theme of an unresolved dialectic between the idea of monarchy and the idea of republicanism. At the turning point of the Revolution, in 1792, when the King was overthrown, there had been no significant outbreak of popular protest; and in January 1793, when the King was condemned to death and executed, there was still no such manifestation, even though Danton had been convinced that the army and the country did not want the King to die. Nevertheless, the idea and the appeal of monarchy refused to go away. At one level this can be explained as the result of outside intervention: Louis XVIII succeeded to the throne because a European coalition handed it to him after Napoléon was defeated. Furet goes further, arguing that 'the history of the entire French nineteenth century can be considered the history of a struggle between the Revolution and the Restoration, as exemplified by such episodes as 1815, 1830, 1848, 1870, the *Commune*, May 16, 1877'.[7]

But the history of the French nineteenth century can also be seen as part of the struggle between the secular value system which the Revolutionaries developed and the deeply embedded religious roots of the Catholic Church. The Revolutionary cause had been seriously damaged for most ordinary people in France by the campaign of the Revolutionaries against the Church, and even more by the campaign of the *sans-culottes* against Christianity itself. The fall of Robespierre meant the abandonment of both of these campaigns, as well as of his invented counter-Cult of the Supreme Being. Christianity and the Church quickly revived in France, and in 1801 Napoléon and Pope Pius VII signed an agreement which officially recognised Catholicism as the religion of the great majority of the French people, though not as the state religion of France.

But this was just a truce between the claims of the state and those of the Church, not a peace; and peace did not come until 1905, with the negotiation of a Concordat and the passage of the French law on the separation of Church and state. The principle of *laïcité* (secularism) has been one of the central tenets of French civic law ever since and is enshrined in the first article of the Constitution of the Fifth Republic, which is still in force: 'France is an indivisible, secular [*laïque*], democratic and social Republic. It ensures equality before the law of all citizens without distinction of origin, race or religion. It respects every belief.'[8] In that sense, the struggle between the Revolution and the Catholic Church has been formally resolved for the past century; though not, of course, that between the state and more fundamentalist and 'jihadist' sects. French secularism has recently met its most significant challenge in the realm of public education, where the ideal of *laïcité* has come into conflict with the claims of Islamic culture.

It is often said that the French Revolution finally came to rest with the Third Republic, and that is what Furet appears to believe; but it seems to me that the traumas caused by the French Revolution continued to create deep disturbances in French society long after that. The deepest was, of course, the long-running Dreyfus affair. In 1894, in the slipstream of the political turbulence following the defeat of France in the Franco-Prussian War and the collapse of the Second Empire, a highly placed French army staff officer fabricated evidence against a fellow officer, Alfred Dreyfus, a Jew from Alsace, implicating him in espionage for the Germans. Dreyfus was tried and sentenced to deportation. Evidence undermining his conviction gradually mounted until it was irresistible; but the army opposed the reopening of the case for many years because France was riven with conservatism, Catholicism, paranoia and above all anti-Semitism. Dreyfus was finally acquitted in 1906, at the end of twelve years of a deep and bitter controversy which split French society from top to bottom.

Even after the Third Republic there remained a deep nostalgia for monarchy, long after there was any realistic chance of another restoration. At Verdun there is a vast monument to the many thousands of French soldiers who died in that epic and long-running battle of World War I. It is surmounted by a tall lookout tower in the shape of an artillery shell, which you can climb to look out over the ruined countryside. At the bottom of the tower, just above the first step, there is a wooden plaque which reads: 'To the dead of Verdun, Known and Unknown. The French royal family.'[9] This is clearly unofficial: when the monument was erected in 1937 (by private subscription), France was still a Republic and there was no French royal family with any status. On the other hand, no one prevented the installation of this plaque, and no one has taken it down; it is there still. Moreover, some nostalgia for monarchy survived, if in attenuated form, for at least another half century. In Paris in the years immediately after World War II, when the public celebrations of Bastille Day came round, every July 14, there were some elegant *quartiers* where some people would always close their shutters in protest.

It is not easy to determine when, or even if, the French Revolution ever came to rest. One may speculate that it could not be over until the French political system could go through a period of major turbulence without a constitutional crisis. By this test, the Third Republic obviously failed: with the defeat of France in 1940, it simply disintegrated. The military details of this perplexing defeat have been much debated; but it seems clear that the completeness of the French collapse cannot be fully explained in purely military terms but only by also invoking the deep political fractures in French society. There have been many analyses of these fractures; among the most eloquent is the vivid and moving picture of them in the novel *Suite française*, by Irène Némirovsky.

The Fourth Republic also failed spectacularly: in 1958 it was paralysed by the postcolonial crisis over Algeria, briskly overthrown by de Gaulle and replaced by his Fifth Republic.

It was in the Fifth Republic that the dynamics of French politics and society seemed to change. The first major challenge to this system came with the student riots and attendant massive wave of workers' strikes in 1968; but the Fifth Republic went through them with impressive stability. Perhaps, by my speculative test, the French Revolution really was coming to an end. If I were to put a date on it, I would say that the French Revolution finally came to rest after almost exactly 180 years, on April 28, 1969, when President de Gaulle resigned in a huff and the Fifth Republic, which he had founded, sailed on without him without a tremor.

So if, after so many years, France had finally emerged from the turbulence churned up by the Revolution, if the French had finally managed to sail past the Scylla and the Charybdis of monarchy and empire, the country should be able to look back with serenity on the sunny days of the great achievements of the early Revolution, as described by Tocqueville:

> That first phase of [17]89, when the love of equality and that of liberty shared their hearts; when they wanted not just to found democratic institutions, but free institutions; not just to destroy privileges, but to recognise and consecrate rights; times of youth, of enthusiasm, of pride, of generous and sincere passions and of which, despite their errors, men will forever cherish the memory, and which, for a long time yet, will disturb the sleep of all those who would wish to corrupt or enslave them.[10]

Tocqueville concluded his masterpiece on the French Revolution with a long peroration on the character and virtues of the French, which will serve for us too:

Good at everything, but excelling only in war; in love with chance, with force, with success, with flash and noise more than with real glory; more capable of heroism than of virtue, of genius than of common sense, likely to think up great plans rather than to carry through great enterprises; the most brilliant and the most dangerous of the nations of Europe, and the one most liable to become in turn an object of admiration, of hatred, of pity, of terror, but never of indifference.[11]

IN PLACE OF A
BIBLIOGRAPHY

In place of a formal bibliography, I have compiled three sets of sources which readers may find useful: the works from which I have quoted most frequently in the text and in the notes and which I believe to be readily available; a brief survey (in French) of the historiography of the French Revolution over the past two centuries and more; and books on the subject, many of which may be of interest, in a mainly uncommented list.

The books most frequently quoted

François Furet, *Penser la Révolution française*, 1978.

François Furet and Denis Richet, *La Révolution française*, 1965–66.

Albert Mathiez, 'Études Robespierristes: La corruption parlementaire sous la Terreur', cours public donné à Besançon, 1911–1912, in *Annales révolutionnaires*, vol. 5, 1912; reprinted as *La corruption parlementaire sous la Terreur* by the Bibliothèque Nationale in BnF Collection ebooks.

———, *La Révolution française*, 3 vols., 1922–24; reprint, 2012.

Jules Michelet, *Histoire de la Révolution française*, 7 vols., 1847–53; reprint in 4 vols., 1952. Gallimard have labelled the 4 volumes as *Histoire de la Révolution française* Tome 1, vol. 1 and vol. 2; and *Histoire de la Révolution française* Tome 2, vol. 1 and vol. 2. Citations in the notes therefore state Michelet (I) or Michelet (II) for clarity.

Albert Soboul, *La Révolution française*, 1965.

———, *Les sans-culottes parisiens en l'an II*, La-Roche-sur-Yon, 1958; 1968.

Alexis de Tocqueville, *L'ancien régime et la Révolution*, 1856, in *Œuvres*, vol. 3, Gallimard, éditions Pléiade.

———, *Souvenirs*, in *Œuvres*, vol. 3, Gallimard, éditions Pléiade.

Jean Tulard, *Histoire de la Révolution française*, Laffont, 1987.

I should also mention three dictionary/encyclopaedias which I found useful:

François Furet and Mona Ozouf (eds), *Dictionnaire critique de la Révolution française*, 1992.

Albert Soboul (ed.), *Dictionnaire historique de la Révolution française*, Éditions PUF, 1989.

Jean Tulard, Fayard, and Fierro, *Histoire et dictionnaire de la Révolution française*, Paris, Robert Laffont, 1987.

A historiography of the French Revolution

Any attempt to read about the French Revolution is bedevilled by the many contradictory passions which the subject has provoked, especially among French historians and especially in the second half of the nineteenth century and the first half of the twentieth. To help navigate these choppy waters, there is the particularly useful and undogmatic *Historiographie de la Révolution française*, which can be found under that title in the French version of *Wikipedia*. I wish I had come upon it before embarking on this project.

A suggested reading list

Florin Aftalion, *L'Économie de la Révolution Française*, 1987.

Elisabeth Badinter and Robert Badinter, *Condorcet*, 1988. A brilliant biography.

Tim Blanning, *The French Revolutionary Wars*, 1996.

Clarence Crane Brinton, *The Anatomy of Revolution*, 1973.

Hugh Brogan, *Alexis de Tocqueville*, 2006.

Howard G. Brown, *War, Revolution and the Bureaucratic State*, 1995.

Edmund Burke (1729–97), *Reflections on the Revolution in France*, 1790.

François René, vicomte de Chateaubriand (1768–1848), *Mémoires d'outre-tombe*. A melancholy post-Revolutionary masterpiece.

Guy Chaussinand-Nogaret, *La noblesse au XVIIIᵉ siècle*, 1976. Translated by Doyle, 1985.

Richard Cobb, *Death in Paris*, 1978.

———, *Reactions to the French Revolution*, 1972.

———, *A Sense of Place*, 1975.

———, *Tour de France*, 1976.

Alfred Cobban, *The Myth of the French Revolution*, 1955.

———, *The Social Interpretation of the French Revolution*, 1963.

It was Cobban, an English historian, who pioneered the intellectual attack which undermined the dominant French Marxist take on the Revolution.

Robert Darnton, *The Business of Enlightenment*, 1987.

———, *The Forbidden Best-Sellers of Pre-Revolutionary France*, 1997.

———, *George Washington's False Teeth*, 2003.

———, *The Great Cat Massacre*, 1984.

———, *The Kiss of Lamourette*, 1990.

Darnton was an American historian who wrote wonderfully about pre-Revolutionary France.

William Doyle, *Oxford History of the French Revolution*, 2nd ed., 2002.

David Hackett Fischer, *The Great Wave: Price Revolutions and the Rhythm of History*, 1996.

François Furet (ed.), *Les orateurs de la Révolution française*, Pléiade, 1989.

———, *Le passé d'une illusion*, 1995.

———, *La Révolution, 1770–1880: De Turgot à Jules Ferry*, 1988.

François Furet and Mona Ozouf (eds), *Dictionnaire critique de la Révolution française*, 1992.

François Furet and Denis Richet, *La Révolution française*, 1965–66.

Jacques Godechot, *La grande nation*, 1956.

———, *Les institutions de la France de 1789 à 1870*, 1951.

———, *Les révolutions, 1770–1799*, PUF, 1963.

Christopher Hibbert, *The French Revolution*, 1980.

Jonathan Israel, *Democratic Enlightenment*, 2011.

———, *Enlightenment Contested*, 2006.

———, *Radical Enlightenment*, 2001.

P. M. Jones, *The Peasantry in the French Revolution*, 1988.

John Keane, *Tom Paine: A Political Life*, 1995.

Hervé Le Bras and Emmanuel Todd, *L'invention de la France*, 1981. This exploration of the deep historical, regional and social diversity of France and the stability of the value systems in different regions is illuminating for any understanding of Revolutionary France.

Marcel Marion, *Histoire financière de la France depuis 1715*, vols. 1–4, 1914–25.

Albert Mathiez, *La Révolution française*, 3 vols., 1922–24; reprint, 2012.

Claude Mazauric, *Sur la Révolution française*, 1970.

Jules Michelet, *Histoire de la Révolution française*, 7 vols., Gallimard Pléiade, 1847–53.

Roland Mousnier, *Les institutions de la France sous la monarchie absolue, 1598–1789*, 2 vols., 1974–80.

Tom Paine, *The Age of Reason*, 1794.

———, *Common Sense*, 1776.

———, *The Rights of Man*, 1791.

R. R. Palmer, *The Age of the Democratic Revolution*, 1959. An essential book on pre-Revolutionary Europe.

———, *Twelve Who Ruled*, 1941. Though ill organised and not well written, this is still the foundation text on the *Comité de salut public*.

Palmer was a groundbreaking American historian of the period who wrote far too little.

George Rudé, *The Crowd in History: A Study of Popular Disturbances in France and England, 1730–1848*, 1963.

————, *The Crowd in the French Revolution*, 1959–67.

————, *Revolutionary Europe*, 1964.

Rudé, a Canadian historian, made a career sidestepping the question of what to think about the *sans-culottes* and what to call them.

Simon Schama, *Citizens*, 1989.

René Sedillot, *Le coût de la Révolution française*, 1987. Essential reading, with Aftalion.

Abbé Emmanuel Joseph Sieyès, *Qu'est ce que le Tiers-État?*, 1789.

Albert Soboul, *Dictionnaire historique de la Révolution française*, 1989.

————, *La 1re République*, 1968.

————, *La Révolution française*, 1965.

————, *Les sans-culottes parisiens en l'an II*, La-Roche-sur-Yon, 1958; 1968.

Madame de Staël, *Considérations sur la Révolution française*, 1818.

Timothy Tackett, *Atlas de le Révolution française*, 1996.

————, *Becoming a Revolutionary: The Deputies of the French National Assembly and the Emergence of a Revolutionary Culture (1789–1790)*, Princeton, Princeton University Press, 1996.

Joseph L. Talmon, *The Origins of Totalitarian Democracy*, 1952.

Alexis de Tocqueville (1805–59), *L'ancien régime et la Révolution* (1856), in *Œuvres*, vol. 3., Pléiade.

————, *De la démocratie en Amérique*, pt. 1, 1835.

————, *De la démocratie en Amérique*, pt. 2, 1840.

————, *Souvenirs*, Gallimard, Pléiade, *Œuvres*, vol 3, 1999.

Emmanuel Todd, *Le destin des immigrés*, 1994.

————, *L'invention de l'Europe*, 1990.

————, *La nouvelle France*, 1988.

Jean Tulard, *Histoire de France, vol. 4, Les révolutions de 1789 à 1851*,1985.

Jean Tulard, *Histoire de la Révolution française*, Laffont, 1987.

Michel Vovelle, *La Révolution contre l'Église*, 1988.

Eugene Weber, *Peasants into Frenchmen*, 1976. Weber complements Todd and traces the slow forging, over the nineteenth century, of the French into a more or less single nation.

Arthur Young, *Travels in France*, 1792.

A NOTE ON THE
CHILDREN OF LOUIS XVI

On May 16, 1770, Louis of France married Marie-Antoinette, the youngest daughter of the Austrian ruler Maria Theresa. He was fifteen years old and the Dauphin of France; she was fourteen.

Many years passed, and they did not have children. There was much speculation as to why this might be, some of it ill intentioned: Marie-Antoinette was not just foreign but Austrian.

Part of the speculation was that the two young people were inexperienced and unfamiliar with each other. There were also rumours that Louis was sexually incompetent and even that some physical condition, such as phimosis, may have physically impeded him from having normal sexual relations. The Austrian novelist Stefan Zweig, allegedly under the influence of his friend Sigmund Freud, canvassed this theory in the late nineteenth century, with the additional conjecture that a surgical operation on Louis' foreskin eventually cured his phimosis. Today, most historians treat these theories with scepticism; Louis was undoubtedly inexperienced when he married, but he may not have suffered from phimosis, and he probably did not have a surgical operation.

In 1774 Louis succeeded to the throne, and he eventually had four children by Marie-Antoinette, only one of whom, a daughter, long outlived her parents:

Marie-Thérèse, December 19, 1778–October 19, 1851
Louis Joseph (Dauphin), October 22, 1781–June 4, 1789
Louis Charles (Louis XVII), March 27, 1785–June 8, 1795

Sophie Hélène, July 9, 1786–June 19, 1787

Louis Joseph, the first son, automatically became the Dauphin, but he died in childhood. Louis Charles, his younger brother, succeeded him as Dauphin, and after the execution of their father in 1793, royalists regarded him as the rightful King, Louis XVII. But he remained in prison, and there were many stories, mostly gossipy and speculative, but plausible, about how various jailors mistreated him. He almost certainly died in prison, probably on June 8, 1795, at the age of ten; there were inevitably rumours that he survived and escaped.

Louis' fourth child, Sophie, born in 1786, lived less than a year. But his first child, a daughter, Marie-Thérèse, survived into her seventies, well into the nineteenth century.

A NOTE ON THE FRANCHISE FOR WOMEN

In France, women did not get the right to vote until 1944; and as a symptom of the fact that it was still, despite its Revolutionary heritage, a Catholic country, other women's rights, like birth control and abortion, were delayed longer there than in some more northern or formerly Protestant countries. In even more profoundly Catholic and therefore more conservative European countries, it took longer for women to gain the vote: in Italy in 1946 and in Greece in 1952; and longer still, of course, in those entrenched tax havens and bastions of male privilege: San Marino, in 1959; Monaco, in 1962; Andorra, in 1970; Switzerland, in 1971; and Liechtenstein, in 1984.

THE COUPS D'ÉTAT
OF THE FRENCH
REVOLUTION

The disintegration of the French Revolution was characterised by frequent coups d'état. This is not the orthodox story. All accounts of the broadly Revolutionary period speak of coups d'état, but they almost always mean the series of four coups d'état which took place after the fall of Robespierre, in the closing years of the century, during the prolonged instability of the *Directoire*:

1. 18 Fructidor An V (4 September, 1797);
2. 22 Floréal An VI (11 May 1798);
3. 30 Prairial An VII (18 June 1799);
4. 18 Brumaire An VIII (9 November, 1799), the final coup which brought
    Napoléon to power.

In fact, the main period of the Revolution, 1789–1794, was regularly and frequently punctuated, after the overthrow of the monarchy, (August 10, 1792), by what can only be described as coups d'état.

This list underlines how, as the Revolution went downhill, the Revolutionaries steadily dismantled, piece by piece, the structure of institutional law which they had themselves created during the previous three years:

1. August 9–10, 1792: *Commune Insurrectionnelle*: overthrow of monarchy;
2. August 11, 1792: *Comité de Surveillance de la Commune;*
3. August 17, 1792: *Tribunal du 17 août,* to try defenders of the Tuileries;

4. March 10, 1793: *Tribunal Révolutionnaire;*

5. March 21, 1793: *Comités de surveillance révolutionnaires*

6. April 6, 1793: *Comité de Salut Public, > Comités de Gouvernement;*

7. June 2, 1793: insurrection of *sans-culottes;* overthrow of *Girondins;*

8. September 4, 1793: *sans-culottes* invade the *Convention;* start of *Terreur;*

9. September 5, 1793: *Armées révolutionnaires;*

10. September 17, 1793: *loi des suspects;* mass arrests;

11. October 10, 1793: abandonment of the new Constitution: *'gouvernement révolutionnaire jusqu'à la paix'*

12. October 24–30: trial of *Girondins;* new emergency decree permitting jurors to convict if their 'consciences' permit; *Girondins* condemned to death;

13. December 4, 1793: *loi du 14 frimaire;* total central government;

14. March 21–24, 1794: trial of *Hébertistes;* 18 condemned to death;

15. April 2–5: trial of *Dantonistes;* new emergency decree silencing any accused who 'insulted' justice; *Dantonistes* condemned to death;

16. June 10, 1794: *loi du 22 prairial;* removing all defence from the accused;

17. July 27–28, 1794: *9–10 thermidor:* Robespierre declared an outlaw; 107 Robespierrists executed.

THE FRENCH TEXT OF THE DECLARATION OF THE RIGHTS OF MAN OF 1789

Les Représentants du Peuple Français, constitués en Assemblée nationale, considérant que l'ignorance, l'oubli ou le mépris des droits de l'Homme sont les seules causes des malheurs publics et de la corruption des Gouvernements, ont résolu d'exposer, dans une Déclaration solennelle, les droits naturels, inaliénables et sacrés de l'Homme, afin que cette Déclaration, constamment présente à tous les Membres du corps social, leur rappelle sans cesse leurs droits et leurs devoirs ; afin que les actes du pouvoir législatif, et ceux du pouvoir exécutif, pouvant être à chaque instant comparés avec le but de toute institution politique, en soient plus respectés ; afin que les réclamations des citoyens, fondées désormais sur des principes simples et incontestables, tournent toujours au maintien de la Constitution et au bonheur de tous.

En conséquence, l'Assemblée nationale reconnaît et déclare, en présence et sous les auspices de l'Etre suprême, les droits suivants de l'Homme et du Citoyen.

Art. 1er. Les hommes naissent et demeurent libres et égaux en droits. Les distinctions sociales ne peuvent être fondées que sur l'utilité commune.

Art. 2. Le but de toute association politique est la conservation des droits naturels et imprescriptibles de l'Homme. Ces droits sont la liberté, la propriété, la sûreté, et la résistance à l'oppression.

Art. 3. Le principe de toute Souveraineté réside essentiellement dans la Nation. Nul corps, nul individu ne peut exercer d'autorité qui n'en émane expressément.

Art. 4. La liberté consiste à pouvoir faire tout ce qui ne nuit pas à autrui : ainsi, l'exercice des droits naturels de chaque homme n'a de bornes que celles qui assurent aux autres Membres de la Société la jouissance de ces mêmes droits. Ces bornes ne peuvent être déterminées que par la Loi.

Art. 5. La Loi n'a le droit de défendre que les actions nuisibles à la Société. Tout ce qui n'est pas défendu par la Loi ne peut être empêché, et nul ne peut être contraint à faire ce qu'elle n'ordonne pas.

Art. 6. La Loi est l'expression de la volonté générale. Tous les Citoyens ont droit de concourir personnellement, ou par leurs Représentants, à sa formation. Elle doit être la même pour tous, soit qu'elle protège, soit qu'elle punisse. Tous les Citoyens étant égaux à ses yeux sont également admissibles à toutes dignités, places et emplois publics, selon leur capacité, et sans autre distinction que celle de leurs vertus et de leurs talents.

Art. 7. Nul homme ne peut être accusé, arrêté ni détenu que dans les cas déterminés par la Loi, et selon les formes qu'elle a prescrites. Ceux qui sollicitent, expédient, exécutent ou font exécuter des ordres arbitraires, doivent être punis ; mais tout citoyen appelé ou saisi en vertu de la Loi doit obéir à l'instant : il se rend coupable par la résistance.

Art. 8. La Loi ne doit établir que des peines strictement et évidemment nécessaires, et nul ne peut être puni qu'en vertu d'une Loi établie et promulguée antérieurement au délit, et légalement appliquée.

Art. 9. Tout homme étant présumé innocent jusqu'à ce qu'il ait été déclaré coupable, s'il est jugé indispensable de l'arrêter, toute rigueur qui ne serait pas nécessaire pour s'assurer de sa personne doit être sévèrement réprimée par la loi.

Art. 10. Nul ne doit être inquiété pour ses opinions, même religieuses, pourvu que leur manifestation ne trouble pas l'ordre public établi par la Loi.

Art. 11. La libre communication des pensées et des opinions est un des droits les plus précieux de l'Homme : tout Citoyen peut donc parler, écrire, imprimer librement, sauf à répondre de l'abus de cette liberté dans les cas déterminés par la Loi.

Art. 12. La garantie des droits de l'Homme et du Citoyen nécessite une force publique : cette force est donc instituée pour l'avantage de tous, et non pour l'utilité particulière de ceux auxquels elle est confiée.

Art. 13. Pour l'entretien de la force publique, et pour les dépenses d'administration, une contribution commune est indispensable : elle doit être également répartie entre tous les citoyens, en raison de leurs facultés.

Art. 14. Tous les Citoyens ont le droit de constater, par eux-mêmes ou par leurs représentants, la nécessité de la contribution publique, de la consentir librement, d'en suivre l'emploi, et d'en déterminer la quotité, l'assiette, le recouvrement et la durée.

Art. 15. La Société a le droit de demander compte à tout Agent public de son administration.

Art. 16. Toute Société dans laquelle la garantie des Droits n'est pas assurée, ni la séparation des Pouvoirs déterminée, n'a point de Constitution.

Art. 17. La propriété étant un droit inviolable et sacré, nul ne peut en être privé, si ce n'est lorsque la nécessité publique, légalement constatée, l'exige évidemment, et sous la condition d'une juste et préalable indemnité.

A NOTE ON MONEY
AND INFLATION

Politics and economics

During much of the nineteenth century and well into the twentieth, most historians said little about the economic or financial dimensions of the French Revolution. Astonishingly, some did not even mention these factors at all.

In some cases this may have been a question of political orthodoxy: some French historians may have regarded the Revolution as a purely political event, even a heroic political event, a triumph of liberation and republicanism, and they wanted to narrate it that way. It may also have been a question of ignorance, or at least of the narrowness of the way historians were then educated; many did not believe that they were required (or even qualified) to speak about economics. But whatever the reason or combination of reasons, nineteenth-century historians seriously understated the importance of the economic dimension of the French Revolution.

In the early twentieth century, things started to change. Pioneers on the subject were Pierre Caron, just before the First World War, and, even more, Marcel Marion just after it, with his multivolume *Histoire financière de la France depuis 1715*. But study of the economic aspects of the Revolution did not really start to flourish until the 1930s, with Fr. Braesch, Ernest Labrousse and Georges Lefebvre. Since then, the subject of the economic impact of the French Revolution has become absolutely mainstream. The run-up to the bicentenary of its start, in 1989, inevitably prompted several fundamental studies, including those by Florin Aftalion and René Sédillot.

Today it is generally acknowledged that the Revolution was profoundly affected by economic factors, most especially the sudden eruption, in 1792–93, of steep inflation caused by the Revolutionaries' massive issue of their new paper currency, the *assignat*, as the main source of the government's revenue; and that the resulting economic and political upheaval was one of the most fundamental factors which sent the French Revolution spiralling downhill and probably one of the principal reasons why it descended into conflict, Terror and central despotism.

What is particularly striking about the outbreak of violent inflation in France is that it was an isolated and short-lived event in an economic landscape that had, for a century, been astonishingly stable and was generally astonishingly stable for another century afterward, until the First World War. As Thomas Piketty has shown, in his *Capital in the Twenty-First Century* (see English edition translated by Arthur Gold-hammer, especially p. 104), most of the countries of Western Europe enjoyed a long period of low monetary inflation, lasting for most of the eighteenth and most of the nineteenth century. As a result, they also enjoyed an equally long period of price sta-bility, with monetary values remaining little changed or at least recognisably similar.

One of the consequences was that in the nineteenth century, British novelists like Jane Austen and French novelists like Honoré de Balzac could describe social and economic situations in monetary terms, secure in the knowledge that readers would recognise the meaning and value of these references. In the twentieth century, by con-trast, monetary stability collapsed, and in these new circumstances, novelists ceased to be able to describe social and economic situations in necessarily understandable monetary terms.

Yet against this general background of monetary stability, as David Hackett Fischer has underlined (see *The Great Wave*, pp. 117–42), there were significant eco-nomic tensions, which increased spasmodically but insistently during the second half of the eighteenth century, especially in France: rises in the price of wheat and other cereals essential for food, and a sharp increase in unemployment, resulting partly from a slowdown in the world economy and exacerbated in France by the government's financial crisis and its attempts to cut back on spending.

Currency systems in England and France

There was long a remarkable similarity, for long-term historical reasons, between the structures and even the terminologies of the currencies of Britain and France.[1] In France the main unit was the *livre*, meaning 'pound' (originally of silver), which was subdivided into twenty *sous* (*sol* in the singular), themselves broken down into twelve *deniers*. In Britain the main unit was the pound, subdivided into twenty shil-lings, themselves broken down into twelve pennies or pence. These similarities were carried even further in the shorthand abbreviations: in both countries the coinage was known as *L* or £, *S* and *D* (in decreasing denominations), the only difference being that in France these initials corresponded directly to the names of the coins, whereas in Britain the names of the coins in circulation had long broken away from their Latinate origins.

These historic links were lost first on December 7, 1793, when the *Convention* decided to decimalise the French currency, dividing the *livre* into 100 *centimes*; again on April 7, 1795, when the *Convention* decided to change the name of the currency from *livre* to *franc*; again in 1971, when the English pound was decimalised (into 100 pennies); and again in 1999, when the French *franc* was abandoned in favour of the euro. Yet despite the centuries-old change in denominations, in France people still say *Je n'ai pas de sous*, meaning 'I've no cash'.

Monetary stability in France before and after the Revolution

In France in the eighteenth century, the main monetary unit was the *livre Tournois*, whose metallic value had been set, in 1726, at 4.5 grams of fine silver.

With the massive issue of *assignats* starting in 1789, the new paper currency progressively drove out the metallic coinage, which gradually disappeared from circulation and into the hands of hoarders and speculators. But the new paper currency was widely distrusted and steadily depreciated. Over its first five years, the value of the *assignat* fell steeply, and by March 1795 it was worth only 8 per cent of its original parity with the metallic currency, accompanied by a corresponding but wildly erratic inflation in the price of goods.

After the extreme spasm of the Terror and the fall of Robespierre in July 1794, France soon returned to another century of monetary stability. By the Law of *18 germinal an III* (April 7, 1795), Robespierre's successors formally did away with the old *livre Tournois*, replacing it with the new *franc Germinal*.

Even so, the *assignats* staggered on for another year, until February 19, 1796, when their printing press was formally destroyed. But their memory was kept alive by the creation of yet another paper currency, the so-called *mandat territorial*, but that too collapsed in value, even faster than the *assignat*, lasting barely a year before France returned fully to the rigorous discipline of a purely metal currency.

Significantly, Robespierre's successors decided that the *franc Germinal* would have exactly the same metal content as the old *livre Tournois*, 4.5 grams of fine silver. One of the results was that France in practice reverted to the monetary system of the *ancien régime*. The metal content of French currency remained unchanged from then until 1914, which meant that (apart from the violent interruption of the middle period of the Revolution) it was unchanged for nearly 200 years.[2]

A NOTE ON THE *COMITÉ*
DE SALUT PUBLIC

The following is a list of the members of the *Comité de salut public* from July 10, 1793, to the fall of Robespierre, on July 28, 1794.

Bertrand Barère was a thirty-eight-year-old lawyer from Tarbes near Toulouse, a clever man and a good talker, a middle-of-the-roader and a survivor, who had risen to prominence in the *Convention*, where he had presided over the trial of the King. He joined the CSP when it was formed, on April 6, 1793, and played an important role on it, dealing with foreign affairs and military and naval questions. Some *Jacobins* criticised him for his moderation, but Robespierre defended him: 'I declare that I have seen Barère as a weak man but never the enemy of the public good.'

Jacques Nicolas Billaud-Varenne was a thirty-seven-year-old lawyer from La Rochelle who spent most of his energy trying, not very successfully, to be a poet and playwright. He was an awkward man who found it difficult to make friends in politics. After the overthrow of the King, in August 1792, he secured a position as the *procureur* of the *Commune*; he seems to have endorsed the prison massacres in September of that year and may have played some part in organising them. At the *Convention*, he voted for the death of the King. He joined the CSP on September 6, 1793, at the same time as his friend Jean-Marie Collot d'Herbois; both arrived as supporters of Hébert, but once there they supported the policies of Robespierre and shared the responsibility for the elimination of the *Hébertistes* and Danton. After the fall of Robespierre, Billaud-Varenne was deported to French Guiana; Bonaparte later pardoned him, but he chose not to return to France and died in Haiti.

Lazare Carnot was a forty-year-old engineer officer from Burgundy (Côte d'Or) who was elected to the *Assemblée nationale législative* and had an important part in its Military Committee. He continued to play an influential role in military affairs at the *Convention* but spent most of his time as an *envoyé en mission* with the armies. Between two of these missions, he voted for the death of the King. He was elected to the CSP on August 4, 1793, despite the hostility of Robespierre, who had known him when he was stationed in Arras and disliked him; he returned the compliment and later contributed to Robespierre's overthrow. Carnot played a key role in the reorganisation of the armies and got the popular nickname 'The Organiser of the Victory' (*l'Organisateur de la Victoire*).

Jean-Marie Collot d'Herbois was a forty-four-year-old travelling actor, part-time playwright and one-time director of the theatre in Lyon. He played a leading role in the insurrection of August 10, 1792, as a member of the *Commune* and, like his friend Billaud-Varenne, endorsed the September prison massacres. He was elected to the *Convention* and spoke in favour of the death of the King, though he was absent on the day of the vote. The *Convention* sent him, with Joseph Fouché, to punish the rebels of Lyon, where they allowed the massacres of the Plaine des Brotteaux. With Billaud-Varenne, he played a leading part in the overthrow of Robespierre. Afterwards he escaped the guillotine but was deported to French Guiana, where he caught a fever and died in 1796.

Georges Auguste Couthon was a lawyer and a Robespierrist member of the *Convention*. In his early thirties he became partially paralysed and was confined to a wheelchair. Soon after voting for the death of the King, he was elected to the CSP, on May 30, 1793.

Marie Jean Hérault de Séchelles was a thirty-four-year-old lawyer from the nobility, an *avocat* at the Châtelet law court in Paris. He was rich, handsome and clever and a rapid climber in the Revolution; the fact that he was a close relative of the duchesse de Polignac did not prevent him from claiming to have been one of the *vainqueurs de la Bastille*. Elected to the *Assemblée nationale législative* and to the *Convention*, he was by turns *Feuillant*, *Girondin* and *Montagnard*. He was a popular member of the *Convention* and was several times elected as its President; but he was absent from Paris as an *envoyé en mission* during the trial of the King. Robespierre hated and despised him, for being too rich, too handsome and too clever, far too frivolous and above all enviably easy with women.

André Jean-Bon Saint-André was a forty-four-year-old from Montauban who had been withdrawn from his Jesuit school by his Calvinist father and almost sent off on a naval career; instead he decided in 1773 to become a Protestant preacher at Castres. He was elected to the *Convention*, where he started by sitting with the *Girondins* but soon joined the *Montagnards* and voted for the death of the King. In the CSP, he was responsible for naval policy. He was known for his honesty, his effectiveness and his frankness.

Jean-Baptiste Robert Lindet was a forty-seven-year-old lawyer from Bernay in Normandy. He started out as a *Girondin* in the *Assemblée nationale législative* and switched to the *Montagne* when he was elected to the *Convention*. He wrote the charges of the 'crimes' of Louis XVI, and he voted for the death of the King. Like Barère, he joined the CSP when it was formed, on April 6, 1793, and he remained a member until the fall of Robespierre. In the CSP he was responsible for financial policy and for food supplies, but he also spent time as an *envoyé en mission*, first to Lyon in June 1793, where he tried to be a conciliator, which got him into trouble all round and caused his recall to Paris, and then to deal with the uprising in Normandy. On his return to Paris at the end of October he saved a number of people from the guillotine, and he refused to sign the arrest warrant for Danton. He was not a friend of Robespierre.

Claude Antoine Prieur de la Côte d'Or was another engineer officer from Burgundy (Côte d'Or), like Carnot, promoted to Captain in 1791. He was still young, only twenty-nine years old, but he had already been elected to the *Assemblée nationale législative* and then to the *Convention*, where he voted for the death of the King. He worked closely with Carnot and was co-opted to the CSP on August 14, 1793, at Carnot's instigation, to help with the reorganisation of the armies.

Pierre Louis Prieur de la Marne was a thirty-seven-year-old lawyer from Châlons-sur-Marne. He was elected to the *Convention*, where he joined the *Montagnards* and voted for the death of the King, but he spent most of his time away from Paris as an *envoyé en mission*, first at Orléans and then with various armies: *des côtes de Cherbourg*, *du Nord*, *des Ardennes*, *de la Moselle*, *des côtes de Brest* and Rennes.

Maximilien Robespierre was a thirty-five-year-old lawyer from Arras, the leader of the *Montagnards* and by now the dominant political figure in the *Convention*.

Louis Saint-Just was a twenty-six-year-old lawyer from Reims and a loyal supporter of Robespierre in the *Convention*. He had been a member since 1792 and had demanded and voted for the death of the King. He played an important role in the fight against the *Girondins*, in the setting up of the Revolutionary government and in the downfall of Danton.

Jacques Alexis Thuriot was a forty-year-old lawyer from Paris. He was elected to the *Assemblée nationale législative*, where he took radical positions against refractory priests and *émigrés*; but he opposed the establishment of the *Tribunal révolutionnaire* as a member of the *Convention*, in which capacity he voted for the death of the King. He joined the CSP on July 10, 1793, but left it on September 20 after a clash with Robespierre; the *Montagne* then had him expelled from the *Jacobin* Club. At *thermidor* he played a crucial role because it was he, as the current President of that dramatic session of the *Convention*, who silenced Robespierre by preventing him from speaking.

A NOTE ON DEATH AND
THE REVOLUTION

In the course of my research for this book, I gradually accumulated a list of names. This list was not filtered by any criterion: the most famous, the most infamous, or anything else; it was just the names of all the people who happened to crop up in the course of my reading, which meant that it was just about anyone who did anything, so that any of the various historians could mention him or her.

In the end, my list ran to 290 names; and I checked out what became of these 'names' of the Revolution. In particular, I checked out how they died; and I found that 84 of them (or 29 per cent), died on the guillotine; and that 41 (or 14 per cent), died violently in some other way, in some cases by suicide to avoid the guillotine. What this seemed to suggest, in a completely unscientific way, was that anyone who did *anything* in the Revolution that could come to the attention of the later historians had a 43 per cent chance of a violent death.

List of characters:

	Executed	Died violently
Aclocque, André Arnoult		
Albitte, Antoine Louis		
Alexandre, Charles Alexis		
Amar, Jean-Pierre Andre		
Anthoine (or Antoine), François Paul Nicolas		
Antonelle, Pierre Antoine, marquis d'		

	Executed	Died violently
Arthur, Robert Jean-Jacques	✝	
Artois, Charles Philippe, comte d'		
Audouin or Audoin, François Xavier		
Audouin (or Audoin), Pierre Jean, called le sapeur du Bataillon des Carmes		
Augereau, Charles Pierre François		
Babeuf, François Noel, called Gracchus	✝	
Bailly, Jean Sylvain	✝	
Bara, François Joseph		✝
Barbaroux, Charles Jean-Marie	✝	
Barbe de Marbois, François		
Barère de Vieuzac, Bertrand		
Barnave, Antoine Pierre Joseph Marie	✝	
Barras, Paul François Jean Nicolas, vicomte de		
Barthelemy, Balthazard François, marquis de		
Basire, Claude	✝	
Batz, Jean-Pierre, baron de		
Baudin, Pierre Charles Louis		
Baudot, Marc Antoine		
Beaurepaire, Nicolas Joseph		✝
Bergasse, Nicolas		
Bernadotte, Jean Baptiste Jules		
Bertier de Sauvigny, Louis Benigne François de		✝
Besenval, Pierre Joseph Victor		
Beurnonville, Pierre de Riel, comte, then marquis de		
Billaud-Varenne, alias of Jacques Nicolas Billaud		
Biron, Armand Louis de Gontaut (formerly duc de Lauzun), duc de	✝	
Birotteau, Jean Bonaventure Blaise Hilarion	✝	
Boisgelin, Jean-de-Dieu Raymond de		
Boissy d'Anglas, François Antoine, comte de		
Bonchamp, Charles Melchior Artus, marquis de		
Bonneville, Nicolas de		
Bouchotte, Jean-Baptiste Noel		
Bouillé, François Claude Amour, marquis de		
Boulanger, Servais Baudouin	✝	
Bourbotte, Pierre	✝	
Bourdon de l'Oise, François Louis		✝
Bourdon de la Crosnière, Léonard		
Boursault-Malherbe, alias of Jean-Francois Boursault		

	Executed	Died violently
Boyer-Fonfrède, Jean-Baptiste	✝	
Brissot, Jacques Pierre	✝	
Buzot, François Nicolas Leonard		✝
Calonne, Charles Alexandre de		
Cambaceres, Jean-Jacques Regis de		
Cambon, Joseph		
Camus, Armand Gaston		
Carnot, Lazare Nicolas Marguerite		
Carra, Jean-Louis	✝	
Carrier, Jean-Baptiste	✝	
Carteaux, Jean-Baptiste François		
Chabot, François	✝	
Chalier, Joseph	✝	
Chambon de Montaux, Nicolas		
Charette, alias of François Athanasée de Charette de la Contrie	✝	
Chasset, Charles-Antoine		
Châtelet, du, Louis Marie Florent, duc	✝	
Chaumette, Pierre Gaspard	✝	
Chénier, Andre Marie de	✝	
Chénier, Marie Joseph Blaise de		
Choudieu, Pierre René		
Clavière, Étienne		✝
Cloots, Jean-Baptiste (called Anarcharsis Cloots), baron	✝	
Coffinhal, Jean-Baptiste	✝	
Collot d'Herbois, alias of Jean-Marie Collot		✝
Condorcet, Marie Jean Antoine Nicolas de Caritat, marquis de		✝
Corday, Marie Anne Charlotte de	✝	
Coupe de l'Oise, Jacques-Michel		
Courtois, Edme Bonaventure		
Couthon, Georges Auguste	✝	
Custine, Adam Philippe, comte de	✝	
Danton, Georges Jacques	✝	
Daunou, Pierre Claude Francois		
David, Jacques Louis		
Defermon, Jacques		
Delacroix, Jean-Francois	✝	
Delaunay, Joseph l'ainé, called Delaunay d'Angers	✝	
Desfieux, François	✝	

	Executed	Died violently
Desmoulins, Camille	✠	
Dillon, Arthur, comte de	✠	
Dobsen, Claude Emmanuel		
Drouet, Jean-Baptiste		
Dubois-Crancé, Edmond Louis Alexis		
Du Chatelet, Louis Marie Florent, duc	✠	
Ducos, Jean-Francois	✠	
Dufourny de Villiers, Louis Pierre		
Dugommier, alias of Jacques Coquille		
Duhem, Pierre Joseph		
Dumas, Rene Francois	✠	
Dumas, Thomas Alexandre Davy de la Pailleterie, called Alexandre		
Dumouriez, alias of Charles-Francois du Perrier		
Dupont de Nemours, Pierre Samuel		
Duport, Adrien		
Duquesnoy, Ernest Dominique Francois Joseph		✠
Durand de Maillane, Pierre Toussaint		
Duroy, Jean-Michel	✠	
Espagnac, Marc Rene Marie d'Amarzit de Sahuguet, abbe d'	✠	
Fabre d'Eglantine, alias of Philippe Francois Nazaire Fabre	✠	
Fauchet, Claude	✠	
Feraud, Jean Bertrand		✠
Flesselles, Jacques de,		✠
Fleuriot-Lescot, Jean-Baptiste Édouard	✠	
Fouche, Joseph		
Foulon, Joseph Francois		✠
Fouquier-Tinville, alias of Antoine Quentin Fouquier	✠	
Fournier, Claude, called Fournier l'Américain et Fournier l'Héritier		
Freron, Stanislas Louis Marie		
Frey, Siegmund Gottlob Dobroujka-Schoenfeld, called Junius	✠	
Garat, Dominique Joseph		
Gasparin, Thomas Augustin de		
Gensonne, Armand	✠	
Gerle, Christophe Antoine, Dom		
Gorsas, Antoine Joseph	✠	

	Executed	Died violently
Goujon, Jean-Marie Claude Alexandre		✝
Grangeneuve, Jean Antoine Lafargue de	✝	
Grégoire, Henri Baptiste, abbé		
Guadet, Marguerite Élie	✝	
Guillotin, Joseph Ignace		
Hanriot, François	✝	
Hardy, Antoine Francois		
Hébert, Jacques Rene	✝	
Hérault de Séchelles, Marie Jean	✝	
Herman, Martial	✝	
Hoche, Louis Lazare,		
Houchard, Jean Nicolas	✝	
Huguenin, Sulpice		
Hulin, Pierre Augustin		
Isnard, Henri Maximin		
Javogues, Claude	✝	
Jean-Bon Saint-André, alias of André Jeanbon		
Jourdan, Jean-Baptiste		
Jourdan Coupe-Tête, alias of Mathieu Jouve Jourdan	✝	
Julien, Jean, called Julien de Toulouse		
Jullien, Marc Antoine, called Jullien de la Drôme		
Jullien, Marc Antoine, fils, called Jullien de Paris		
Kellermann, Francois Etienne Christophe		
Kersaint, Armand Guy Simon de Coetnempren, comte de	✝	
Kervelegan, Augustin Bernard Francois Legoazre de		
Kleber, Jean-Baptiste		✝
Laclos, Pierre Ambroise Francois Choderlos de		
Lacombe, Claire, called Rose		
La Fayette, Marie Joseph Paul Yves Roch Gilbert Motier, marquis de		
La Harpe, Jean-Francois de		
Laignelot, Joseph Francois		
Lakanal, Joseph		
Lally-Tollendal, Trophime Gérard, marquis de		
La Marck, Auguste Marie Raymond, prince d'Arenberg, comte de		
Lamballe, Marie-Thérèse de Savoie-Carignan, princesse de		✝
Lameth, Alexandre Theodore Victor de		
Lameth, Charles Malo Francois de		✝

	Executed	Died violently
Lameth, Theodore		✝
Lanjuinais, Jean-Denis		
Laplanche, Jacques Leonard Goyre de		✝
Laporte, alias of François Sebastien Christophe Delaporte		
La Révellière-Lépeaux, Louis Marie de		
La Rochefoucauld-Liancourt, Francois Alexandre Frederic, duc de		
La Rochefoucauld, Dominique de		
La Rochejaquelin, Henri du Vergier, comte de		✝
Lasource, alias of Marc David Alba	✝	
Latour-Maubourg, Marie Charles Cesar de Fay, comte de		
Laveaux, Jean Charles Thiebault		
Lavoisier, Antoine Laurent	✝	
Lazowski, Claude-François		
Lebas, Philippe Francois Joseph		✝
Le Bon, Guislain Francois Joseph	✝	
Lebrun, Charles Francois		
Le Chapelier, Isaac Rene Guy	✝	
Leclerc, Jean Theophile Victoire		
Lecointre, Laurent		
Lecoulteux de Canteleu, Jean Barthelemy		
Lefebvre, Francois Joseph		
Legendre, Louis		
Legray, Francois Vincent		
Lejeune, Sylvain Phalier		
Léon, Pauline		
Le Peletier de Saint-Fargeau, Louis Michel		✝
Lequinio, Louis Marie, marquis de		
Letourneur, Louis Etienne Francois Honore		
Levasseur, Rene		
Lhuillier (or Lullier), Louis Marie		
Lindet, Jean-Baptiste Robert		✝
Lindet, Robert Thomas		
Louchet, Louis		
Loustalot, Elysee		
Louvet, Jean-Baptiste		
Maignet, Etienne Christophe, called Publicola		
Mailhe, Jean		
Maillard, Stanislas Marie, called *Tape Dur*		
Malesherbes, Chrétien Guillaume de Lamoignon de		
Mallet du Pan, Jacques	✝	

	Executed	Died violently
Malouet, Pierre Victor		
Mandat, Antoine Jean Gailliot, marquis de		
Manuel, Louis Pierre		☩
Marat, Jean-Paul	☩	
Marceau, alias of François Severin Marceau-Desgraviers		☩
Marmontel, Jean-François		
Massena, Andre		
Maure, Nicolas		
Maury, Jean Siffrein, abbé		☩
Mazuel, Albert		
Mehee de la Touche, Jean-Claude Hippolyte	☩	
Merlin de Douai, alias of Philippe Antoine Merlin		
Merlin de Thionville, alias of Antoine Christophe Merlin		
Mirabeau, Honoré Gabriel Riquetti, comte de		
Momoro, Antoine François		
Monge, Gaspard Louis	☩	
Montesquiou-Fézensac, Jean Gabriel Maurice Rocques, called le comte de Montesquiou-Fézensac		
Moreau, Jean Victor		
Mounier, Jean-Joseph		
Narbonne-Lara, Louis Marie Jacques, comte de		
Necker, Jacques		
Neufchateau, François de		
Orléans, Louis-Philippe Joseph, called Philippe Égalité, duc d',		
Osselin, Charles Nicolas	☩	
Pache, Jean Nicolas	☩	
Panis, Étienne Jean		
Pare, Jules François		
Paris, Philippe Nicolas Marie de		
Payan, Claude-François		☩
Pereyra, Jacob	☩	
Pétion, Jérôme	☩	
Philippeaux, Pierre Nicolas		☩
Pichegru, Jean-Charles	☩	
Precy, Louis François Perrein, comte de		☩
Prieur-Duvernois, Claude Antoine, called Prieur de la Cote-d'Or		
Prieur, Pierre Louis, called Prieur de la Marne		
Proli, Pierre Joseph Berchtold		

	Executed	Died violently
Provence, Louis-Stanislas Xavier, comte de	✝	
Puisaye, Joseph Geneviève, comte de		
Rabaut Saint-Etienne, alias of Jean Paul Rabaut		
Rebecqui,François Trophime	✝	
Reubell (or Rewbell), Jean-François		✝
Reveillon, Jean-Baptiste		
Robert, Pierre François Joseph, called Robert-Rhum		
Robespierre, Augustin Bon Joseph, called le Jeune		
Robespierre, Maximilien Marie Isidore de	✝	
Roederer, Pierre Louis	✝	
Roland de la Platière, Jean-Marie		
Roland, Jeanne Marie Philipon, épouse Roland,		✝
Romme, Gilbert	✝	
Ronsin, Charles Philippe		✝
Rossignol, Jean Antoine	✝	
Roux, Jacques		
Rovère de Fontvielle, Joseph Stanislas François Xavier Alexis		✝
Royer, Claude, curé, Enragé, (Mathiez)		✝
Ruhl, Philippe Jacques		
Saint-Huruge, Victor Amédée de la Fage, marquis de		✝
Saint-Just, Louis Antoine de		
Saint-Simon, Claude-Henri de Rouvroy, comte de	✝	
Saliceti, Christophe		
Salle, Jean-Baptiste		
Santerre, Antoine Joseph	✝	
Sergent, Antoine François		
Servan, Joseph		
Sèze, Raymond de, called Romain		
Sièyes, Emmanuel Joseph		
Simon, Antoine		✝
Simond, Philibert	✝	✝
Soubrany, Pierre Amable	✝	
Stofflet, Nicolas	✝	
Talleyrand-Périgord, Charles Maurice de	✝	✝
Tallien, Jean Lambert		✝
Target, Guy Jean-Baptiste		✝
Théroigne de Méricourt, Anne Josèphe (born Anne Josèphe Terwagne)		
Thibaudeau, Antoine Claire		

	Executed	Died violently
Thirion, Didier		
Thouret, Jacques Guillaume		
Thuriot, Jacques Alexis	✚	
Treilhard, Jean-Baptiste		
Tronchet, François-Denis		
Turreau de Garambouville, Louis Marie		
Turreau de Linières, Louis		
Vadier, Marc-Guillaume Alexis		
Valazé, ou Dufriche-Valazé, Charles Éléonore		
Varlet, Jean-François	✚	
Vergniaud, Pierre Victurnien		
Viala, Joseph Agricol	✚	
Vilatte, Joachim		✚
Vincent, François Nicolas	✚	
Virieu, François Henri, comte de	✚	
Voulland, Jean Henri		✚
Westermann, François Joseph		
Wimpffen, Louis-Felix, baron de	✚	
Ysabeau, Claude Alexandre		

NOTES

1 Introduction

1. François Bluche, *La véritable hiérarchie sociale de l'ancienne France*; Guy Chaussinand-Nogaret, *La noblesse au XVIIIe siècle*; Roland Mousnier, *Les institutions de la France sous la monarchie absolue, 1598–1789*, 2 vols., 1974–1980.

2. Furet was long the doyen of the first generation of post-Marxist historians of the French Revolution after World War II. See his *La Révolution française*, coauthored with Denis Richet (2 volumes, 1965), and *Penser la Révolution française* (1978).

3. The *Encyclopédie* was the spearhead of the Enlightenment in France. Edited by Jean Le Rond d'Alembert and Denis Diderot, it set out to provide a critical description of the whole of the known world.

4. Jean Calas was a Toulouse Protestant who in 1762 was accused by local Catholics of having murdered one of his sons. There was no evidence against him, but he was convicted and sentenced to death on the wheel. Voltaire heard of the case and was outraged by its injustice and sectarian intolerance. He campaigned tirelessly for a review and after three years secured from the King's Council a posthumous exoneration of Calas and compensation for his widow.

5. « la société française du XVIIIe siècle est à la recherche désespérée de mandataires. En effet, elle est trop « développée », comme on dirait aujourd'hui, pour être maintenue, comme au siècle précédent, dans le silence et l'obéissance à l'Etat Elle s'est trouvée naturellement portée, à la mort de Louis XIV, vers

la réanimation des circuits traditionnels, et notamment du rôle des parlements. Mais comme ces mêmes parlements multiplient, tout au long du siècle, les preuves de leur conservatisme, comme ils condamnent *L'Encyclopédie*, et *L'Émile* et le malheureux Calas, ils ne constituent pas, pour une société « éclairée », le meilleur des mandataires C'est pourquoi la société du XVIIIe siècle s'est progressivement constitué d'autres porte-parole : les philosophes et les hommes de lettres La littérature assume dès lors la fonction politique » Furet, *Penser la Révolution française,* pp. 65–66.

6. Tocqueville (1805–59) is widely regarded as the touchstone of all commentators on the French Revolution. See his *L'ancien régime et la Révolution* (1856).

7. « Si l'on songe maintenant que cette même nation française, si étrangère à ses propres affaires et si dépourvue d'expérience, si gênée par ses institutions et si impuissante à les amender, était en même temps alors, de toutes les nations de la terre, la plus lettrée et la plus amoureuse du bel esprit, on comprendra sans peine comment les écrivains y devinrent une puissance politique et finirent par y être la première. » Tocqueville, *L'ancien régime et la Révolution,* p. 175.

8. See R. R. Palmer, *The Age of the Democratic Revolution*.

9. To be precise, Bastille Day officially commemorates the *Fête de la Fédération* celebrated on July 14, 1790, the first anniversary of the fall of the Bastille.

2 *États généraux*

1. This is the origin of the modern tradition of referring to journalists as 'the Fourth Estate'.

2. See 'A Note on the Children of Louis XVI', page 257.

3. « Nous avons besoin du concours de nos fidèles sujets pour Nous aider à surmonter toutes les difficultés où Nous Nous trouvons relativement à l'état de Nos finances, et pour établir, suivant nos vœux, un ordre constant et invariable dans toutes les parties du gouvernement qui intéressent le bonheur de nos sujets et la prospérité de Notre royaume. Ces grands motifs Nous ont déterminé à convoquer l'Assemblée des États de toutes les provinces de notre obéissance, tant pour Nous conseiller et Nous assister dans toutes les choses qui seront mises sous nos yeux, que pour Nous faire connaître les souhaits et doléances de nos peuples, de manière que par une mutuelle confiance et par un amour réciproque entre le souverain et ses sujets, il soit apporté le plus promptement possible un remède efficace aux maux de l'État, que les abus de tous genre soient réformés et prévenus par de bons et solides moyens qui assurent la félicité publique et qui nous rendent à Nous particulièrement, le calme et la tranquillité dont Nous sommes privés depuis si longtemps. » 'Lettre de convocation des États généraux à Versailles', January 24, 1789.

4. Tocqueville, *L'ancien régime et la Révolution*, p. 45.

5. « Quand je secoue ma terrible hure, il n'y a personne qui ose m'interrompre ! »

6. *Lettres de cachet* were a typical absolutist instrument of the *ancien régime*. The King could simply sign one of these letters, and the person named in it could be imprisoned, perhaps in the Bastille, or sent into exile indefinitely, without trial.

In practice the system was widely extended: a noble or high-placed commoner could have his own son imprisoned or exiled by getting a *lettre de cachet* from the King.

7. Marie Jean Antoine Nicolas de Caritat, marquis de Condorcet (1743–94), was an aristocrat, an intellectual leader of the Enlightenment, a mathematician, a member of the *Académie des sciences*, a friend of Voltaire and editor of his works and *le dernier des philosophes*, according to the historian Jules Michelet. In the *Convention*, he generally followed the *Girondins*; in the trial of the King, he voted against the death penalty, in favour of an appeal to the people and for indefinite imprisonment.

8. Laclos was a former artillery officer from the minor nobility who left the army in 1788 at the age of forty-seven after a very modest career and joined the staff of the duc d'Orléans. *Les liaisons dangereuses* had been published in 1782; the first edition, of 2,000 copies, sold out within a month, and it was reprinted many times in the next two years.

9. « Le plan de cet écrit est assez simple. Nous avons trois questions à nous faire.
1° Qu'est-ce que le Tiers état? – TOUT.
2° Qu'a-t-il été jusqu'à présent dans l'ordre politique? – RIEN.
3° Que demande-t-il? — À ÊTRE QUELQUE CHOSE » Emmanuel Joseph Sieyès, *Qu'est-ce que le tiers état ?* 1792.

10. Marie Joseph Paul Yves Roch Gilbert Motier, marquis de La Fayette (1757– 1834), came from an ancient and immensely wealthy noble family. He joined the Black Musketeers in 1771 when he was fourteen and married the duchesse Adrienne de Noailles in 1774 when he was seventeen and she fifteen. In 1777, in the face of the total opposition of his father-in-law, he bought a ship at his own expense and sailed to America, where he offered his services to the rebels. Congress, in recognition of the nobility of his ancestry, made him a major general, though without any troops to command. He returned to France in 1785, the romantic 'Hero of Two Worlds'.

11. Jean Tulard, Fayard, and Fierro, *Histoire et dictionnaire de la Révolution française*, p. 806.

12. *Jeu de paume*, known in English as real tennis or royal tennis, was an early forerunner of tennis, played across a net in an enclosed and awkwardly shaped indoor court.

13. Mathiez, *La Révolution française*, p. 71.

14. « Le Roi sortit, la Noblesse et le clergé suivirent. Les Communes demeurèrent assises, tranquilles, en silence. Le maître des cérémonies entre alors, et d'une voix basse, dit au président : « Monsieur, vous avez entendu l'ordre du Roi ? » Il répondit : « … L'Assemblée s'est ajournée après la séance royale ; je ne puis la séparer sans qu'elle en ait délibéré. » Puis, se tournant vers ses collègues voisins de lui : « Il me semble que la nation assemblée ne peut pas recevoir d'ordre. » Michelet I (1), p. 119.

15. « Nous sommes ici par le vœu de la nation; la force matérielle pourrait seule nous faire désemparer. » Tulard asserts that these were the words spoken

by Mirabeau, and definitely not the Michelet-*Moniteur* version more widely popularised: 'We are here by the will of the people, we can only be made to leave by the force of bayonets' (« Nous sommes ici par la volonté du peuple, nous n'en sortirons que par la force des baïonnettes »). Tulard, Fayard, and Fierro, *Histoire et dictionnaire de la Révolution française*, p. 769.

16. « Nous avons entendu les intentions qu'on a suggérées au Roy ; et vous, Monsieur, qui ne sauriez être son organe auprès de l'Assemblée nationale, vous qui n'avez ici ni place, ni voix, ni droit de parler, vous n'êtes pas fait pour nous rappeler son discours. Allez dire à ceux qui vous envoient que nous sommes ici par la volonté du peuple, et qu'on ne nous en arrachera que par la puissance des baïonnettes. » Quoted in Michelet I (1), p. 119.

17. Furet, *Penser la Révolution française*, p. 181.

3 The Fall of Necker

1. The *Gardes françaises* were a long-established elite corps of 3,600 men, formed in 1563 to protect Charles IX.

6 Declaration of the Rights of Man

1. For the French original, see 'The French Text of the Declaration of the Rights of Man of 1789', page 261.

7 The King Moves to Paris

1. « L'aigle marche toujours seul, le dindon fait troupe. »

2. « La nation existe avant tout, elle est à l'origine de tout. Sa volonté est toujours légale, elle est la loi elle-même. »

3. See 'The French Text of the Declaration of the Rights of Man of 1789', page 261.

4. « Elle contient de très bonnes maximes propres à guider vos travaux, mais des principes susceptibles d'applications et même d'interprétations différentes ne peuvent être justement appréciés, et n'ont besoin de l'être qu'au moment où leur véritable sens est fixé par les lois auxquelles ils doivent servir de première base. » Tulard, Fayard and Fierro, *Histoire et dictionnaire de la Révolution française*, p. 53.

5. « La réponse du roi est destructive; non seulement de toute Constitution, mais encore du droit national à avoir une Constitution. Celui qui peut imposer une condition à une constitution a le droit d'empêcher cette constitution ; il met sa volonté au dessus du droit de la nation. »

6. « On dit qu'il y a un contrat social entre le roi et la nation. Je nie le principe. Le roi ne peut que gouverner suivant les lois que la nation lui présente. »

7. « Qu'ils mangent de la brioche ! »

8. The most famous source of the saying is Book 6 of Rousseau's *Confessions* (1765), written a quarter of a century before the Revolution: 'Finally I recalled the retort of a great princess who was told that the peasants had no bread, and who replied: "Let them eat brioche."' But the *Confessions* are notoriously unreliable, and in any case Rousseau attributes the saying only to an unnamed 'great princess', not

to Marie-Antoinette, who was at the time of writing only nine years old and living with her family in Vienna. Moreover, there is no evidence that anyone during the Revolution ascribed this saying to her; the first such attribution appeared in a book published fifty years later, *Les guêpes* (1843), by Alphonse Karr.

9. « Nous ramenons le Boulanger, la boulangère et le petit mitron. »

8 The Assembly Starts to Govern France

1. « Louis par la grâce de Dieu, roi de France et de Navarre ».
2. « Louis par la grâce de Dieu et la loi constitutionnelle de l'État, roi des Français ».
3. In France at the time, the symbol £, an old-fashioned version of the letter *L*, denoted the main unit of currency, the *livre*. The next, smaller unit was the *sol*, or *sous* in the plural, of which there were twenty in each *livre*; and the smallest was the *denier*, of which there were twelve in each *sol*. I make no attempt to translate French monetary values of the late eighteenth century into European monetary values of the early twenty-first century, since the operation is impossible. See 'A Note on Money and Inflation', page 264.
4. Marion, *Histoire Financière de la France* (1914–1921), pp. 130–39.
5. Ibid.

9 The Revolutionaries Reform the Church

1. In 1598, Henri IV brought a halt to the long-running and murderous wars of religion between Catholics and Protestants in France by signing the Edict of Nantes, which made considerable concessions to the Protestants, including all their civil rights, as well as freedom of conscience and freedom of worship. But in 1685, under relentless pressure from Catholics, Louis XIV revoked the Edict of Nantes, withdrawing all these privileges and resuming the traditional policy of persecuting Protestants. More than 200,000 Protestants fled abroad, mainly to Geneva, Holland, Prussia and England.

10 The Flight of the King

1. « Alors et dans ce cas, leurs dites Majestés   sont résolues d'agir promptement, d'un mutuel accord, avec les forces nécessaires pour obtenir le but proposé en commun. » Pillnitz Declaration, from *Dictionnaire Historique de la Révolution française*, p. 844.
2. For more details of the slave revolt, see chapter 11, page 81.

11 The Rush to War

1. In the eighteenth century, Frenchmen often had names which may appear feminine; in most cases, they had Catholic resonances – for example, Marie.
2. Soboul et al, p. 917.
3. « Il ira loin, car il croit tout ce qu'il dit. »

4. Michelet II (1), p. 1178.

5. « La guerre est toujours le premier voeu d'un gouvernement puissant qui veut devenir plus puissant encore… C'est pendant la guerre que le pouvoir exécutif déploie la plus redoutable énergie, et qu'il exerce une espèce de dictature qui ne peut qu'effrayer la liberté naissante ; c'est pendant la guerre que le peuple oublie les délibérations qui intéressent essentiellement ses droits civils et politiques, pour ne s'occuper que des événements extérieurs, qu'il détourne son attention de ses législateurs et de ses magistrats, pour attacher tout son intérêt et toutes ses espérances à ses généraux et à ses ministres… C'est pendant la guerre que l'habitude d'une obéissance passive, et l'enthousiasme trop naturel pour les chefs heureux, fait, des soldats de la patrie, les soldats du monarque ou de ses généraux. Dans les temps de troubles et de factions, les chefs des armées deviennent les arbitres du sort de leur pays, et font pencher la balance en faveur du parti qu'ils ont embrassé. Si ce sont des Césars ou des Cromwells, ils s'emparent eux-mêmes de l'autorité… »
Robespierre, discours contre la guerre, au Club des Jacobins, le 18 décembre, 1791.

6. « La plus extravagante idée qui puisse naître dans la tête d'un politique, est de croire qu'il suffise à un peuple d'entrer à main armée chez un peuple étranger, pour lui faire adopter ses lois et sa constitution. Personne n'aime les missionnaires armés ; et le premier conseil que donnent la nature et la prudence, c'est de les repousser comme des ennemis. »

7. « la cause d'Avignon est celle de l'univers, elle est celle de la liberté ».

8. « Puisque la guerre est déclarée, je suis d'avis aussi de conquérir le Brabant, les Pays-Bas, Liège, la Flandre, etc. La seul chose qui doive nous occuper désormais, ce sont les moyens d'exécuter cette utile entreprise, c'est-à-dire, dans ce moment, il faut faire, comme je l'ai proposé plusieurs fois, non plus la guerre de la Cour, mais la guerre du peuple, il faut que le peuple français se lève désormais et s'arme tout entier, soit pour combattre au-dehors, soit pour veiller le despotisme au-dedans. »

12 The Overthrow of the Monarchy

1. « Cette arme est en quelque sorte sacrée. »

2. Michelet I (1), p. 912.

3. Michelet I (2), p. 905–906.

4. Tulard, Fayard, and Fierro, *Histoire et dictionnaire de la Révolution française*, p. 343.

5. « Je vois bien que M de La Fayette veut nous sauver ; mais qui nous sauvera de M de La Fayette ? »

6. Mathiez, *La Révolution française* (2012), p. 205–206.

7. Michelet I (2), p. 947.

8. Ibid., p. 944; Tulard, *Histoire de la Révolution française*, p. 345.

9. Tulard, *Histoire de la Révolution française*, p. 100–101.

10. « s'il était fait la moindre violence à leurs Majestés le Roi et la Reine et à la famille royale, [les souverains] en tireront une vengeance exemplaire en livrant la ville de Paris à une exécution militaire et à une subversion totale, et les révoltés coupables aux supplices qu'ils auront mérités. » Quoted in Soboul et al, p. 162.

11. Michelet I (1), pp. 950–51; Hibbert, *The French Revolution*, p. 154; Mathiez, *La Révolution française* (2012), p. 207.

12. « Comme Marat il contribua à préparer les esprits à l'insurrection du 10 août, dont il ne fut cependant pas l'organisateur. » Quoted in Soboul et al, p. 917.

13. Furet, *Penser la Révolution française,* p. 100–101.

14. Soboul et al, p. 268.

15. Ibid., p. 268.

16. Tulard, Fayard, and Fierro, *Histoire et dictionnaire de la Révolution française*, p. 102.

17. Michelet I (2), p. 996; quoted in Mathiez, *La Révolution française* (2012), pp. 218, 221.

18. ibid., p. 909.

13 The *Commune insurrectionnelle*

1. « Le peuple, qui nous envoie vers vous, nous a chargés de vous déclarer qu'il vous investissait de nouveau de sa confiance, mais il nous a chargés en même temps de vous déclarer qu'il ne pouvait reconnaître pour juges des mesures extraordinaires auxquelles la nécessité et la résistance à l'oppression l'ont porté, que le peuple français, votre souverain et le nôtre, réuni dans ses assemblées primaires. » Quoted in Mathiez, *La Révolution française* (2012), p. 218.

2. Mathiez, *La Révolution française* (2012), p. 249.

3. Michelet I (2), p. 906.

4. Article 1 of the new penal code: « Les délits du même genre seront punis par le même genre de peine, quels que soient le rang et l'état du coupable. »

5. Michelet I (2), pp. 1044–45.

6. « Ce fanatique énergumène nous inspirait à nous-mêmes une sorte de répugnance et de stupeur. Lorsqu'on me le montra pour la première fois je le considérai avec cette curiosité inquiète qu'on éprouve en contemplant certains insectes hideux. Ses vêtements en désordre, sa figure livide, ses yeux hagards avaient je ne sais quoi de rebutant et d'épouvantable qui contristait l'âme. » Quoted in Tulard, Fayard, and Fierro, *Histoire et dictionnaire de la Révolution française*, p. 970.

7. He followed the Revolutionary fashion of adopting a nom de guerre borrowed from classical Greece or Rome, taking the surname Anaxagoras, after the fifth-century BC Presocratic Athenian philosopher.

8. Michelet II (1), pp. 834, 315.

9. Mathiez, *La Révolution française* (2012), p. 21.

10. « avec le pouvoir de suspendre provisoirement tant les généraux que tous autres officiers et fonctionnaires publics, civils et militaires, et même les faire mettre

en état d'arrestation, si les circonstances l'exigent, ainsi que de pourvoir à leur remplacement provisoire. » Quoted in Mathiez, *La Révolution française*, p. 220.

11. « On nous apprend, Monsieur, que l'on forme le projet de se transporter dans les prisons de Paris pour y enlever tous les prisonniers et en faire une prompte justice. » Quoted in Mathiez, *La Révolution française* (2012), p. 223.

12. « Les prisons regorgent de scélérats; il est urgent d'en délivrer la société sur le champ. »

13. « Le dernier parti, qui est le plus sûr et le plus sage, est de se porter en armes à l'Abbaye, d'en arracher les traîtres, particulièrement les officiers Suisses et leur complices, et de les passer au fil de l'épée. » Quoted in Tulard, Fayard et Fierro, *Histoire et dictionnaire de la Révolution française* (2012), p. 105.

14. « La Section, considérant les dangers imminents de la patrie et les manœuvres infernales des prêtres, arrête que tous les prêtres et personnes suspectes, enfermés dans les prisons de Paris, Orléans et autres, seront mis à mort. » Quoted in Michelet I (2), p. 1050; and Mathiez, *La Révolution française* (2012), p. 235.

15. « Je jure d'être fidèle à la nation, de maintenir de tout mon pouvoir la liberté, l'égalité, la sûreté des personnes et des propriétés, et de mourir s'il le faut, pour l'exécution de la loi. »

16. « Le tocsin qu'on va sonner n'est point un signal d'alarme, c'est la charge sur les ennemis de la patrie. Pour les vaincre, Messieurs, il nous faut de l'audace, encore de l'audace, toujours de l'audace, et la France est sauvée! »

17. The *Mairie* was separate from the *Hôtel de ville*, the vast and rather magnificent building (entirely rebuilt after a fire in 1871) which stood on the Right Bank somewhat to the east of the Louvre and housed the large hall for the meetings of the assembly of the *Commune* and its principal offices.

18. This prison of the Abbaye no longer exists; it was pulled down in 1854 to make way for the construction of the boulevard Saint-Germain.

19. « Je me fous bien des prisonniers; qu'ils deviennent ce qu'ils pourront! » Quoted in Mathiez, *La Révolution française* (2012), p. 237; and Tulard, *Histoire et dictionnaire de la Révolution française* (1987), p. 744.

20. « La Commune de Paris se hâte d'informer ses frères des départements qu'une partie des conspirateurs féroces détenus dans ses prisons a été mise à mort par le peuple; actes de justice qui lui ont paru indispensables pour retenir par la terreur des légions de traîtres cachés dans ses murs, au moment où il allait marcher à l'ennemi; et sans doute, la nation entière, après la longue suite de trahisons qui l'ont conduite sur les bords de l'abîme, s'empressera d'adopter ce moyen si nécessaire de salut public » Quoted in Mathiez, *La Révolution française* (2012), p. 239.

14 The *Convention*

1. « La royauté est abolie en France. » Quoted in Tulard, Fayard, and Fierro, *Histoire et dictionnaire de la Révolution française*, p. 348.

2. 'Peasant' is a literal translation of the French word *paysan*, meaning simply 'someone who lives in the *pays*, or countryside'.

3. Michelet II (1), p. 20.
4. Ibid., p. 20.
5. Ibid., p. 23.
6. Mathiez, *La Révolution française* (2012), p. 249.
7. Michelet II (1), p. 41.
8. Paine drafted his pamphlet *Le siècle de la raison* in the spring of 1793 and issued it clandestinely that spring or summer. In October he considerably revised the manuscript, and he brought out the expanded English edition, *The Age of Reason*, in February 1794. See John Keane, *Tom Paine* (1995, 1996), p. 389.
9. Robespierre had an early copy of *Le siècle de la raison*, on which he scribbled a reminder to himself: « Demander que Thomas Paine soit décrété d'accusation, pour l'intérêt de l'Amérique autant que de la France. » 'Demand that Thomas Paine be arrested and charged, in the interest of America as much as of France'. Ibid., pp. 389, 599 note 16.
10. Ibid., pp. 400–414.
11. « Personne n'ose nommer les traîtres. Eh bien ! moi, pour le salut du peuple, je les nomme ; je dénonce le liberticide Brissot, la faction de la Gironde ; je les dénonce pour avoir vendu la France à Brunswick et pour avoir reçu d'avance le prix de leur lâcheté. » Quoted in Tulard, *Histoire de la Révolution française*, p. 602.
12. Mathiez, *La Révolution française* (2012), p. 271.
13. Ibid., p. 302.
14. « Le parti qu'on vous a dénoncé, dont l'intention est d'établir la dictature, c'est le parti de Robespierre, voilà ce que la notoriété publique nous a appris à Marseille. » Quoted in Mathiez, *La Révolution française* (2012), p. 303.
15. Tulard, Fayard et Fierro, *Histoire et dictionnaire de la Révolution française* (1987), pp. 115, 609.
16. « Toutes ces choses étaient illégales, aussi illégales que la Révolution, que la chute du trône et de la Bastille, aussi illégales que la liberté elle-même. On ne peut vouloir une révolution sans une révolution. » Quoted in Tulard, Fayard, and Fierro, *Histoire et dictionnaire de la Révolution française*, p. 115.

15 The War in 1792: From Valmy to Jemappes

1. I am grateful to my friend the writer Edmund Fawcett for this detail.
2. Tulard, Fayard et Fierro, *Histoire et dictionnaire de la Révolution française* (1987), p. 121.
3. « Brave nation Belge, nous entrons sur votre territoire pour vous aider à planter l'arbre de la liberté, sans nous mêler en rien à la Constitution que vous voudrez adopter ! Pourvu que vous adoptiez la souveraineté du peuple et que vous renonciez à vivre sous des despotes quelconques, nous serons vos frères, vos amis, vos soutiens. Nous respecterons vos propriétés et vos lois. » Quoted in Tulard, *Histoire de la Révolution française*, p. 123.
4. « La France a renoncé aux conquêtes et cette déclaration doit rassurer le gouvernement anglais sur l'entrée de Dumouriez en Belgique » ; « Nous

ne voulons pas nous ingérer à donner à aucun peuple telle ou telle forme de gouvernement. Les habitants de la Belgique choisiront celle qui leur conviendra le mieux. » Quoted in Mathiez, *La Révolution française*, p. 351.

5. « J'ai beau battre les Autrichiens, cette superbe expédition se terminera mal, parce qu'on contrarie tous mes plans, parce qu'on tyrannise le pays, parce que des spéculateurs avides, soutenus par les bureaux de la Guerre, accaparent toutes les subsistences, sous prétexte de nourrir l'armée, et la laisse manquer de tout. » Quoted in Tulard, Fayard et Fierro, *Histoire et dictionnaire de la Révolution française* (1987), p. 124.

6. « La Convention nationale déclare, au nom de la nation française, qu'elle accordera fraternité et secours à tous les peuples qui voudront recouvrir leur liberté et charge le pouvoir exécutif de donner aux généraux les ordres nécessaires pour porter secours à ces peuples et défendre les citoyens qui auraient étés vexés ou qui pourraient l'être pour la cause de la liberté. » Quoted in Mathiez, *La Révolution française* (2012), p. 358.

7. « Le salut de la République est dans la Belgique ; ce n'est que par l'union de ce riche pays à notre térritoire que nous pouvons rétablir nos finances et continuer la guerre. » Quoted in Tulard, Fayard et Fierro, *Histoire et dictionnaire de la Révolution française* (1987), p. 124.

8. Michelet I (2), p. 1255.

9. Michelet II (1), p. 81–82.

10. « Il faut nous déclarer pouvoir révolutionnaire dans les pays où nous entrons ; il est inutile de nous cacher ; les despotes savent ce que nous voulons. Point de demi-révolution ! Tout peuple qui ne voudra pas ce que nous proposons ici sera notre ennemi et méritera d'être traîté comme tel ! » Quoted in Tulard, Fayard et Fierro, *Histoire et dictionnaire de la Révolution française* (1987), p. 124.

11. Mathiez, *La Révolution française* (2012), p. 362.

16 The Trial of the King

1. « L'unique but du comité fut de vous persuader que le roi devait être jugé en simple citoyen; et moi, je dis que le roi doit être jugé en ennemi, que nous avons moins à le juger qu'à le combattre, et que, n'étant plus rien dans le contrat qui unit les Français, les formes de la procédure ne sont point dans la loi civile, mais dans la loi du droit des gens

« Pour moi, je ne vois point de milieu: cet homme doit régner ou mourir

« rien au monde ne peut légitimer cette usurpation; et de quelque illusion, de quelques Conventions que la royauté s'enveloppe, elle est un crime éternel, contre lequel tout homme à le droit de s'élever et de s'armer

« On ne peut point régner innocemment: la vérité est trop évidente. Tout roi est un rebelle et un usurpateur …

« Citoyens, le tribunal qui doit juger Louis n'est point un tribunal judiciaire: c'est un conseil, c'est le peuple, c'est vous; et les lois que nous avons à suivre sont celles du droit des gens. C'est vous qui devez juger Louis; mais vous ne pouvez être à son égard une cour judiciaire, un juré, un accusateur; cette forme civile de jugement le rendrait injuste; et le roi, regardé comme citoyen, ne pourrait être jugé, par les mêmes bouches qui l'accusent. Louis est un étranger parmi nous, il n'était pas citoyen avant son crime; il ne pouvait voter; il ne pouvait porter les armes; il l'est encore moins depuis son crime: et par quel abus de la justice même en feriez-vous un citoyen, pour le condamner?…

« Tout ce que j'ai dit tend donc à vous prouver que Louis XVI doit être jugé comme un ennemi étranger. J'ajoute qu'il n'est pas nécessaire que son jugement à mort soit soumis à la sanction du peuple …

« Louis a combattu le peuple: il est vaincu. C'est un barbare, c'est un étranger prisonnier de guerre.

« Vous avez vu ses desseins perfides; vous avez vu son armée; le traître n'était pas le roi des Français, c'était le roi de quelques conjurés. Il faisait des levées secrètes de troupes, avait des magistrats particuliers; il regardait les citoyens comme ses esclaves; il avait proscrit secrètement tous les gens de bien et de courage. Il est le meurtrier de la Bastille, de Nancy, du Champ-de-Mars, de Tournai, des Tuileries: quel ennemi, quel étranger nous a fait plus de mal? Il doit être jugé promptement: c'est le conseil de la sagesse et de la saine politique; c'est une espèce d'otage que conservent les fripons.

« On cherche à remuer la pitié; on achètera bientôt des larmes; on fera tout pour nous intéresser, pour nous corrompre même. Peuple, si le roi est jamais absous, souviens-toi que nous ne serons plus dignes de ta confiance, et tu pourras nous accuser de perfidie. »

2. Michelet II (1), p. 74.
3. « Il ne se fait payer que pour être de son avis ». Quoted in Furet, *Penser la Révolution française,* p. 86.
4. « C'est un crime pour une nation de se donner un roi Il ne faut pas s'envelopper d'une équivoque. L'assemblée n'a pas décrété qu'il y aurait un procès en forme; seulement elle a décidé qu'elle prononcerait elle-même le jugement ou la sentence du ci-devant roi. Je soutiens que, d'après les principes, il faut le condamner sur-le-champ à mort, en vertu d'une insurrection. »
5. « Défendu par Malesherbes, Tronchet et De Seze, 'Louis Capet' fut reconnu coupable de conspiration contre la liberté de la nation et d'attentat contre la sûreté de l'État, au terme d'un procès extrêmement inéquitable. Les pièces à conviction avaient été rassemblées à l'insu du roi dans l'intention avouée de le montrer coupable. On avait écarté du dossier toutes les pièces qui pouvaient représenter un moyen de défense pour l'accusé. L'acte énonciatif de ses 'crimes' et les pièces à conviction avaient été imprimés, affichés, envoyés dans les départements Les témoins qui auraient pu déposer pour la défense avaient été massacrés dans les prisons les 2 ou 3 septembre, 1792, ou exécutés à Versailles avec les prisonniers de la Haute Cour d'Orléans. Les témoignages innocentant Louis XVI et les pièces les accompagnant ne furent pas communiqués au roi non plus qu'à ses avocats » F. Gendron, quoted in Soboul et al, p. 686.
6. After the overthrow of the monarchy on August 10, 1792, the Revolutionaries decided to invent a name for the King, in order symbolically to minimise his

status. From then on, he was called Louis Capet, an allusion to Hugues Capet, ostensibly the founder of the Bourbon dynasty.

7. Mathiez, *La Révolution française* (2012), pp. 331–32.
8. Michelet II (1), p. 146.
9. Ibid., p. 160.
10. This large open space, started in 1757 and finished in 1772, towards the end of the reign of Louis XV, was at first called place Louis–XV. In 1792, three years after the start of the Revolution, it was renamed place de la Révolution; and in 1795, after the fall of Robespierre, it was renamed again, place de la Concorde.

17 *Girondins* and *Montagnards*

1. « Je dis que c'est en vain qu'on veut faire craindre de donner trop d'étendue à la République. Ses limites sont marquées par la nature. Nous les atteindrons toutes des quatre coins de l'horizon, du côté du Rhin, du côté de l'Océan, du côté des Alpes. Là doivent finir les bornes de notre République, et nulle puissance humaine ne pourra nous empêcher de les atteindre. » Quoted in Tulard, Fayard et Fierro, *Histoire et dictionnaire de la Révolution française* (1987), p. 125.
2. Soboul et al, pp. 563–64.
3. « On veut un despotisme plus affreux que celui de l'anarchie. Je rends grâces de chaque moment de vie qui me reste à ceux qui me le laissent encore Qu'ils me donnent seulement le temps de sauver ma mémoire, d'échapper au déshonneur, en votant contre la tyrannie de la Convention ! Quand vous avez reçu des pouvoirs illimités, ce n'était pas pour usurper la liberté publique. Si vous confondez tous les pouvoirs, si tout est ici, où finira ce despotisme, dont je suis las moi-même ? » Quoted in Michelet II (1), pp. 254, 260.
4. Michelet II (1), p. 260.
5. « contre lesquels il y aura de fortes présomptions de complicité avec les ennemis de la liberté, de l'égalité, et du gouvernement républicain. » Quoted in Tulard, Fayard et Fierro, *Histoire et dictionnaire de la Révolution française* (1987), p. 132.

18 The Fall of the *Girondins*

1. « coupables du crime de félonie envers le peuple souverain ».
2. « Vos propriétés sont menacées et vous fermez les yeux sur ce danger. On excite la guerre entre ceux qui ont et ceux qui n'ont pas, et vous ne faites rien pour la prévenir. Quelques intrigants, une poignée de factieux vous font la loi, vous entraînent dans des mesures violentes et inconsidérées, et vous n'avez pas le courage de résister ; vous n'osez pas vous présenter dans vos sections pour lutter contre eux. Vous voyez tous les hommes riches et paisibles quitter Paris, et vous demeurez tranquilles » Quoted in Mathiez, *La Révolution française* (2012), p. 396.
3. « Je demande que les individus de la famille d'Orléans dite Egalité, soient traduits devant le tribunal révolutionnaire, ainsi que Sillery, sa femme, Valence,

et tous les hommes spécialement attachés à cette maison; que ce tribunal soit également chargé d'instruire le procès de tous les autres complices de Dumouriez. Oserai-je nommer ici des patriotes tels que Brissot, Vergniaud, Gensonné, Guadet?–Je renouvelle en ce moment la même proposition que j'ai déjà faite à l'égard de Marie-Antoinette d'Autriche. Je demande que la Convention nationale s'occupe ensuite sans relâche des moyens tant de fois annoncés de sauver la patrie, et de soulager la misère du peuple. » Robespierre to the *Convention*, April 10, 1793.

4. « Autrefois le savon ne valait que 12 sols, aujourd'hui il en vaut 40. *Vive La République !* Le sucre 20 sols, aujourd'hui 4 livres. *Vive La République*. » Quoted in Soboul, *La Iʳᵉ République* (1968), p. 61.

5. « Qu'on n'objecte pas le droit de propriété ! Le droit de propriété ne peut être le droit d'affamer ses concitoyens. Les fruits de la terre, comme l'air, appartiennent à tous les hommes. Nous venons demander : 1. La fixation du maximum du prix du blé dans toute la République ; 2. L'anéantissement du commerce des grains ; 3. La suppression de tout intermédiaire entre le cultivateur et le consommateur ; 4. Un recensement général de tout le blé après chaque récolte. » Quoted in Tulard, Fayard et Fierro, *Histoire et dictionnaire de la Révolution française* (1987), p. 138.

6. « Vous avez des aristocrates dans les sections ; chassez-les ! Vous avez la liberté à sauver, proclamez les droits de la liberté, et déployez toute votre énergie. Vous avez un peuple immense de *sans-culottes*, bien purs, bien vigoureux, ils ne peuvent quitter leurs travaux, faites-les payer par les riches ! » Robespierre to the *Jacobins*, May 8, 1793, quoted in Mathiez, *La Révolution française* (2012), p. 397.

7. « en matière de conspiration, il est absurde de demander des faits démonstratifs ».

8. « Quand le peuple est opprimé, quand il ne lui reste plus que lui-même, celui-là serait un lâche qui ne lui dirait pas de se lever. C'est quand toutes les lois sont violées, c'est quand le despotisme est à son comble, c'est quand on foule aux pieds la bonne foi et la pudeur, que le peuple doit s'insurger. Ce moment est arrivé. » Robespierre to the *Jacobins*, May 26, 1793, quoted in Mathiez, *La Révolution française* (2012), pp. 402–403.

9. « … fortes présomptions de complicité avec les ennemis de la liberté, de l'égalité, et du gouvernement républicain. » Quoted in Tulard, Fayard et Fierro, *Histoire et dictionnaire de la Révolution française* (1987), p. 132.

19 The Civil Wars of 1793

1. « Si j'avance, suivez-moi ; si je recule, tuez-moi ; si je meurs, vengez-moi. »

2. « Il n'y a plus de Vendée. Je viens de l'enterrer dans les marais de Savernay. J'ai écrasé les enfants sous les pieds des chevaux, et massacré les femmes. Je n'ai pas un prisonnier à me reprocher. J'ai tout exterminé. » Quoted in Tulard, Fayard et Fierro, *Histoire et dictionnaire de la Révolution française* (1987), p. 363.

3. Quoted in Mathiez, *La Révolution française* (2012), p. 302.

4. Marat lived in a two-room apartment, which he rented from a private landlord, on the first floor of a house at 20 rue des Cordeliers; it was appropriately near the École de Médecine (since he had long aspired to recognition as a doctor). He was in his bath, writing on a plank desk laid across it, because he suffered from a painful skin condition that was alleviated by being in water.

5. Soboul et al, p. 689.

6. Saliceti (1757–1809) was a *député* from Corsica and long deeply involved in Corsican affairs.

7. « Lyon perdra son nom, elle sera appelée Ville-Affranchie. Elle sera détruite, tout ce qui fut habité par le riche sera démoli, il ne restera que la maison du pauvre, les habitations des patriotes égarés ou proscrits, les édifices spécialement employés à l'industrie et les monuments consacrés à l'humanité et à l'instruction publique. Il sera élévé sur les ruines de Lyon une colonne qui attestera à la postérité les crimes et la punition des royalistes de cette ville avec cette inscription : Lyon fit la guerre à la liberté ; Lyon n'est plus. » Quoted in Soboul et al, p. 693.

8. Soboul et al, p. 695.

9. Tulard, Fayard, and Fierro, *Histoire et dictionnaire de la Révolution française*, p. 625.

20 The *Gouvernement révolutionnaire*

1. « Il faut une volonté *une*. Il faut qu'elle soit républicaine ou royaliste. Pour qu'elle soit républicaine, il faut des ministres républicains, des papiers républicains, des députés républicains, un gouvernement républicain. Les dangers intérieurs viennent des bourgeois, pour vaincre les bourgeois, il faut rallier le peuple. Tout était disposé pour mettre le peuple sous le joug des bourgeois, et faire périr les défenseurs de la République sur l'échafaud. » Quoted in Mathiez, *La Révolution française* (2012), p. 416.

2. « Quand le peuple se lève, ne doit-il pas avoir un but digne de lui? De chétives marchandises doivent-ils l'occuper ? Le peuple doit se lever, non pour recueillir du sucre, mais pour terrasser les brigands. »

3. « Art. 1er. La propriété est le droit qu'a chaque citoyen de jouir et de disposer de la portion des biens qui lui est garantie par la loi.
« Art. 2. Le droit de propriété est borné, comme tous les autres, par l'obligation de respecter les droits d'autrui. »

4. « Art. 1er. Le but de toute association politique est le maintien des droits naturels et imprescriptibles de l'homme, et le développement de toutes ses facultés.
« Art. 2. Les principaux droits de l'homme sont celui de pourvoir à la conservation de son existence, et la liberté. »

5. See 'A Note on the Franchise for Women', page 267.

6. « La résistance à l'oppression est la conséquence des autres droits de l'homme ».

7. « Quand le gouvernement viole les droits du peuple, l'insurrection est pour le peuple, et pour chaque portion du peuple, le plus sacré des droits et le plus indispensable des devoirs. »

8. « La liberté n'est qu'un vain fantôme quand une classe d'hommes peut affamer l'autre impunément ; l'égalité n'est qu'un vain fantôme quand le riche exerce le droit de vie et de mort sur ses semblables. » Quoted in Tulard, Fayard, and Fierro, *Histoire et dictionnaire de la Révolution française*, p. 800.

9. « Tous ceux qui aiment la franchise et la probité ne s'effarouchent pas des *bougres* et des *foutres*, dont je larde, par-ci et par-là, mes joies et mes colères. » Quoted in Tulard, Fayard et Fierro, ibid., p. 872.

10. « Tant que les Comités usurperont tous les pouvoirs, nous n'aurons jamais de gouvernement, ou nous en aurons un détestable   Nous n'aurons jamais de liberté, notre Constitution ne sera qu'un chimère tant que les ministres ne seront que des galopins aux ordres des derniers balayeurs de la Convention. » *Le Père Duchesne*, no. 275, quoted in Mathiez, *La Révolution française* (2012), p. 451.

11. « Il est à craindre que cette Commission ne s'occupe plutôt d'inimitiés personelles que de surveillance loyale et ne devienne ainsi un véritable Comité de dénonciation. Ce n'est pas d'aujourd'hui que je m'aperçois qu'il existe un système perfide de paralyser le *Comité de salut public*, en paraissant l'aider dans ses travaux. » Quoted in Mathiez, ibid., p. 453.

12. Tulard, Fayard, and Fierro, *Histoire et dictionnaire de la Révolution française*, p. 161.

13. Mathiez, *La Révolution française* (2012), p. 453.

14. Ibid., p. 455.

15. « Ce ne sont pas des promesses qu'il nous faut, c'est du pain, et tout de suite. » Mathiez, ibid., p. 455.

16. « Et, moi aussi, j'ai été pauvre et par conséquent je sais ce que c'est que les pauvres ! C'est ici la guerre ouverte des riches contre les pauvres, ils veulent nous écraser, eh bien ! il faut les prévenir, il faut les écraser nous-mêmes, nous avons la force en main ! » Quoted in Mathiez, ibid., p. 455.

17. Soboul et al, p. 978.

18. Mathiez, *La Révolution française* (2012), p. 454.

19. « l'armée révolutionnaire qui, selon le mot de la Commune, *mettra la terreur à l'ordre du jour* » Quoted in Michelet II (1), p. 574.

20. Quoted in Tulard, Fayard, and Fierro, *Histoire et dictionnaire de la Révolution française*, p. 361.

21. « Dans les circonstances où se trouve la République, la Constitution ne peut être établie ; on l'immolerait par elle-même, elle deviendrait la garantie des attentats contre la liberté, parce qu'elle manquerait de la violence nécessaire pour les réprimer. » Quoted in Tulard, Fayard et Fierro, *Histoire et dictionnaire de la Révolution française* (1987), p. 148.

22. « Ce dernier est soumis à des règles moins uniformes et moins rigoureuses, parce que les circonstances où il se trouve sont orageuses et mobiles et surtout parce qu'il est forcé de déployer sans cesse des ressources nouvelles et rapides pour répondre à des dangers nouveaux et pressants   Il faut organiser le despotisme de la liberté pour écraser le despotisme des rois. » Quoted in Tulard, Fayard et Fierro, *Histoire et Dictionnaire de la Révolution française* (1987), p. 149.

23. A full list of the members can be found in 'A Note on the *Comité de salut public*', page 268.
24. See 'A Note on Death and the Revolution', page 271.

21 The *Terreur*

1. Estimate by Richard Cobb. See Soboul et al, p. 41.
2. Soboul et al, p. 123.
3. « La notoriété publique accuse un citoyen de crimes dont il n'existe point de preuves écrites, mais dont la preuve est dans le cœur de tous les citoyens indignés. » Quoted in Soboul, *Les sans-culottes parisiens*, p. 253.
4. Tocqueville, *L'ancien régime et la révolution*, p. 227.
5. « ... tous ceux qui par leurs écrits se sont montrés partisans de la tyrannie, du fédéralisme et ennemis de la liberté. »
6. Tulard, Fayard, and Fierro, *Histoire et dictionnaire de la Révolution française*, p. 1125.
7. « La Société des Jacobins est le véritable comité de recherches de la nation   Non seulement c'est le Grand Inquisiteur, qui épouvante les aristocrats, c'est encore le grand réquisiteur qui redresse les abus et vient au secours de tous les citoyens. » Quoted in Soboul, *La Iʳᵉ République*, p. 117.
8. Michelet II (1), p. 38.
9. Michelet II (1), p. 692.
10. In May and June 1793, the insurrectionists had demanded the arrest of twenty-two *Girondin* Deputies, plus the members of the Committee of Twelve, on the grounds that they had been led astray; and some of the others were still on the run.
11. Michelet II (1), p. 614.
12. Ibid., p. 616.
13. « Liberté, que de crimes on commet en ton nom ! » Quoted in Tulard, Fayard, and Fierro, *Histoire et dictionnaire de la Révolution française*, p. 1074.
14. « Égalité était peut-être le seul membre qui pût se récuser. » Quoted in Tulard, Fayard, and Fierro, *Histoire et dictionnaire de la Révolution française*, p. 1074.
15. « En vérité, ceci a l'air d'une plaisanterie. » Quoted in Soboul et al, p. 801.
16. Michelet II (1), p. 130.

22 The Spasm of Religion to the Fall of Danton

1. Tocqueville, *L'ancien régime et la Révolution*, ch. 3.
2. For Desmoulins, see Soboul, *La Iʳᵉ République*, p. 117; for Michelet II (1), p. 38.
3. « le gouvernement provisoire de la France serait révolutionnaire jusqu'à la paix. » Quoted in Tulard, Fayard, and Fierro, *Histoire et dictionnaire de la Révolution française*, p. 361.
4. Michel Vovelle, in Soboul et al, pp. 327–30.
5. « La mort est un éternel sommeil. »

6. Maillard was a one-time bailiff's clerk who had made his name in 1789 as a 'Conquerer of the Bastille' but was by now mainly a street brawler and regular participant in all available Revolutionary demonstrations. From August to October 1793 he was also a part-time local police spy. He died of consumption on April 15, 1794, aged thirty-one.

7. « Le comité de salut publique a cru que pour établir la République il avait besoin un moment de la jurisprudence des despotes. »

8. « Ouvrez les prisons à 200 000 citoyens que vous appelez suspects, car, dans la Déclaration des Droits, il n'y a point de maisons de suspicion Vous voulez exterminer tous vos ennemis par la guillotine ! Mais y eut-il jamais plus grande folie ! Croyez-moi, la liberté serait consolidée et l'Europe vaincue si vous aviez un Comité de Clémence ! »

9. « Le but du gouvernement constitutionnel est de conserver la République ; celui du gouvernement révolutionnaire est de la fonder Sous le régime constitutionnel, il suffit presque de protéger les individus contre l'abus de la puissance publique ; sous le régime révolutionnaire, la puissance publique elle-même est obligée de se défendre contre toutes les factions qui l'attaquent Ces notions suffisent pour expliquer l'origine et la nature des lois que nous appelons révolutionnaires. Ceux qui les nomment arbitraires ou tyranniques sont des sophistes stupides ou pervers qui cherchent à confondre les contraires. »

10. « Brûler n'est pas répondre. »

11. « On a brûlé ce livre chez nous. L'opération de le brûler a été aussi odieuse que celle de le composer. Il y a des choses qu'il faut qu'une administration sage ignore. Brûler un livre de raisonnement, c'est dire : 'Nous n'avons pas assez d'esprit pour lui répondre.' » Voltaire, *Idées républicaines*, para. XXXIX, in *Mélanges*, Bibliothèque de la Pléiade, no. 152, Paris, Gallimard (1961), p. 515.

12. « Il est temps de marquer nettement le but de la Révolution, et le terme où nous voulons arriver Quel est le but où nous tendons ? La jouissance paisible de la liberté et de l'égalité Mais comme l'essence de la République ou de la démocratie est l'égalité, il s'ensuit que l'amour de la patrie embrasse nécessairement l'amour de l'égalité Non seulement la vertu est l'âme de la démocratie, mais elle ne peut exister que dans ce gouvernement Si le ressort du gouvernement populaire dans la paix est la vertu, le ressort du gouvernement populaire en révolution est à la fois *la vertu et la terreur* : la vertu, sans laquelle la terreur est funeste ; la terreur, sans laquelle la vertu est impuissante. La terreur n'est autre chose que la justice prompte, sévère, inflexible ; elle est donc une émanation de la vertu … »

13. « La force des choses nous conduit peut-être à des résultats auxquels nous n'avons points pensés. L'opulence est dans les mains d'un assez grand nombre d'ennemis de la Révolution, les besoins mettent le peuple qui travaille dans la dépendance de ses ennemis Les propriétés des patriotes sont sacrées, mais les biens des conspirateurs sont là pour tous les malheureux. Les malheureux sont les puissances de la terre. Ils ont le droit de parler en maîtres aux gouvernements qui les négligent. » Quoted in Mathiez, *La Révolution française* (2012), p. 548.

14. « l'extrême disproportion des fortunes est la source de bien des maux et de bien des crimes. »

15. « On n'emporte pas la patrie à la semelle de ses souliers. »

16. « Je suis ici pour secourir les citoyens, et non pour tuer les patriotes. »

17. « Tout prévenu de conspiration qui résistera ou insultera à la justice nationale sera mis hors des débats sur-le-champ. »

18. « Tu montreras ma tête au peuple ; elle en vaut la peine. » Quoted in Michelet II (1), p. 808.

23 The Fall of Robespierre

1. Soboul, *La Ire République*, p. 119.

2. « La Révolution est glacée ». Soboul, ibid., p. 112.

3. « Ceux qui auront secondé les projets des ennemis de la France, en persécutant et calomniant le patriotisme, ceux qui auront cherché à inspirer le découragement, à dépraver les mœurs, à altérer la pureté et l'énergie des principes révolutionnaires, tous ceux qui, par quelque moyen que ce soit, et de quelque dehors qu'ils se couvrent, auront attenté à la liberté, à l'unité, à la sûreté de la République, ou travaillé à en empêcher l'affermissement. »

4. The term *fournées* derives from the French word for 'oven' (*four*) and means 'batches of bread'.

5. « Les têtes tombaient comme des ardoises. » Quoted in Soboul et al, p. 122.

6. Soboul, *La Ire République*, p. 123. Soboul does not, however, draw the same conclusions from his figures that I do.

7. « Il ne faut pas vous dissimuler que nous sommes perdus si vous n'entrez pas bien vite en pays ennemi pour avoir des subsistances et des effets de tout genre, car la France ne peut soutenir longtemps l'état forcé où elle se trouve en ce moment Il faut vivre au dépens de l'ennemi ou périr. » Quoted in Mathiez, *La Révolution française* (2012), p. 584.

8. « Nous devons vivre aux dépens de l'ennemi, nous n'entrons pas chez lui pour lui porter nos trésors. » Quoted in Mathiez, *La Révolution française* (2012), p. 586.

9. « Il faut dépouiller le pays, et le mettre dans l'impuissance de fournir aux ennemis les moyens de revenir. » Quoted in Mathiez, *La Révolution française* (2012), p. 587.

10. Mathiez, *La Révolution française* (2012), p. 587.

11. « Nous ne voulons garder que ce qui peut assurer notre propre frontière, c'est-à-dire à gauche toute la West-Flandre et la Flandre Hollandaise, à droite le pays d'entre Sambre et Meuse, et au milieu seulement ce qui est en deçà de l'Escaut et de la Haisne. » Quoted in Mathiez, *La Révolution française* (2012), p. 588.

12. Mathiez, *La Révolution française* (2012), p. 588.

13. « … révolutionnaire jusqu'à la paix. » Quoted in Tulard, Fayard, and Fierro, *Histoire et dictionnaire de la Révolution française*, p. 361.

14. Mathiez, *La Révolution française* (2012), p. 603.

15. Michelet II (1), p. 593.

16. Mathiez, *La Révolution française* (2012), pp. 591–92.

17. Mathiez, ibid., p. 601.

18. « un turbot farci ». Quoted in Tulard, Fayard, and Fierro, *Histoire et dictionnaire de la Révolution française*, p. 1131.

19. Mathiez, *La Révolution française* (2012), pp. 592–93.

20. « Disons donc qu'il existe une conspiration contre la liberté publique; qu'elle doit sa force à une coalition criminelle qui intrigue au sein même de la Convention; que cette coalition a des complices dans le comité de sûreté générale et dans les bureaux de ce comité qu'ils dominent; que les ennemis de la République ont opposé ce Comité au comité de salut public, et constitué ainsi deux gouvernements; que des membres du comité de salut public entrent dans ce complot

« Quel est le remède à ce mal? Punir les traîtres, renouveler les bureaux du comité de sûreté générale, épurer ce comité lui-même, et le subordonner au comité de salut public; épurer le comité de salut public lui-même, constituer l'unité du gouvernement sous l'autorité suprême de la Convention nationale. »

21. « Il faut en finir : le décret d'arrestation contre Robespierre ! » Quoted in Tulard, Fayard, and Fierro, *Histoire et dictionnaire de la Révolution française*, p. 956; for a longer account of this dramatic event, see also Mathiez, *La Révolution française* (2012), pp. 612–13.

22. Mathiez, *La Révolution française* (2012), p. 616.

23. Furet, pp. 98–100.

24 The Aftermath

1. 'Revolutionary until the peace'. Quoted in Tulard, Fayard, and Fierro, *Histoire et dictionnaire de la Révolution française*, p. 361.

2. R. R. Palmer, *Twelve Who Ruled*, (1941, 2005), pp 381–382.

3. « le désarmement des hommes connus dans leurs section comme ayant participé aux horreurs commises sous la tyrannie ». Quoted in Soboul, *La 1ère république* (1968), p. 172.

4. Soboul, ibid., pp. 174–77; Tulard, *Histoire de la Révolution française*, pp. 190–92.

5. Soboul, *La 1ère république* (1968), p. 177.

6. Under this treaty, Austria gave up its possessions in the Low Countries and on the left bank of the Rhine, which were annexed to France. It also gave up possession of Milan but was compensated with Venice, the Veneto and the Archbishopric of Salzburg.

7. Pichegru escaped from French Guiana, reached England and in February 1804 returned secretly to France. There, with the rebel Georges Cadoudal, he conspired against Bonaparte. But Bonaparte made short work of them. They were discovered and arrested; Cadoudal was executed on June 25, 1804; and Pichegru was found strangled in his cell on April 5, 1804. Bonaparte also suspected (wrongly) that Louis, the duc d'Enghien, who was a Bourbon and thus a distant relative of the executed King of France, was part of the conspiracy and had him kidnapped abroad, in Baden, where he was living; brought back to France under arrest; and judicially murdered by court martial. This provoked the lapidary comment

C'est pire qu'un crime, c'est une faute ('It's worse than a crime, it's a mistake'), variously attributed to Joseph Fouché, Napoléon's chief of police; to a one-time Revolutionary, Antoine Boulay de la Meurthe; and even sometimes to Talleyrand.

25 Epilogue

1. Furet, *Penser la Révolution française*, p. 35.
2. Ibid., p. 137.
3. Tocqueville, *Souvenirs*, vol. III, pp. 779–80.
4. Tocqueville, *L'ancien régime et la révolution*, p. 99.
5. This enumeration does not correspond to that of the French government's *Conseil d'État*, but that is because the *Conseil d'État* list includes the Constitution of June 24, 1793, which was consigned to oblivion by Robespierre and never put in force.
6. The *Conseil d'État* list of the Constitutions of France does not make any mention of the Constitution of the Vichy régime; like the Constitution of June 24, 1793, it was consigned to oblivion and never enacted.
7. Furet, *Penser la Révolution française*, p. 17. The crisis of May 16, 1877, exposed the deep splits in French society and the weakness of the Constitution of the Third Republic. After the fall of the Second Empire, a Republic was formally established in 1875, but the *parlement* was deeply divided among Republicans, monarchists and Bonapartists. The crisis exploded when Marshal Patrice de MacMahon, the President and a monarchist, attempted to form a government opposed to the Republican majority of the Chamber of Deputies. He called elections, but the Republicans again had a majority. MacMahon finally submitted to the will of the majority.
8. « La France est une République indivisible, laïque, démocratique et sociale. Elle assure l'égalité devant la loi de tous les citoyens sans distinction d'origine, de race ou de religion. Elle respecte toutes les croyances. »
9. « Aux morts de Verdun, Connus et Inconnus. La famille royale française. »
10. Tocqueville, *L'Ancien Régime et la Révolution*, vol. III, p. 46.
11. Ibid., p. 231.

A Note on Money and Inflation

1. From the marriage of Henry II of England to Eleanor of Aquitaine in 1152 until the end of the Hundred Years' War in 1453, a large part of the territory of France, including most of Aquitaine, was under the control of the English monarchy, and the affairs of England and France were intimately connected.
2. See Tulard et al, p. 830.

LIST OF ILLUSTRATIONS

1. The opening of the États généraux, May 5, 1789. Contemporary Dutch engraving. (Granger, NYC/Alamy.)
2. Honoré Gabriel Riqueti, comte de Mirabeau before Dreux Breze Joseph Désiré Court, 1797. (Peter Horree/Alamy.)
3. The famous Tennis Court Oath (le serment du jeu de Paume). (Image: The Art Archive/Alamy.)
4. A cartoon symbolising the final reconciliation of the three Estates. (Image: Bibliothèque nationale de France.)
5. Camille Desmoulins speaking at the Palais Royal, July 12, 1789, engraved by Pierre Gabriel Berthault. (Bibliotheque Nationale, Paris, France/Bridgeman Images.)
6. 'Prise de la Bastille' (The storming of the Bastille), chalk lithograph, coloured, by Hippolyte Lalaisse. (Image: akg-images.)
7. Parisian market women march to Versailles. (Image: Bibliothèque nationale de France.)
8. Parisians protest in Versailles. (Image: Bibliothèque nationale de France.)
9. A political allegory, depicting the long-running debate over the role of the King's veto. (Image: Bibliothèque nationale de France.)
10. Pierre Victurnien Vergniaud, (1753–93). (Image: Public domain.)
11. Jacques Pierre Brissot, (1754–93). (Image: Public domain.)
12. Paul François Jean Nicolas, vicomte de Barras, (1755–1829). (Image: Public domain.)

13. Charles Maurice de Talleyrand, (1754–1838). (Image: Public domain.)

14. Emmanuel Joseph Sieyès, (1748–1836). (Image: Public domain.)

15. Charles-François du Périer Dumouriez, (1739–1823). (Image: Public domain.)

16. Louis XVI with his wife, Marie-Antoinette, and their family. (Leemage/Getty Images.)

17. The Palace of Versailles by Pierre Denis Martin, (akg-images/Jean-Claude Varga).

18. The Palais des Tuileries, drawn by Texier and engraved by Jourdan. (Image: Bibliothèque nationale de France.)

19. The overthrow of the Tuileries on August 10, 1792. (Image: Public domain.)

20. 'The Triumph of Marat', painting by Louis-Léopold Boilly (akg-images/De Agostini Picture Lib./G. Dagli Orti).

21. The emotional night session of August 4–5, 1789. (Private collection, Paris. akg-images.)

22. Georges Danton, (1759–94). (Image: Public domain.)

23. Maximilien Robespierre, (1758–94). (Image: Public domain.)

24. September 2, 1792: massacre of a group of priests at the Église des Carmes. (Image: Bibliothèque nationale de France.)

25. Robespierre's arrest. (Image: Bibliothèque nationale de France.)

26. January 21, 1793: the execution of Louis XVI. (Chronicle/Alamy.)

27. 'The battle of Valmy' by Horace Vernet. (Photo by Art Media/Print Collector/ Getty Images.)

28. Marie Antoinette (1755–93), pictured at the time of her trial (Paul Popper/ Popperfoto/Getty Images).

29. The guillotining of Jacques Brissot on October 31, 1793 (Classic image/Alamy).

30. The Two Only Make One: Satirical print depicting Louis XVI and Marie-Antoinette as a monstrous conjoined animal (Pictorial Press Ltd/Alamy).

31. 'Liberty Leading the People', 1830, by Eugène Delacroix (Heritage Images/Getty Images).

Endpapers and chapter opening decorations: The Turgot Map of Paris c. 1734–1736

INDEX

A

Acte additionnel, 248

Aftalion, Florin, 263

agents-nationaux, 220

Aiguillon, Armand, duc d', 31

Aix-en-Provence, 235

Alexandre, Charles, 95

Algeria, 251

Amarzit, Marc René Marie d', abbé
d'Espagnac, 217

America
Bill of Rights, 36
Constitution, 36
Declaration of Independence, 35
Revolution, 8
War of Independence, 6
see also United States

ami du peuple, L' (newspaper), 106

Amiens, 237

ancien régime, 2, 5, 21, 32, 52, 106, 110–11

Anselme, Jacques Bernard d', General, 131

Anthoine, François, 94, 95, 99

anticlericalism, 60–61

anti-Semitism, 60, 250

aristocracy *see* nobility

Armonville, Jean-Baptiste, 122–23

army, 22, 87–88
Armée catholique et royale d'Anjou, 165
armée de l'Italie, 242
armée de l'Ouest, 166, 174
armée de Sambre-et-Meuse, 223–24
Armée des côtes maritimes, 166
Armée révolutionnaire, 183, 190, 191, 218
battle of Valmy, 130–31
as a career, 2
conscription, 145–46, 164, 194
control of, 110
and death of Louis XVI, 141
and Dreyfus affair, 250
emigration of officers, 69, 84, 88
Gardes françaises, 23
growth of, 223
military service, 194
mutiny of, 88
and political process, 248
Regiment of Flanders, 41, 45, 47

reorganisation, 147
Royal Allemand regiment, 24, 26
royalist, 88
supplies for, 133
volunteers, 88, 90
see also fédérés; Garde nationale; militias;
   Swiss Guards
Artois, Charles Philippe, comte d', 23, 28,
   66, 69
assignats, 54–55, 56–58, 81, 135, 177, 199,
   237, 264, 265
atheism, 124, 207
Audouin, François Xavier, 107
Augereau, Charles, General, 243
Austen, Jane, 264
Austria
   occupation of Low Countries, 87
   Partition of Poland, 89, 93
   war with France, 86, 88, 89, 131–32,
      149, 151, 223–24, 242–43
Avignon, 85–86, 235

B

Bailly, Jean Sylvain, 18, 20, 28, 42, 47, 73
Balzac, Honoré de, 264
Barbaroux, Charles Jean-Marie, 180, 201,
   203
Barentin, Charles Louis de, 17
Barère, Bertrand, 45, 155–56, 186, 226,
   229, 233–34, 236, 237, 267
Barnave, Antoine, 18, 41, 79
Barras, Paul François, vicomte de, 123,
   171–72, 213, 221, 226–27, 230, 240, 242,
   243
Basel, Peace of (April 5, 1795), 242
Basire, Claude, 216
Bastille, 27–28, 29
Bastille Day, 8, 92, 250
Beauharnais, Alexandre de, General, 236
Beauharnais, Joséphine de, 236, 241
Belgium, 131–32, 133, 134–35, 145, 149,
   223–25
bells, 114
Bentham Jeremy, 124
Bertier de Sauvigny, Louis Bénigne
   François, 27

Beurnonville, Pierre de Riel, comte de,
   150, 151, 182
Billaud-Varenne, Jacques Nicolas, 122,
   184, 186, 189, 226, 228, 229, 233, 236, 267
Birotteau, Jean Bonaventure Blaise
   Hilarion, 152, 180
bishops, 3, 16, 61, 63, 64, 115, 122, 186; *see
   also* Gobel, Jean-Baptiste Joseph, Bishop
   of Paris
Blanc, Louis, 245, 247
Boissy d'Anglas, François Antoine, 238
Bonaparte, Napoléon *see* Napoléon I
bonds *see assignats*
Bordeaux, 168–69, 171
Bouche de fer (magazine), 73
Bouchotte, Jean-Baptiste Noël, 154–55,
   182
Bouillé, François Claude Amour, marquis
   de, 66–67, 68, 69, 88
Boulay de la Meurthe, Antoine, 298n25:7
Bourbons, 39, 246
bourgeoisie
   careers, 2, 3–4, 12
   and class war, 237
   demonstrations by, 234–35
   economic condition of, 180–81
   liberal principles of, 163
   and politics, 5, 150
   and religion, 208
   Robespierre and, 176
   victory of, 239
Boyer-Fonfrède, Jean-Baptiste, 80, 142,
   202
Braesch, Fr., 263
bread, 23, 42, 46–47, 158, 185, 237, 238
Breteuil, Louis Auguste Le Tonnelier,
   baron de, 24, 28
Brissot, Jacques-Pierre, 14, 80, 81, 85, 86,
   90, 96–97, 125, 126, 148, 152, 156, 202
Brissotins, 80, 81
Britain
   currency, 264, 265
   population, 16
   see also England
Brunswick, Karl Wilhelm Ferdinand,
   Duke of, 89, 93, 109, 130

Brunswick Manifesto, 97
Burke, Edmund, 6–7, 72
Buzot, François Nicolas Léonard, 128,
    142, 148–49, 156, 180, 203

C

Cabarrus, Thérésa, 236
Cadoudal, Georges, 298n25:7
cahiers de doléances, 10–12
Calas family, 4
calendar: Revolutionary, 206–7
Cambon, Pierre Joseph, 134–35, 145,
    155–56, 227, 228
Campoformio, Treaty of, 242–43
capital punishment,106; see also death
    penalty; guillotine
Carnot, Lazare, 123, 147, 184, 223, 224,
    226, 234, 268
Caron, Pierre, 263
Carpentras, 85
Carra, Jean-Louis, 95, 113, 142, 202
Carrier, Jean-Baptiste, 173–74, 193, 221,
    226–27, 236
Carteaux, Jean-Baptiste François, 171
Catholicism, 112, 165, 249, 266; see also
    Church; papists
Cercle social, 48, 73
Chabot, François, 212, 213, 214, 216
Chalier, Joseph, 169, 172
Charette, François, 242
Charles X, King, 246, 247
Charters, 248
Chartres, Louis-Philippe, duc de (later
    King Louis-Philippe) 151–52, 204
Chaumette, Pierre Gaspard, 107, 181,
    185–86, 187, 201–2, 208, 219
Cholet, 164, 166
Christianity: anti-Christian campaign,
    207–9, 249
Church
    as a career, 2
    conflict with, 32–3
    National Assembly and, 114
    property, 53–55, 56, 61, 120–21, 135, 199
    reform of, 59–65
    revival of, 249

schism in, 112
and state, 249
and taxes, 32
see also Catholicism; clergy; religion
churches
    anti-Christian campaign, 207, 208
    bells, 114
    Versailles, 19
citizenship, 75, 81, 104
class war, 158, 186, 234, 237, 238
Clavière, Étienne, 14, 86, 90, 110, 125, 155,
    161
clergy 3
    campaign against, 113, 207–8
    Constitution civile du clergé, 61
    and Declaration of the Rights of Man,
        60
    deportation of, 90
    election of, 61–62, 65
    emigration of, 28, 65
    and États généraux, 9, 10, 11, 12, 16, 17,
        18, 19
    execution of, 198
    imprisonment of, 112–13, 115
    living conditions of, 54
    massacre of, 115
    oaths of loyalty, 62, 63–65, 122
    privileges of, 15
    repression of, 84
    salaries of, 61
    and taxation, 32, 60–61
    see also anticlericalism; bishops; priests
Clermont-Tonnerre, Stanislas Marie
    Adelaide, duc de, 40
Cloots, Anacharsis, 123, 124, 209
clubs, 48, 78, 189, 266
    Club Breton (later Club Jacobin), 41, 48,
        71
    Club des citoyennes républicaines
        révolutionnaires, 196
    Club des Cordeliers, 48, 71, 72–73, 107,
        215
    Les Feuillants, 72, 79, 90, 93, 96, 100
    see also Jacobins; sociétés populaires
Coblenz, 67, 97
Coffinhal, Jean-Baptiste, 231

coinage, 57, 58, 71, 135, 264, 265; *see also* currency

Collot d'Herbois, Jean-Marie, 122, 172, 186, 189, 193, 221, 226, 228, 233, 236, 267, 268

colonies, 51, 71, 80–81, 113

Comité de défense générale, 151, 153

Comité de salut public (Committee of Public Safety, CSP), 123, 153, 154–56, 160–61, 167, 178, 184–85, 188, 189, 202, 210, 213, 215–16, 218, 219, 220–21, 226, 227–28, 233–34, 267–69

Comité de sûreté générale (CSG), 192, 215, 218–19, 227, 234, 239

Comité exécutif, 155

Comité exécutif provisoire, 110

comités de surveillance, 108–9, 115, 116, 146, 149, 192

comités révolutionnaires, 157, 192, 234

commerce, 3–4; *see also* trade

Commissions exécutives, 220

commoners, 4, 9, 10, 11–12, 13, 19, 21, 33, 106; *see* also *tiers état*

Communes
1870, 248, 249
and conscription, 146
and *décrets de ventôse*, 215
definition, 52
Insurrectionary, 101, 103, 105, 106–8, 110, 112, 113, 119, 121, 127, 161, 162
Paris *see under* Paris

Compagnie des Indes, 212, 213

Comtat Venaissin, 85

Condé, Louis Antoine Henri, prince de, 28, 71

Condorcet, Marie Jean Antoine Nicolas de Caritat, Marquis de, 14, 57, 203

Conseil d'État, 298n5

Conseil exécutif provisoire, 220

conservatives, 44, 51

Constitutions, 11, 12, 19, 22, 34, 35, 38, 39, 42, 43, 44, 50–51, 53, 62–63, 69, 74, 79, 83, 89, 120, 149, 248
1793, 177–79, 187–88
1795, 239–241
Fifth Republic, 249

Constitutional Guard, 90

Consulate, 243

Conti, Louis François Joseph de Bourbon, prince de, 28

Convention
balance of power, 233
and *Comité de salut public* (CSP), 184–85, 188, 220–21
Committee of Twelve, 160, 161, 162
and *Commune insurrectionnelle*, 118, 161–62
and *Compagnie des Indes*, 212
and corruption, 213–14
and currency, 264–65
decree of April 1, 1793, 152
decree of 'friendship', 133–34
deputies' immunity from prosecution, 162–3
Directoire, 240, 242, 243
and disarmament of 'suspects', 152
elections to, 104
foreign supporters of, 123–24
and French expansion, 145
and parliament, 240
and price control, 159, 186
and property rights, 180
and provisional government, 188, 207
and revolutionary government, 233
and Revolutionary Tribunal, 196–97
Revolutionary war principles, 135
and Robespierre's arrest, 228–230
Robespierre's speech to (July 26 (*8 thermidor*), 1794), 227–28
sans-culottes' intimidation of, 237
subcommittees, 110, 123, 146, 149, 151, 153
and trial of Danton, 216–17
and trial of Louis XVI, 137–38
and Vendéen rebellion, 166

Corday, Charlotte, 168

Cordeliers see under clubs

Corneille, Pierre, 76

corruption, 56, 133, 150, 172, 199, 212, 213–14, 221

corvées, 11, 31

Council of Ministers, 111, 155, 220

counter-revolutionaries, 105
countryside, 16, 30, 75, 114; *see also* peasants
coups d'état, 242–43, 246, 248, 259–260
courts, 4; *see also parlements*
Couthon, Georges Auguste, 162, 178, 184, 189, 193, 228, 229, 230, 268
Crêtois, 233
currency, 81–82, 264–65
    paper, 55, 57, 58, 264, 265
    see also *assignats*
Custine, Adam Philippe, comte de, 131, 183

D

Danican, Louis Michel, General, 240
Danton, Georges Jacques, 42
    and clemency policy, 222
    and *Club des Cordeliers*, 48, 71, 73, 98
    and *Comité de salut public*, 184, 185
    and *Comité exécutif*, 155
    and conquest of Belgium, 133, 134
    and corruption, 213
    as deputy Chief Executive of Paris, 91, 95, 100, 110, 111
    disillusionment of, 232
    and Dumouriez, 152
    emigration to England, 247
    fall of, 216–17
    and *Girondins*, 152, 161
    and Louis XVI, 14, 249
    as Minister of Justice, 51, 114–15, 116, 122, 197, 213
    'natural frontiers' speech, 144–45
    and Prussian invasion, 117
    Revolutionary reputation, 106
    trial of, 209–10, 226
    and war policy, 150–51, 155, 223
Dantonistes (*Indulgents*), 210, 212, 216
Daunou, Pierre Claude François, 233
de Gaulle, Charles, 248, 251
death penalty, 106, 111, 113, 142, 190, 194, 196, 198–99, 201, 202–3, 204, 208, 209, 217, 219, 222, 239
    see also executions; guillotine

Debry, Jean, 142
Déclaration des droits de l'homme et du citoyen (pamphlet), 179, 183
Declaration of the Rights of Man, 6, 18, 22, 34–39, 44, 45, 56, 60, 79, 114, 178, 248
    French text, 261–62
décrets de ventôse, 215
Delacroix, Jean-François, 133, 150–51, 155, 212, 216
Delaunay, Joseph, 212, 214, 216
democracy, 6, 28, 61–62, 72, 214, 245
départements
    and conscription, 145–46
    and *Convention*, 125, 167
    dioceses, 61
    elections, 122
    formation of, 52
    National Assembly representatives, 111
    Paris, 91, 92, 110, 128
    unrest in, 168, 171
deportations, 90, 113, 189, 193, 233, 234, 236, 239, 243, 250
Desmoulins, Camille, 43, 48, 73, 76, 122, 159, 197, 200, 206, 212, 216, 222
    Le Vieux Cordelier, 210–11
Desmoulins, Lucile, 219
Dictionnaire historique de la Révolution française, 140
Dillon, Arthur, comte de, 219
Dillon, Théobald, General, 87
dress, 25–26, 235, 236
Dreux- Brézé, Henri Évrard, marquis de, 20
Dreyfus affair, 250
Ducos, Jean-François, 79–80, 142, 202
Dufriche de Valazé, Charles-Éléonor, 202
Dumas, René François, 197, 198, 229
Dumouriez, Charles François, General, 86, 87, 90, 131–32, 133, 139, 149, 150–51, 152–53, 216
Duplay, Maurice, 73–77, 94
Dupont de Nemours, Pierre, 54, 57
Duport, Adrien, 41, 79
economy, 33, 56, 80, 148, 158, 179, 236, 237; *see also* inflation

E

Edgeworth, Henry, 143

elections

clergy, 64

Constitution (1793), 179

and *Convention*, 121–22

départements, 52, 122

foreign, 135

fructidor, 1797, 242–43

intimidation at, 121–22

of Mayor of Paris, 76, 122, 133

municipal, 42–43

National Assembly, 119, 120

National Legislative Assembly, 74–75

parliamentary, 240–41, 242

see also suffrage

electorate, 239–241

emigration, 28–29, 69

émigrés, 82, 83–84, 93, 97, 152, 180, 215,
247–48

employment, 75, 108; *see also*
unemployment

Encyclopédie, 4, 219

Enghien, Louis, duc d', 298n25:7

England

and American War of Independence, 6

democracy, 6

emigration to, 247–48

and First Coalition, 136

gentry, 3

Industrial Revolution, 4

neutrality of, 70

Paine's *The Rights of Man* in, 72

political rights, 36

post-Civil War, 247

wars, 51, 145, 170, 171, 185, 224

see also Britain

Enlightenment, 4–5, 219

Enragés, les (The Infuriated), 155, 181,
194, 196

envoyés en mission, 146–47, 151, 166, 170,
171, 172, 173, 191, 193, 213, 221, 226,
227, 228, 233–34

États généraux (Estates General), 9, 14,
16–21, 53

cahiers de doléances, 10–12, 54

députés, 18, 127

orders, 10, 12–13

executions, 106, 143, 173, 174, 223, 230–31,
242; *see also* death penalty; guillotine

F

Fabre d'Églantine, Philippe, 146, 207, 212,
213–14, 216, 227

Favras, Thomas de Mahy, marquis de,
66–67

fédérés, 90, 93, 94, 95, 97–98, 101, 115

Féraud, Jean Bertrand, 238

Fête de la Fédération (July 14, 1790), 62, 63,
280n9

Fête de la Liberté et de la Raison
(November 10, 1793), 186

feudalism, 30–33, 158, 180

Feuillants, Les, 72, 79, 90, 93, 96, 100

finances, public, 53–58; *see also* taxation

Fischer, David Hackett: *The Great Wave*,
264

Flesselles, Jacques de, 26, 27

Fleuriot-Lescot, Jean-Baptiste Édouard,
229

Fleurus, 223–24

food, 43, 57, 191

shortages, 42, 58, 70–71, 80, 81, 117, 147,
158, 177, 179, 185, 208, 215, 237, 264

see also bread

Fouché, Joseph, 172–73, 186, 193, 221, 268,
298n25:7

Foullon, Joseph, 27

Fouquier-Tinville, Antoine Quentin,
197–98, 217, 222, 234

Fournier, Claude, 92, 95

Francis II, Emperor, 88, 89

Franklin, Benjamin, 14

Frederick William II, King of Prussia, 68,
69–70, 89

Frenchness, 21

Fréron, Louis-Stanislas, 113, 171, 221,
226–27, 235

Furet, François, 4, 7–8, 21, 91, 99, 100,
106, 231, 245, 249, 250

G

Garat, Dominique, 154

Garde nationale, 28, 42, 43, 45, 47, 62, 73, 80, 87, 88, 91, 93, 96, 105, 109, 115, 193, 238, 239

gender, 36, 75; *see also* suffrage; women

Geneva, 6, 212, 283n9:1

Genlis, Charles Alexis Brulart Sillery, marquis de, 202

Gensonné, Armand, 80, 125, 141, 152, 156, 180, 202

gentry, 3; *see also* nobility

Germany, 145; *see also* Prussia

Girondins, 79–80, 81, 85, 90, 91, 93, 96, 100, 110, 122, 124, 125, 126–27, 129, 133, 136, 137, 141, 146, 147, 148, 150, 152, 154, 155–56, 156–57, 158–59, 160, 161–62, 163, 167, 171, 175, 176, 178, 201–3, 216, 233

Gobel, Jean-Baptiste Joseph, Bishop of Paris, 208, 219

Goethe, Johann Wolfgang von: *Kampagne in Frankreich*, 131

Gorsas, Antoine Joseph, 95, 113, 180

Gouges, Olympe de, 196

government
central, 176, 218
constitutional, 211
instability of, 246–47
local, 42, 52, 61, 81, 110; *see also* *communes*; *départements*
national, 110
provisional, 188, 207
revolutionary, 211, 233
Vichy, 248

Goyre de Laplanche, Jacques Léonard, 186

Grande Peur, la (the Great Fear), 30–31211111

Grave, Pierre Marie, marquis de, 89

Greer, Donald, 192, 198

Gresham, Thomas, 57

Grouchy, Sophie de, 196

Guadet, Marguerite Élie, 80, 92, 125, 141, 142, 152, 156, 159, 180, 201, 202–3

Guillotin, Joseph Ignace, 106

guillotine, 106, 173, 198, 222, 239

Guizot, François, 7, 245, 247

Guzman, Andreas Maria de, 217

H

Hamelin, Fortunée, 236

Hamilton, Alexander, 8, 124

Hanriot, François, 161, 162, 229, 230

Hardouin-Mansart, Jacques, 19

Hardy, Antoine François, 141

Hébert, Jacques René, 107, 113, 160, 181–82, 183–84, 185, 186, 201–2, 209, 215

Hébertistes, 185, 187, 208, 209, 215, 218, 220, 226

Henri IV, King, 283n9:1

Hérault de Séchelles, Marie Jean, 162, 178, 189, 217, 268

Herman, Martial Joseph, 197, 198, 202, 217

Hibbert, Christopher, 7

Hochard, Lazare, 194

Hoche, Louis Lazare, 151

Hood, Samuel, Admiral, 170, 171

Houchard, Jean Nicolas, 194

Huguenin, Sulpice, 103

I

Incroyables, les (the Unbelievables), 122; *see also* *muscadins*

Indulgents, 216, 232; *see also* *Dantonistes*

Industrial Revolution, 3–4

inflation, 263–64

Isnard, Maximin, 142, 203

Italy, 145

J

Jacobins, 72, 78–79, 82, 83, 85, 86, 89, 90, 91, 92, 93, 94, 95, 97, 99, 107, 108, 122, 124, 125, 126, 156, 157, 169–170, 178, 186, 191, 199–200, 206, 216, 220, 230, 234–35

Jaurès, Jean, 7, 245

Jemappes, 132, 137, 144

jeunesse dorée, 234–35

Jews, 60, 217; *see also* anti-Semitism

Jourdan, Jean-Baptiste, General, 223–24

Jourdan, Mathieu Jouve, 86

journalists, 113; *see also* magazines; newspapers; press freedom
Junius, Sigmund and Emmanuel, 217

K

Kléber, Jean-Baptiste, Lieutenant-General, 224
Kock, Jean Conrad de, 209

L

Laboureau, Jean-Baptiste, 209
Labrousse, Ernest, 263
Laclos, Pierre Ambroise Choderlos de: *Qu'est-ce que le tiers état? (What Is the Third Estate?)*, 15
Lacombe, Claire, 194–95
Lafargue de Grangeneuve, Jean Antoine, 202
La Fayette, Marie Joseph Paul Yves Roch Gilbert Motier, marquis de, 15, 22, 28, 45, 46, 47, 73, 74, 79, 82, 84, 87, 89, 90, 92–93, 238
Lally-Tollendal, Trophime Gérard, marquis de, 40
La Marck, August Marie, comte de, 139
Lamartine, Alphonse de, 245
Lameth, Alexandre Theodore Victor de, 41, 79
Lameth brothers, 81, 84
land redistribution, 120–21; *see also* property
landowners, 3
Lanjuinais, Jean-Denis, 141, 156, 180, 203, 233
La Porte, Arnaud de, 106
La Révellière-Lépeaux, Louis Marie de, 242, 243
La Rochejaquelein, Henri du Vergier, comte de, 165
Lasource, Marc-David, 122, 128, 142, 152, 156, 166–67, 202
Launay, Bernard de Jourdan, marquis de, 27
law
  as a career, 3–4, 5, 16
  Church and state, 249

constitutional, 227
  in Declaration of the Rights of Man, 37
  Law of 22 *prairial* (June 10, 1794), 221–22, 227, 234
  Law of Suspects, 190, 192, 196, 198, 210
  trade unions and, 70, 219
Law, John, 55
Lazowski, Claude-François, 95
Lebas, Philippe François, 229, 230, 231
Lebrun, Pierre, 134
Lebrun-Tondu, Pierre, 155
Le Chapelier, Isaac René Guy, 70, 219
Leclerc, Jean-Théophile, 194
Lefebvre, Georges, 263
Legendre, Louis, 92
Le Mans, 174
Léon, Pauline, 196
Leopold II, Emperor, 69–70, 88, 89
Le Peletier, Michel, 169
Lequinio, Marie Joseph, 186
Lescot-Fleuriot, Jean-Baptiste Édouard, 220
Lessart, Jean-Marie de, 86
lettres de cachet, 13, 14
Levasseur, René, 107
Lhuillier, Louis Marie, 158–59
Liberté, égalité, fraternité slogan, 2, 38, 183
liberty, 36, 37, 148, 149, 181, 188
Lindet, Jean-Baptiste Robert, 140, 171, 216, 234, 269
literature, 5
Longwy fortress, 109, 114, 117
Louchet, Louis, 229
Louis XIII, King, 9–10
Louis XIV, King, 2, 4, 283n9:1
Louis XV, King, 2, 3
Louis XVI, King
  authority of, 20–21
  and bourgeoisie, 5, 6
  capitulation of, 28, 29
  and Civil Constitution of the Clergy, 64
  and Constitution, 50–51, 69, 74, 83
  correspondence, 139
  and counter-revolution, 22–23, 24
  and Declaration of the Rights of Man, 44, 45, 46, 47

and demonstration (June 20, 1792), 92
escape from Paris, 67–68
and *États généraux*, 9, 10, 13, 17, 18,
    19–20
execution of, 143
finances, 53
marriage, 257
and National Assembly, 40, 41, 51–52,
    90
and nobles, 3, 5
oath of loyalty by, 62
overthrow of, 93, 94, 95–97, 101, 104,
    112, 119–120, 154
and Protestants' rights, 60
removal to Paris, 47, 49, 66
role of, 83
trial of, 105, 137–143, 156
and war, 82, 84
Louis XVII, King *see* Louis Charles,
    Dauphin
Louis XVIII, King, 249
Louis Charles, Dauphin (Louis XVII),
    201, 257
Louis Joseph François Xavier, Dauphin,
    201, 257, 258
Louis Napoléon, Emperor *see* Napoléon
    III, Emperor
Louis-Philippe, King, 246, 247; *see also*
    Chartres, Louis-Philippe, duc de
Louis, Antoine, 106
Louvet, Jean-Baptiste, 128, 180, 203, 233
Low Countries, 87; *see also* Belgium
Lückner, Nicolas, count, 87
Lyon, 169, 172, 173, 193, 235, 268

M
MacMahon, Patrice de, Marshal, 298n24:7
Madison, James, 8
magazines, 73
Mailhe, Jean, 142
Maillard, Stanislas Marie, 46, 116, 209
Malesherbes, Chrétien Guillaume de
    Lamoignon de, 219
Malouet, Pierre Victor, baron, 40, 57
Mandat, Antoine Jean Gailliot, marquis
    de, 100

Manifeste des Enragés, 180
Manuel, Louis Pierre, 91, 95, 100, 101,
    122, 137
Marat, Jean-Paul
    appearance, 107
    and *Club des Cordeliers*, 71, 73
    and *Comité de surveillance*, 109, 115
    and *Commune insurrectionnelle*, 106–7
    and *Convention*, 156
    death of, 168
    and *Girondins*, 162
    impeachment of, 156–57
    and *La bouche de fer*, 48
    as a pamphleteer, 43, 106
    as a rabble-rouser, 113, 117
Marceau, François Séverin, Lieutenant-
    General, 224
Marie-Antoinette, Queen, 10, 19, 23, 46,
    89, 90, 93, 201, 257
Marie-Thérèse, princess, 10, 257, 258
Marion, Marcel, 263
Marseillaise, La, 96
Marseille, 169–170, 171, 235
Marx, Karl, 231
Mathiez, Albert, 7, 91, 93–94, 110, 127,
    136, 185, 186, 192, 215, 224, 226, 231
Maury, Jean Siffrein, abbé, 54
Mazauric, Claude, 99
Mediterranean Fleet, 170, 185
Menou, Jacques, General, 240
Merlin de Douai (Philippe Antoine
    Merlin), 243
Merlin de Thionville (Antoine Christophe
    Merlin), 234
Michelet, Jules, 7, 20, 77, 82, 91, 95, 100,
    105, 106–7, 108, 115, 121, 134, 138–39,
    141, 148, 149, 186, 200, 202, 204, 206,
    245
Military Commission, 239
militias, 24, 26–27, 28; *see also Garde
    nationale*
Mirabeau, Honoré Gabriel Riqueti, comte
    de, 13–14, 18, 24, 54, 56, 57, 82, 139, 213,
    216
    L'appel à la nation provençale (*The
        Appeal to the Provençal Nation*), 14

'Mirabeau's Retort' (*La réplique de Mirabeau*), 20–21

moderates, 40, 56–57, 169, 219; *see also* Plaine, la

Momoro, Antoine François, 73, 183, 209

Monarchiens, 40

monarchists, 90, 92; *see also* royalists

monarchy
  absolute, 5, 10, 21
  authority of, 110–11
  Bourbon, 246
  and Constitution, 44
  constitutional, 18, 50, 69
  exclusionary policies, 1, 5–6
  July, 152, 246
  and loans, 24
  nostalgia for, 250
  overthrow of, 119, 245
  and republicanism, 249
  see also Restoration

monasteries, 48, 60

money *see* coinage; currency

Moniteur, Le (newspaper), 20–21, 189

Montagnards, 106, 124, 125, 126–28, 129, 133, 136, 140, 147, 148, 150, 152–53, 156–57, 159, 160, 166, 167, 175, 176, 177, 178, 180, 183, 187–88, 197, 219, 232, 233, 238, 239

Montané, Jacques, 197

Montesquiou-Fézensac, Jean Gabriel Maurice Rocques, comte de, 56, 131

Montmédy, 67

Mounier, Jean-Joseph, 18, 40, 46, 47

muscadins, 234, 235, 237; *see also* Incroyables, les

N

Nancy, 10

Nantes, 173, 174, 193, 198, 221, 236
  Edict of, 283n9:1

Napoléon I (Napoléon Bonaparte)
  and Catholicism, 249
  and Constitution, 248
  and coup d'état (1799), 232, 246, 248
  and government, 111
  and human rights, 39
  marriage, 236
  military career, 123, 171, 172, 240, 242–43
  and rebels, 298n25:7

Napoléon III, Emperor, 246, 247–48, 248

nation: definition of, 44

National Assembly, 19
  and *assignats*, 58
  authority of, 18, 93, 167
  and Church property, 54–55
  and clergy, 90, 113–14
  collapse of power of, 103–4
  and *Comité exécutif provisoire*, 110
  and Constitution, 22, 41, 53, 74, 79
  and Declaration of the Rights of Man, 34
  and demonstration (June 20, 1792), 92
  députés, 18, 34, 35, 38, 100, 122–23, 125, 141
  Ecclesiastical Committee, 59–60
  elections (August 26, 1792), 119
  factions, 49
  and *fédérés*, 98
  and feudalism, 31–32, 33
  and government, 50–58, 111
  and King's Constitutional Guard, 90
  Le Manège meeting chamber, 77–78, 92
  Loi Le Chapelier, 70
  and Louis XVI, 24, 51–52, 68, 69, 72, 73, 94, 95, 101
  and Paine, Thomas, 72
  and Paris *Commune*, 158–59
  and Prussian invasion, 114–15, 117
  removal to Paris, 48
  Robespierre and, 78, 82, 105
  and *Sections*, 96
  and sovereignty, 40–41
  voting rights in, 75–76
  and war, 86

National Constituent Assembly (*Assemblée nationale constituante*), 74, 75, 76, 81, 119, 158

national debt, 56

National Legislative Assembly (*Assemblée nationale législative*), 74, 75–76, 77–79, 96, 109–10, 119, 123–24, 127, 158

navy, 223; *see also* Mediterranean Fleet

Necker, Jacques, 13, 17, 19, 24, 28, 53, 57

Némirovsky, Irène: *Suite française*, 250
newspapers, 20–21, 106, 107, 113, 155, 160,
   182, 200; *see also* journalists; magazines;
   press freedom
Nièvre, 186
Nîmes, 122, 169, 235
Noailles, Louis, vicomte de, 31
nobility
   emigration of, 28–29
   and *États généraux*, 9, 10, 11, 12, 16, 17,
     18, 19, 20
   execution of, 106, 198
   feudal system, 33
   and King's finances, 53
   and the law, 5
   nobles d'épée, 3, 12
   nobles d'extraction, 3
   noblesse de robe, 4, 12
   privileges, 15
   Vendéen rebellion, 165
Normandy, 168, 171

O
oaths: swearing of, 62–63, 64–65, 113
O'Hara, Charles, Major, 170
orateur du peuple, L' (newspaper), 113
Orléans, Louis-Philippe Joseph, duc d',
   17, 21, 72, 122, 151, 152, 203–4

P
Pache, Jean Nicolas, 107, 133, 150, 154,
   156, 167, 183, 220
Paine, Thomas, 123
   Rights of Man, The, 71–72
   siècle de la raison, Le (*The Age of
     Reason*), 124
Palloy, Pierre François, 27
pamphlets, 13, 14–15, 43, 44, 71–72, 189
Panis, Étienne, 109, 115, 116, 228
papists, 85–86
Paris
   Bastille Day protests, 250
   Champ de Mars massacre, 73, 74
   Commune, 27, 42–43, 49, 91, 95, 97, 99,
     101, 111, 112, 115, 157, 160, 167, 220
   Couvent des Carmes, 115

   demonstrations in, 91–93, 185–86
   département of, 91, 92, 110, 128
   food shortages, 147
   government of, 42–43
   Hôtel de ville, 26, 27, 28, 46, 47, 49, 99,
     100, 229, 230, 286n17
   insurrections in, 95–103, 112, 240
   Les Invalides military hospital, 27
   Mairie, 115
   and Marseille, 170
   Notre Dame Cathedral, 186
   Palais de Justice, 115
   Palais Royal, 17, 23, 24, 43, 48
   Parlement, 5–6, 9, 12
   Place de la Concorde, 143
   poverty in, 148
   Saint-Germain-des-Prés abbey, 23
   Sections, 42–43, 49, 71, 91, 92, 96, 97, 98,
     99, 100, 105, 109, 113, 121, 141, 157,
     176, 179, 229–230
   Terror, 229–230
   Tuileries Gardens, 24
   Tuileries Palace, 47, 92, 100, 101,
     120–21, 139
   see also prisons
Pâris, Philippe de, 142
Parlements, 4, 5–6, 9, 12
parliament, 240, 242
Payan, Claude François de, 219–220
peasants, 30–31, 32, 58, 120–21, 165, 194
Père Duchesne, Le (newspaper), 107, 155,
   160, 182, 183, 209
Pereyra, Jacob, 209
Pétain, Philippe, 248
Pétion, Jérôme, 14, 45, 56, 74, 76, 91, 92,
   93, 98, 99, 100, 125, 137, 142, 180, 201,
   203
   Lettre aux Parisiens, 156–57
Philipon, Jeanne Marie, 203
Philippe Égalité *see* Orléans, Louis-
   Philippe Joseph, duc d'
Philippeaux, Pierre Nicolas, 216
philosophes, 4
Pichegru, Jean-Charles, General, 194, 224,
   237–38, 243
pikes, 91, 115

Piketty, Thomas: *Capital in the Twenty-First Century*, 264
Pitt, William, the Younger, 227
Pius VI, Pope, 64
Pius VII, Pope, 249
Plaine, la, 155, 228–29, 233
Pointe, Noël, 123
Poland: partition of, 89, 131, 242
police, 37, 108, 109, 149, 226; *see also Comité de sûreté générale*
population, 3, 15–16, 192
poverty, 75, 148, 169, 215–16
press freedom, 20, 196
price controls, 159, 186, 187, 190–91, 208, 214–15, 237
Priestley, Joseph, 124
priests, 3, 16; *see also* clergy
Prieur, Pierre Louis (Prieur de la Marne), 234, 269
Prieur-Duvernois, Claude Antoine, comte (Prieur de la Côte d'Or), 184, 226, 234, 269
prisoners, 115–17, 120, 173, 192, 215, 222, 233, 234, 235
prisons
  Abbaye, 115, 116
  Bastille, 8, 27–28, 29
  Châtelet, 116
  Conciergerie, 113, 115, 116
  'Conspiracy of the Prisons', 219
  invasion of, 112
  La Salpêtrière, 116
  Luxembourg, 124
  massacres, 104
  Saint-Firmin, 116
  Temple, 101, 201
procureurs, 219–220
Proly, Pierre, 209
propaganda, 182
property
  Church, 54–55, 61, 199
  in Constitution, 178
  in Declaration of the Rights of Man, 37–38
  of *émigrés*, 84, 180
  redistribution of, 215

Robespierre and, 157, 159
'sacred rights' of, 31
Protestants, 60, 283n9:1
Provence, Louis-Stanislas Xavier, comte de, 23, 28, 67, 84, 97, 170
Prussia
  battle of Valmy, 131
  invasion of France, 93, 104–5, 114, 117
  population, 16
  withdrawal of, 242
Public Education Committee, 206
purges, 109

Q
Quinet, Edgar, 245, 247

R
Rabaut Saint-Étienne (Jean-Paul Rabaut), 122
Reason, Cult of, 207
Rebecqui, François Trophime, 128
Récamier, Jeanne, 236
religion
  anti-Christian campaign, 207–9
  and death penalty, 199
  religious rights, 114
  Revolution compared to, 205–6
  tolerance of, 60
  see also Catholicism; Christianity; Church; Protestants
rentiers, 24
Republic
  declaration of (September 21, 1792), 206
  idea of, 72–73, 74, 128, 176
  Second, 246, 247
  Third, 247, 248, 250–51
  Fourth, 248, 251
  Fifth, 249, 251
Républicain, Le (journal), 71, 73
republicans/ republicanism, 71, 72–73, 249; *see also* clubs: *Club des Cordeliers*
Restoration, 246, 247, 248, 249
Reubell, Jean-François, 242
Revolution: legacy of, 245–252
Revolution (1830), 39
Revolution (1848), 247

Révolutions de France et de Brabant, Les
    (newspaper), 200
Riel, Pierre de, 150
rights
    equal, 20, 36, 181
    human, 39
    property, 31, 37–38, 54–55, 61, 84, 157,
        159, 178, 179
    religious, 114
    social, 178, 179
    voting, 75–76
    see also American Bill of Rights;
        *Déclaration des droits de l'homme et
        du citoyen*; Declaration of the Rights
        of Man
Rivarol, Antoine, 47
Robespierre, Augustin, 171, 229, 230
Robespierre, Maximilien Marie Isidore
    de, 208–9
    appearance, 26, 82, 105, 107
    arrest of, 229–230
    on Avignon, 85
    and Barras, 172
    and Brissot, 126
    and Carnot, 268
    character, 73–74, 226
    class war strategy, 159, 160, 234
    and *Comité de salut public*, 184, 185
    on Constitution, 44
    and corruption, 213, 214
    and counter-revolutionary conspiracy,
        227–28
    and Danton, 216
    and *Dantonistes*, 212
    death of, 189, 230
    and death of Louis XVI, 136, 139–140
    on Declaration of Rights, 178
    and *départements*, 110
    and Desmoulins, 210–12
    on Dumouriez and Gironde, 152
    election to *Convention*, 122, 127
    and *Enragés*, 194, 196
    and executions, 189
    and Extraordinary Tribunal, 105
    and *Girondins*, 118, 157, 162, 175, 201
    government control by, 220

and Hébert, 209
and Hérault de Séchelles, 268
incorruptibility of, 199
influence of, 45
and Insurrectionary *Commune*, 105, 106
and *Jacobins*, 126, 199–200
and Law of Suspects, 192
as leader of Paris *Commune*, 219, 220
on liberty, 188
and Marat, 107, 109
and National Assembly, 78
as an orator, 82
and Paine, 124
and Paris demonstration (June 20,
    1792), 91
on Philippe Égalité, 203–4
on pikes, 91
and policy change, 180
power of, 125, 128
on property rights, 157
and protest movement, 93–95, 98–99, 100
*Rapport sur les principes du gouvernement
    révolutionnaire*, 211
and Revolutionary Tribunal, 197–98
and Roux, 181, 232
and *sans-culottes*, 177, 220
and 'a single will' ideal, 175–76
and *Terror*, 186–87, 214, 218, 225–26
threats to, 226–29
and war, 82–83, 85, 86, 89, 95
'War Against the Factions', 205, 209–10
on wealth inequality, 215
Rochambeau, Jean-Baptiste Donatien de
    Vimeur, comte de, 87, 89
Roland, Jean-Marie, 86, 90, 110, 125, 133,
    154, 161
Roland de la Platière, Jean Marie, 51, 203
Ronsin, Charles Philippe, General, 183,
    186, 191, 209, 215
Rouen, 237
Rouget de l'Isle, Claude, Captain, 96
Rousseau, Jean-Jacques, 37, 48, 76, 176
    Confessions, 282n8
    Du contrat social, 211–12
Roux, Jacques, 107, 148, 158, 179–180, 181,
    185, 194

royalists, 88, 92, 109, 113, 139, 147, 165, 169, 170, 235, 240; *see also* monarchists
Royer, Jean-Baptiste, 186
Russia, 15, 89

S
Saint-André, André Jean-Bon, 234, 268
Saint-Domingue, 71, 80–81
Saint-Fargeau, Louis Michel Le Peletier de, 142
Saint-Huruge, Victor Amédée de la Fage, marquis de, 92
Saint-Just, Louis, 138–39, 147, 178, 180, 184, 188, 189, 215, 216, 217, 220, 221, 226–27, 228, 229, 230, 269
Saliceti, Christophe, 171
Salle, Jean-Baptiste, 180
sans-culottes, 29, 81, 90, 95, 99, 101–2, 107–8, 112, 115, 129, 133, 148, 156, 157, 158, 159, 161, 167, 171, 175, 176, 177, 184, 185, 190, 191, 194, 208, 220, 232, 235, 237, 239
    definition of, 25–26
    insurrectional committee (*Comité insurrectionnelle*), 95, 100
Santerre, Antoine Joseph, 42, 91, 92, 95, 105, 112
Savenay, 174
Schama, Simon, 7
Schiller, Friedrich, 124
Schmitt, T., 106
Second Empire, 246
secularism, 249–250
Sedan, 248
Sédillot, René, 263
Sergent, Antoine François, 116
Servan, Joseph, 90, 110
Sieyès, Emmanuel Joseph, *abbé*, 14–15, 18, 122, 243
    Qu'est-ce que le tiers état? 44
silk industry, 169
Simoneau, Jacques, 81
slave trade, 14, 81
slaves, 36, 71
Soboul, Albert, 7, 100, 192, 239
social fractures, 250

social life: post-Revolutionary, 236
Société des amis des Noirs, 14, 81
sociétés populaires, 184, 191, 220
Sophie Hélène, princess, 258
sovereignty, 6, 37, 40, 41, 44, 245
Spain, 51, 145
speculation, 55
speech: post-Revolutionary, 235–36
Stofflet, Nicolas, 165, 242
suffrage: universal male, 95, 104, 120, 179; *see also* elections
Swiss Guards, 47, 101, 105, 113, 116

T
Talleyrand- Périgord, Charles Maurice de, 14, 16–17, 54, 57, 64, 91, 298n25:7
Tallien, Jean Lambert, 221, 226–27, 229, 234, 237
Talon, Antoine, 139
tax 'farmers', 26
taxation, 2, 11, 18, 19, 20, 31, 32, 37, 54, 55–56, 60–61, 81, 239–240
Terror, 6–7, 58, 81, 149, 153, 190–204, 218–19, 221, 232, 245
    end of, 234
    Grand Terreur, 222
    origin of, 186
    Terreur blanche, 235
Thermidoriens, 233, 239, 240
Thiers, Adolphe, 7, 245
Third Estate *see tiers état*
Thouret, Jacques Guillaume, 74, 219
Thuriot, Jacques Alexis, 149, 188, 189, 269
tiers état, 9, 11,12, 13, 14,15, 16, 17, 18, 19–20, 28, 62, 198–99; *see also* commoners
tithes, 32, 54
Tocqueville, Alexis de, 5, 7, 192, 205–6, 245, 246, 248, 251–52
    L'ancien régime et la Révolution, 11
Toulon, 170, 171, 172, 185, 213, 221
Toulouse, 169
Toussaint-L'Ouverture, François-Dominique, 81
towns, 16, 75
trade, 71; *see also* commerce; slave trade
trade unions, 70, 219

trials, 116
  Carrier, Jean-Baptiste, 236
  conspiracy, 219
  Custine, comte de, 183
  Danton, 216–17, 226
  Dantonistes, 214
  Girondins, 167, 186, 201–3
  Hébertistes, 209
  Louis XVI, 105, 137–143, 149, 156
  Marie-Antoinette, 201
  Orléans, duc d', 203–4
  show, 199, 208, 218, 219–222
tribunals, 112
  Extraordinary Tribunal, 105–6, 197
  Revolutionary Tribunal (*Tribunal
    révolutionnaire*), 104, 148, 149, 152,
    156, 193, 196, 197–99, 201–4, 210,
    218–19, 234
Triumvirate, 79
Tulard, Alphonse, 100
Tulard, Jean, 7, 8, 142, 185, 281n15
Turreau, Louis Marie, General, 174, 193

U
unemployment, 29, 69, 158, 169, 179
United Nations, 36
United States: Convention, 104; *see also*
  America

V
Vadier, Marc-Guillaume Alexis, 226,
  236–37
Valmy, battle of, 104–5, 125, 130
Varlet, Jean-François, 92, 148, 194
Vendée, 146, 164–66, 173, 192, 193, 242
Verdun, 109, 114, 117, 250
Vergniaud, Pierre, 79–80, 93, 96, 101, 125,
  141, 142, 156, 167, 180, 202
Versailles
  church of Notre Dame de Saint-Louis,
    19
  États généraux, 9, 17–20
  invasion of, 47
  Louis XVI in, 10
  nobility and, 2, 28
  procession to, 46–47

Real Tennis Court (*salle du Jeu de
  paume*), 19, 62
  Revolution starts in, 8
  salle des Menus Plaisirs, 19, 20
Vichy regime, 248
Vieux Cordelier, Le (pamphlet), 210, 211
Vincent, François Nicolas, 73, 182–83,
  209, 215
Voltaire, 71, 211, 212, 219, 279n1:4
voting, 75, 104, 121, 123, 140, 142; *see also*
  elections; suffrage
Vovelle, Michel, 207–8

W
wage controls, 191, 215
war, 82–83, 84–85, 86, 87–91, 93, 125, 130–
  33, 144, 149–151, 223–25, 242, 248
  civil, 112, 164, 166–174, 192–93
  enrichment from, 136, 172
  officers and, 224
  and peace, 51
  Revolutionary, 135
  and *Terror*, 225
  Vendée, 164–66
  victories (1793–4), 194
  World, 248, 250
  see also Valmy, battle of
'War Against the Factions', 205, 209–10
War Ministry, 108, 133, 150, 155
Washington, George, 8, 124
Westermann, François, General, 95, 164,
  193, 217
Wilberforce, William, 124
Wimpfen, Félix, 168
women
  and Church, 120–21
  and death penalty, 203
  and elections, 120, 179
  and franchise, 266
  as protesters, 194
  rights of, 36, 75
  social life of, post-Revolution, 236

Z
Zweig, Stefan, 257